MAGAZINES:

A Bibliography for Their Analysis, with Annotations and Study Guide

By
Fred K. Paine
and
Nancy E. Paine

The Scarecrow Press, Inc.
Metuchen, N.J., & London
1987

This book is typeset in 12 pitch Gothic Bold and Document Italic typefaces via laser printer.

Available on PC compatible 5 1/4" floppy disk from the authors, c/o H.B.E. 449 Church Street, Wethersfield, Connecticut 06109

Library of Congress Cataloging-in-Publication Data

Paine, Fred K., 1938-
Magazines : a bibliography for their analysis with annotations and study guide.

Includes index.
1. Periodicals, Publishing of--Bibliography.
2. Periodicals, Publishing of--United States--Bibliography. 3. Periodicals--History--Bibliography.
4. American periodicals--History--Bibliography.
I. Paine, Nancy E., 1942- . II. Title.
Z6940.P24 1987 [PN4734] 016.0705'72 86-29825
ISBN 0-8108-1975-9

Dedicated to publishers, editors, business people, librarians, educators, students and all who care about the readers served by magazines, and to the potential they have for making American life still better.

Acknowledgments

The authors are indebted to many--those who have labored over the original works cited herein, & to librarians from Yale and the universities of Illinois, Pennsylvania State, Minnesota, Ohio State and Kent State, and the State Library of Connecticut.

We also offer thanks to our daughter, Judy, who did without many attentions and much time her mother and father would otherwise have been able to give her, and who typed some entries.

In particular, we acknowledge the bright, caring and steadfast programming and computer/production guidance of J.C. Givens and his remarkable, selfless toil. His work and that of Scarecrow publisher William R. Eschelman turned the authors' research into physical reality.

For the inevitable error in an effort of this detailed, interwoven complexity, the authors alone must stand responsible. We invite corrections, additions and suggestions.

MAGAZINES: A BIBLIOGRAPHY FOR THEIR ANALYSIS WITH ANNOTATIONS AND STUDY GUIDE

TABLE OF CONTENTS

PREFACE

USES & PURPOSES OF THIS BIBLIOGRAPHY

This book has been prepared for all those who are interested in magazines or have a managerial, journalistic, librarian's, researcher/student's, professional, personal or academic reason for studying them.

It is a reference guide to help find valuable tools for studying magazines.

This bibliography lists more than 2,200 magazine, newspaper and journal articles, books, and dissertations written about magazines--selected from some 15,000 works examined.

The focus of this volume is on material printed after 1978, although some key pieces published prior to that year are included.

Despite its length, this effort has been selective, and the listings included are but a fraction of those reviewed in preparing this work. Yet it seeks to cover most areas of the field. Where little writing has been done, pieces of less weight are included since they appear to be the best available.

The year 1978 ended the period covered by J. H. Schacht's BIBLIOGRAPHY FOR THE STUDY OF MAGAZINES, published by the College of Communications at the University of Illinois. It is a selective list of articles and books, divided by subject, briefly annotated, and used by students of magazine journalism at home and abroad over the years. Of course much has been written since 1978, and many industry and business changes have occurred.

It is past time for a new bibliography--to emphasize new material about magazines, highlight the most important past material, and provide a reference guide in what has become the computer age.

The present work is, in a sense, a chronicle of the industry today. It is a tool with which to access other information sources. But it is also a means of learning in and of itself.

Simply by reading index, entries, and annotations, experienced professionals and newcomers can learn much about the breadth and scope of the American magazine in terms both of its business and content. What is said (and not said) in print about today's U.S. magazines is significantly demonstrated by the present volume. This second and less obvious use should not be overlooked. NOR SHOULD THE INDEX, which substantially cross-references content of most items listed.

Hopefully this bibliography will complement Professor Schacht's work, but its intent is not to duplicate his approach.

THIS BOOK HAS TWO DIVISIONS

PART I

Chapter 1 is a bibliography of magazines, newspapers, and journals that regularly include material about magazines and the magazine industry.

Annotations explain the publication's character relevant to magazines. The particular slant of the periodical must be kept in mind. Special issues or regular columns of value to magazine researchers are noted, as are some indexes which serve them.

Chapter 2 lists reference books in two sections. The first includes bibliographies, directories, handbooks, statistical sources. The second is a list of indexes which give the reader access to material published in and about magazines. Entries in these sections are annotated with reference to their particular value in examining magazines.

PART II

This is a selected bibliography of some 2,220 magazine, journal and newspaper articles, books, and dissertations about magazines.

Included are materials dealing with:

a. The magazine business (such as, circulation, distribution, promotion, revenue sources, management)

b. Magazine writing, layout and production
c. Magazine content
d. Magazine audience
e. The social functions and effects of magazines
f. Magazine advertising
g. Law
h. Ethics
i. History
j. Types of magazines (for example, trade, women's, computer, non-profit, house, specialized)
k. Editors
l. Specific magazine titles

Items on U.S. sales of foreign magazines and foreign sales of U.S. magazines have been included. Foreign magazines have been largely excluded.

Most entries are annotated except when titles are self explanatory or in under two percent of the cases when the authors have been unable to physically examine the item itself or reviews thereof.

No attempt has been made to include everything written about magazines. A publication such as FOLIO: THE MAGAZINE FOR MAGAZINE MANAGEMENT that deals solely with magazines has its own index.

This book is not meant to index such a publication, but to include noteworthy articles only, allowing the reader to peruse the magazine itself for other material matching his/her special needs.

Entries for the bibliography were found through search of all the indexes listed in Chapter II of this volume. In addition, JOURNALISM QUARTERLY includes a regular feature, "Articles on Mass Communication in U.S. and Foreign Journals," and these entries have also been considered for inclusion.

In significant measure, the starting date for materials in this work is January 1, 1979. although overview historical works and some particularly useful books and articles before that date are included. Excluded before 1979 are biographical materials on individual magazines and their editors, writing guides, and nearly all materials included in the J. H. Schacht bibliography. Articles with short-run, non-trend statistics are largely excluded.

Some British and Canadian studies, particularly those dealing with content analyses and social functions of magazines are included. Primarily these are studies indexed in tools handily available in the U.S. and containing material relevant to studies of U.S. magazines.

Material about events in Canadian and British magazine industries has been avoided. The few selections included are mainly generalizable to American magazines and/or contribute to communications theory overall.

So much is written about magazines it is impossible to include more than a most significant minority. The tendency has been toward increased comprehensiveness after 1980 and increasing selectivity in earlier years. It is inevitable that personal interests will bias selection of materials. Thus primary reference sources are included so the reader may further expand his/her own area of investigation.

Books on specific publishers or magazine titles listed in BOOKS IN PRINT or the CUMULATIVE BOOK INDEX have not been sought out for inclusion since they are so readily located by specific name in those references. Major reviewed books on specific magazines and publishers have been included.

Selected M.A. and Ph.D. theses from JOURNALISM ABSTRACTS were included. Selections were based on significance of conclusions and importance of the topics studied. Annotations are based on abstracts rather than personal inspection.

A majority of the theses are content analyses of magazines and study sex-ethnic-racial roles or coverage of selected issues. A few theses were profiles or histories of specific magazine titles, types or journalists.

No effort was made to locate every book written on article writing or free-lancing since 1980. A number of such books are included in the bibliography, but most are quite similar in content, stressing the importance of market analysis, fundamentals of writing, and successfully "selling" queries and manuscripts. Some are written by teachers, others by writers; most are practical, how-to guides.

PART II items are arranged alphabetically within 31 chapters and subcategories. Both books and articles are included in the same list. Each entry is numbered.

The index provides cross references to entries by subject.

ENTRIES WILL NOT BE INDEXED BY THE CHAPTER SUBJECT HEADING. For example, all history entries that appear in the chapter on history will not also be indexed under "history." Any entries appearing elsewhere in the book, and also dealing with history, will be indexed under "history."

THUS, USE OF THE INDEX IS NECESSARY FOR COMPLETE INFORMATION EXTRACTION FROM THIS BIBLIOGRAPHY.

The subject heading "content analysis" is not because most of these entries are classified under content, history, and ethics, Chapters 4, 9, and 13. While these chapters include more than content analysis, many of these chapters' entries use that methodology.

With a few exceptions, articles dealing with magazine content were classed under Chapter 4, "Content," if they dealt with magazines subsequent to 1950, even if they included years prior. Those studies dealing with coverage of a single historical issue, such as the holocaust or the stockmarket crash, or content published only before 1950 are located in Chapter 9, "History."

ITEMS WILL BE INDEXED BY ITEM NUMBER, AND NOT BY PAGE NUMBER.

There are of course many different ways of looking at magazines, and numerous journals, as we have seen, through which to do it. One might, for example, look at magazines in terms of:

a. Writing, editing, design and production
b. Business management--money making
c. Advertising in them or buying space
d. Distribution, display and sales
e. Selection and access by librarians
f. As a vehicle of sociological study
g. As a popular culture medium
h. History--contemporary or general
i. Law, ethics, free press in a democracy
j. Use in educational institutions
k. Innumerable magazine content categories
l. Types of specialized magazines

This bibliography focuses most sharply on the journalistic and business aspects of magazines. Readers with such a focus can broaden their outlook by looking into other areas as listed above to see how they relate to magazine journalism.

TOWARD A DEFINITION OF "MAGAZINE"

There may be as many definitions of the word "magazine" as there are ideas conveyed in a large issue of one. Frank Luther Mott, scholarly historian and noted authority on magazines, defined a magazine as a "bound pamphlet issued more or less regularly ... containing a variety of reading matter and ... a strong connotation of entertainment."[1]

Most contemporary definitions include some or all of these requirements:

a. Issued periodically. (Many sources, such as the IMS/AYER DIRECTORY OF PUBLICATIONS, require a frequency of at least four times a year.)
b. Bound with a paper cover.
c. Containing a variety of feature articles, stories, literature, etc., by many writers.
d. Possibly including art, photographs, advertising.

Such criteria for a "magazine" may become troublesome when we apply them to the wide variety of contemporary magazines.

What is a magazine and what is not? There have been magazines with hard covers, such as AMERICAN HERITAGE, and those appearing more like newspapers, such as the original ROLLING STONE, PARADE, and the NATIONAL ENQUIRER. Some magazines, such as the decade-old "60 MINUTES" or "20/20" are television magazines far from printed pages.

The new-word supplement to the third edition of Webster's unabridged dictionary, 9,000 WORDS, adds this definition for the term "magazine": "A radio or television program presenting several short segments on a variety of topics."

There are magazines which appear irregularly or infrequently, some only once a year, such as the Christmas/craft annuals published by McCALL'S or BETTER HOMES & GARDENS.

Definitions in terms of form may be roughly satisfactory, but they treat magazines as physical commodities instead of as vehicles for ideas, understanding, and reader service. Better magazines primarily seek to serve readers, rather than to manipulate them or sell ideologies or products.

The essence of a magazine is content. The feature article is the fundamental building block of today's magazine.

Whether printed or broadcast, magazines deal with ideas, trends, events, interpretation, facts. They communicate in language readily comprehensible to reasonably well-defined audiences to produce understanding while being entertaining. Content is usually presented as a series of vignettes, articles or segments brief enough to be absorbed by an audience member in a short time. Information is notably shorter and more compressed than in books, yet more detailed and developed than most feature films or television documentaries.

The etymology of the term "magazine" supports this content definition. The word derives from the French noun, "magasin," meaning storehouse, which was Anglicized in 1731 in the title of the London periodical, GENTLEMEN'S MAGAZINE, 110 years before the first U.S. magazines were born.

As used then, the term was descriptive of the publication's content rather than its format, and some publications of that time period in newspaper format were called magazines if they contained a broad variety of content.[2]

What distinguishes magazines from newspapers? Magazines tend to be national, while most newspapers have local circulation. Magazines tend to be more specialized in terms of content and audience, while newspapers have general content with broad audience appeal. Magazines cut across physical boundaries to capture specific, well-defined readers. Newspapers circulate within particular geographic areas appealing to a mass audience.

Magazines have longer deadlines, which allow greater in-depth investigation, research, analysis, and writing. Often more space per issue is devoted to a single feature than in a newspaper. Significance rather than immediacy is central.

The conventions of "objectivity" apply less restrictively in magazines. Fairness is the goal. Helping readers understand rather than simply presenting a "laundry list of facts" is more important in magazines. Dean Osborn Elliott of the Columbia University School of Journalism suggests magazines use "beneficial subjectivity" far more often than newspapers.[3] Viewpoint is usual, editorializing the exception, the distinction continuing to resist precise definition.

Magazines are more permanent than newspapers, though less so than books. On the other hand, they are more timely than books, though less timely than newspapers. They offer easy readability and availability. Those with a cover or subscription price are inexpensive, though less so, discounting inflation, than a decade or so ago. They are clippable, informative, entertaining, easily handled and read in a variety of circumstances and places. They are generally more attractive than newspapers, printed on slick paper, and often with more numerous color pictures.

Magazines have both reflected and helped form the fabric of American culture since the days of Benjamin Franklin when AMERICAN MAGAZINE and Franklin's own GENERAL MAGAZINE first appeared in 1741. Although early magazines were published for wealthy, educated readers, magazines of the late nineteenth century began to appeal to larger mass audiences by reducing their prices and accepting advertising to offset costs.

The character of American magazines has not remained stable. It has changed over the decades to match the needs of audiences, publishers, and advertisers, and to survive in the face of severe competition from such other media as radio and television. Yet the changes have generally been gradual, stable, planned.

With the advent of television and the decline of large, financially burdened mass circulation magazines like LIFE and LOOK, magazines adapted by becoming more specialized and narrowcasting their audiences to offer advertisers a financially reasonable alternative to mass audience advertising techniques of network television.

Magazines are an "important part of the written record of American civilization."[4] They are an invaluable research source to social scientists studying American culture, as they are a permanently preserved record of our tastes, habits, interests, achievements, fads, fashion, opinions, events, values. Magazines are a barometer of contemporary culture at any given point in time. They offer viewpoints on a contemporary world that has long ago passed by.

Magazines are important to study for other reasons, too. Today they cover every business, academic, and social interest--from supermarkets and Sears to mass communication research and jogging. The number of magazines is increasing yearly, according to the IMS/AYER DIRECTORY OF PUBLICATIONS, perhaps the most widely recognized and used source of statistics regarding the number of magazines existing. Since 1950, the number of magazines has doubled, and in 1985 had reached 11,090 titles as defined by AYER'S. Interestingly, the number of newspapers has declined yearly from 13,461 titles in 1932 to 9,134 in 1985.

Magazines are an important part of daily living, serving to educate, inform, and entertain the approximately 75 percent of the adult American population that reads magazines.[5]

Magazines serve the business community as well, by providing a major vehicle for national advertising copy needed to stimulate sales. The business press also serves industry by providing information on new techniques and products and by acting as a forum for the exchange of ideas and news of industry members and conferences.

Magazines are published to serve most individuals in America--young or old, black or white, professional, laborer, hobbyist, new mother or retired teacher, would-be writer or experienced magazine publisher. The industry is dynamic and exciting. Those within the industry are sometimes celebrities in their own right, like Norman Cousins, Helen Gurley Brown or Hugh Hefner.

Being published as a magazine writer is a hope shared by thousands of Americans, from homemaker to student. What happens to magazines, how they grow, where they're going, what they contain, and the problems they face--all are of great interest to magazine and ad industry professionals, journalism students, social researchers, and magazine readers.

Exposure to a magazine is unlikely to instantly change a person's opinions or perspective, but over the course of a lifetime, magazines may have a profound effect on the reader.[6] Most magazine scholars agree on basic functions magazines serve.

Magazines provide information--from how-to skills to career advice to new product information in the form of advertising. People frequently read magazines to learn how to behave--what to wear, proper ettiquette, how to fit into a particular social milieu. Thus magazines become agents of socialization. They reflect and teach acceptable social behavior, and reinforce the status quo in the process.

Magazines provide information on timely events, as well as interpretation, explanation, and understanding of those events and the major social issues of the day. Which political or social happenings are important for public consideration are brought to our attention as part of an agenda-setting role of the mass media.

Magazines provide a forum for the exchange of ideas and discussion. Through the use of advice columns, letters to the editor, and submission of true experience stories, magazines still allow reader participation.

Magazines are a major medium of entertainment. From celebrity journalism to sexual fantasy, they offer readers both informative enjoyment and escapism.

Yet for all that magazines have been studied, analyzed, and written about, their number and purposes remain as elusive as their precise definition. Responsible organizations in the field have declared there are 200 magazines while others, equally responsible, estimate their number at more than 100,000.

Government figures are based on association data, industry sources, and publications put out by and for those in the magazine business. This yields a strong bias toward counting only those publications which contain advertising--strongly correlated with the profit motive.

The 200 figure is of course limited to a narrow category of widely-available "consumer" or general-interest slick-paper monthlies and weeklies.

The 100,000 estimate includes such publications as "house organs," the business press, and highly-specialized, "narrowcast," folded and bound sheets down to but not including newsletters.

Yet if the essence of a magazine is content and not form--if it can be broadcast, for example--then how can one logically eliminate even "newsletters" if their content be thoughtful and prepared with the readers' best interests paramount?

So the argument is endless, and in a sense academic. What counts for each individual is an understanding of his or her own definition based on a system of personal values and knowledge, to which, it is hoped, this volume may contribute.

FOOTNOTES

[1]Frank Luther Mott, A HISTORY OF AMERICAN MAGAZINES, 1841-1850, 5 vols (Cambridge, Mass: Harvard University Press, 1930), 1:7.

[2]Roland E. Wolseley, UNDERSTANDING MAGAZINES, 2d ed. (Ames, Iowa: Iowa State University Press, 1969), p. 7.

[3]Osborn Elliott, "Subjectivity in Journalism," in THE NEWS MEDIA--A SERVICE AND A FORCE, ed. by Festus Justin Viser (Memphis: Memphis State University Press, 1970), p. 29.

[4]James Playsted Wood, MAGAZINES IN THE UNITED STATES, 3d ed. (New York: Ronald Press, 1971), p. 472.

[5]Lieberman Research, HOW AND WHY PEOPLE BUY MAGAZINES: A NATIONAL STUDY OF THE CONSUMER MARKET FOR CONSUMER MAGAZINES (Port Washington, N.Y.: Publishers Clearinghouse, 1977), p. 29.

[6]Theodore Peterson, MAGAZINES IN THE TWENTIETH CENTURY (Urbana, Ill.: University of Illinois Press, 1964), p. 441.

Chapter 1

JOURNALS, MAGAZINES & NEWSLETTERS

Diverse publications carry articles about magazines. Access to these may be gained through the indexes listed in Chapter II or through the bibliography in Part II.

Space and time limitations have prevented listing every article about magazines found in these publications. Below is a selected list of periodicals that carry numerous articles about magazines, and a brief annotation describing the particular focus and approach of each.

If the publication is indexed, one or two readily available indexes are indicated. Consult ULRICH'S PERIODICAL DIRECTORY or Katz's MAGAZINES FOR LIBRARIES to determine other places where publications are indexed.

Selections include not only media periodicals, but those which include critical reviews, scholarly research, and statistics. The effort has been to show a wide variety of approaches available for the study of magazines.

ADVERTISING AGE: THE INTERNATIONAL NEWSPAPER OF MARKETING. 1930-. Crain Communications. Chicago, Ill.

A slick, stapled tabloid written for advertising, marketing, and sales promotion industries, this twice-weekly publication includes numerous articles on magazines. Although the focus is on advertising, there are many articles on new magazines, redesigns of existing titles, targeted magazine audiences, growth of the magazine industry, profiles, promotion campaigns.

Articles tend to be short, geared to advertisers and media space buyers. ADVERTISING AGE covers all media, nationally and internationally.

Some articles seem to be little more than public relations releases from magazine publishers, announcing planned changes in design or launches of new magazines.

Special sections regularly highlight specific types of media, products, markets. Yearly there is a special section on consumer magazines. Sunday supplements, city and regional magazines, the business press have also been highlighted.

ADVERTISING AGE is indexed in the BUSINESS PERIODICALS INDEX, the BUSINESS INDEX, and TOPICATOR.

CAPPELL'S CIRCULATION REPORT: THE NEWSLETTER OF MAGAZINE CIRCULATION. 1982-. Whitaker Newsletters. 24 Prospect St., Westfield, N.J.

Six-page newsletter published twenty times yearly for magazine circulation personnel. Condensed style. Frequent statistics. Overviews of circulation trends for various magazine types.

Lists top ten circulation magazines and analyzes common characteristics. Based on magazine successes, offers advice for improving circulation. Emphasis on analysis of circulation data. Like most newsletters prepared for industry use, subscription cost is high.

CO-EVOLUTION QUARTERLY. 1974-. Point Foundation. Sausalito, Calif.

A general interest periodical of interest to magazinists only because it contains several reviews of magazines in each issue. Reviews are brief and include a signed evaluation and occasional comments from the magazine's publisher.

Indexed in the HUMANITIES INDEX.

COLUMBIA JOURNALISM REVIEW. 1961-. Columbia University, School of Journalism. New York, N.Y.

Emphasis on critical analysis of print and broadcast media. Oriented to issues rather than research, theory, or money-making techniques. Covers such topics as editorial-advertising influences, press objectivity, government controls, role of media, problems at individual publications.

Offers a variety of articles dealing with magazines. "Chronicle" presents suggestive briefs on happenings in magazines and newspapers. "Darts and Laurels" praises and chastises individual editors and publications. Readable and thought-provoking.

Indexed in the HUMANITIES INDEX and TOPICATOR.

COMMUNICATION RESEARCH. 1974-. Sage Publications. Beverly Hills, Calif.

Occasional articles on magazines. Generally focuses on magazines as part of the overall media of communication rather than on specific titles or editors. Heavily research oriented.

Often deals with the application, advantages and disadvantages of a specific research technique. Articles tend to be lengthy, and have excellent bibliographies and research references.

Selectively indexed in COMMUNICATION ABSTRACTS.

EDITORS ONLY: THE NEWSLETTER FOR MAGAZINE EDITORS. 1982-. Editors Only. P.O. Box 2597, Waterbury, Conn.

Monthly eight-page newsletter for publication editors. Advice, how-to tips from experts and other editors on writing, picture editing, management. News of the industry and announcements of workshops, association meetings, conferences. Salary surveys.

FOLIO: THE MAGAZINE FOR MAGAZINE MANAGEMENT. 1972-. Folio Magazine Publishing Corporation. Six River Bend, Box 4949, Stamford, Conn.

Aimed at professional magazine publishers, this trade magazine is a vast, useful source on the business of magazines. How-to features and consultants' advice on management, circulation, production, sales, art direction, editing. Industry news on money, labor, paper, and postal costs. Practical, profit-oriented copy dominant.

Offers understanding of professional jargon, thinking, short- and long-term trends. Copy is occasionally less than polished. Regular features highlight biographies of professionals, births and deaths of magazines.

Some recent issues have focused on one specific function, such as production, circulation, paper. Annual features include salary surveys for all categories of magazine professionals, and the separately published FOLIO 400, an annual statistical report on the top four hundred revenue-producing consumer magazines. An annual Suppliers issue (May) provides extensive data on those who sell products, equipment, and services to (profit-making/ad-carrying) magazines.

Folio Magazine Publishing Corporation produces numerous books on magazine business functions, including the HANDBOOK OF MAGAZINE PUBLISHING which reprints the best articles from the magazine. FOLIO also sponsors professional conferences.

Also publishes CATALOG AGE for those publishers.

Numerous FOLIO articles have been cited in Part II of this volume, but we have not provided a complete index to FOLIO content.

For additional references, consult FOLIO and its annual index. Also indexed in the BUSINESS INDEX and TOPICATOR.

THE GALLAGHER REPORT: "A Confidential Letter to Marketing, Sales, Advertising and Media

Executives." 1951-. Gallagher Report, Inc. 230 Park Ave., New York, N.Y.

Canny newsletter, in gossipy style, full of predictions, coming personnel changes, financial successes and failures with some specific dollar amounts, forthcoming magazine start-ups and shifts. Covers ad/marketing concerns, so only significant minority of clipped comment in this four-pager is on magazines. Surprisingly significant insights find trends in what seems merely current activity reports. Weekly.

INSIDE PRINT (see also MAGAZINE AGE)

INSIDE PRINT, formerly MAGAZINE AGE, is now published by FOLIO. Aimed at ad executives in and out of agencies, but under new title, publication discusses advertising in magazines AND newspapers.

JOURNAL OF ADVERTISING. 1972-. American Academy of Advertising. (See next entry annotation.)

JOURNAL OF ADVERTISING RESEARCH. 1960-. Advertising Research Foundation. New York, N.Y.

These two journals are similar with regard to content carried about magazines. Both are scholarly journals focusing primarily on ad research.

Articles deal with research techniques, advertising effectiveness, recall, effects of ad placement. Focus is on advertising; magazines are important only as the vehicle for advertising.

Both are indexed in BUSINESS PERIODICALS

INDEX. JOURNAL OF ADVERTISING is also indexed in TOPICATOR.

JOURNAL OF AMERICAN CULTURE. 1967-. Bowling Green Popular Press. Bowling Green State University, Bowling Green, Ohio. (See next annotation.)

JOURNAL OF POPULAR CULTURE. 1973-. Popular Culture Association. Bowling Green State University, Bowling Green, Ohio.

These two scholarly journals carry occasional articles about magazines as vehicles of popular culture. Emphasis is frequently on history or content, with consideration of popular themes or heroes. Approach is usually non-quantitative. Indexed in the HUMANITIES INDEX.

JOURNAL OF COMMUNICATION. 1951-. Annenberg School of Communications. Philadelphia, Pa.

This academic journal is concerned with the study of communication theory, practice, and policy, and is aimed at those interested in research, policy development, public impact of communication studies. Interdisciplinary approach. Carries only occasional articles about magazines. Articles tend to be brief, emphasizing research findings rather than methodology. Articles frequently have excellent bibliographies to provide a jump-off point for further research.

Prior to 1983, indexed in the EDUCATION INDEX; from 1982, indexed in SOCIAL SCIENCES INDEX. Also in TOPICATOR.

JOURNALISM HISTORY. 1974-. California State University, Journalism Department. Northridge, Calif.

Brief articles on the history of all aspects of journalism, including magazines. Articles tend to be about particular magazines and/or editors, describing content, issues, and social impact. "Communication History Abstracts" is an excellent bibliographic reference source to articles in other journals, many of which relate to magazines.

Indexed in the HUMANITIES INDEX.

JQ: JOURNALISM QUARTERLY. 1924-. Association for Education in Journalism. Ohio University, Athens, Ohio.

Frequent feature articles and "Research in Brief" about magazines. Emphasis on quantitative research. Many include complex statistical designs. Articles cover a wide range of subjects--including history, types of magazines, magazine advertising, content, functions, theory.

A regular feature is a briefly annotated list of articles on journalism published in other periodicals, arranged by subject with index. Book reviews also arranged by subject. Both are highly useful for locating material on magazines.

Indexed in the HUMANITIES INDEX. Access to early issues through JQ's own cumulated indexes.

LIBRARY JOURNAL. 1876-. R. R. Bowker. New York, N.Y.

Of interest to magazinists in this respected journal for librarians is a regular feature by Bill Katz entitled "Magazines." The author of MAGAZINES FOR LIBRARIES presents title by title review of newer magazines. Magazines reviewed generally not brand-new but one or two years old. Reviews are evaluative, aimed at librarians, and selection of titles is mostly favorable.

Indexed in LIBRARY LITERATURE.

MADISON AVENUE. 1958-. Madison Avenue Publishing Corporation. New York, N.Y.

As its subtitle indicates, this is a magazine of "Marketing Thought and Advertising Strategy," aimed at advertisers and media buyers. Magazines frequently featured since they carry many ads.

Occasional features on specific titles or types of magazines and their advantages to advertisers. "Sales Call" is a regular feature that provides a sales presentation to the reader, often featuring a specific magazine or magazine network, prepared by the management and sales staff of the publication itself.

Prior to August 1985, "Media Times: New and of Note" offers news of new magazines and changes in old titles. It was replaced, with the publication's redesign, by the briefer feature "MADISON AVENUE Flips through Magazines."

Indexed in the BUSINESS PERIODICALS INDEX.

MAGAZINE AGE: "Bringing Advertiser and Agency Management Inside Print." 1980-. Name changed end of 1985 to INSIDE PRINT.

Bought by FOLIO (see annotation) in October 1984. Name changed end of 1985 to INSIDE PRINT. Primarily concerned with advertisers and advertising, with, despite its title, only some emphasis on magazines.

Much discussion of ad rates, demographics, marketing specific types of products, ad positioning. Early issues have occasional reviews of magazines for advertiser selection.

Especially note the "Annual Buyer's Guide to Consumer Magazines" (starting July 1981). Offers profiles and comparative tables on 174 large consumer and farm magazines with introduction, audience, circulation rankings, statistical profiles, new magazines, those with fastest growth, most ad pages for specified products, etc. Also an index. Covers some 100 pages yearly!

MARKETING & MEDIA DECISIONS. 1966-. Decision Publications. New York, N.Y.

Analyzes and offers judgments about on-going concerns relating to placement of advertising dollars in various media. Aimed at professionals in the advertising industry.

Frequent, magazine-related content with advertising slant on such subjects as magazine images, ad rates, growth areas, editors and their achievements. A "Magazines" column by varied ad-industry executives appears in most issues.

Indexed in the BUSINESS PERIODICALS INDEX and TOPICATOR.

MEDIA MANAGEMENT MONOGRAPHS. 1978-. Published

by Jim Mann & Associates. 9 Mount Vernon Drive, Gales Ferry, Conn.

Each useful issue is a sixteen-page booklet on a single topic. Published ten times yearly. Includes an interview with a magazine publishing executive, followed by an analysis of the interview by publisher and media consultant Jim Mann and a brief checklist for readers' use in reviewing their publications' positions. Style is succinct, almost clipped.

Format designed for quick, easy reading with maximum comprehension. Content offers insights into publishing by specific magazines on a variety of interesting and pertinent problems.

Subjects include reader loyalty, how editorial helps advertising, research, spin-offs, starting new magazines. Backlist available. As with many industry newsletters, subscription rates tend to be high. Quality is excellent with professional/managerial orientation in view.

MIN: MEDIA INDUSTRY NEWSLETTER. 1948-. MIN Publishing, Inc. 18 East 53rd Street, New York, N.Y.

Eight-page newsletter, published fifty times per year for media-marketing industry. Strongly but not exclusively magazine-oriented. Content emphasizes news from the industry rather than how-to and management advice.

Covers personnel changes, mergers and acquisitions, publication financial data, industry outlook. Statistics about advertising pages, ad revenue, circulation.

Emphasis on business and advertising rather than editorial aspects of magazines.

NEW YORK MAGAZINE. 1968-. New York Magazine Co. New York, N.Y.

City magazine which frequently carries profiles of editors, publishers, and magazines of the New York metropolitan area. Although content is geographically limited, a wide range is offered in the U.S. magazine-publishing capital.

Some selections are lengthy features, others appear in "On Madison Avenue," a regular column about advertising that frequently considers magazine-related topics such as magazine redesigns or a boom in specific magazine categories.

Indexed in the READERS' GUIDE TO PERIODICAL LITERATURE and the MAGAZINE INDEX.

NEWSWEEK. 1933-. Newsweek Inc. New York, N.Y. (See annotation below.)

TIME. 1923-. Time Inc. New York, N.Y.

These weekly news magazines include occasional articles on magazines. Length ranges from a few column inches to two pages. Often profiles editors, publishers, or magazines; often deals with commemorative occasions or events (e.g, anniversaries, launches, deaths, acquisitions). TIME and NEWSWEEK frequently duplicate coverage.

Indexed in the READERS' GUIDE TO PERIODICAL LITERATURE and the MAGAZINE INDEX.

PUBLISHING TRADE: "Serving Non-Consumer Publications." 1983-. 464 Central, Northfield, Ill.

Six times yearly. Slender, slick volume with substantial emphasis on magazines, personnel, editorial, design, ad, promotion, research, collections, mail, start-up concerns. Formerly for the non-consumer executive now shifting to serve consumer magazines with circulations under 100,000.

Elemental and needed advice for smaller magazine publishers, editors, and would-be executives. Selections from this trade magazine are not included in Part II because the publication is not readily available in many libraries and is not indexed. Claimed circulation 11,000.

QUILL. 1912-. Society of Professional Journalists/Sigma Delta Chi. Chicago, Ill.

Although greater emphasis is placed on news reporting and newspapers than on magazines, QUILL considers many issues applicable to all print media. Focus is on contemporary issues and problems, such as law, free press, government control, ethics, censorship. Also carries association news and announcement of awards such as the National Magazine Awards, established by American Society of Magazine Editors.

Indexed in the HUMANITIES INDEX.

SERIALS LIBRARIAN. 1976-. Haworth Press. New York, N.Y.

Edited for serials librarians. Of greatest interest to the magazinist is a regular column on government serials which discusses content of various classes of government periodicals. Also frequently contains annotated lists of periodicals on specific topics.

Indexed in LIBRARY LITERATURE.

SERIALS REVIEW. 1975-. Pierian Press. Ann Arbor, Mich.

Although edited for librarians, all magazinists will find reviews and overview articles of great interest. Each issue divided into two sections--"Reviews and Recommendations" and "Collection Management Resources."

The review section is divided by category of magazine, such as little, regional, newsstand magazines, and government periodicals. Review articles cover magazines similar in content, ranging from wrestling magazines to comic books.

Articles not only review specific titles, but may overview a type of magazine, such as men's military magazines, or deal at length with one major periodical, such as ATLANTIC MONTHLY.

Selected SERIALS REVIEW articles have been included in Part II of this volume. Readers interested in briefer reviews should peruse other issues of SR.

The first issue of each volume indexes reviews in the previous volume. Also indexed in LIBRARY LITERATURE.

WASHINGTON JOURNALISM REVIEW. 1977-. Washington Communications Corporation. Washington, D.C.

National focus as the name implies. Some articles on magazines, although newspapers are featured more often than any other medium. Articles on magazines most often cover individual editors, publications, people in the news.

Journalistic not business or advertising perspective, though content lacks the critical slant found in COLUMBIA JOURNALISM REVIEW. Informative, upbeat, entertaining style, and lengthy articles.

Somewhat negative reviews (in MAGAZINES FOR LIBRARIES and SERIALS REVIEW) and non-inclusion in a major indexing service unfortunately make this difficult to locate in all but the largest or most specialized libraries. WJR features on magazines have been cited in Part II.

WILSON LIBRARY BULLETIN. 1914-. H. W. Wilson. Co., Bronx, N.Y.

Written for librarians, this publication carries a regular feature reviewing magazine genres, with reference to specific titles. Begun as a regular feature in 1982, "Magazines," by Gail Pool, continues but no longer appears in every issue. Articles are brief, dealing with a broad range of magazine types from trade to humor.

Emphasis is not on evaluative reviews of particular titles, but on understanding magazine publishing and the relationship of specific titles to the whole field.

Selected articles by Pool have been included in Part II of this volume. Perusal of other issues of WLB may be helpful to the reader.

Indexed in LIBRARY LITERATURE and the EDUCATION INDEX.

THE WRITER. 1887-. The Writer, Inc. Boston, Mass. (See annotation below.)

WRITER'S DIGEST. 1919-. F & W Publishing Corporation. Cincinnati, Ohio.

Two monthly publications written for writers, with heavy emphasis on magazine free-lancing. Both feature suggestions for developing article ideas, marketing free-lanced pieces, querying editors. Both offer notes on specific magazines seeking free-lanced articles, with payment and submission details. Articles generally brief. Very few selections from these magazines have been included in Part II.

Readers interested in learning basic writing techniques and free-lancing are encouraged to peruse these magazines, then move on to larger directories and issues of lesser-known magazines themselves, which must be studied to succeed.

The WRITER is indexed in READERS' GUIDE TO PERIODICAL LITERATURE.

Chapter 2

SELECTED REFERENCE SOURCES

From directories listing hundreds of published consumer magazines to indexes of their content, reference tools of various kinds assist the magazine researcher. Below is a selected list of some general reference books particularly helpful in the study of magazines.

The annotations make no attempt to give complete descriptions, but to briefly suggest how they might be used for researching magazines. Directories of special interest magazines have not been included in this section, but in Part II.

Only the major, comprehensive magazine directories have been listed here. This section is divided into three parts:

a. Statistical Sources.
b. Indexes and Abstracts.
c. Directories, Bibliographies and Others.

Statistical Sources

AUDIT BUREAU OF CIRCULATIONS. 900 North Meacham Road, Schaumburg, Illinois, 60195.

As an authority on magazine circulation, ABC is a major source of circulation data. The organization offers special low-cost memberships to schools that enable professors to distribute much valuable statistical information to their students. Industry memberships are considerably more expensive.

Of particular value is the annual "Magazine Trend Report" which provides five-year circulation and advertising data for 128 U.S. and 49 Canadian magazines. Magazines are listed by type (e.g., automotive, business & finance, general editorial, science). Data include average paid circulation, percentages of newsstand and subscription sales, number of subscriptions sold and how many are sold by mail and at the basic rate, single copy and subscription prices, advertising rates, cost per thousand, and guaranteed circulation. Comparisons easily made between magazines of similar types.

Also available are circulation reports on individual magazine titles.

FOLIO 400. Annual. Folio Magazine Publishing Corporation. New Canaan, Conn.

Published since 1979 each October by the publishers of FOLIO: THE MAGAZINE FOR MAGAZINE MAN-

AGEMENT. Originally bound within the monthly issue, the FOLIO 400 is now separately bound with approximately five hundred pages and index tabs.

It ranks top revenue publications in the U.S. Aimed at the advertising and marketing industries, it includes brief profiles for each magazine title and comparisons of titles in each of numerous subject categories (e.g., in-flight, black, computing, news, three categories for men's books).

Data include number of ad pages, ad revenue, average circulation, total revenue with percent change from the previous year noted. Also ranks the top fifty consumer magazines by each of several criteria (e.g., ad revenue, ad pages, subscription revenue, newsstand revenue, circulation, amount of change).

Other lists rank the fastest-growing consumer magazines. Bar graphs and pie charts illustrate revenue and circulation sources for all FOLIO 400 publications with comparisons for years since 1979. An invaluable statistical reference source for consumer magazines.

STUDY OF MEDIA AND MARKETS. Annual. Simmons Market Research Bureau. New York, N.Y.

Multi-volume survey report on readership of approximately 120 consumer magazines. Considers social, occupational, racial, age, financial, etc. status of readers. Projects number of readers per magazine based on interviews with more than 19,000 American adults. Measures reach and frequency, multi-media audiences, duplication of audiences.

Other volumes deal with specific consumer products and relate their use (by brand and genre) to magazine reading. One could find a percentage indicating how many readers of ATLANTIC MONTHLY smoke cigarettes, for example.

An extensive statistical study. Over the years significant controversy has been generated regarding SMRB methodolgy. See Part II of this volume, Chapter 6, "Audience," for additional information.

CENSUS OF MANUFACTURES. Published every five years, in years ending in two and seven. U.S. Department of Commerce. Bureau of the Census.

Of interest to magazinists is the report, "Newspapers, Periodicals, Books, and Miscellaneous Publishing." Accompanying text describes each segment of the publishing industry and also provides brief explanation of the tabulations and data collection procedures. The bulk of the report is statistical tables. Relevant data are classed under Periodicals, industry 2721.

Consistent tendency to look in terms of magazines as a manufactured product--paper, ink, machinery needed to manufacture, number of persons employed in various categories (e.g., professional and blue-collar).

Historical tables compare industry-wide data from various years on the number of employees, payroll, production, work hours, value of shipments. Periodical production compared by state. Of particular value are statistics on total industry receipts (advertising and circulation revenue) and circulation, broken down by type of magazine (consumer, business, farm) and type of circulation (controlled, newsstand, subscription).

Although there is a tendency to feel bogged down by too many tables and statistics, the persistent researcher will find a wealth of information here. Comparing these reports over time is valuable for study of industry trends.

U.S. INDUSTRIAL OUTLOOK. Annual. U.S. Department of Commerce. Bureau of Industrial Economics.

Of relevance to magazinists is the section on periodicals found in the chapter "Printing and Publishing." This section has for many years been separately authored by Rose Marie Zummo Bratland (a name for serious researchers to remember), of the Office of Consumer Goods.

Includes a separate set of references. Two or three pages describe trends and the overall growth or decline in the periodical industry for consumer, business, and farm publications.

Production and paper costs, ad and circulation revenues, subscription and newsstand circulation trends are presented with frequent tables and graphs accompanying tables and graphs.

Statistics derived from Bureau of Census and industry/association sources. Invaluable comparisons and trend study may be made by examining these chapters over the years.

Indexes & Abstracts

Indexes are most commonly used to access the content of periodicals. Other research has used indexes as a source of data. Applying content analysis techniques to index content by counting entries under specific subject headings has been used by some social scientists as a measure of important social concerns, particularly as it reflects the agenda setting function of the press. See entry 1, Chapter 3, describing the Greenfield Index. See also entries indexed under READERS' GUIDE.

BUSINESS PERIODICALS INDEX. 1958-. H. W. Wilson. Bronx, N.Y.

An index to the complete content of selected business periodicals. Numerous advertising industry periodicals containing magazine-related content are indexed here, including MADISON AVENUE, MARKETING & MEDIA DECISIONS, ADVERTISING AGE, JOURNAL OF ADVERTISING, JOURNAL OF ADVERTISING RESEARCH.

General business publications are indexed here, including BUSINESS WEEK, FORBES, FORTUNE, and publishing industry periodicals including PUBLISHERS WEEKLY and EDITOR & PUBLISHER. Unfortunately, FOLIO: THE MAGAZINE FOR MAGAZINE MANAGEMENT is not yet indexed here.

Primary subject headings relevant to magazines are audience research--periodicals, advertising in magazines, periodicals, house organs, periodical publishers and publishing, with cross-references to names of specific publications.

Indexing by subject only, not author/title. Articles accessed through this index are business-related, offering financial, ad, distribution, management, publishing, and ownership information and news.

COMMUNICATION ABSTRACTS. 1978-. Sage Publications. Beverly Hills, Calif.

Selective abstracts of communication-related articles from a variety of sources, ranging from academic journals to book sections. Entries of interest to magazinists are indexed under magazines, magazine readership, magazine advertising.

Includes ten to thirty items per year on magazines. Most have a scholarly research focus. Selections drawn from such journals as JOURNALISM QUARTERLY, JOURNAL OF COMMUNICATIONS, PUBLIC OPINION QUARTERLY, JOURNAL OF ADVERTISING. Each selection has a descriptive annotation outlining approach and findings.

DISSERTATION ABSTRACTS INTERNATIONAL. 1938-. Xerox University Microfilms. Ann Arbor, Mich.

An index and abstracting service in two parts. Index volumes list citations to abstracts by subject, keyword index, and author. Accession number locates abstract in companion volumes. Abstracts are prepared by dissertation authors. Dissertations available through University Microfilms, although abstracts themselves offer concise summaries. Of particular interest are dissertations in mass communications.

HUMANITIES INDEX. 1974-. H. W. Wilson. Bronx, N.Y.

A subject and author index to journals in the humanities. Indexed titles relevant to magazines are JOURNALISM QUARTERLY, JOURNALISM HISTORY, JOURNAL OF POPULAR CULTURE, JOURNAL OF AMERICAN CULTURE, COLUMBIA JOURNALISM REVIEW. Search under the subheading periodicals. Indexed articles are oriented primarily towards journalism, research, history, popular culture.

JOURNALISM ABSTRACTS. 1963-. Association for Education in Journalism and Mass Communications. Place varies.

Abstracts of mass communication and journalism dissertations and theses from fifty-four universities in U.S. and Canada. Abstracts are author-prepared. Arranged alphabetically in two parts, Ph.D. dissertations and Master's theses. Author and subject indexes.

Search under the subhead magazines. Includes research theses only, not creative projects. Many dealing with magazines are content analyses. About half the papers listed during the period covered by this bibliography are included in this volume. Selection was based on subject and on value of the information included within the abstract itself.

NEXIS. Mead Data Central. New York.

High specificity, high cost information search via comprehensive(!) on-line, full-text retrieval system. Covers vast numbers of newspapers, magazines. Keyword(s) offer instant access for and by wire services, other printed sources filed in databank (next day filing claimed on daily papers, weekly or better for weekly publications, etc.)

McGraw-Hill and many, many other publications input material and some access at (1981) rates of $25-90 per hour. Worth watching as industry may increase its use of NEXIS, possibly replicating information and error more than under present system as speed increases.

MAGAZINE INDEX. (IAC Magazine Index.) Information Access Corporation. Menlo Park, Calif.

Updated frequently. Purports to accurately index content of 435 (actually 370, perhaps fewer) magazines on a prompt basis. Microfilmed currently (five years); microfiche for earlier issues. Covers 1959-1970 and 1973-date, with some in progress for period between. Online database.

While neither error-free nor as comprehensive as one might be led to believe, this microform version of READERS' GUIDE TO PERIODICAL LITERATURE nonetheless has great potential and some utility now. Search under periodicals and periodical publishing.

NEW YORK TIMES INDEX. Annual. New York Times Company. New York. (And other newspaper indexes.)

The NEW YORK TIMES contains sporadic but often excellent discussions of publishing, events, and advertising concerns in the magazine capital of the world.

A useful column titled "Advertising," by Philip H. Dougherty, often covers magazines with reports of conventions, speeches, individuals, innovations.

Use of index is a virtual must. Complete but often a year behind. Articles are listed alphabetically by subject, chronologically within a single subject. Search under the subject heading, magazines.

The NEWSPAPER INDEX on microform from Information Access indexes the past five years, and claims immediacy. However, there are some citation errors and possible subject access problems.

In addition, the WASHINGTON POST and LOS ANGELES TIMES both publish their own indexes and often carry articles related to magazines.

READERS' GUIDE TO PERIODICAL LITERATURE. 1900-. H. W. Wilson Co. Bronx, N.Y.

An author and subject index to 160 general interest periodicals. Search under heading, periodicals. One disadvantage--references to specific magazine titles are not cross referenced under the general heading, periodicals.

Among magazines indexed that frequently carry magazine-related content are TIME, NEWSWEEK, NEW YORK, FORBES. Focus of indexed articles tends to be news-oriented, covering lawsuits, mergers, new editions, and occasionally magazine profiles.

RESOURCES IN EDUCATION: RIE. 1974-. Oryx Press, Phoenix, Ariz. (E.R.I.C.)

This is the abstract journal for the Educational Resources Information Center, otherwise known as ERIC. A two-part index and abstract. Abstracts are indexed by author, subject, type of material (e.g., dissertations, opinion papers, reports), publishing institution.

Abstracts in separate volumes summarize speeches, papers, documents, pamphlets not generally available through ordinary channels. Articles from such relevant journals as JOURNALISM QUARTERLY are indexed in the companion, CURRENT JOURNALS IN EDUCATION.

Documents can be ordered through ERIC at a reasonable cost. Numerous research papers on magazines and journalism are indexed here. Time and space limitations prevent inclusion in Part II.

SOCIAL SCIENCES INDEX. 1965-. H. W. Wilson. Bronx, N.Y.

An author and subject index to journals in the social sciences. Occasional sociological research studies use magazines for data collection, and such articles are indexed here.

TOPICATOR. 1965-. P.O. Box 99, Florissant, Colorado.

A classified article guide to twenty publications in advertising/communications/ marketing. Published bi-monthly. Annual index gives quick reference guide to content. Index but not citations are cumulated annually. Indexed publications of interest to magazinists include ADVERTISING AGE, FOLIO, COLUMBIA JOURNALISM REVIEW,

EDITOR & PUBLISHER, GRAPHIC ARTS MONTHLY, JOURNAL OF ADVERTISING, JOURNAL OF COMMUNICATIONS, MARKETING & MEDIA DECISIONS.

WALL STREET JOURNAL INDEX. Annual. Dow Jones Books. Princeton, N.J.

For articles about magazines in the WALL STREET JOURNAL, consult volume II for the general news index. Articles are arranged alphabetically by subject (see magazines) and chronologically within subject categories. Entries include a brief synopsis of content and item's location in the newspaper. Articles range from news briefs to lengthy, in-depth magazine profiles. Feature articles on magazines generally appear in columns one, four or six, while column five most often contains news briefs.

Directories, Bibliographies & Others

AMERICA'S CORPORATE FAMILIES. Parsippany, N.J.: Dun & Bradstreet, 1986.

Valuable source for tracing ultimate ownership of individual publishing houses. Alphabetical list of parent companies with subsidiaries. Indexed by geographic location, industry classification, subsidiary or division name. Not limited to publishers.

Blum, Eleanor. BASIC BOOKS IN THE MASS MEDIA. 2d ed. Urbana: University of Illinois Press, 1980.

An excellent selected bibliography of basic source materials on mass communication. A chapter on magazines includes basic reference tools (e.g., bibliographies, directories) and texts. Another chapter annotates the primary indexes to the periodical literature of mass communication.

Blum, retired long-time University of Illinois journalism librarian, deserves special respect and attention in communication bibliography, as does the branch library there.

BUSINESS PUBLICATION RATES AND DATA. See Standard Rate and Data Service.

CONSUMER MAGAZINE AND AGRI-MEDIA: RATES AND DATA. See Standard Rate and Data Service.

ENCYCLOPEDIA OF ASSOCIATIONS. 1986. 20th ed. Detroit, Mich.: Gale Research Co., 1985.

Published since 1959, annually since 1972, this directory lists associations by type. Name and key word indexes. Each entry provides address, founding date, staff size, membership, and brief description of purposes and goals. Lists publications offered by each association. Provides access to list of various advertising, magazine, journalism, publishing associations by subject.

Harrison, William T. U.S. REGIONAL PUBLICATIONS DIRECTORY. Haverford, Pa.: Bradley Communications, 1986.

Profiles of 2,121 city, state and regional magazines, tabloids, newsletters and directories in twenty-nine subject categories from agriculture to printing to women's interests.

Has geographic coverage index to distinguish circulation area from corporate headquarters area.

Edited by William T. Harrison. More extensive list of titles than some sources. Zip codes, subject, ad rates, key personnel.

IMS/AYER DIRECTORY OF PUBLICATIONS. Fort Washington, Pa.: IMS Press, 1869-.

Directory of magazines and newspapers by place of publication. Includes consumer and trade magazines, daily and weekly newspapers, newsletters, but excludes house organs. No subject access.

Publications based in U.S., Canada, some other areas. Entry shows circulation, prices, ad rates, editor, publisher, date established.

Of particular value to magazine researchers is the statistical tabulation appearing in the front of each annual volume. It gives the number of newspapers and magazines included in the current and previous directory.

AYER'S has come to be recognized as a leading source for the "number of magazines" quoted by the Magazine Publishers Association as well as in some Congressional reports. It is possible to use earlier volumes (in 1932 AYER DIRECTORY separated periodicals from newspapers in its count) to develop historical and trend data.

Katz, Bill, and Katz, Linda Sternberg. MAGAZINES FOR LIBRARIES. 4th ed. New York: R. R. Bowker, 1982.

Annotated list of 6,500 periodicals, arranged by subject. Citations include full bibliographic information, scope and focus of content, indexing, evaluation, and suggested audience. Although prepared for librarians, its critical evaluations and descriptions are valuable for everyone interested in magazines.

MAGAZINE INDUSTRY MARKETPLACE 1986: THE DIRECTORY OF AMERICAN PERIODICAL PUBLISHING. 6th ed. New York: R. R. Bowker, 1985.

A directory of people, publishers, services, publications. Lists of magazines include title, address, personnel, frequency of publication, circulation, advertising information.

Other sections of the volume provide bibliography of reference literature on magazines, associations, events and exhibits, advertising and public relations agencies, a wide range of services and suppliers including photographers, translators, direct mail promoters, manufacturers, and circulation fulfillment and distribution services.

Lists back-date periodical dealers and includes a telephone-address directory of names and organizations.

Marconi, Joseph V. INDEXED PERIODICALS. Ann Arbor, Mich.: Pierian Press, 1976.

A guide to 170 years of coverage in thirty-three indexing services. Alphabetical list of magazines, with history of publication dates, title changes, and indexing. Its publication date limits its current usefulness, but historical value is vast.

Schmittroth, John, Jr. ABSTRACTING AND INDEXING SERVICES DIRECTORY. 3 vols. Detroit: Gale Research Co., 1982-1983.

This directory was published in three issues between 1982-1983 and includes a total of 1760 citations to abstracting journals, indexes, digests. AISD is a list of recurring publications that "provide summaries of and/or references to multiple sources of published literature in a particular subject area or of a specific type."

It is arranged alphabetically by index title within each of the three issues. Cumulative keyword subject and publication title indexes appear in each issue.

Entries include arrangement, content, description, and scope of the index as well as the subjects covered and ordering information. Magazine researchers may find it useful to identify indexes and abstracting services dealing with journalism, mass communication, magazines, etc.

SOURCES OF SERIALS. 2d ed. New York: R. R. Bowker, 1981.

A geographical directory of serials publishers and corporate authors worldwide. Lists titles published by each organization. Titles of approximately 100,000 periodicals appearing in the several Ulrich's directories appear here. Index to publishers, not to titles. Consult Ulrich's directories to determine publisher and use this directory to discover what other periodicals emanate from the same source.

STANDARD PERIODICAL DIRECTORY, 1983-1984. 8th ed. New York: Oxbridge Communications, 1982.

Now in its eighth edition, this directory has been published since 1964. It currently provides a list of over 60,000 U.S. and Canadian periodical titles, including consumer and trade magazines, newletters, house organs, directories, etc.

Arranged by subject of periodical and indexed by title. Each entry includes publication title, previous titles, publisher, address, phone, names of key personnel, year established, frequency of issue, price, circulation (including newsstand and subscription data), readership, size, advertising rates.

Often contains a short, descriptive statement (lacking in other major directories) about the magazine. Helpful in locating titles of various publications on the same subject, in gathering statistical data on circulation, comparing newsstand and subscription circulations.

Standard Rate and Data Service. CONSUMER MAGAZINE AND AGRI-MEDIA: RATES AND DATA. Wilmette, Ill.: SRDS, Inc., 1919-.

Monthy publication detailing advertising rates

and data for more than 1,200 U.S. consumer magazines and 200 farm journals. Also of relevance is BUSINESS PUBLICATION RATES AND DATA, a similar publication for the business press.

Organized by subject of magazines with a title index. Entries include magazine editorial profile, publisher, address, personnel names and titles, advertising rates, discounts and specifications, circulation. Written for advertising buyers.

Current issues used in combination with past issues provide much information on the success or failure of specific titles, as new magazines and subject trends may be traced. See entries 2 and 333 in the bibliography for citations to research based on SRDS information.

Schacht, J. H. A BIBLIOGRAPHY FOR THE STUDY OF MAGAZINES. Urbana: University of Illinois, College of Communication, 1979.

Briefly annotated, selective bibliography of materials about magazines. Lists over 1100 journal and magazine articles and books. Includes old materials as well as items published as late as 1979. Annotations are very brief, non-evaluative clarification of content. Entries arranged by subject. No index. Invaluable for locating earlier materials. Prior edition, dated 1972, was far briefer. The 1972 edition is available through ERIC.

Sicignano, Robert, and Prichard, Doris, eds. SPECIAL ISSUES INDEX: SPECIALIZED CONTENTS OF BUSINESS, INDUSTRIAL, AND CONSUMER JOURNALS.

Westport, Conn.: Greenwood Press, 1982. (See annotation below.)

Uhlan, Miriam, ed. GUIDE TO SPECIAL ISSUES AND INDEXES OF PERIODICALS. 3d ed. New York: Special Libraries Association, 1985. (See annotation below.)

GUIDE TO INDUSTRY SPECIAL ISSUES. 1st ed. Cambridge, Mass.: Ballinger Publishing Co., 1984.

These three directories provide similar information and roughly comparable format. They are alphabetical listings of periodicals that offer special issues. Each lists periodicals by title with corresponding special issues, their dates of publication and subject focus. All have subject indexes. None claims to be comprehensive, and so all three are well-used in concert.

Unlike the other volumes, the GUIDE TO INDUSTRY SPECIAL ISSUES offers indexes by geographic area, industry, publisher, statistical content.

ULRICH'S INTERNATIONAL PERIODICALS DIRECTORY: A CLASSIFIED GUIDE TO CURRENT PERIODICALS, FOREIGN AND DOMESTIC. New York: R. R. Bowker, 1932-.

This guide lists more than 69,000 titles of magazines published more often than annually and arranged under 557 broad subject headings.

Title index in Volume II. Entries include frequency of publication, publisher's name and address, and Dewey Decimal number. When available, has information on whether publication has advertising or book reviews, and where it is indexed and abstracted.

Includes a list of cessations since last issue of ULRICH'S and an index to international organizations. ULRICH'S QUARTERLY gives prompt information on cessations, title changes, and new titles.

The companion volume IRREGULAR SERIALS AND ANNUALS gives data on publications issued at irregular frequencies or yearly, including such items as conference proceedings.

A comprehensive, authoritative list, useful in locating hard-to-find and foreign titles.

No ad or circulation data.

Wolseley, Roland E., and Wolseley, Isabel. THE JOURNALIST'S BOOKSHELF. 8th ed. Indianapolis, Ind.: R. J. Berg, 1986.

A selected, critically annotated bibliography of 2,368 books about U.S. print journalism. Includes many older titles, as well as some new. Sections relevant to magazines include "Magazines in General" and "Magazine Writing."

Other sections include magazine-related materials. Of particular value are the sections on biography, history, free-lance journalism, editing. This is a good source to locate biographies of journalists and histories both general and for specific magazines.

WORKING PRESS OF THE NATION. 5 vols. Chicago: National Research Bureau. 1947-.

An annual directory. Of interest to magazinists are volume 2, MAGAZINE DIRECTORY, and volume 5, INTERNAL PUBLICATIONS DIRECTORY. Both are lists of publications. Volume 2 lists magazines by title in three categories, business, farm, and consumer. Within broad types, entries are arranged by specific subjects, and include address, phone number, year established, publication frequency, page size, subscription rate, types of publicity materials accepted, free-lance pay scale, printing process, wire services used, circulation size and type, owner, personnel names, reader profile, deadlines. Information is submitted by the publisher. Subject and title indexes.

Volume 5 is a directory of more than 3,000 company-sponsored publications, listed alphabetically by organization. Indexes to titles, type of industry, and editorial interest. Entry includes sponsor name, address and telephone number, publication name, description, frequency, size, publicity materials accepted, free-lance pay scale, lead time, editor. All information is provided by publications' sponsors.

WRITER'S MARKET. Annual. F & M Publications, Cincinnati, Ohio. 1930-

Widely available guide mainly for beginning and would-be magazine free-lance writers. Index and brief bibliography. Associated with WRITER'S DIGEST magazine, and has similar "just write and you'll sell" philosophical undertone.

Includes description and requirements of magazines using free-lance material. Each entry consists of a few paragraphs supplied by the magazine via yearly questionnaire.

WRITER'S MARKET has two drawbacks. First, it apparently seeks to be all things to all writers--of short stories, poetry, plays, fillers and gags--as well as article writers.

Second, many listings are for more familiar and available (and hence more competitive) magazines. Would-be writers thus send to publications less likely to buy because of their popularity with free-lancers. Off-beat markets, unfamiliar on newsstands, and study of numerous issues thereof, being necessary to consistent sales, the book can lead new writers in wrong directions, since they tend to feel "knowledgable" based on few paragraphs.

WRITER'S MARKET is a good first-look source for the writer who chooses less widely-known magazines dealing incidentally, not primarily, in subjects with which writer has much expertise.

Chapter 3

GENERAL OVERVIEW

1 Beniger, James R. "Media Content as Social Indicators: The Greenfield Index of Agenda-Setting." COMMUNICATION RESEARCH 5 (October 1978) : 437-453.

The Greenfield Index, based on counting periodical index entries, is useful in measuring social change, agenda setting, and attention by the media.

2 Bowers, Anne Palmer. "The Life Expectancy of American Consumer Magazines." M.A. thesis, University of Georgia, 1979.

Statistical documentation of magazine life cycles over twenty-five-year period. STANDARD RATE AND DATA SERVICES used as primary information source. Publications with large circulations and small prices lived longest. Average healthy life span was between 10 and 20 years. Documents the rise in "mass" special interest magazines.

3 Burnett, Leo. "The Mission of Magazines." SATURDAY REVIEW 42 (December 26, 1959) : 22.

Critique of marketing trends in the magazine industry which may overshadow editorial integrity.

4 "Business Publishers Starting Own 'Journalism Schools.'" FOLIO 15 (February 1986) : 32.

Publishers offer legitimate complaint that university "J-Schools" do little to teach business magazine publishing. Chilton and North American cited as having begun low-cost quickie programs.

5 Carter, Robert A. "Breaking In." PUBLISHERS WEEKLY 224 (November 25, 1983) : 28-32.

College and university publishing programs (as opposed to journalism education) and their value to job seekers in book and magazine publishing.

6 Click, J. William, and Baird, Russell N. MAGAZINE EDITING AND PRODUCTION. 4th ed. Dubuque, Iowa: Wm. C. Brown, 1986.

This academically preeminent text focuses on layout/production and editorial planning, although the industry is surveyed from research to circulation. Other chapters discuss law, publication success and failure, and trends towards special interest magazines. Also of interest is brief chapter on ethics. "Pressures and Responsibilities" facing editors and publishers include social class pressures, advertiser influence, editorial bias. Glossary and brief bibliography.

7 Compaine, Benjamin M. "Magazines." In WHO OWNS THE MEDIA?, pp. 127-178. Edited by Benjamin M. Compaine. White Plains, N.Y.: Knowledge Industry Publications, 1979.

Excellent overview of the magazine industry. Considers everything from the role of magazines to group ownership, from advertising revenue to starting a new magazine. Conclusions supported by detailed statistics.

8 Cook, Charles R. "Employment Trends in the U.S. Printing and Publishing Industry." PRINTING AND PUBLISHING, U.S. Department of Commerce 21 (Fall 1980) : 3-7.

Includes newspapers, periodicals, books, printing, etc. Provides total employment and earnings 1974-79.

9 Donath, Bob. "Magazines Hang their Hats on Special Interest, Shun War on TV." ADVERTISING AGE 45 (November 18, 1974) : 32+.

Trends in magazine publishing, from easing of competition with television to rise in cover prices and advertising rates.

10 Dreyfack, Madeleine. "Home and Technology Magazines Booming." MARKETING & MEDIA DECISIONS 16 (December 1981) : 68-70+.

Booming magazines for 1980-1981 included home, shelter, technology, cable, and regional magazines. Do-it-yourselfers promote growth of home and shelter magazines.

11 Elliott, Stuart J., and Emmrich, Stuart. "Mass and Class Clash for Readers, Ads." ADVERTISING AGE 53 (November 8, 1982) : 10.

Controversy over which type of magazine is stronger--mass or class. Although many mass magazines are successful, the balance probably favors class magazines. More new magazines and repositioned old ones aim for affluent, educated audiences.

12 Fabrikant, Geraldine. "Sobering Year for Magazines; Many Face Ad Declines." NEW YORK TIMES, 14 September 1985, p. 31+.

Ad rates have increased but ad pages have declined. Advertising revenue contributes higher share of operating costs than subscription revenue because the cost of obtaining new ads is less than the cost of obtaining new subscriptions.

13 Ford, James L. C. MAGAZINES FOR MILLIONS: THE STORY OF SPECIALIZED PUBLICATIONS. Carbondale, Ill.: Southern Illinois University

Press, 1969.

Comprehensive. All kinds of specialized magazines, including shelter, children's, leisure, religious, farm, business. Covers house organs and publications serving associations and industries. Many brief profiles of specific titles. Old but never entirely replaced by another volume.

14 Gingrich, Arnold. "The Facts of Life and Death in the Magazine World." QUILL 51 (October 1963) : 21-23.

Excerpts from AEJ speech August 28, 1963. Observations from ESQUIRE publisher regarding magazine problems and future trends. Predicts magazine-making will grow more difficult, and increasingly local, topical, authoritative, intellectual, daring, and specialized in content.

15 Hafferkamp, Jack. "Prognosis Bodes Well for a Steady Recovery." ADVERTISING AGE 54 (October 17, 1983) : M9+.

After recession effects, magazines are again a growth industry. Advertising pages rise as network tv audience declines. Special interest magazines proliferate. Research determines reader needs.

16 Hanson, J. J. "MPA and ABP Should Merge: The Magazine Industry is too Small to be Represented by as many Associations as Now Exist."

One column reviews ABP and other magazine-related associations, name changes, membership. Offers glimpse of industry size.

17 Haroldsen, Edwin O., and Harvey, Kenneth E. "Frowns Greet New J-Grads in Magazine Job Market." JOURNALISM EDUCATOR 34 (July 1979) : 3-8+.

Magazine editors' ideas for improving journalism curricula. Their displeasure with quality of journalism grads.

18 "Have We Been Here Before?" FORBES 109 (May 15, 1972) : 52-56.

Comparison of today's reformers with yesterday's muckrakers.

19 Holder, Dennis. "The Decade of Specialization." WASHINGTON JOURNALISM REVIEW 3 (November 1981) : 28-32.

Overview article details growth in specialized magazines, lifestyle changes which spawn new magazine titles, postal service problems, cable television competition. Part of WJR special report: "Magazines in the 80s." See also entry 20.

20 Holder, Dennis. "Magazines in the Eighties." In READINGS IN MASS COMMUNICATION: CONCEPTS AND ISSUES IN THE MASS MEDIA, pp. 375-385. Edited

by Michael Emery and Ted Curtis Smythe. Dubuque, Iowa: Wm. C. Brown, 1983.

Trends discussed include increasing specialization, new types of women's magazines, increasing advertising content in relation to editorial, industry growth. Reprint of WASHINGTON JOURNALISM REVIEW article, November 1981. See also entry 19.

21 "The Hot Magazines Aim at Special Targets." BUSINESS WEEK (May 2, 1970) : 64-65+.

Mass magazines are struggling, but specialized magazines thrive in 1970.

22 Hulin-Salkin, Belinda. "Viewing the Future in a New Light." ADVERTISING AGE 56 (October 3, 1985) : 15-16.

Newsstand sales are down, ad pages are down, mergers are common in the magazine industry. After years of growth, the industry has reached a plateau.

23 Husni, Samir Afif. "Success and Failure of New Consumer Magazines in the United States: 1979-1983." Ph.D. dissertation, University of Missouri, 1983.

Two functions of consumer magazines are defined: social and commercial. A typical issue of a new magazine is constructed. Major differences between successful and unsuccessful new magazines include cover price and frequency of publication.

24 Inge, M. Thomas, ed. HANDBOOK OF AMERICAN POPULAR CULTURE. 3 vols. Westport, Conn.: Greenwood Press, 1978-1981.

A reference volume with separately titled and authored chapters on a wide variety of popular culture vehicles, including magazines and the pulps. Each section includes an extensive bibliography.

25 Isaacs, Stephen. "Magazines: The Medium Gets the Message." WASHINGTON POST, 2 January 1972, p. E1.

Four-part series, appearing January 2-5, 1972, on the "economic and editorial revolution in magazines" during the 1970s. Discusses higher reader costs, tailoring magazines to match an audience, and other changes.

26 "Journalism: Where the Jobs Are." MS. 11 (September 1982) : 75-76.

Advantages of working for the trade press, including magazines, newsletters, and newspapers. Names and addresses of major publishing houses.

27 Kenyon, Robert E., Jr. "New QUALIFIED J-Grads DO Land Magazine Jobs." JOURNALISM EDUCATOR 34

(January 1980) : 20-22+.

How magazine educators can better prepare students to compete for magazine jobs.

28 Klingel, John. "What's in a (Magazine's) Name?" FOLIO 15 (January 1986) : 151-152+.

Anecdotal look at some unusual magazine names and their surprising effect on readers.

29 Kobak, James. "Magazines Sail Through." MARKETING & MEDIA DECISIONS 18 (Fall 1983, Special) : 41-42+.

Financial data to back Kobak's opinion that magazines survived the recession very well.

30 Kronenfeld, Michael R., and Thompson, James A. "Impact of Inflation on Journal Costs." LIBRARY JOURNAL 106 (April 1, 1981) : 714.

Comparison of journals and magazines over the years 1967-1979 shows periodical costs have been rising more rapidly than other costs.

31 Love, Barbara. "1980s: The Real Test." FOLIO 8 (September 1979) : 45-46+.

Forecast for the 1980s: a mild recession won't hurt the industry, great changes in printing and production techniques, more competition from television as it begins to segment audiences, higher circulation prices.

32 Love, Barbara. "The Past 10 Years: Tracking the Industry's Performance." FOLIO 11 (September 1982) : 60-64+.

An excellent twenty-four-page summary of industry trends, 1972 to 1982. Economics, advertising, circulation, production, editorial, postal statistics are displayed in numerous graphs and charts.

33 Lukovitz, Karlene. "The Next 10 Years: 24 Predictions for the Future." FOLIO 11 (September 1982) : 96-97+.

Sixteen pages of predictions from magazine experts.

34 "Magazines." ADVERTISING AGE 51 (June 16, 1980) : S1-S47.

For the first time AA devotes an entire section to magazines, including consumer, business, and farm publications. Articles deal with entrepreneurs, booming business in specialized magazines, newsstand sales, computers, alternate delivery systems, the maturity market, political press repositioning.

35 "Magazines." ADVERTISING AGE 52 (October 19, 1981) : S1-S72.

Lengthy special section on magazines includes articles on fashion magazines, women's magazines old and new, black magazines, WASHINGTON MONTHLY, INSIDE SPORTS, APARTMENT LIFE'S transformation to METROPOLITAN HOME, SMITHSONIAN, MOTHER JONES, READER'S DIGEST, MOTHER EARTH NEWS, the news magazines' search for unique identities.

36 "Magazines." ADVERTISING AGE 53 (October 25, 1982) : M9-M66.

The theme of this special AA section is the increase in specialized magazines over the past decade. Articles deal with numerous special interests treated by magazines, such as computers, daytime television, men's fashions, public television, military adventure, art, weddings, affluence. Other articles deal with magazine consultants and expansion into video and television.

37 "Magazines." ADVERTISING AGE 54 (October 17, 1983) : M9-M76.

This special report on magazines forecasts a steady economic recovery. Articles on numerous types and titles of magazines, including serious magazines, finance magazines, news magazines.

38 "Magazines." ADVERTISING AGE 55 (March 26, 1984) : M9-M60.

This special report considers the difference between special interest and general interest magazines today. Individual articles on magazines specializing in such subjects as muscle-building, computers, physical fitness, medicine, weight loss, babies. Emphasis on assessment of specialized magazines as advertising vehicles.

39 "Magazines." ADVERTISING AGE 56 (October 3, 1985) : 15-56.

Special report on magazines with articles covering celebrity journalism, steadily growing future of the industry, innovative graphic style. Articles on specific magazine titles include NATIONAL GEOGRAPHIC, SMITHSONIAN, SATURDAY REVIEW, AMERICAN HERITAGE. Review of trendy new types of specialized magazines, e.g., automotive, parents, outdoor.

40 "Magazines: Specialty Publications to have Heyday." ADVERTISING AGE 55 (November 29, 1984) : 16.

Poll of media directors suggests comeback for mass magazines and continued vitality of specialized magazines.

41 Mandelbaum, Sara. "The Foundation that Gives More than Money." MS. 11 (July-August 1982) : 43.

MS. Foundation has awarded grants to the Reproductive Rights Project.

42 Memory, David M. "Magazines as Resources in the Secondary Classroom." CLEARING HOUSE 58 (September 1984) : 22-27.

Advantages of magazines in secondary school education and ideas for their use. Includes a list of magazine titles recommended by the author, and a good bibliography of sources on classroom use of magazines.

43 Mogel, Leonard. THE MAGAZINE: EVERYTHING YOU NEED TO KNOW TO MAKE IT IN THE MAGAZINE BUSINESS. Englewood Cliffs, N.J.: Prentice Hall, 1979.

One man's opinion. A quickly-read overview of practical publishing useful to beginning and intermediate students. Factual research and substantiation for judgments in short supply, but useful concepts are raised based on author's considerable experience. Focus on large scale consumer publications.

44 Pace, Eric. "The Gloss Fades from Magazines." NEW YORK TIMES, 10 January 1982, p. F1+.

Problems magazines face include recession, high postal rates, poor management.

45 Paganetti, JoAn. "New Tech Bends Magazines Out of Shape." ADVERTISING AGE 54 (October 17, 1983) : M64-M65.

While traditional slick-paper magazines are not likely to disappear, new periodicals in a variety of shapes are likely, e.g., videodisc, videotex. Some of the advantages for readers and advertisers are listed.

46 Peterson, Theodore. MAGAZINES IN THE TWENTIETH CENTURY. 2d ed. Urbana: University of Illinois Press, 1964.

Classic history of consumer magazines covering 1900-1963. Deals with effects of advertising, economics of the industry, problems (e.g., those exemplified by Curtis and the SATURDAY EVENING POST). Of great merit is the final chapter which sums up the functions, effects, roles of magazines. Index but no bibliography.

47 Reese, Diane. "Research: PCs Heighten Demand." FOLIO 14 (September 1985) : 94-100.

PCs fuel the trend towards increasing research by magazines. Most research supports advertising sales, and involves extensive questioning of readers and/or manipulation of data from syndicated services. Other research supports the editorial function and management planning.

48 Rehm, Jack. "Slowdown has Little Effect on Magazines." ADVERTISING AGE 50 (October 8, 1979) : S31.

Magazines were minimally affected by the late

1970s recession. Future predictions include continued high advertising spending, higher costs to readers, expansion of private delivery systems.

49 Reuss, Carol. "Magazine Classes should Examine Split-Run Editions." JOURNALISM EDUCATOR 32 (January 1978) : 13-14.

Explores student opportunity to publish brief regionally-oriented articles in split-run editions.

50 Rottenberg, Dan. "Nattering Nabobs of Narcissism." QUILL 73 (November 1985) : 34-37.

A new formula in magazine publishing: catering to the ego factor. Most readers' immediate concern is themselves, and the most successful publications serve this "growing nationwide egocentric obsession." This may be a factor in the success of new local business magazines like MANHATTAN, INC. Rottenberg asks: "Beyond the relentless hype, is narcissistic journalism really so terrible." The answer seems to be a qualified "no."

51 Rucker, Bruce W. "Magazines and Teenage Reading Skills: Two Controlled Field Experiments." JOURNALISM QUARTERLY 59 (Spring 1982) : 28-33.

Subscriptions to high interest magazines improved reading skills of eighth grade students and stimulated interest in reading.

52 Sanoff, Alvin P. "America's Press: Too Much Power for too Few?" U.S. NEWS & WORLD REPORT 83 (August 15, 1977) : 27-33.

Discussion of ownership concentration in newspapers, magazines, tv, books. Magazines are moving towards conglomerates the least.

53 Schiller, Herbert I. "Recreation and Entertainment: Reinforcement for the Status Quo." In THE MIND MANAGERS, pp. 79-103. Boston: Beacon Press, 1973.

The role of magazines in reinforcing popular culture is discussed with reference to TV GUIDE and NATIONAL GEOGRAPHIC. These publications are not as value-free as one might believe.

54 Schmidt, Dorey, ed. JOURNAL OF AMERICAN CULTURE 3 (Spring 1980).

Special issue on popular culture and magazines. All articles in the issue relate to magazines, many with a historical slant.

55 Snow, Robert P. CREATING MEDIA CULTURE. Beverly Hills, Calif.: Sage Publications, 1983.

Discussion of the way mass media have created the media culture in which we live, and the effects of the media on our lives. Individual chapters relate to different types of media, with Chapter 5 covering novels and magazines.

Functions of magazines include teaching social rules, referencing norms and values particularly for people belonging to special interest groups, providing role models. Magazines can also be status symbols for their readers.

56 Taft, William H. AMERICAN MAGAZINES FOR THE 1980S. New York: Hastings House, 1982.

A sweeping magazine text that offers a "panoramic view" of the magazine industry today. Historical background and current trends are interwoven in numerous chapters on the various types of magazines, including news, business, women's, men's, city, science, sports, shelter, farm, religious, minority magazines as well as tabloids and Sunday supplements. Briefly covers research, production, advertising, circulation. Numerous references to specific editors and magazine titles. Short but worthy bibliography and extensive index.

57 Tan, Alexis S., and Scruggs, Kermit Joseph. "Does Exposure to Comic Book Violence Lead to Aggression in Children?" JOURNALISM QUARTERLY 57 (Winter 1980) : 579-583.

Hypothesis that comic book violence leads to aggressive behavior in children is not supported.

58 Tebbel, John W. OPPORTUNITIES IN MAGAZINE PUBLISHING. Skokie, Ill.: VGM Career Horizons, 1980.

Senior magazine historian and scholar offers simple overview of magazine field. Covers the types of jobs available in all areas of specialized and consumer magazines, from advertising sales to production, from editing to circulation. Includes brief notes on preparation for a magazine career.

59 "There's New Life in the Mass Magazines." BUSINESS WEEK (October 13, 1973) : 84+.

New mass magazines are specialized magazines. Another look at the trend towards specialized publications from a 1973 vantage point.

60 "Time Runs Out." NATION 237 (October 1, 1983) : 261.

Some interesting comparisons on how the $47 million Time Inc. spent on TV-CABLE WEEK could have kept more than half a dozen worthy publications alive for a decade. Critique of editing by research instead of for thinking humans. Brief but thoughtful.

61 Tobin, Richard L. "Big Magazines--Dead Like the Dodo: But Special Periodicals (PLAYBOY, FIELD AND STREAM) Likely to Survive." BOSTON SUNDAY GLOBE, 17 December 1973, p. A3.

Intelligent page reviewing history and status of mass appeal and somewhat specialized consumer magazines, comparing purposes, costs, and other media.

62 Wolseley, Roland E. THE CHANGING MAGAZINE. New York: Hastings House, 1972.

Brief look at the changes in magazines which occurred in the early 1970s. Updated the more extensive and impressive UNDERSTANDING MAGAZINES.

63 Wolseley, Roland E. UNDERSTANDING MAGAZINES. 2d ed. Ames, Iowa: Iowa State University Press, 1969.

A classic text which emphasizes the decline of mass appeal consumer magazines and the rise of specialized magazines. Covers business and editorial functions, social responsibilities and effects, and various types--from men's to company to news magazines. Splendid, considering its age.

64 Wood, James Playsted. MAGAZINES IN THE UNITED STATES. 3d ed. New York: Ronald Press, 1971.

What magazines are and how they exert social and economic influence. Covers history of magazines, showing the relationship between the industry and various social phenomena over the decades. A classic one-volume history covering 1741 onward.

65 Yovovich, B. G. "Reflections of Reader's Tastes." ADVERTISING AGE 52 (November 9, 1981) : S14+.

New magazine types reflect social tastes. Trends include magazines aimed at working women, fashion-conscious men, quality markets, general finance interests, cable tv subscribers, do-it-yourselfers.

66 Yovovich, B. G. "Sun Also Rises on Affluent Magazine Sector: Changes in Life Styles, Publishing Fuel Surge in Upscale Reading." ADVERTISING AGE 54 (April 4, 1983) : M24+.

The 1970 decline in mass circulation magazines and increase in specialized magazines has focused publishers' interest on readers with large discretionary incomes. The rising number of young affluents and their interest in education and information has stimulated demand for affluent magazines.

Chapter 4

MAGAZINE CONTENT

Editorial

67 Albrecht, Milton C. "Does Literature Reflect Common Values?" AMERICAN SOCIOLOGICAL REVIEW 21 (December 1956) : 722-729.

A classic content analysis of 1950s magazine fiction. Thematic differences found for three cultural levels studied, although all magazines reflected such American family values and norms as importance of marriage based on personal affection, superiority of male status, monogamy, fidelity, nuclear family independence.

68 Anderson, Ronald E., and Jolly, Elaine. "Stereotyped Traits and Sex Roles in Humorous Drawings." COMMUNICATION RESEARCH 4 (October 1977) : 453-484.

Study of male and female sex roles in cartoons from SATURDAY EVENING POST, SATURDAY RE-

VIEW, and PLAYBOY, 1952-1972, defined five stereotypes. Excellent bibliography and citation of previous research.

69 Astor, David. "Changing Roles For Women in Comics." EDITOR & PUBLISHER 116 (April 16, 1983) : 31-32.

Trend in feminist portrayals of women in comics comes largely from young progressive cartoonists.

70 Babcock, William A. "Environmental Pollution Coverage in NEWSWEEK from 1969 through 1975." Ph.D. dissertation, Southern Illinois University, 1979.

Comparison of NEWSWEEK's coverage of environmental pollution with indices of public and government concern about pollution showed little correlation. Study concludes NEWSWEEK is not a good indicator of public concern with the environment.

71 Baeher, Helen, ed. WOMEN AND MEDIA. Oxford: Pergamon Press, 1980.

Of interest are three qualitative studies of women's magazines which describe the female image particularly in regard to work outside the home. One article deals with confession magazines. Reprint of vol. 3, no. 1, 1980 issue of WOMEN'S STUDIES INTERNATIONAL QUARTERLY. See also entries 120, 141, and 187.

72 Bahn, Adele K. "Changes and Continuities in the Transitional Status of Bride into Wife: A Content Analysis of Bridal Magazines. 1967-1977, The Decade of the Women's Movement." Ph.D. dissertation, City University of New York, 1979.

Continuity in content in bridal magazines viewed as significant to the media's role as socialization agents. Bridal magazines gave little attention to career planning and work after marriage.

73 Barber, Simon. "Let's Get Physical: The New Woman's Niche on the Newsstand." WASHINGTON JOURNALISM REVIEW 4 (September 1982) : 40-43.

Physical fitness is a new trend in women's magazine content.

74 Barrett, Edward W. "Sex, Death and Other Trends in Magazines." COLUMBIA JOURNALISM REVIEW 13 (July-August 1974) : 24-26.

Magazine contest judge offers observations on trends. Content and new titles mirror social fads and interests, city and regional magazines show increased vitality, there is less consumer protection reporting than in other media. Even though dated, offers salient views on magazine trends.

75 Bayer, Tom. "Carbine Shoots Down Women Stereo-

types." ADVERTISING AGE 52 (March 30, 1981) : 70.

Summary of speech by MS. editor, Patricia Carbine, in which she defines new stereotypes of women found in magazines. These include the super female, the woman who takes over a man's job, the woman who walks out of the home for a career.

76 Beckwith, Barbara. "He-Man, She-Woman: PLAYBOY and COSMO Groove on Genes." COLUMBIA JOURNALISM REVIEW 22 (January-February 1984) : 46-47.

Mass circulation magazine treatment of new sociobiological theories. Do men and women think, act, feel differently because of genetic differences?

77 Belkaoui, Janice Monti. "Images of Arabs and Israelis in the Prestige Press, 1966-74." JOURNALISM QUARTERLY 55 (Winter 1978) : 732-738+.

Content analysis of articles about Arabs and Israelis in news magazines and New York Sunday newspapers, 1967-1973. Commentary on how media images were created.

78 Bledsoe, Robert L.; Handberg, Roger; Maddox, William S.; Lenox, David R.; and Long, Dennis A. "Foreign Affairs Coverage in Elite and Mass Periodicals." JOURNALISM QUARTERLY 59 (Autumn 1982) : 471-474.

Content analysis of politcal and news magazines found a world image characterized by conflict, with little effort to tie events together.

79 Botts, Linda, ed. LOOSE TALK: THE BOOK OF QUOTES FROM THE PAGES OF ROLLING STONE MAGAZINE. New York: Quick Fox, 1980.

Collection of quotes from RS. JOURNALISM QUARTERLY reviewer writes that the selections illustrate the magazine's place "in the history of popular culture and provide a fascinating and entertaining view of American entertainment and celebrity." (JQ, Summer 1981.)

80 Bowman, James S., and Hanaford, Kathryn. "Mass Media and the Environment Since Earth Day." JOURNALISM QUARTERLY 54 (Spring 1977) : 160-165.

Major articles on the environment in eight high-circulation magazines were counted. Authors conclude magazines had minimal coverage of environmental issues, failing to fulfill the leadership role of giving information to readers.

81 Boyles, Isabel H. "The WASHINGTON POST Pressman's Strike: How the Press Covered the Press." MASS COMM REVIEW 4 (Winter 1977) : 7-12.

Coverage of the newspaper strike in various magazines is reviewed. Includes NATIONAL REVIEW, TIME, NEWSWEEK, NEW REPUBLIC.

82 Brenders, David A., and Robinson, James D. "An Analysis of Self-Help Articles: 1972-1980." MASS COMM REVIEW 11 (Fall 1985) : 29-36.

Content analysis of 137 self-help articles in popular magazines, 1972-1980. Many self-help articles create and solve their own problems. Most sought problem and solution within the individual. Majority of articles directed towards both men and women.

83 Brooks, A. Russell. "CLA JOURNAL As a Mirror of Changing Ethnic and Academic Perspectives." CLA JOURNAL 26 (March 1983) : 265-276.

How editorial content of the CLA JOURNAL reflected social change from the 1930s to today.

84 Bryant, Margaret M. "New Words from POPULAR MECHANICS." AMERICAN SPEECH 52 (Spring-Summer 1977) : 39-46.

Dictionary of new words coined in POPULAR MECHANICS, with introductory remarks on the type of new words most often seen in magazines.

85 Bugeja, Michael J. "Periodicals Publishing More About Journalism Education." JOURNALISM QUARTERLY 54 (Summer 1977) : 382-385.

Journalism periodicals show increased coverage of journalism education from 1955 to 1975.

86 Butler, Matilda, and Paisley, William. "Equal Rights Coverage in Magazines." JOURNALISM QUARTERLY 55 (Spring 1978) : 157-160.

Analysis of ERA articles in thirty-nine women's magazines 1976 as indexed in READERS' GUIDE.

87 Butler, Matilda, and Paisley, William. "Magazine Coverage of Women's Rights." JOURNAL OF COMMUNICATION 28 (Winter 1978) : 183-186.

Magazine articles on women's rights indexed in the READERS' GUIDE were counted from 1922-1976. A rapid increase in number of articles began about 1970.

88 Butler, Matilda, and Paisley, William. WOMEN AND THE MASS MEDIA: SOURCEBOOK FOR RESEARCH AND ACTION. New York: Human Sciences Press, 1980.

Comprehensive treatment of women and the mass media, from content roles to employment. Chapter on magazines and newspapers summarizes existing research of both advertising and editorial copy, and concludes with five propositions that characterize research results.

89 Calbreath, Dean. "Kovering the Klan: How the Press Gets Tricked Into Boosting the KKK." COLUMBIA JOURNALISM REVIEW 19 (March-April 1981) : 42-45.

Klan tactics get increased magazine, newspaper, and television coverage.

90 Canape, Charlene. "Playing Politics in a Big Way." ADVERTISING AGE 53 (July 26, 1982) : M2-M3+.

A select group of five magazines (ATLANTIC, ESQUIRE, NEW YORK TIMES MAGAZINE, HARPER'S, ROLLING STONE) are increasing and improving political coverage. Unlike news magazines, these publications probe behind the headlines rather than report the news.

91 Cancian, Francesca M., and Ross, Bonnie L. "Mass Media and the Women's Movement: 1900-1977." JOURNAL OF APPLIED BEHAVIORAL SCIENCE 17 (January-February-March 1981) : 9-26.

Quantity of media coverage about women was measured in the READERS' GUIDE and NEW YORK TIMES. Highest coverage was found during women's sufferage and current women's liberation movement. Reasons are suggested for the time lag observed between growth of movement and increased coverage. Thematic analysis of coverage is also included.

92 Cerulo, Karen A. "Television, Magazine Covers, and the Shared Symbolic Environment: 1948-1970." AMERICAN SOCIOLOGICAL REVIEW 49 (August 1984) : 566-570.

Content analysis of LIFE and LOOK magazine covers shows increased use of symbols during the period when television was developing. This may be related to effect of television in increasing the public's shared symbolic environment.

93 Clark, Rebecca L. "How Women's Magazines Cover Living Alone." JOURNALISM QUARTERLY 58 (Summer 1981) : 291-294.

Content analysis of six women's magazines found all covered the subject equally. Articles were mostly of an indirect, helping nature, implying living alone was less desirable than marriage.

94 Clarke, Peter, and Esposito, Virginia. "A Study of Occupational Advice For Women in Magazines." JOURNALISM QUARTERLY 43 (Autumn 1966) : 477-485.

Occupational articles for women in COSMOPOLITAN, MADEMOISELLE, and GLAMOUR, 1963-1964, frequently used traditionally male career motivations. Female readers showed little preference for careers recommended by the magazines.

95 Cockburn, Andrew. "Graphic Evidence ... of Nuclear Confusion." COLUMBIA JOURNALISM REVIEW 22 (May-June 1983) : 38-41.

Comparison of graphs showing relative nuclear stengths of U.S.S.R. and U.S. as they have appeared in magazines and newpapers.

96 Coleman, Marilyn; Ganong, Lawrence H.; and Gingrich, Ronald. "Stepfamily Strengths: A Review of Popular Literature." FAMILY RELATIONS 34 (October 1985) : 583-588.

Qualitative literature review of stepfamily life as covered in self-help books, magazine articles, and adolescent fiction. Magazine articles since 1975 selected from READERS' GUIDE ranged over thirty-six different magazines. Major emphasis of articles was on problems connected with stepfamily life.

97 Crooke, Robert. "The Editorial Challenge: From Auto Repairs to Frost and Faulkner." MAGAZINE AGE 1 (February 1980) : 26-28+.

Part of special section on marketing to women. How women's magazines adjust content to non-traditional women's roles. Examples from LADIES' HOME JOURNAL, GLAMOUR, BETTER HOMES & GARDENS, and others.

98 Culbertson, Hugh M., and Thompson, Lujuan. "A Comparison of THE QUILL and COLUMBIA JOURNALISM REVIEW Relative to Three Critical Perspectives." MASS COMM REVIEW 11 (Winter-Spring 1984) : 12-21.

Content analysis of QUILL and CJR for all issues of 1965, 1970, 1975, 1979. Differences between the two journals were small. Both covered primarily traditional ideas, focusing less on interpretation and even less on activism.

The external press critic, CJR, tended towards more critical approach than the internal press critic, QUILL.

99 Curry, Timothy Jon, and Clarke, Alfred C. "Developing Visual Literacy: The Use of Magazine Advertisements Depicting Gender Roles." TEACHING SOCIOLOGY 10 (April 1983) : 361-369.

Use of magazines in the classroom to analyze changing images of men and women.

100 Deahl, Maureen E. "The Independent Candidate--Campaign 80: A Content Analysis of the Coverage of John B. Anderson in Three News Magazines." M.A. thesis, North Texas State University, 1982.

Anderson received mildly negative coverage, amounting to 17 percent of the total campaign coverage. Rather than creating a third party candidate, the news magazines may have hurt his campaign by limiting number and length of articles about him.

101 Dennis, Everette E. "Utopian Values in Journalistic Content and Organizational Structure." JOURNAL OF POPULAR CULTURE 8 (Spring 1975) : 724-734.

Utopian values in media content as well as in publications' organizational structures. Examples drawn from muckraking magazines in the early 1900s, counter culture media in the 1960s and 1970s, and MS. magazine.

102 Einsiedel, E. F., and Bibbee, M. Jane. "News Magazines and Minority Candidates--Campaign 76." JOURNALISM QUARTERLY 56 (Spring 1979) : 102-105.

Political candidate coverage in news magazines in 1976 was unbiased and similar. Third party candidate McCarthy received much less attention than Ford and Carter.

103 Elliott, Stuart J. "Novel Approach to NEWSWEEK Special." ADVERTISING AGE 54 (February 21, 1983) : 69.

NEWSWEEK's fiftieth anniversary issue describes America's history 1933-1985 from the perspective of five small town families.

104 Fannin, Rebecca. "Whatever Happened to the 'Fashion' Books?" MARKETING & MEDIA DECISIONS 18 (January 1983) : 64-67.

Content of fashion magazines has broadened with the changing role of women in society.

105 Farley, Jennie. "Women's Magazines and the Equal Rights Amendment: Friend or Foe?" JOURNAL OF COMMUNICATION 28 (Winter 1978) : 187-192.

In 1976 thirty-nine women's magazines joined forces to promote ERA. The article reports the number of articles published and devises an advocacy score for each magazine to measure its positive/negative coverage of the issue.

106 Fedler, Fred. "TIME and NEWSWEEK Favor John F. Kennedy, Criticize Robert and Edward Kennedy." JOURNALISM QUARTERLY 60 (Autumn 1983) : 489-496.

TIME and NEWSWEEK present similar images of the Kennedys.

107 Ferguson, Marjorie. "Imagery and Ideology: The Cover Photographs of Traditional Women's Magazines." In HEARTH AND HOME: IMAGES OF WOMEN IN THE MASS MEDIA, pp. 97-115. Edited by Gaye Tuchman, Arlene Kaplan Daniels, and James Benet. New York: Oxford University Press, 1978.

The function and content of magazine covers on the three largest circulating British women's magazines. Covers are "consciously classless" and present the face of the "traditional woman."

108 Fisher, David Eugene. "Aggression as a Function of Sex and Socioeconomic Status in Popular Magazine Fiction in the School Library." Ph.D. dissertation, University of Missouri, 1978.

Content analysis of fiction in McCALL'S and

ESQUIRE, 1958-1977. Men were more likely to be aggressive than women. No significant changes were found in the expression of aggressive behavior for men or women over the period of the study.

109 Flora, Cornelia Butler. "Changes in Women's Status in Women's Magazine Fiction: Differences by Social Class." SOCIAL PROBLEMS 26 (June 1979) : 558-569.

Changing female role 1970-1975 is explored in a content analysis of fiction in four middle- and working-class magazines (TRUE STORY, MODERN ROMANCES, REDBOOK, COSMOPOLITAN). Later fiction legitimizes paid jobs for middle-class women while providing positive reinforcement for traditional roles for working-class women. Author relates fictional value changes to real life economics.

110 Flora, Cornelia Butler. "The Passive Female: Her Comparative Image by Class and Culture in Women's Magazine Fiction." JOURNAL OF MARRIAGE AND THE FAMILY 33 (August 1971) : 435-444.

Content analysis of female image in 1970 magazine fiction. Passive female behavior rewarded across cultural and class lines, but is more strongly idealized in Latin American than in U.S. fiction, for working class than for middle class women.

111 Folkerts, Jean, and Lacy, Stephen. "Journalism History Writing, 1975-1983." JOURNALISM QUARTERLY 62 (Autumn 1985) : 585-588.

Content analysis of eighty-two JQ articles on journalism history 1976-1983. Authors' approaches were generally traditional.

112 Fowler, Gilbert Len, Jr., and Smith, Edward J. "Readability of Delayed and Immediate Reward Content in TIME and NEWSWEEK." JOURNALISM QUARTERLY 59 (Autumn 1982) : 431-434+.

Immediate-reward stories, e.g., crime, disaster, entertainment, were generally more readable than delayed-reward stories, e.g., public affairs, economics, science.

113 Fowler, Gilbert L., Jr., and Smith, Edward J. "Readability of Newspapers and Magazines over Time." NEWSPAPER RESEARCH JOURNAL 1 (November 1979) : 3-8.

Flesch readability formula applied to magazine and newspaper content in three randomly-selected one-year periods, 1904, 1933, 1965. Magazines analyzed were ATLANTIC, HARPER'S, COSMOPOLITAN. Readability was easier and more constant in magazines than newspapers.

114 Franzwa, Helen H. "Working Women in Fact and Fiction." JOURNAL OF COMMUNICATION 24 (Spring 1974) : 104-109.

Roles of female characters in magazine fiction, 1940-1970, show little change. Wife and mother role predominates.

115 Fridriksson, Lianne. "A Content Analysis of the Darts and Laurels Column in COLUMBIA JOURNALISM REVIEW." MASS COMM REVIEW 11 (Fall 1985) : 2-7.

Content analysis of fifteen years of CJR's "Darts and Laurels" found only slightly more criticisms than praises. Most abused ethical principle was conflict of interest, most praised was thorough investigative reporting.

116 Funkhauser, G. Ray. "Levels of Science Writing in Public Information Sources." JOURNALISM QUARTERLY 46 (Winter 1969) : 721-726.

The lower the educational level of a magazine's audience, the more its science writing aimed for enjoyment and interest of the reader.

117 Galas, Judith Catherine. "The Image of Women in Magazine Fiction: A Demographic Look at Four Women's Magazines." M.S. thesis, University of Kansas, 1982.

Study of fictional heroines in women's magazines (GOOD HOUSEKEEPING, LADIES' HOME JOURNAL, McCALL'S, and REDBOOK) in the 1970s found no large differences between fictional occupations and readers' occupations. About 40 percent of each group were housewives.

118 Geise, L. Ann. "The Female Role in Middle Class Women's Magazines From 1955 to 1976: A Content Analysis of Nonfiction Selections." SEX ROLES 5 (February 1979) : 51-62.

Women were not portrayed as "narrow creatures, interested only in home and family" in LADIES' HOME JOURNAL and REDBOOK. Changes in attitudes toward working women paralleled societal changes.

119 Gershman, Carl. "Rise and Fall of the New Foreign-Policy Establishment." COMMENTARY 70 (July 1980) : 13-24.

Changes in U.S. foreign policy as seen in the pages of the journal of the Council on Foreign Relations, FOREIGN POLICY, founded IN 1970.

120 Glazer, Nona. "Overworking the Working Woman: The Double Day in a Mass Magazine." WOMEN'S STUDIES INTERNATIONAL QUARTERLY 3 (no. 1, 1980) : 79-93.

Qualitative analysis of WORKING WOMAN magazine. Study of the dual female role as career woman and homemaker identified three role models. Concludes that portrayal of employed women supports view of continued female subordination.

121 Goldstein, Patrick. "Magazine Covers: Are Blacks Blacked Out?" EBONY 39 (January 1984) : 65-69.

National magazines don't feature black entertainers on covers. Chart illustrates how few covers on seven magazines featured blacks. Reprinted from the LOS ANGELES TIMES. See entry 122.

122 Goldstein, Patrick. "Magazine Covers: Are Blacks Blacked Out?" LOS ANGELES TIMES, 4 September 1983, sec. Cal., p. 3+.

Black entertainers, regardless of their success have generally not appeared on magazine covers. Many team up with white stars to be featured on national magazine covers. See also entry 121.

123 Goodman, Sandy. "Can NEWSWEEK Really Separate Fact From Opinion?" COLUMBIA JOURNALISM REVIEW 7 (Summer 1968) : 26-29.

Use of language and value-laden words in NEWSWEEK turn factual copy into opinion. Complete objectivity impossible for NEWSWEEK and anyone else.

124 Halasz, Piri. "Art Criticism (And Art History) in New York: The 1940s vs 1980s; Part Two: The Magazines." ARTS MAGAZINE 57 (March 1983) : 64-73.

Magazine coverage of art: the 1940s compared with the 1980s. Discusses art magazines as well as news and general interest magazines.

125 Hall, Dennis R. "A Note on Erotic Imagination: HUSTLER As a Secondary Carrier of Working

Class Consciousness." JOURNAL OF POPULAR CULTURE 15 (Spring 1982) : 150-156.

Analysis of HUSTLER reveals it reenforces working class culture. It may be defiant, but it is not revolutionary, and according to the author is actually a conservative magazine.

126 Hall, Dennis R. "The Venereal Confronts the Venerable: PLAYBOY on Christmas." JOURNAL OF AMERICAN CULTURE 7 (Winter 1984) : 63-68.

How PLAYBOY's content celebrates Christmas, with particular emphasis on cartoons. Author suggests PLAYBOY "seeks not to destroy middle-class values, but to alter and guide" them.

127 Hart, Roderick P.; Turner, Kathleen J.; and Knupp, Ralph E. "A Rhetorical Profile of Religious News: TIME, 1947-1976." JOURNAL OF COMMUNICATION 31 (Summer 1981) : 58-68.

Content analysis of TIME magazine's coverage of religion. Of particular note was the increase in intra-church skirmishing and the over-representation of Jews and Catholics. Various reasons are suggested for TIME's differential treatment of denominations.

128 Hatch, Mary G., and Hatch, David L. "Problems of Married Working Women as Presented By Three Popular Working Women's Magazines." SOCIAL FORCES 37 (December 1958) : 148-153.

Qualitative analysis of articles dealing with problems of working wives in MADEMOISELLE, GLAMOUR, and CHARM, 1956-1957. Child care and housework problems were recognized, but conflict between husband and wife as workers, the physical and emotional strains on working wives, and the need for early vocational training were not noted.

129 Henry, Susan. "Juggling the Frying Pan and the Fire: The Portrayal of Employment and Family Life in Seven Women's Magazines, 1975-1982." SOCIAL SCIENCE JOURNAL 21 (October 1984) : 87-107.

Magazines inconsistently portray the employed woman as a "superwoman." Some recognize women work a "double day," but are negligent in suggesting realistic alternatives.

130 Hoffman, Phyllis Pfeffer. "Women's Magazines: 20 Years of Change in COSMOPOLITAN, LADIES' HOME JOURNAL, McCALL'S, REDBOOK and WOMAN'S DAY." M.S. thesis, West Virginia University, 1984.

Broad subject areas of coverage did not change significantly between 1960 and 1980, but focus of the articles did. Articles intending to help women with homemaking skills decreased, while those intending to help with employment outside the home increased. Female image was unrealistic.

131 Honey, Maureen. "The Confession Formula and Fantasies of Empowerment." WOMEN'S STUDIES 10 (no. 3, 1984) : 303-320.

Contrary to established theories of confession magazine functions, Honey suggests the confession formula is one offering mixed messages. It encourages working-class female self-respect and strength but clouds the true nature of female victimization. A qualitative content analysis.

132 Johns-Heine, Patricke, and Gerth, Hans H. "Values in Mass Periodical Fiction, 1921-1940." PUBLIC OPINION QUARTERLY 13 (Spring 1949) : 105-113.

Classic content analysis of magazine fiction, 1921-1940, indicates trends in occupations and values. Based on premise that mass fiction is a useful index to social values.

133 Johnson, Karen S. "The Honeymoon Period: Fact or Fiction?" JOURNALISM QUARTERLY 62 (Winter 1985) : 869-876.

Quantitative and qualitative content analysis of two newspapers and TIME and NEWSWEEK. Three-month periods following presidential elections were studied. Analysis showed coverage of presidents is not as positive as generally suggested.

134 Jones, T. S. "A Media Definition of Alcoholism." In STUDIES IN MASS COMMUNICATION AND TECHNOL-

OGY, pp. 130-139. Edited by S. Thomas. Norwood, N.J.: Ablex Publishing Corporation, 1984.

Content analysis of twenty-five articles on alcoholism in popular news and women's magazines, 1960-1979. Both types of magazines showed alcoholism as a disease and addiction, and offered cures and therapies. Alcoholics described as out of control, shameful, lonely.

135 King, Robert L. "And Then He Was Gone." COLUMBIA JOURNALISM REVIEW 19 (January-February 1981) : 51.

Journalistic word choice irresponsibly equates some political figures with the hero image of the Lone Ranger.

136 Kirkhorn, Michael J. "Nuclear Arms Reporting: Not With a Bang, But a Whisper." QUILL 71 (July-August 1983) : 11-16.

How magazines have handled the nuclear weapons issue. Includes news magazines, general interest magazines, the defense community trade magazine, AVIATION WEEK & SPACE TECHNOLOGY.

137 Koger, Daniel Allan. "The Liberal Opinion Press and the Kennedy Years in Viet Nam: A Study of Four Journals." Ph.D. dissertation, Michigan State University, 1983.

Four journals present diverse opinions about U.S. involvement in Viet Nam. Two were strongly anti-Communist supporting U.S. military intervention, one was opposed, and the fourth altered its opinion between 1960 and 1963 from favoring military action to advocating negotiated settlement.

138 LaFollette, Marcel Evelyn Chotkowski. "Authority, Promise, and Expectation: The Images of Science and Scientists in American Popular Magazines, 1910-1955." Ph.D. dissertation, Indiana University, 1979.

Content analysis of eleven general interest magazines. Frequency of coverage and image over the decades is traced from 1910 to 1955. Overall the scientist's image emphasized his intellect, strength, endurance, patience, perseverance, energy.

139 Lagoni, Laurel S., and Cook, Alicia Skinner. "Stepfamilies: A Content Analysis of the Popular Literature, 1961-1982." FAMILY RELATIONS 34 (October 1985) : 521-525.

Content analysis of thirty articles on stepparenting in five parenting magazines 1961-1982. READERS' GUIDE used as initial source for locating articles. Number of articles did not increase over time. Content focused on needs of children. Stepparenting articles did not appear in magazines in proportion to the rise of the stepfamily lifestyle itself. Popular magazine articles tend to reflect the quantity and content of professional literature on the subject.

140 Lazer, Charles, and Dier, S. "The Labor Force in Fiction." JOURNAL OF COMMUNICATION 28 (Winter 1978) : 174-182.

Occupational distribution of men and women in ATLANTIC MONTHLY and SATURDAY EVENING POST fiction is compared with government statistics. Fictional roles are glamorized. Proportion of working women in fiction relatively unchanged since 1940.

141 Leman, Joy. "'The Advice of a Real Friend.' Codes of Intimacy and Oppression in Women's Magazines 1937-1955." WOMEN'S STUDIES INTERNATIONAL QUARTERLY 3 (no. 1, 1980) : 63-78.

Qualitative analysis of British women's magazines describes the woman-to-woman editorial intimacy characterizing the medium 1937-1955. Various themes and trends are described, particularly relating to the developing image of the working woman.

142 Lemert, James B., and Ashman, Marquerite Gemson. "Extent of Mobilizing Information in Opinion and News Magazines." JOURNALISM QUARTERLY 60 (Winter 1983) : 657-662.

Liberal opinion magazines contained more mobilizing information than news magazines. Mobilizing information allows reader to act on existing attitudes.

143 Lentini, Cecelia. "Publications Changing to Suit Times." ADVERTISING AGE 51 (March 17, 1980) : S4+.

Fashion magazines now include content beyond fashion to satisfy broadened reader interest. Changes in types of products advertised in specific fashion magazines.

144 Lentz, Richard Glenn. "Resurrecting the Prophet: Dr. Martin Luther King, Jr., and the News Magazines." Ph.D. dissertation, University of Iowa, 1983.

Coverage of Martin Luther King Jr. 1956-1968 in TIME, NEWSWEEK, and U.S. NEWS & WORLD REPORT. Each magazine presented a different image of King. After his death, the image was reinterpreted "to preserve the integrity of a symbol" representing national ideals.

145 Lopate, Carol. "Jackie!" In HEARTH AND HOME: IMAGES OF WOMEN IN THE MASS MEDIA, pp. 130-140. Edited by Gaye Tuchman, Arlene Kaplan Daniels, and James Benet. New York: Oxford University Press, 1978.

Qualitative analysis of women's magazine content about Jackie Kennedy Onassis. Differences found in magazine content aimed at working and middle class readers. Also observed is distinction between gossip and news in celebrity v. news magazines. How women's magazines are integrated into the political framework.

146 Loughlin, Beverly. "Women's Magazine Short-Story Heroines." JOURNALISM QUARTERLY 60 (Spring 1983) : 138-142.

Content analysis of fiction, 1979-1981, found conservative female image of wife and mother. Although half the heroines worked, their jobs were unimportant to them.

147 Lowe, Sylvia Owen. "Birth Control Coverage by Selected Women's Magazines: 1960-1980." M.A. thesis, California State University, Northridge, 1984.

Qualitative content analysis of McCALL'S, LADIES' HOME JOURNAL, and GOOD HOUSEKEEPING. Coverage of oral contraceptives lacked skepticism, investigative reporting, completeness, and timeliness.

148 Luh, Wen-shwu Maria. "Attitude of the Three National American Magazines Toward Chinese Civil War, 1946-1949." M.S. thesis, Iowa State University, 1981.

Content analysis of news magazine coverage of the Chinese Civil War. TIME and NEWSWEEK presented more balanced coverage than U.S. NEWS & WORLD REPORT because they presented more detailed and complete reports from differing viewpoints.

149 Lundburg, Lea J. "Comprehensiveness of Coverage of Tropical Rain Deforestation." JOURNALISM QUARTERLY 61 (Summer 1984) : 378-382.

Analysis of eight comsumer magazine articles using a new content analysis technique of grouping facts and information into five categories. Analysis showed much pertinent information was omitted from the articles.

150 McFadden, Maureen. "Why Some Magazines are Replacing Fiction with Fact." MAGAZINE AGE 4 (July 1983) : 22-26.

Magazine fiction is being replaced by increased service information. Reasons include advertiser demand, tv's success with serial fiction, low newsstand response to fiction.

151 Maddox, William S., and Robins, Robert. "How PEOPLE Magazine Covers Political Figures." JOURNALISM QUARTERLY 58 (Spring 1981) : 113-115.

Shift of concern from hero worship to demand for information about celebrities. PEOPLE magazine plays agenda setting role in covering and making political celebrities.

152 Matthews, Mary L. "Roles Portrayed by Women in News Magazines." M.A. thesis, University of North Carolina at Chapel Hill, 1982.

Content analysis of photos in TIME and NEWSWEEK 1940 to 1980 shows little change over time. Women were infrequently portrayed in all roles except entertainer and spouse. Sample of photos from MS. 1980 reflected a broad range of female activities.

153 Maurer, Gilbert C. "Never a Crocodile." MARKETING & MEDIA DECISIONS 16 (November 1981, Supplement) : 72+.

Summary of speech given by author, president of Hearst Magazines, emphasizing the importance of content in magazines.

154 Mitteness, Linda S. "Historical Changes in Public Information about the Menopause." URBAN ANTHROPOLOGY 12 (Summer 1983) : 161-179.

Content analysis of magazine articles dealing with menopause 1900-1976. Articles selected from READERS' GUIDE. Prior to 1950, menopause was given positive and negative evaluation and considered a natural event seldom requiring medical intervention. After 1950, content grew more negative, medical treatment was viewed as increasingly more necessary.

155 Moore, Wayne S.; Bowers, David R.; and Granovsky, Theodore A. "What Are Magazine Articles Telling Us About Insects?" JOURNALISM QUARTERLY 59 (Autumn 1982) : 464-467.

Analysis of selected articles about insects from nature, shelter, women's, general interest, and other magazines found 80 percent were negative.

156 Nelson, Michael. "Evaluative Journalism: A New Synthesis." VIRGINIA QUARTERLY REVIEW 58 (Summer 1982) : 419-434.

Contrast between nineteenth century partisan journalism and twentieth century objective journalism. Does the WASHINGTON MONTHLY offer a synthesis of the two that might be called "evaluative journalism?"

157 Newkirk, Carole Ruth. "Female Roles in Non-Fiction of Three Women's Magazines." JOURNALISM QUARTERLY 54 (Winter 1977) : 779-781.

Little change in female roles in MADEMOISELLE, REDBOOK, and MS., 1961-1974. MADEMOISELLE and REDBOOK tend toward domestic role, while MS. tends toward social activist and non-domestic roles.

158 Nord, David Paul. "An Economic Perspective on Formula in Popular Culture." JOURNAL OF POPULAR CULTURE 3 (Spring 1980) : 17-31.

The role of formula in popular magazines and other media. By staying with tested formulas, popular culture producers minimize risk, lower cost of production, raise profits. Evidenced by the rise of mass circulation magazines like LIFE that offended no one, preserved the status quo, used the tried and true.

159 Pasher, Edna. "The Dominant Metaphors of Education in Selected Educational Magazines."

Ph.D. dissertation, New York University, 1981.

Analysis of essays in EDUCATIONAL LEADERSHIP and PHI DELTA KAPPAN revealed most commonly used metaphors referring to the school environment were: business, government and military, competition.

160 Pasley, Kay, and Ihinger-Tallman, Marilyn. "Portraits of Stepfamily Life in Popular Literature: 1940-1980." FAMILY RELATIONS 34 (October 1985) : 527-534.

Content analysis of articles on stepfamilies indexed in READERS' GUIDE, 1940-1980. Most articles appeared in general interest and women's magazines. Over time, magazines have shown increasing interest in remarriage and stepparenting, but have not substantially broadened their appeal beyond the female audience. Articles have more references to authoritative sources and present an increasingly diverse picture of this family lifestyle.

161 Patterson, Oscar III. "Television's Living Room War in Print: Vietnam in the News Magazines." JOURNALISM QUARTERLY 61 (Spring 1984) : 35-39+.

Magazines gave less attention to Vietnam war news from 1968 to 1973 than television did. Magazine content and photos were not excessively concerned with the dead and wounded.

162 Paxson, Avis Jeanette Reynolds. "Occupational Information in REDBOOK, LADIES' HOME JOURNAL, and GOOD HOUSEKEEPING." M.A. thesis, University of Texas, 1983.

Content analysis of occupational articles 1970-1980 revealed a slight increase in work-related articles, but not large enough to indicate a repositioning effort on the part of the magazines studied. Women were portrayed in all occupational fields.

163 Perry, David K. "Foreign Industrial Disputes in TIME and NEWSWEEK, 1966-1973." JOURNALISM QUARTERLY 58 (Autumn 1981) : 439-443.

News magazine coverage of foreign industrial disputes is not in direct proportion to days lost in strikes.

164 Phillips, E. Barbara. "Magazine Heroines: Is MS. Just Another Member of the FAMILY CIRCLE?" In HEARTH AND HOME: IMAGES OF WOMEN IN THE MASS MEDIA, pp. 116-129. Edited by Gaye Tuchman, Arlene Kaplan Daniels, and James Benet. New York: Oxford University Press, 1978.

Content analysis of heroines (occupational role, social role, writers' attitudes towards) in non-fiction features from MS. and FAMILY CIRCLE. FAMILY CIRCLE represents dominant culture, while MS. offers a minority view parallel to emerging feminist role. MS. sees women as different and better than men, not as females in traditional male roles.

165 Prisco, Dorothy D. "Women and Social Change As Reflected in a Major Fashion Magazine." JOURNALISM QUARTERLY 59 (Spring 1982) : 131-134.

Content analysis of MADEMOISELLE magazine 1970-1980 reflects the changing image of the American woman.

166 Pugh, David G. "History as an Expedient Accommodation: The Manliness Ethos in Modern America." JOURNAL OF AMERICAN CULTURE 3 (Spring 1980) : 53-68.

Characterization of modern "he-men" in male magazines includes such qualities as brutality, pathological hatred, self-assertion. He-men need machines (e.g., cars, motorcycles) to retain and assert manliness. How the he-man image derived from historical frontier.

167 Reid, Leonard N. "SPORTS ILLUSTRATED's Coverage of Women in Sports." JOURNALISM QUARTERLY 56 (Winter 1979) : 861-863.

Content analysis of twenty years of SPORTS IIUSTRATED shows women's sports coverage did not increase from 1956 to 1976. Data suggest a cultural lag between changing role of women and the magazine's coverage.

168 Reo, M. Christenson. "The DIGEST on Urban Renewal." COLUMBIA JOURNALISM REVIEW 4 (Summer 1965) 45-46.

Professor of government offers critical appraisal of READER'S DIGEST coverage of urban renewal. The DIGEST looks backward rather than forward, and sets forth its opinions only, avoiding other opinions on the issue. Facing page is a READER'S DIGEST ad offering a statement of praise for the magazine.

169 Reynolds, Paula Kay Cozort. "Opinion Journals and the Women's Movement, 1968-1977." Ph.D. dissertation, University of Texas, 1982.

Content analysis of articles about the women's movement in six serious magazines 1968-1977. Articles divided by coverage of three ideologies existing in the women's movement--legalist, separatist, androgynist. Most space dealt with the legalists, representing the most conservative beliefs.

170 Rich, Jonathon T. "A Measurement of Comprehensiveness In News-Magazine Science Coverage." JOURNALISM QUARTERLY 58 (Summer 1981) : 248-253.

Analysis of coverage of two events showed TIME'S coverage more complete than that of NEWSWEEK or U.S. NEWS.

171 Robinson, Gertrude Joch. "The Media and Social Change: Thirty Years of Magazine Coverage of Women and Work (1950-1977)." ATLANTIS 8 (Spring 1983) : 87-111.

Counting and sampling of READERS' GUIDE articles indexed under "Women: Employment, Equal Rights and Occupations," 1950-1977. Also content analysis of GOOD HOUSEKEEPING, CHATELAINE, TIME, LADIES' HOME JOURNAL, READER'S DIGEST, MACLEAN'S. Concludes media are good indexes of public opinion but less reliable in monitoring social change.

172 Rossi, Lee D. "The Whore Vs. the Girl-Next-Door: Stereotypes of Woman in PLAYBOY, PENTHOUSE, and OUI." JOURNAL OF POPULAR CULTURE 9 (Summer 1975) : 90-94.

Skin magazines present an image of women that is compatible with traditional American sex roles --dependent on men and non-threatening to male domination. A non-quantitative comparison of female images in several men's magazines.

173 Rothman, Stanley; Lichter, Linda S.; and Lichter, S. Robert. "Watching the Media Watchdog." PUBLIC OPINION 7 (April-May 1984) : 19-20+.

Content analysis of COLUMBIA JOURNALISM REVIEW, 1972-1981, found liberal slant and anti-establishment tone in critical articles. Authors criticize CJR for lack of the "objectivity and 'value-free' journalism that its editors preach."

174 Ruggiero, Josephine, and Weston, Louise C. "Work Options for Women in Women's Magazines: The Medium AND the Message." SEX ROLES 12 (March 1985) : 535-547.

Comparison of female role and work options in six traditional women's magazines (e.g., LADIES' HOME JOURNAL, COSMOPOLITAN) and four new ones (e.g., MS., SAVVY). New magazines less likely to depict women as homemakers. In established magazines majority of women work for pay, but in traditional occupations.

175 Schoenfeld, A. Clay. "The Environmental Movement as Reflected in the American Magazine." JOURNALISM QUARTERLY 60 (Autumn 1983) : 470-475.

Traces the environmental issue from its inception to popularity through magazine content.

176 Schoenfeld, A. Clay. "The Press and NEPA: The Case of the Missing Agenda." JOURNALISM QUARTERLY 56 (Autumn 1979) : 577-585.

The National Environmental Policy Act was passed in 1969 without newspapers and magazines having performed an agenda setting role.

177 Scott, Joseph E., and Franklin, Jack L. "The Changing Nature of Sex References in Mass Circulation Magazines." PUBLIC OPINION QUARTERLY 36 (Spring 1972) : 80-86.

Study of cultural changes with regard to sex as portrayed in magazines 1950-1970. A content analysis of seven high circulation general interest magazines. Authors conclude magazines reflect changing attitudes towards sex but have not been responsible for liberalizing sexual values.

178 Sentman, Mary Alice. "Black and White: Disparity in Coverage by LIFE Magazine from 1937 to 1972." JOURNALISM QUARTERLY 60 (Autumn 1983) : 501-508.

Content analysis of LIFE magazine, 1937-1972, finds blacks were not shown in everyday life situations.

179 Singletary, Michael W.; Boland, Raymond; Izzard, William; and Rosser, Terry. "How Accurate Are News Magazines' Forecasts?" JOURNALISM QUARTERLY 60 (Summer 1983) : 342-344.

Content analysis of NEWSWEEK and U.S. NEWS & WORLD REPORT found forecasts more often accurate than not, comparable to error rate in newspapers.

180 Smith, Edward J. "Journalism Education Issues Covered in Two Publications." JOURNALISM QUARTERLY 57 (Autumn 1980) : 491-495.

Journalism education issues covered in JOURNALISM QUARTERLY and JOURNALISM EDUCATOR, 1924-1973.

181 Smith, M. Dwayne. "Portrayal of Elders in Magazine Cartoons." GERONTOLOGIST 19 (August 1979) : 408-412.

Content analysis of cartoons in eight women's, men's, and general interest magazines found more negative portrayals of the elderly when compared with other age groups.

182 Smith, M. Dwayne., and Matre, Marc. "Social Norms and Sex Roles in Romance and Adventure Magazines." JOURNALISM QUARTERLY 52 (Summer 1975) : 309-315.

Analysis of fiction in adventure and romance magazines 1973 shows characters supported traditional male and female stereotypes. Comments on the social functions of these magazines.

183 Smith, Ron F., and Decker-Amos, Linda. "Of Lasting Interest? A Case Study of Change in the Content of the READER'S DIGEST." JOURNALISM QUARTERLY 62 (Spring 1985) : 127-131.

Content analysis comparison of DIGEST content 1940, 1960, and 1980 suggests consistency in the DIGEST'S editorial formula. Number of articles on controversial issues was consistently between 16 percent and 20 percent of total. Between 10 percent and 14 percent of the articles showed women in traditional roles. Articles offering solutions to problems and suggestions for self-improvement increased over time.

184 Solimine, Michael E. "Newsmagazine Coverage of the Supreme Court." JOURNALISM QUARTERLY 57 (Winter 1980) : 661-663.

Content analysis of TIME, NEWSWEEK, and U.S. NEWS & WORLD REPORT found high quality but low quantity coverage of the Supreme Court.

185 Stepp, Carl Sessions. "Looking Out For #1: Magazines That Celebrate Success." WASHINGTON JOURNALISM REVIEW 7 (November 1985) : 41-44.

Magazines featuring success and affluence have had a good year. Analysis of trendy magazine topics, and how successful publications have developed them.

186 Sterud, Eugene L. "Changing Aims of Americanist Archaeology: A Citations Analysis of AMERICAN ANTIQUITY--1946-1975." AMERICAN ANTIQUITY 43 (April 1978) : 294-302.

Analysis of the journal's content over time reflects shifting theoretical focus of the discipline.

187 Stewart, Penni. "He Admits ... But She Confesses." WOMEN'S STUDIES INTERNATIONAL QUARTERLY 3 (no. 1, 1980) : 105-114.

Qualitative analysis of male and female portrayals in confession magazines (TRUE STORY and TRUE CONFESSIONS) and notes on the development and functions of confession magazines as a type.

188 Stone, Gerald C., and McCombs, Maxwell E. "Tracing the Time Lag in Agenda-Setting."

JOURNALISM QUARTERLY 58 (Spring 1981) : 51-55.

Discussion of the agenda setting function of the mass media. TIME and NEWSWEEK were analyzed to determine which issues the media selected for public attention. A delay of two to six months was found before these issues were emphasized in local newspapers.

189 Strodthoff, G. G.; Hawkins, R. P.; and Schoenfeld, A. Clay. "Media Roles in a Social Movement: A Model of Ideology Diffusion." JOURNAL OF COMMUNICATION 35 (Spring 1985) : 134-153.

Content analysis of 3056 articles in AUDUBON, ENVIRONMENT, TIME, SATURDAY REVIEW, 1959-1979. Considers the roles of specialized and general interest magazines in the crystallization and diffusion of new ideas in the development of social issues.

190 Suplee, Curt. "ESQUIRE: Steinbeck to Steinham; The Way We Were in 50 Years of Words." WASHINGTON POST, 19 May 1983, p. C1+.

Critique of ESQUIRE's fiftieth anniversary issue deplores the debasing of American taste as reflected in ESQUIRE's pages and the self-congratulatory attitudes of its editors.

191 Suplee, Curt. "Sugar and Spices and Princess Di." WASHINGTON POST, 1 December 1982, p. C1+.

Celebrity interest is high everywhere, especially in magazines. Critical review of magazine content themes and brief news notes.

192 Tarpley, J. Douglas. "American Newsmagazine Coverage of Supreme Court." JOURNALISM QUARTERLY 61 (Winter 1984) : 801-804+.

Most Supreme Court stories dealt with decisions; 47 percent were media-related cases. Many decisions go unreported.

193 Tobin, Richard L., and Weaver, David. "At This Point In Time." QUILL 68 (April 1980) : 12+.

Survey of magazine and newspaper editors on language use. Comparison of the two media.

194 "Traditional Magazines Reflect Changing Roles, Values of Women." LEADING EDGE: A BULLETIN OF SOCIAL TRANSFORMATION 1 (September 8, 1980) : 4.

195 Tsang, Kuo-jen. "News Photos in TIME and NEWSWEEK." JOURNALISM QUARTERLY 61 (Autumn 1984) : 578-584+.

Analysis of news photos from 1971, 1976, and 1980 found more U.S. photos than international ones. U.S. photos were more likely to depict nonviolence than international photos.

196 Tuchman, Gaye. "Women's Depiction By the Mass Media." SIGNS 4 (Spring 1979) : 528-542.

An overview and critique of research on the female image in the mass media. How women are presented in media content, why the media are sexist, and the effects of the media.

197 Whitney, Melinda J. "Sex-Role Stereotypying in the Contents of Four Magazines for Children." M.A. thesis, University of Nevada, 1980.

Men and boys were pictured more frequently and shown in wider variety of activities than women. Men had more occupations to choose from than women. Women were subordinate to men in fictional roles.

198 Wilson, Susannah J. "The Image of Women in Canadian Magazines." MASS MEDIA AND SOCIAL CHANGE, pp. 231-245. Edited by Elihu Katz and Thomas Szecsko. Beverly Hills, Calif.: Sage Publications, 1981.

Overview of the social role of magazines. Content analysis of fiction and personality profiles in MACLEAN'S and CHATELAINE, 1930-1969. Content reflected the pervasive but not subtle changes in the female role over time as communcators sought to be contemporary.

199 Wulfemeyer, K. Tim. "How and Why Anonymous Attribution is Used by TIME and NEWSWEEK." JOURNALISM QUARTERLY 62 (Spring 1985) : 81-86+.

Content analysis of TIME and NEWSWEEK 1982 revealed 80 percent of national and international articles contained anonymous attribution.

200 Yardley, Jonathon. "VANITY's Ultra-Rich Fare; The Medium Sends an Ostentacious Message." WASHINGTON POST, 7 March 1983, p. C1+.

This review of VANITY FAIR's inaugural issue suggests incongruity between editorial and advertising content. Editorial reveals commitment to culture and left-of-center political viewpoint, while advertising is committed only to stroking an affluent self-indulgent readership. Qualitative analysis of themes used in advertising to the rich.

201 Yates, Norris. "Vocabulary of TIME Magazine Revisited." AMERICAN SPEECH 56 (Spring 1981) : 53-63.

Discussion of words used by TIME, with particular emphasis on formation of new words.

202 Zureik, Elia T., and Frizzell, Alan. "Values in Canadian Magazine Fiction: A Test of the Social Control Thesis." JOURNAL OF POPULAR CULTURE 10 (Fall 1976) : 359-376.

Content analysis of purposively selected Canadian magazines. Magazine fiction reinforced dominant social values which characterize all "North Ameria in particular and capitalist consumer-oriented societies in general."

Advertising

203 Bland, M. Susan. "Henrietta the Homemaker and Rosie the Riveter: Images of Women in Advertising in MACLEAN'S Magazine, 1939-50." ATLANTIS 8 (Spring 1982) : 61-86.

War-time advertisements did not show a changing female role even though illustrating women's war work. War images did not appear until 1941. Post-1947 ads did not show women working outside the home. Most ads directed towards housewives. Content themes included importance of eliminating drudgery, improving and saving marriages, catching a man, pursuing beauty and youth, attaining social status.

204 Breed, Warren, and De Foe James R. "Themes in Magazine Alcohol Advertisements: A Critique." JOURNAL OF DRUG ISSUES 9 (Fall 1979) : 511-522.

Content analysis of alcohol ads in thirteen national magazines in 1976 found most frequent themes related the product brand with a desired outcome, particularly a desired life style. Most common themes were wealth, success, social approval, pleasure, sex.

205 Brown, Bruce W. "Family Intimacy in Magazine Advertising 1920-1977." JOURNAL OF COMMUNICATION 32 (Summer 1982) : 173-183.

Content analysis of general interest magazine advertising showed an increase in portrayal of family intimacy.

206 Brown, Bruce W. IMAGES OF FAMILY LIFE IN MAGAZINE ADVERTISING: 1920-1978. New York: Praeger Publishers, 1981.

Content analysis of magazine advertising in general interest magazines showed increase in intimacy between spouses and between siblings. Sociological slant to theoretical background and analysis. Excellent bibliography.

207 Castledine, Susan Eloise. "Depictions of Men and Women in TIME Magazine Advertisements: 1923-1980. M.A. thesis, California State University, Northridge, 1980.

Comparison of male and female roles in TIME's ads over fifty-seven-year period. Men were shown in greater variety of paid occupations while women were shown most often as secretaries. No significant changes over time. Traditional roles for both sexes predominated.

208 Colfax, J. David, and Sternberg, Susan Frankel. "The Perpetuation of Racial Stereotypes: Blacks in Mass Circulation Magazine Advertisements." PUBLIC OPINION QUARTERLY 36 (Spring 1972) : 8-18.

Content analysis of ads in READER'S DIGEST, LOOK, LIFE, LADIES' HOME JOURNAL, 1965-1970.

Despite increased use of black models, ads perpetuated racial stereotypes by portraying blacks in roles which distorted reality and confirmed stereotypes.

209 DeVoe, Jane L. "An Analysis of the Roles Portrayed by Males in Magazine Advertisements." M.S. thesis, San Jose State University, 1984.

In both 1982 and 1972 ads in seven popular magazines with male and female readership (e.g., READER'S DIGEST, EBONY, ESQUIRE, REDBOOK) showed male models more often in non-working activity. Working males increased in 1982, with more professional roles in 1972 and more laborers in 1982.

210 England, Paula, and Gardner, Teresa. "Sex Differentiation in Magazine Advertisements: A Content Analysis Using Log-Linear Modeling." In CURRENT ISSUES AND RESEARCH IN ADVERTISING, pp. 253-268. Edited by James H. Leigh and Claude R. Martin Jr. Ann Arbor, Mich.: Graduate School of Business Administration, University of Michigan, 1983.

Content analysis of 2000 magazine ads 1960-1979 in VOGUE, LADIES' HOME JOURNAL, PLAYBOY, and TIME revealed much sex-typing in ads, with little change between 1960 and 1979. Ads showed more sex-typing than real-life roles.

211 England, Paula; Kuhn, Alice; and Gardner, Teresa. "The Ages of Men and Women in Magazine Adver-

tisements." JOURNALISM QUARTERLY 58 (Autumn 1981) : 468-471.

Ads in five magazines, 1960-1979, show female models younger than male models.

212 Fox, Harold L., and Renas, Stanley R. "Stereotypes of Women in the Media and their Impact on Women's Careers." HUMAN RESOURCE MANAGEMENT 16 (Spring 1977) : 28-31.

Comparison of male-female roles in television and magazine advertising. Few methodological details provided.

213 Gantz, Walter; Gartenberg, Howard; and Rainbow, Cindy K. "Approaching Invisibility: The Portrayal of the Elderly in Magazine Advertisements." JOURNAL OF COMMUNICATION 30 (Winter 1980) : 56-60.

The elderly are under-represented in U.S. magazine ads.

214 Harmon, Robert R.; Razzouk, Nabil Y.; and Stern, Bruce L. "Information Content of Comparative Magazine Advertisements." JOURNAL OF ADVERTISING 12 (no. 4, 1983) : 10-19.

Ads comparing two or more products contained more information than non-comparative ads.

215 Healey, John S., and Kassarjian, Harold H.

"Advertising Substantiation and Advertiser Response: A Content Analysis of Magazine Advertisements." JOURNAL OF MARKETING 47 (Winter 1983) : 107-117.

Following FTC ruling that advertising claims must be supported by evidence, advertisers tended to offer more verification of claims in ads or reduce the number of claims made. A content analysis of ads in popular magazines, 1971 and 1976.

216 Humphrey, Ronald, and Schuman, Howard. "The Portrayal of Blacks in Magazine Advertisements, 1950-1982." PUBLIC OPINION QUARTERLY 48 (Fall 1984) : 551-563.

Comparison of frequency and social characteristics of blacks and whites in ads in TIME and LADIES' HOME JOURNAL, 1950 and 1980. Blacks are no longer represented as servants, but are underrepresented. Whites are portrayed as authority figures.

217 Kassarjian, Harold H. "The Negro and American Advertising, 1946-1965." JOURNAL OF MARKETING RESEARCH 6 (February 1969) : 29-39.

Content analysis of ads in mass circulation magazines 1946, 1956, 1965. Less than 1 percent of total ads included blacks. Frequency of blacks decreased in 1956 and increased in 1965 to the 1946 level. Most often portrayed as service workers and entertainers.

218 Kelly, Mary Patricia. "The Images of Women in Advertising of Six Magazines from 1940 through 1980." M.A. thesis, University of Montana, 1983.

Content analysis of female image in advertising of six magazines, from PLAYBOY to McCALL'S. Images of women did not change significantly in the forty years studied, and women were not presented differently to different types of readers.

219 Kern, Marilyn Louise. "A Comparative Analysis of the Portrayal of Blacks and Whites in White-Oriented Mass Circulation Magazine Advertisements During 1959, 1969 and 1979." Ph.D. dissertation, University of Wisconsin, 1982.

Integrated ads appeared more frequently in 1969 and 1979 than in 1959. Integrated ads showing blacks and whites in social and work interaction also increased after 1959.

220 Kvasnicka, Brian; Beymer, Barbara; and Perloff, Richard M. "Portrayals of the Elderly in Magazine Advertisements." JOURNALISM QUARTERLY 59 (Winter 1982) : 656-658.

Elderly subjects appeared in 8 percent of the ads in eight general interest and senior citizens' magazines.

221 Laczniak, Gene R. "Information Content in Print Advertising." JOURNALISM QUARTERLY 56 (Summer 1979) : 324-327+.

Magazine advertising research studies compared, with careful attention to defining an informative ad. Research is divided on whether print ads are more persuasive or informative.

222 Leonard-Spark, Arlene Janet. "A Content Analysis of Food Ads Appearing in Women's Consumer Magazines in 1965 and 1977." Ed.D. dissertation, Columbia University Teachers College, 1980.

Although the number of food ads increased between 1965 and 1977, all advertising increased and food ads in 1977 were a smaller proportion of total advertising pages than in 1965. Natural food ads increased. Most ads depict women in homemaker roles.

223 Lloyd, Kate Rand. "Stereotypes Don't Pay." ADVERTISING AGE 53 (July 26, 1982) : M14+.

Why advertiser stereotypes of working women don't work. Lessons from WORKING WOMAN magazine.

224 Lysonski, Steven. "Female and Male Portrayals in Magazine Advertisements: A Re-examination." AKRON BUSINESS AND ECONOMIC REVIEW 14 (Summer 1983) : 45-50.

Content analysis of ads in twenty-two men's, women's, and general interest magazines shows undramatic change in female role between 1975 and 1980. Women portrayed as less dependent on men, more career-oriented, although stereotyped images still persist.

225 Marquez, F. T. "Advertising Content: Persuasion, Information or Intimidation?" JOURNALISM QUARTERLY 54 (Autumn 1977) : 482-491.

Twice as many magazine and newspaper ads are persuasive rather than informative. Focus of ad depended primarily on type of product advertised.

226 Moriarty, Sandra Ernst. "Trends in Advertising Typography." JOURNALISM QUARTERLY 59 (Summer 1982) : 290-294.

The most fashionable-appearing ads are often the least readable, and appear more frequently in special interest magazines rather than general interest and trade magazines.

227 Moriarty, Sandra Ernst, and McGann, Anthony F. "Nostalgia and Consumer Sentiment." JOURNALISM QUARTERLY 60 (Spring 1983) : 81-86.

Content analysis of advertising in twelve consumer and trade magazines, 1959-1979, found nostalgia increased in periods of decreased public confidence.

228 Mulcahy, Sheila Hogan. "Female Images in Women's and General Interest Magazine Advertising, 1905-1970: A Content Analysis." M.A. thesis, University of Wisconsin, 1980.

Traditional, stereotypical female images dominated advertising over time. Role of "domestic drudge and decorative sex mate" increased over time despite real-life trends to the contrary.

229 Pendleton, Jennifer. "MS. Editor Slaps New Ad Image of Women." ADVERTISING AGE 55 (October 29, 1984) : 73.

Summary of speech by MS. editor Patricia Carbine. Women appear in erotic, romantic advertising that may offer a harmful image of dependency, decoration, male possessiveness.

230 Pittatore, Oddina. "The Image of Italy in Ads in Five U.S. Magazines." JOURNALISM QUARTERLY 60 (Winter 1983) : 728-731.

Contemporary image of Italy includes sophistication, art, craftsmanship, and sex.

231 Pollay, R. W. "The Subsidizing Sizzle: A Descriptive History of Print Advertising, 1900-1980." JOURNAL OF MARKETING 49 (Summer 1985) : 24-37.

Content analysis of advertisements from largest circulating magazines, 1900-1980. Ads encouraging purchase of products represented 80 percent of total; 75 percent used human subjects; 66 percent communicated benefits of product use.

232 Pollay, R. W. "Twentieth-Century Magazine Advertising: Determinants of Informativeness." WRITTEN COMMUNICATION 1 (January 1984) : 56-77.

Content analysis of 2000 magazine advertisements covering the twentieth century. Ads increased in informativeness over the century, but varied with decade, page size, product, format, and rhetorical style.

233 Reed, Brenda Lee. "Patterns of Advertisers' Support and Attack of the Women's Movement in Four Mass Market Women's Magazines." M.A. thesis, University of Pennsylvania, 1983.

Content analysis of ads in COSMOPOLITAN, REDBOOK, McCALL'S, and VOGUE. Most ads supported the women's movement regardless of product advertised. Number of ads in "expanding" markets (e.g., cars, insurance, career services) increased more than those in "threatened" markets (e.g., clothing, cosmetics).

234 Reid, Leonard N., and VandenBergh, Bruce G. "Blacks in Introductory Ads." JOURNALISM QUARTERLY 57 (Autumn 1980) : 485-488.

Although other research suggests more blacks are being used in ads, this study reports it is not so in ads for new products.

235 Ritter, Diana. "Nudes in Ads: What are they Selling." MAGAZINE AGE 3 (May 1982) : 60-61+.

Review of magazine ads featuring nudes suggests a trend towards increasing use of nude models. Is there a double standard for nudity in editorial and advertising? Many feature lingerie and cosmetics in women's and fashion magazines. They sell products not sex.

236 Rossi, Susan R., and Rossi, Joseph S. "Gender Differences in the Perception of Women in Magazine Advertising." SEX ROLES 12 (May 1985) : 1033-1039.

Comparison of male and female response to magazine ads showing men and women as equals and women as sex objects. Men rated both types of ads as appealing. Women gave "sexist ads" lower appeal ratings than "non-sexist" ads.

237 Sarel, Dan. "Trends in Factual Claims in Ads in Magazines: 1958, 68, 78." JOURNALISM QUARTERLY 61 (Autumn 1984) : 650-654+.

Majority of ads in NEW YORKER, NEWSWEEK, and READER'S DIGEST contain both factual and non-factual claims over all three years studied.

238 Schorin, Gerald A., and Vandenbergh, Bruce G. "Advertising's Role in the Diffusion of Country-Western Trend in the U.S." JOURNALISM QUARTERLY 52 (Autumn 1985) : 515-522.

The differences between fads and social trends--fads are transitory and related to a single expression; trends are longer-term, related to other developments, consistent with values and lifestyles, modifiable for adoption by various groups. Study of country-western trend includes discussion of treatment by all media, counting of READERS' GUIDE articles on the subject, and content analysis of ads in sixteen magazines ranging from MOTOR TREND to VOGUE. Trend not reported in magazines prior to 1973. Two clusterings of country-western ads found--in 1974 and between 1978 and 1981.

239 Seldin, Joseph J. "A Long Way To Go Baby." NATION 224 (April 16, 1977) : 464-466.

Feminists have a long way to go before eliminating insulting female stereotypes in advertising.

240 Skelly, Gerald U., and Lundstrom, William J. "Male Sex Roles in Magazine Advertising, 1959-1979." JOURNAL OF COMMUNICATION 31 (Autumn 1981) : 52-57.

Trend shows a less stereotyped portrayal of men in advertising in 1979. In women's magazines, male models are decorative, not involved in "manly" activities. Useful bibliography on sex role stereotyping.

241 Soley, Lawrence. "The Effect of Black Models on Magazine Ad Readership." JOURNALISM QUARTERLY 60 (Winter 1983) : 686-690.

Color or presence of models does not affect magazine ad readership.

242 Soley, Lawrence., and Reid, Leonard N. "Satisfaction With the Informational Value of Magazine and Television Advertising." JOURNAL OF ADVERTISING 12 (no. 3, 1983) : 27-31.

Consumers who rated the informational value of magazine and television advertising were more satisfied with magazine advertising.

243 Stern, Bruce; Krugman, Dean M.; and Reskik, Alan. "Magazine Advertising: An Analysis of its Information Content." JOURNAL OF ADVERTISING RESEARCH 21 (April 1981) : 39-44.

Content analysis and comments on the value of ads to consumers. Research suggests 86 percent information utility in consumer magazine ads versus 49 percent in television advertising (comparative data from earlier study).

244 Strickland, Donald E.; Finn, T. Andrew; and Lambert, M. Dow. "A Content Analysis of Beverage Alcohol Advertising. I. Magazine Advertising." JOURNAL OF STUDIES ON ALCOHOL 43 (July 1982) : 655-682.

Content analysis of alcohol ads in 1978 magazines found most common themes were product-related, e.g., quality, good taste. Least common themes were sexual and life-style oriented. Also dealt with models and types of magazines carrying ads. Excellent critical review of literature on alcohol advertising.

245 Tankard, James W., Jr., and Pierce, Kate. "Alcohol Advertising and Magazine Editorial Content." JOURNALISM QUARTERLY 59 (Summer 1982) : 302-305.

Magazines with few alcohol ads took a negative view of using alcohol beverages.

246 VandenBergh, Bruce G.; Krugman, Dean M.; and Salwen, Michael B. "The Temptation To Puff: Puffery in Automotive Advertising 1930-1980." JOURNALISM QUARTERLY 60 (Winter 1983) : 700-704.

Analysis of TIME ads showed decrease in puffery as FTC regulatory pressure increased.

Chapter 5

EDITING & THE CHANGING MAGAZINE

Editing & Editors

---

247 Arth, Marvin, and Ashmore, Helen. THE NEWSLETTER EDITOR'S DESK BOOK. 3d ed. Shawnee Mission, Kansas: Parkway Press, 1984.

A handbook for the independent newsletter and magazine editor-publisher. Covers all the basics briefly, from law to layout, targeting the audience to formula stories.

248 Beach, Mark. EDITING YOUR NEWSLETTER. 2d ed. New York: Van Nostrand Reinhold, 1983.

How to publish a newsletter, from setting goals to layout. A practical handbook.

249 Boykin, John. "The Editor as Photographer." FOLIO 15 (March 1986) : 106-112.

On often-overlooked reality: Specialized as staff members may be, editor-photographers are needed by many magazines. "Word-people" versus "picture-people" isn't cost efficient thinking.

250 Carlson, Walter. "Copy Flow: Editors' Secrets." FOLIO 13 (July 1984) : 46-47.

Setting editorial deadlines to meet printer's deadlines.

251 Carlson, Walter. "Increasing Reader Involvement." FOLIO 13 (November 1984) : 85-86+.

Letters to the editor, contests, coupons are ways to get readers involved.

252 Carlson, Walter. "Researching Readers' Needs." FOLIO 13 (September 1984) : 63-64+.

Editorial research as used by several publishers to determine interests and needs of readers.

253 "Checks Stem Libel Suits." FOLIO 14 (March 1985) : 38.

NEW YORK magazine avoids libel suits with careful editing, fact-checking, and legal consultation.

254 Delaney, Rachelle. "Making the Most of Editorial Advisory Boards." FOLIO 12 (July 1983) : 60-62.

Comprised of practicing professionals, the editorial board gives an editor feedback on how well his trade magazine is covering the industry it serves.

255 Diamond, Edwin. "Take a Great Editor, Add Great Writers, Throw Caution to the Wind." NEXT 2 (January-February 1981) : 54-57.

256 "The Editorial Audit: A Sales Tool That May Be Coming of Age." FOLIO 11 (September 1982) : 8.

Editorial audit is a statistical analysis of editorial content.

257 "Editorial Pages Expand to Match Increases in Advertising Pages." FOLIO 13 (April 1984) : 16.

As advertising pages increase, magazines must find more editorial copy to maintain established advertising-editorial ratios.

258 Elliott, Osborn. THE WORLD OF OZ. New York: Viking Press, 1980.

Harvard graduate and dean of Columbia University school of journalism recalls his years (1961-1975) as editor of NEWSWEEK. Covers Vietnam, Nixon, Agnew, and the trials of depth journalism in those years of useful excursion into cover-up and even occasional advocacy.

259 Feinberg, Andrew. "The Magazine Business: Editing by Statistics." THE PRESS 9 (December 1981) : 30.

Opinion piece by magazine free-lancer laments the importance of audience demographics in determining magazine content. Editing by statistics lacks life, variety, sparkle, freshness.

260 Fry, John. "Regionalizing Your Editorial." FOLIO 10 (May 1981) : 78-80+.

Most added costs of regionalizing editorial are editorial rather than production costs. Regionalization increases service to the reader, and may boost circulation and make rising cover prices more acceptable.

261 Gage, Theodore J. "Magazines With Solid Niches Notch Success." ADVERTISING AGE 53 (November 8, 1982) : M33-M34.

High circulation is not as important for magazine success as finding the right audience, understanding the audience, and carefully pursuing it. A magazine needs to have more specific demographic information about its audience, including buying power, education, etc.

262 Glenn, George A. "The Art of Being on Time: Part I." FOLIO 6 (April 1977) : 16+.

Tips for the editor on meeting deadlines include thinking mathematically about production checkpoints, scheduling, self-discipline, and using bulletin boards and/or printed programs.

263 Glenn, George A. "The Art of Being on Time: Part II." FOLIO 6 (June 1977) : 68+.

Example of how the plan outlined in Part I has worked for a publication with a serious deadline problem. See entry 262.

264 Hershey, Lenore. BETWEEN THE COVERS: THE LADY'S OWN JOURNAL. New York: Coward-McCann, 1983.

Gossipy autobiogrqaphy of former LADIES' HOME JOURNAL editor. In between the recipes and name-dropping (from Lynda Bird Johnson to Walt Disney) are statements about her editorial policy and LHJ's coverage of the women's movement.

265 Hubbard, J. T. W. MAGAZINE EDITING: HOW TO ACQUIRE THE SKILLS YOU NEED TO WIN A JOB AND SUCCEED IN THE MAGAZINE BUSINESS. Englewood Cliffs, N.J.: Prentice-Hall, 1982.

Lively, once-over-lightly approach characterizes this magazine text. Covers everything from writing to starting your own magazine, and includes practical exercises, sample edited copy, and recounted experiences from magazinists.

266 Hudson, Howard Penn. PUBLISHING NEWSLETTERS. New York: Charles Scribner's Sons, 1982.

How to start, manage, design, print, sell newsletters.

267 Jacobi, Peter. "The Art of Magazine Editing: An Introduction." FOLIO 12 (September 1983) : 83-84+.

The editor assembles various writings into a coherent whole. He is a conductor, and must understand his audience.

268 Jones, Alex. "Editing and Libel: TIME's Methods in Sharon Spur Debate About Journalism Standards." NEW YORK TIMES, 8 January 1985, p. B4.

Procedures in copy preparation used by news magazines (where reporting is separated from writing) are questioned.

269 Kanes, John, and Kanes, Martha. "The Girls in the Executive Suite." SAVVY 4 (July 1983) : 11.

Regarding aggressive women editors employed on early 1960s VOGUE.

270 Kanner, Bernice. "Mighty Mack." NEW YORK 16 (March 21, 1983) : 18+.

Brief biographical and personality profile of John Mack Carter, editor of GOOD HOUSEKEEPING.

271 Lehtinen, Merja H. K. "Creating Workable Editorial Schedules." FOLIO 14 (July 1985) : 86-91.

How-to specifics on achieving efficiency, excellence, lowered editorial employee turnover.

272 Lipman, Joanne. "At the NEW YORKER, Editor and a Writer Differ on Facts." WALL STREET JOURNAL, 18 June 1984, p. 1+.

The NEW YORKER is a magazine that carefully checks all facts and is well-known for its accuracy. Disagreement between editorial philosophy and writer Alastair Reid's narrative style, composite characters and situations. Journalistic pros and cons of Reid's style.

273 Lott, David. "12 Ways to Energize Editorial." FOLIO 13 (March 1984) : 90-91+.

Ideas for better editing and attracting readers.

274 Ludwig, Myles Eric. "Achieving Magazine 'Brand Personality'." FOLIO 12 (January 1983) : 66-67.

Successful magazine publishing requires identity, credibility, and positioning. Acquiring this "brand personality" depends on content, strategy, and design. Brief examples illustrating the concept from GEO, NEW YORKER, PEOPLE, and NEW YORK.

275 Lukovitz, Karlene. "Staying on Schedule: How Do 'Other' Magazines Do It?" FOLIO 10 (August 1981) : 73-79.

Production managers, consultants, and publishers offer ideas for meeting deadlines. These include granting ad production deadline extensions reluctantly, having adequate staff, getting specific reasons for each deadline breakage that occurs. Such ideas are fleshed out in varied ways useful to the less sophisticated production person.

276 Machalaba, Daniel. "Carving Out Identity is the Crucial Task For a New Magazine." WALL STREET JOURNAL, 24 March 1980, p.1+.

One-year-old GEO magazine is suffering identity problems.

277 Machalaba, Daniel. "Does Saul Bellow Stand on His Head? Ask a Fact Checker." WALL STREET JOURNAL, 15 December 1981, p. 1+.

Fact-checking helps avoid libel suits.

278 Mann, Jim. "How to Take Your Magazine's Temperature." FOLIO 6 (April 1977) : 44-48.

How to notice editorial vitality and/or declining health in a magazine. Thoughtful.

279 Mayes, Herbert R. THE MAGAZINE MAZE. Garden City, N.Y.: Doubleday, 1980.

Autobiography of Herbert Mayes, who began his career in trade publications, moved through the Hearst Corporation to the editorship of GOOD HOUSEKEEPING, and in 1958 to the editorship of McCALL's. Provides insights into magazine editing, business, and history.

280 Meskil, John. "Circulation Is the Only Problem." MARKETING & MEDIA DECISIONS 18 (October 1983) : 92+.

Health of magazine may be measured using three criteria: editorial vitality, circulation, advertising growth.

281 Parker, Hershel. "Norman Mailer's Revision of the ESQUIRE Version of AN AMERICAN DREAM and the Aesthetic Problem of Built-In Intentionality." BULLETIN OF RESEARCH IN THE HUMANITIES 84 (Winter 1981) : 405-430.

How ESQUIRE's printing of Mailer's AN AMERICAN DREAM in 1963 differs from that of Dial Press in 1964.

282 "Periodic 'Audits' of Magazine Editorial Spark Improvements." FOLIO 11 (December 1982) : 40.

Analysis of all aspects of a publication (depth of information, writing quality, cover, layout, headlines, etc.) to determine if readers' needs are met.

283 Peter, John. "Measuring Your Magazine's Editorial Health." FOLIO 12 (May 1983) : 77-80.

Step-by-step approach for evaluation of a magazine includes analysis of physical characteristics, editing, writing, design.

284 Peter, John. "A Touch of Class." FOLIO 7 (January 1978) : 33+.

The reasons why more magazines are becoming class publications. What makes a "classy" magazine.

285 Peter, John. "The Underestimated Art of Editorial Planning." FOLIO 6 (December 1977) : 44-46+.

How magazine issues are planned and scheduled.

286 Plotnik, Arthur. "The Compulsive Editor." FOLIO 11 (November 1982) : 115-116+.

Comments on the editorial personality, with emphasis on what Plotnik calls "compulsiveness." Examples of how compulsiveness may be functional or dysfunctional.

287 Poltrack, Terence. "Publishers Pursue the Theme Scheme." MARKETING & MEDIA DECISIONS 20 (April 1985) : 73-74+.

Many magazines are using regular issues to cover single topics.

288 Rauch, Howard S. "Measuring Editorial Performance." FOLIO 12 (November 1984) : 123-124+.

Gralla Publications executive discusses hiring and training editors for small magazine staffs. Good quick training for young editors saves supervisory time and yields greater productivity. Use of quantitative standards to measure editorial productivity is suggested.

289 Ranly, Don. MAGAZINE EDITING WORKBOOK. Ames, Iowa: Iowa State University Press, 1984.

Loose-leaf volume of magazine editing exercises designed to simulate on-the-job assignments for students.

290 Ravis, Howard S. "The Art of the Interview." FOLIO 5 (February 1976): 63-66.

Eight magazine editors offer tips for successful interviewing. Emphasis on preparation, establishing rapport, question formulation.

291 Ridder, Pamela. "There are TK Fact-Checkers in the U.S." COLUMBIA JOURNALISM REVIEW 19 (November-December 1980) : 59-62.

The role and duties of a fact-checker.

292 Rivers, William L. MAGAZINE EDITING IN THE '80S. Belmont, Calif.: Wadsworth Publishing, 1983.

The tasks of magazine editors and their relationships with writers are covered simply in this text. Includes a comparison between magazine and newspaper editing, law and ethics, and numerous practical exercises in addition to the basics--copy editing, writing headlines and titles, graphics, picture editing, layout and design. Includes a brief glossary.

293 Rogers, Jane C. "How to Conduct Responsible In-House Research." FOLIO 14 (September 1985) : 102-109.

Practical and specific tips for newcomers to magazine research. Covers all the basics: defining objectives, selecting samples, interview alternatives, data analysis.

294 Salmans, Sandra. "Magazine's Winning Formula." NEW YORK TIMES, 9 May 1984, sec. D, p. 1.

Editorial formula and advertising approach of SUNSET magazine.

295 Silvey, Larry K. "The Making of a Magazine: A Descriptive Analysis of the Total Design of COUNTERMAN." M.A. thesis, University of Akron, 1985.

Lengthy overview of the magazine editing function and methods of visual presentation for both editorial and advertising copy. A case study of COUNTERMAN illustrates an objective and directed approach to magazine design.

296 Swan, Christopher. "HARPER'S Lapham: Good-bye." CHRISTIAN SCIENCE MONITOR, 16 July 1985, p. 1+.

HARPER'S editor Lewis Lapham laments the past heyday of magazine journalism, when money was no object and articles were lengthy and in-depth. Editing for a generation reared on television with no appreciation for discoursive sentences and profound conclusions is completely different.

297 Swartz, Herbert. "Why Some Magazines Never Die." FOLIO 15 (February 1986) : 104-109.

Excellence of editorial and individual drive are among reasons offered for magazine longevity. Practical advice to management as well as knowledge for the beginner is listed and explained.

298 White, Jan. "Art-Edit: Promoting a Team Spirit." FOLIO 19 (September 1984) : 180+.

Rules for writers and designers to use in working together for best results.

299 Wootton, Philip H., Jr. "Confronting the Editorial Mystique." FOLIO 8 (November 1979) : 82-83+.

Tips for publishers on assessing editorial problems when they occur. Difficulties of coping with an editor's "mystique and genius."

New Magazines

---

300 Allen, Bruce. "Innovation on a Shoestring is the Rule for Little Mags." CHRISTIAN SCIENCE MONITOR, 13 August 1984, p. B3+.

Trend in little local magazines starting up on small budgets.

301 Alter, Stewart. "Will a New Magazine Survive? Ayer Forms Committee to Decide." MAGAZINE AGE 1 (March 1980) : 28-31.

Ayer evaluates chances for success of new magazine start-ups. Forecasts assist advertisers deciding to buy or not buy space. But does Ayer contribute to a publication's early demise by predicting failure?

302 "Anatomy of a New Magazine." MARKETING & MEDIA DECISIONS 15 (May 1980) : 64-67+.

Description of new magazine starts: INSIDE SPORTS, NEXT, SCIENCE 80, PANORAMA.

303 Auchmutey, Jim. "Gambling with a Subject: Some Win, Some Lose." ADVERTISING AGE 55 (March 26, 1984) : M24.

Difficulties of publishing specialized magazines. It's easy to start a magazine in response to a fad, but difficult to keep it going.

304 Blair, William S. "COUNTRY JOURNAL." FOLIO 7 (September 1978) : 42+.

Founder of COUNTRY JOURNAL describes how he financed his new magazine.

305 Constantino, Jerry R. "The Anatomy of a Spinoff." FOLIO 7 (January 1978) : 30-32+.

Benefits of creating new magazines from spin-offs of successful publications are illustrated by the example of CRAFTS MAGAZINE.

306 Diamond, Edwin. "Time Inc. Plays Magazine." NEW YORK 17 (November 19, 1984) : 38-41+.

Time Inc.'s magazine development group and how it works. Includes discussion of several ideas for new magazines being considered.

307 Dougherty, Philip H. "Bringing a Magazine to Market." NEW YORK TIMES, 20 November 1981, p. D19.

Birth of AMERICAN HEALTH magazine.

308 "Dreaming the Big Dream." FOLIO 11 (February 1982) : 63-68+.

The story of twelve magazine start-ups from publishers' viewpoints. From PRIME TIME and FISHING TACKLE RETAILER to ON CABLE and SHEET MUSIC MAGAZINE, the top people offer insights on hundreds of details relating to what it takes to make a new magazine succeed in the hurly-burly of high-pressure competition.

309 Ellenthal, Ira. "Learning from a Successful Launch." FOLIO 14 (January 1985) : 167-168+.

Sensible planning accounts for the success of the new computer magazine, FAMILY COMPUTING.

310 Elliott, Stuart J. "Don't Prejudge PICTURE WEEK." ADVERTISING AGE 57 (February 17, 1986) : 24.

Brief editorial by AA magazine reporter. Elliott criticizes the critics of Time Inc.'s PICTURE WEEK who say the proposed magazine is not classy or upscale. Better judge the publication (now being revamped) on its own merits.

311 Elliott, Stuart J. "GOOD FOOD Yet to Simmer." ADVERTISING AGE (January 20, 1986) : 67.

New item on the reintroduction of Triangle Communications' GOOD FOOD, sold at supermarket checkouts.

312 Elliott, Stuart J. "'Launch Fever' Still Lives in the Magazine Game." ADVERTISING AGE 54 (November 7, 1983) : M39-M40.

Brief overview of some new titles and redesigns planned for 1984.

313 Elliott, Stuart J. "No Epilog for Time Development." ADVERTISING AGE 56 (June 3, 1985) : 95.

Time Inc.'s magazine development group is focusing on one project: PICTURE WEEK.

314 Elliott, Stuart J. "PICTURE WEEK Starts Sept. 23." ADVERTISING AGE 56 (July 8, 1985) : 61.

Test marketing of PICTURE WEEK begins in September 1985, after delay since July.

315 Elliott, Stuart J. "TIME Begins PICTURE WEEK Test." ADVERTISING AGE 56 (September 23, 1985) : 92.

Time's new quick-read black and white photo magazine begins newsstand trials in some cities.

316 Elliott, Stuart J. "Time Flies when Testing Magazines." ADVERTISING AGE 56 (March 4, 1985) : 3+.

Time Inc.'s magazine development group and its new ideas are discussed.

317 Elliott, Stuart J. "Time Inc. Readies Snappy PICTURE WEEK." ADVERTISING AGE 56 (May 20, 1985) : 6.

Time's new venture PICTURE WEEK is being launched.

318 Elliott, Stuart J. "Time's Stolley Steps Back into the Picture." ADVERTISING AGE 56 (October 3, 1985) : 20+.

Richard Stolley, formerly of PEOPLE, is managing editor of Time Inc.'s new PICTURE WEEK. Profile and plans for the new magazine.

319 Elliott, Stuart J. "Upscale Magazine Tilts Toward Europe." ADVERTISING AGE 56 (April 22, 1985) : 123.

EUROPEAN TRAVEL GUIDE, another new magazine carving a niche for itself in the crowded affluent market.

320 Fleming, Karl. "The New LOS ANGELES TIMES MAGAZINE." WASHINGTON JOURNALISM REVIEW 7 (April 1985) : 48-51.

The first U.S. Sunday supplement of consumer magazine size, printed on slick paper. To be launched October 6, 1985.

321 Garry, William J. "The Winners ... and the Losers." FREE ENTERPRISE (August 1978) : 38-41.

Analysis of ten new magazines with brief commentary on the success or failure of each one.

322 Gloede, William F. "Putting 'Romance' into Magazine Publishing." ADVERTISING AGE 56 (April 11, 1985) : 9.

Pilot issue of ROMANCE TODAY, a slick, four-color women's magazine, will be distributed in the Sunday edition of the NEW YORK DAILY NEWS.

323 Howland, Jennifer. "Financing: How to Find it." FOLIO 13 (May 1984) : 78+.

Seven pages on how to find financial backing for a new magazine venture.

324 "Jerry's Journal." TIME 120 (September 20, 1982) : 79.

Brief news note on the launching of Jerry Falwell's new monthly, FUNDAMENTALIST REVIEW.

325 Kanner, Bernice. "PRIME TIME Remembers the Forgotten Generation." ADVERTISING AGE 50 (November 12, 1979) : 88.

Birth of PRIME TIME, new magazine for senior citizens. Will it face problems selling ads through agencies that have traditionally avoided older customers?

326 Kanner, Bernice. "Triangle Sets Stage for PANORAMA." ADVERTISING AGE 50 (April 23, 1979) : 3+.

Some details about the test marketing of PANORAMA, an unsuccessful spin-off of TV GUIDE.

327 Kastor, Elizabeth. "And Now, NATIONAL INTEREST: Neoconservatives Plan Foreign Policy Journal." WASHINGTON POST, 10 September 1985, p. E1.

Thin commentary on an ad forecasting the arrival of the new journal and discussion of those "present at the creation." Likely useful only in conjunction with other, later pieces.

328 Kleinfield, N. R. "The Itch to Start a Magazine." NEW YORK TIMES, 2 December 1979, sec. 3, p. 1.

More new magazines fail than survive. Some facts and reasons why.

329 Klingel, John. "Pre-Launch Testing." FOLIO 13 (May 1984) : 122-123+.

Testing marketing strategies and designing circulation management for new magazines.

330 Kobak, James B. "New Magazine Myths." FOLIO 7 (October 1978) : 35-36.

Magazine consultant disproves familiar myths. Suggests failure rate for new magazines is not high, ventures need not be expensive or risky, and profits may be good.

331 Kobak, James B. "Starting ANOTHER Magazine." FOLIO 7 (September 1978) : 51-52+.

Established publishers know little about starting additional magazines. This article discusses the problems, why non-publishers invest in new magazines, and an effective procedure for launching a new title.

332 Kobak, James B. "Startups: Who Succeeds and Why?" FOLIO 13 (May 1984) : 90-92+.

Enterpreneurs fresh to the publishing industry create and develop more new successful magazines than do existing publishers.

333 Kobak, James B. "A Statistical Look at Recent Launches." FOLIO 11 (February 1982) : 88-93.

Obtaining data from STANDARD RATE and DATA SERVICE volumes, a familiar magazine consultant looks at the increased number of start-ups and emphasizes realized possibilities for individual entrepreneurs who dominate. Also counts the seven largest publishers, who account for just 83 of 1,200 new magazines.

334 Kobak, James B. "Writing the Proposal." FOLIO 7 (December 1978) : 61+.

How to define the editorial concept and plans for a new magazine.

335 Laitin, Julie A. "Promoting the New Magazine." FOLIO 13 (May 1984) : 96-98+.

Sales promotion, advertising, public relations, and marketing for a new magazine. A crucial task is positioning or finding the magazine's special niche in the market.

336 Landro, Laura. "Time Embarks on Ambitious Plan to Develop a Range of Magazines." WALL STREET JOURNAL, 18 October 1984, p. 33.

Despite recent failure of TV-CABLE WEEK, Time Inc. has new magazine plans under consideration. Its magazine development group has editorial staff of approximately eighteen.

337 Landro, Laura. "Time, Inc.'s New Photo-Filled Magazine Takes Big Risk in a Crowded Market." WALL STREET JOURNAL, 23 May 1985, p. 33.

Competition is strong and the risks great for the proposed PICTURE WEEK.

338 Landro, Laura. "Time Shifts Emphasis From Developing Mass Magazines to Special-Interest Ones." WALL STREET JOURNAL, 18 February 1986, p. 6.

Time Inc. proposes launching special interest, controlled circulation magazines that cost little to start, carry few risks, make profits quickly, and use available subscriber lists.

339 Leinster, Colin. "The Magazine Mavericks." FREE ENTERPRISE (August 1978) : 33-37.

New magazine success stories of Jann Wenner (ROLLING STONE) and John Shuttleworth (MOTHER EARTH NEWS).

340 Levin, Gary. "Meredith Pushes Launch Plans." ADVERTISING AGE 57 (April 21, 1986) : 114.

Meredith completes $92 million purchase of LADIES' HOME JOURNAL and makes plans to test market MIDWEST LIVING, modeled after SOUTHERN LIVING and SUNSET.

341 Lipstein, Owen J. "Starting Up." FOLIO 10 (July 1981) : 45-46.

Notes on the launch of SCIENCE 81 include editorial research, coping with competition, promotion.

342 "Local Business Magazines Require Big-Time Money." FOLIO 14 (April 1985) : 11.

Increasing funds needed to launch even local business magazines.

343 MacDougall, A. Kent. "Nation's New Magazine Binge is Staggering." LOS ANGELES TIMES, 9 April 1978, sec. 6, p. 1+.

New magazine titles proliferate. Many reflect new interests and changing lifestyles; others imitate successful magazines. Some of the problems their owners face.

344 Mansfield, Stephanie. "County Chic: Bucks in the Backwoods." WASHINGTON POST, 15 December 1983, p. D1+.

The popular "country theme" is reflected in COUNTRY magazine, founded on a shoestring budget in 1980.

345 Marshall, Christy. "Neophytes Set Debut of NEW MAN." ADVERTISING AGE 52 (February 16, 1981) : 30.

Brief announcement of new men's magazine positioned as a service book for the young executive.

346 Martin. Michael B. "Looming Large: Kate and Rob Pulleyn Publish Three Craft Magazines." MONEY 12 (July 1983) : 29.

Brief recount of an individual success story. From a controlled circulation, typewritten newsletter for weavers, two shopkeepers now have a stable of three craft magazines and some financial backing from the Bonnier Group, a Swedish publisher.

347 Molotsky, Irvin. "A New Magazine from Smithsonian." NEW YORK TIMES, 22 September 1985, sec. 1, p. 89.

Brief announcement of Smithsonian's intention to introduce AIR & SPACE, a magazine for the general reader.

348 Neher, Jacques. "PLAYBOY One-Shots May Yield New Books." ADVERTISING AGE 50 (November 19, 1979) : 1+.

Plans for six one-shot GUIDES, and other brief news from Playboy Enterprises.

349 "New Magazine Spin-Offs from Special Issues Lower Publisher Risk." FOLIO 7 (September 1978) : 8-9.

Magazines that begin as special issues of established publications lower start-up costs, reduce risks to publisher, and allow pre-testing new magazine's success with readers and advertisers. Some examples of magazines that began as special issues.

350 Norris, Eileen. "Kansas Boy Grabs an Idea and Runs with it." ADVERTISING AGE 54 (July 18, 1983) : M14+.

Success of RUNNER'S WORLD magazine. Part of a special ADVERTISING AGE MAGAZINE report on "Fitness Marketing." RUNNER'S WORLD exemplifies the report's premise that physical fitness is not a fad but a trend.

351 Obis, Paul. "VEGETARIAN TIMES." FOLIO 7 (September 1978) : 45+.

The editor of VEGETARIAN TIMES describes his launching of a successful magazine.

352 Pendleton, Jennifer. "LOS ANGELES TIMES Leaving Home: New Glossy Expected to Stop Ad Linage Erosion." ADVERTISNG AGE 56 (January 24, 1985) : 36-37.

To counter loss of advertising pages in its Sunday magazine, HOME, the LOS ANGELES TIMES plans a new glossy magazine with broader advertising appeal.

353 "PIC WEEK Back in Developer." ADVERTISING AGE 57 (January 27, 1986) : 92.

Time Inc.'s news and human interest PICTURE WEEK has ended its test for additional revamping. The quick-read, black and white photo magazine received high reader acceptance but trial posed problems for staff.

354 "Popcorn, Kid-Pleaser and More." BLACK ENTERPRISE 12 (January 1982) : 18.

Shoestring start-up of children's magazine POPCORN, founded in 1979 by a mother whose kids were bored by available children's titles.

355 Rohter, Larry. "SPIN: New Music Voice Takes on Rolling Stone." NEW YORK TIMES, 2 June 1985, sec. 1, p. 55.

New pop music magazine hopes to challenge ROLLING STONE. SPIN's editor-publisher is Robert Guccione Jr., son of PENTHOUSE's founder.

356 Scott, Joseph. "Survival Strategy for New Magazines." FREE ENTERPRISE (August 1978) : 42-43.

Composite interview with magazine publishers outlines the major pitfalls in starting a new magazine and suggestions for avoiding them.

357 "Spinoffs Interest BUSINESS WEEK." ADVERTISING AGE 54 (November 14, 1983) : 84.

McGraw Hill is publishing its first magazine spun off from BUSINESS WEEK, BUSINESS WEEK'S GUIDE TO CAREERS.

358 "Time Inc. is Testing a Photo Magazine in 13 U.S. Markets: Launching of PICTURE WEEK Scheduled for Next Year if Market Trial Succeeds." WALL STREET JOURNAL, 23 September 1985, p. 20.

359 "Time Inc. Overhauls Planned Magazine, Delays Market Test." WALL STREET JOURNAL, 3 July 1985, p. 2.

Disappointed by the response from advertisers and consumers, Time Inc. has overhauled its proposed magazine, PICTURE WEEK.

360 "Time Inc. Takes on TV GUIDE." BUSINESS WEEK (April 18, 1983) : 64+.

Launch of Time Inc.'s TV-CABLE WEEK will offer competition for TV GUIDE.

361 "12 Who did it Reveal Lessons Learned from Launches." FOLIO 14 (May 1985) : 88-111.

Personal experiences detailing successes and failures of twelve magazine start-ups, ranging from shoestring to corporate enterprises, regional to national titles, business to consumer publications.

362 "Two-Letter Man." MONEY 11 (March 1982) : 34+.

Newsman Llewellyn King successfully launched two newsletters, WEEKLY ENERGY REPORT and DEFENSE WEEK, on minimum budgets. Briefly written individual financial success story.

363 "Weekly Women's Magazine Launched." FOLIO 10 (February 1981) : 31.

WOMAN'S WORLD will depend on newsstand sales, not subscriptions.

364 Yoffe, Emily. "INSIDE SPORTS: Expansion Team in the Magazine League." WASHINGTON JOURNALISM REVIEW 2 (September 1980) : 56-58.

NEWSWEEK's new sister publication INSIDE SPORTS seemed headed for success in 1980.

Change, Rebirths, Revitalization

---

365 "Back in Circulation." INC. 5 (November 1983) : 122+.

How Mrs. Cory SerVaas, a physician, and her husband bought and revived the SATURDAY EVENING POST. The new POST now offers extensive coverage of medicine, has sponsored medical studies and stop smoking programs, and underwrites cancer research.

366 Barbieri, Richard. "Reviving Old Magazine Titles." VENTURE 5 (September 1983) : 82-83.

Brief commentary on planned revivals of INSIDE SPORTS and SATURDAY REVIEW by new owners.

367 Bonaventure, Peter. "The New LOOK." NEWSWEEK 93 (February 12, 1979) : 55.

The first issue of the revived LOOK magazine has separate covers for east and west editions. Brief review of some problems facing LOOK under new owner Daniel Filipacchi.

368 "BOOK DIGEST Owners Plan to Aim Magazine at Narrower Audience." WALL STREET JOURNAL, 4 June 1980, p. 16.

Repositioning of BOOK DIGEST will reduce circulation and provide demographic control.

369 "Bringing SATURDAY REVIEW in Step With the 80S." FOLIO 14 (May 1985) : 78-80.

Repositioning strategy planned by latest SATURDAY REVIEW owners Paul Dietrich and Frank Gannon.

370 Burrough, Bryan. "Skeptics Fault Plan to Revive Arts Review." WALL STREET JOURNAL, 13 December 1982, p. 13.

SATURDAY REVIEW's new owner is Jeff Gluck, publisher of a profit-making campus newspaper.

371 Carter, Betsy. "Back to LIFE." NEWSWEEK 91 (May 8, 1978) : 93.

The reborn LIFE magazine will aim for an affluent audience, unlike its predecessor. It will have more pictures, snappy text, upbeat stories, and evocative photojournalism.

372 Castro, Janice. "GEO Goes Upbeat-and-Uptown." TIME 118 (November 9, 1981) : 104.

New owners of GEO plan a more positive timeless image. Brief background of new editor, Paige Rense, and her experience at ARCHITECTURAL DIGEST and BON APPETIT.

373 Conway, Flo, and Siegelman, Jim. "The Second Going of HARPER'S WEEKLY." NEW TIMES 7 (October 15, 1976) : 98.

Attempt to revive HARPER'S WEEKLY as a reader participation journal failed.

374 Cook, Bruce. "VANITY FAIR's Chaotic Comeback: Exit Richard Locke, Enter Leo Lerman." WASHINGTON JOURNALISM REVIEW 5 (September 1983) : 22-25.

Problems at Conde Nast's revived VANITY FAIR lead to firings and new faces.

375 Dougherty, Philip H. "Class Act: Marketing VANITY FAIR." NEW YORK TIMES, 9 August 1982, p. D6.

Marketing and promotion for the forthcoming new VANITY FAIR.

376 Dougherty, Philip H. "A 'New Attitude' at CUISINE." NEW YORK TIMES, 18 January 1983, p. D26.

CUISINE searching for a "class" audience and circulation increases.

377 Edel, Richard. "Magazine, Thy Name is VANITY FAIR." LOS ANGELES TIMES, 27 February 1983, sec. Cal., p. 4.

Review of the new VANITY FAIR. Ads are tasteful and well done, but tend to mix too much with editorial material.

378 Edel, Richard. "New Graphics Energize Magazines' Appeal." ADVERTISING AGE 12 (October 17, 1983) : M46-M47.

Magazine redesign can increase a publication's marketability.

379 Ellenthal, Ira. "LIFE Resurrected, and Other Magazine Turnarounds." MAGAZINE AGE 6 (March 1985) : 6+.

Sketches of publishing, turnarounds, ups and downs at PARENTS, REDBOOK, CUISINE, WOMAN'S DAY, MAGAZINE AGE, PARADE.

380 Elliott, Stuart J. "CBS to Fix MECHANIX." ADVERTISING AGE 12 (November 28, 1983) : 45.

Revamp and rename of MECHANIX ILLUSTRATED is part of CBS Publications' new focus on magazines. Other corporate changes include major personnel shifts and planned revamping of other magazines.

381 Elliott, Stuart J. "Changes at FAMILY CIRCLE Aimed at Younger Women." ADVERTISING AGE 54 (July 11, 1983) : 69.

Changes planned for appearance, promotion, and reproduction of FAMILY CIRCLE are a response to revisions at WOMAN'S DAY.

382 Elliott, Stuart J. "HOUSE BEAUTIFUL Undergoes Remodeling." ADVERTISING AGE 57 (February 17, 1986) : 32.

More changes at Hearst's HOUSE BEAUTIFUL after a year of decreased revenues.

383 Elliott, Stuart J. "How Editors Keep their Magazines Fresh." ADVERTISING AGE 54 (October 31, 1983) : 58.

Three editors tell MPA conference about changes made at their magazines: BUSINESS WEEK, ESQUIRE, METROPOLITAN HOME.

384 Elliott, Stuart J. "It's US vs. Them in Checkout-Counter War." ADVERTISING AGE 14 (May 13, 1985) : 14.

New owner of US magazine plans complete revamp. Jann Wenner of ROLLING STONE is new board chairman and editor-in-chief.

385 Elliott, Stuart J. "Magazine Tinkerer Making Family Media Roster Grow." ADVERTISING AGE 56 (February 25, 1985) : 10+.

Robert Riordan's Family Media has bought four ailing magazines in the past two and one-half years--LADIES' HOME JOURNAL, HOMEOWNER, WORLD TENNIS, SAVVY.

386 Elliott, Stuart J. "New Design Fits CHANGING TIMES Name." ADVERTISING AGE 13 (December 13, 1984) : 3+.

Graphics and editorial revamp of CHANGING TIMES was completed over a five-year period to attract younger readers. Brief profile of the magazine's readers and editorial concept.

387 Elliott, Stuart J. "Publisher is 'Only' Change at 'VF'." ADVERTISING AGE 14 (June 3, 1985) : 3+.

VANITY FAIR has its third publisher and third editor since its 1983 rebirth.

388 Elliott, Stuart J. "Revamp is Key to SUCCESS." ADVERTISING AGE 55 (September 10, 1984) : 74+.

New management has selected WORKING WOMAN as a role model for SUCCESS magazine's revamp. SUCCESS will appeal to the complete man, covering all aspects of his lifestyle--business, personal finance, rewards of success.

389 Elliott, Stuart J. "SOAP Book Responds to New Script." ADVERTISING AGE 54 (October 24, 1983) : 26+.

Problems for SOAP OPERA DIGEST due to management's failure to recognize the need for change. New publisher is repositioning to seek a higher demographic audience and conducting research to measure his success.

390 Elliott, Stuart J. "US Colors in Void in Magazine Market." ADVERTISING AGE 14 (June 10, 1985) : 10.

Redesigned US magazine uses color generously to compete for sales with PEOPLE magazine.

391 Elliott, Stuart J. "VANITY FAIR Comes Out for Round Three." ADVERTISING AGE 56 (March 11, 1985) : 83.

Changes in the editorial concept of VANITY FAIR since its relaunch and the installation of its third editor, Tina Brown.

392 Emmrich, Stuart. "Can H & G Home in on Tough Ad Market." ADVERTISING AGE 52 (December 7, 1981) : 64.

HOUSE & GARDEN plans changes to attract an upscale, modern, mobile reader beyond the homemaker.

393 Emmrich, Stuart. "New Team in Place as BUSINESS WEEK Tries to Restabilize." ADVERTISING AGE 54 (January 10, 1983) : 3+.

Personnel changes at BUSINESS WEEK precede redesign and improvement in quality and style of editorial content.

394 Emmrich, Stuart. "Revamp Gamble Appears to be Paying Off for H & G." ADVERTISING AGE 12 (June 6, 1983) : 61+.

HOUSE & GARDEN's complete graphic and editorial remake was designed to attract upscale readers and advertisers and to separate the magazine from its competition. But can the magazine now compete successfully with ARCHITECTURAL DIGEST?

395 Emmrich, Stuart. "Shelter Books Redecorate to Combat Market's Slump." ADVERTISING AGE 52 (September 14, 1981) : 83-84.

Changes made in magazines such as METROPOLITAN HOME, BETTER HOMES & GARDENS, HOUSE & GARDEN, in response to 1981 slump in ad sales.

396 Emmrich, Stuart. "Swipe at VANITY FAIR has N.Y. Media Buzzing." ADVERTISING AGE 54 (April 4, 1983) : 46.

Summary of reviews for VANITY FAIR's first issue. The strong negative criticism of NEW REPUBLIC's Henry Fairlee suggests the magazine was not created for an editorial purpose but for advertising sales.

397 Emmrich, Stuart. " ... While SPORT is Trying its Hand as Forecast Guide." ADVERTISING AGE 53 (July 19, 1982) : 37+.

SPORT is repositioning again. This time it will focus on future rather than past sports events.

398 English, Mary McCabe. "How to Stay SEVENTEEN--and Keep Growing." ADVERTISING AGE 53 (August 2, 1982) : M27-28.

How SEVENTEEN has changed over the years to stay in step with its readers.

399 "Esquire Magazine Set to Change Direction Under New Ownership." WALL STREET JOURNAL, 1 May 1979, p. 33.

Under 13-30 Corporation, ESQUIRE will be redesigned to provide a "clearer male image."

400 Fairlie, Henry. "The Vanity of VANITY FAIR: A Monument to Status Anxiety." NEW REPUBLIC 188 (March 21, 1983) : 25.

Strongly critical review and brief historical sketch of VANITY FAIR old and new.

401 Fannin, Rebecca. "Comeback of the Culture Books." MARKETING & MEDIA DECISIONS 18 (July 1983) : 40-41+.

Publishers are learning how to interest the high-brow reader, and magazines like VANITY FAIR and ESQUIRE are repositioning both format and content to attract upscale readers.

402 Fannin, Rebecca. "Image Revision for Magazines." MARKETING & MEDIA DECISIONS 19 (January 1984) : 54-55+.

Several periodicals have redesigned for more affluent audiences: WOMAN'S DAY, CUISINE, HOUSE & GARDEN, METROPOLITAN HOME.

403 Fannin, Rebecca. "Tina's in Vogue at VANITY FAIR." MARKETING & MEDIA DECISIONS 19 (May 1984) : 72-73+.

VANITY FAIR is receiving more favorable reviews under its third editor Tina Brown, and may regain reders and advertisers lost by earlier unsuccessful issues. Notes on Brown's plans for the magazine.

404 Felker, Clay S. "Life Cycles in the Age of Magazines." ANTIOCH REVIEW 24 (Spring 1969) : 7-13.

How magazines change over time, as audiences, editors, and editorial formulas change.

405 Hafferkamp, Jack. "ROLLING STONE Moves into the Mainstream." ADVERTISING AGE 55 (October 18, 1984) : 13-14.

ROLLING STONE changes with its audience--from yippie to yuppie. Readers are still aged 18 to 34 males, but the interests of that group have changed in ROLLING STONE's seventeen years of publishing.

406 Hammonds, Keith. "A New Publisher Gives GEO Magazine a Facelift." NEW YORK TIMES, 22 August 1982, p. F21.

New GEO owner, Knapp Communications, has given the magazine a new look.

407 "HARPER'S Woos a New Reader." NEW YORK TIMES, 3 August 1984, p. D1+.

HARPER'S new design and marketing approach targets affluent, well-educated business people, not the "armchair intellectuals" it catered to in the past.

408 Harrigan, Anthony. "MODERN AGE in a Changing World." MODERN AGE 26 (Summer-Fall 1982) : 350-353.

On the occasion of twenty-five years of publishing, this conservative journal considers changes in society and the magazine's editorial concept.

409 "HOUSE & GARDEN's New Focus." NEW YORK TIMES, 7 July 1984, p. 33+.

National Magazine Awards won by the redesigned HOUSE & GARDEN.

410 "How will the New LIFE Differ From the Old?" FOLIO 7 (July 1978) : 24.

The new LIFE will be a monthly, rely more heavily on newsstand sales, have smaller circulation, more pictures, pages, color, and cost, and cater to a more affluent audience.

411 Hunter, Bill. "The New Look of BUSINESS WEEK." WASHINGTON JOURNALISM REVIEW 5 (July-August 1983) : 37+.

Intense competition from FORBES, FORTUNE, and other business media have led BUSINESS WEEK to become more "slick, bold, friendly" and less "stick-in-the-mud." The new magazine is more appealing on the newsstand and more organized inside in its effort to attract readers and advertisers.

412 Janssen, Peter A. "ROLLING STONE's Quest for Respectability." COLUMBIA JOURNALISM REVIEW 12 (January-February 1974) : 59-65.

Profile of ROLLING STONE, and how it is evolving with the youth culture it represents.

413 Kaiser, Charles. "The Making of a Magazine." NEWSWEEK 101 (January 3, 1983) : 65+.

Rebirth of VANITY FAIR expected. Like the original VANITY FAIR (1914-1936), the rebirth will be aimed at an affluent audience because such readership is viewed as "recession-proof."

414 Kanner, Bernice. "Reader, Advertiser Services are Keys to ESQUIRE Revamp." ADVERTISING AGE 50 (May 7, 1979) : 6+.

Sketchy plans revealed for ESQUIRE's future by new owners Whittle and Moffitt.

415 Kanner, Bernice. "Starting Over: Magazine Face-lifts." NEW YORK 15 (September 20, 1982) : 22+.

Economic problems and keeping up with the times are two reasons behind the "make-over-mania" in the magazine industry. Some examples used are HOUSE & GARDEN, GEO, APARTMENT LIFE, SPORTS AFIELD.

416 Klein, Howard R. "The Anatomy of a Redesign." FOLIO 12 (February 1983) : 56-62.

Detailed, illustrated account of the redesign of BUILDER magazine. Viewed as a systematic, step-by-step procedure. Considers contents page, logo, magazine structure, features, layout and pictures, typography, back-of-the-book. All changes lead to a consistent, identifiable style.

417 Kobak, James B. "A Magazine's Life Cycle and its Profits." FOLIO 5 (October 1976) : 48+.

Analysis of seven stages in a magazine's development and growth, and their relation to revenue and costs. Examples of magazines at each described stage.

418 Krakow, Marie. "A Book Breaks its Diet and Hopes to Get Fatter." ADVERTISING AGE 55 (March 26, 1984) : 42-43.

WEIGHT WATCHERS magazine is redesigned graphically and editorially to build circulation.

419 Landro, Laura. "Time is Revamping DISCOVER Magazine in Attempt to Stem the Monthly's Losses." WALL STREET JOURNAL, 7 June 1985, p. 8.

Hurt by the boom in computer magazines, DISCOVER is revamping to attract more upscale readers and advertisers.

420 Leff, Laurel. "As Record Sales Sag, ROLLING STONE Gives New Subjects a Spin: Magazine Plays Down Music to Attract Older Readers and a Broad Range of Ads." WALL STREET JOURNAL, 4 June 1981, p. 1+.

ROLLING STONE is becoming more "mainstream" to improve its demographics and continue to meet its readers' needs.

421 "Liberal Magazines Adapting to the 80s." FOLIO 15 (May 1986) : 53-54.

How MOTHER JONES and NEW REPUBLIC are trying to lure advertisers and readers in a conservative social climate. Changes involve new marketing approaches, subtle editorial changes, and redesign.

422 "LOOK Down and Very Possibly Out." TIME 114 (July 16, 1979) : 65.

Problems with the revival of LOOK magazine by Daniel Filipacchi and his contract with Jann Wenner to revitalize the book.

423 Lukovitz, Karlene. "Repositioning." FOLIO 10 (November 1981) : 78+.

Changing a magazine to improve its position is costly and dangerous, if potentially strengthening. Differing opinions are stressed. So is promotion. A list is offered to show when repositioning is unlikely to work.

424 McFadden, Maureen. "HOUSE & GARDEN: A Classic Case of Turnaround." MAGAZINE AGE 6 (March 1985) : 59-60.

Alleges the magazine "is succeeding on repositioning course set three years ago" to upscale demographics.

425 McFadden, Maureen. "Repositioned Magazines: A Last-Ditch Effort or a New Beginning." MAGAZINE AGE 4 (February 1983) : 24-30.

Questions what repositioning is--a few normal adjustments or a major turnaround. Comments on successful and unsuccessful repositionings at GEO, HOUSE & GARDEN, CALIFORNIA (formerly NEW WEST), ESQUIRE, PSYCHOLOGY TODAY, and AMERICAN HOME. Magazines are becoming more vertical--many serve a single subject category (e.g., science). As public interest decreases in that area, repositioning may not be possible and shakeouts will occur.

426 Machalaba, Daniel. "More Magazines Aim for Affluent Readers, But Some Worry that Shake-out is Coming." WALL STREET JOURNAL, 4 October 1982, p. 35+.

Anticipating an increase in high-income households, many magazines are upgrading content and appearance to lure affluent readers and advertisers of expensive products. Will the field become so crowded there will be a shakeout?

427 Marshall, Christy. "BOOK DIGEST Future Reads Better." ADVERTISING AGE 51 (October 27, 1980. : 76.

Solutions to BOOK DIGEST's problems include circulation cutback, class audience repositioning, improved graphics, new sales people, new marketing strategy.

428 Meskill, John. "Reversing Magazine Declines." MARKETING & MEDIA DECISIONS 16 (August 1981) : 88+.

Overall decline in industry health for the first half of 1981 relates to tight economy, comparison with previous high circulation years, adverse effect of cable tv. Magazines need to change content to match lifesyle shifts and to specialize.

429 "MI Seeks Home Edge with New Name." ADVERTISING AGE 55 (July 16, 1984) : 64.

Name change for MECHANIX ILLUSTRATED will occur in stages. The new HOME MECHANIX will reflect inclusion of more home-oriented editorial.

430 Millman, Nancy. "GEO Puts on a New Face." ADVERTISING AGE 53 (April 5,1982) : M2-M3+.

New owner Knapp Communication and new editor Paige Rense attempt to rescue GEO. Background of the fated magazine emphasizes its struggle for an editorial identity, lack of advertising pages, and poor response to direct mail subscription solicitation.

431 Moffitt, Phillip. "Backstage with ESQUIRE: We've Been Back to the Drawing Board." ESQUIRE 93 (March 1980) : 5.

Notes on the redesign of ESQUIRE magazine from its editor.

432 Moffitt, Phillip. "No Magic Moments, No Single Factor Turned ESQUIRE Around." FOLIO 13 (January 1984) : 54+.

ESQUIRE's successful redesign. New owners defined their target audience as professional men and women in their thirties, and redesigned ESQUIRE to match their needs and interests.

433 "New VANITY FAIR Aimed at the 'Soon-to-be-Rich'." LOS ANGELES TIMES, 5 April 1983, sec. 4, p. 2.

Reborn VANITY FAIR receives bad reviews from the critics.

434 Oliver, Belinda J. "REDBOOK Goes for the Jugular." MAGAZINE AGE 6 (February 1985) : 69-71.

REDBOOK's new graphics and vital promotion demonstrate success to some, but leave others with a wait-and-see attitude. Statistics over several years cited.

435 Paskowski, Marianne. "Home Service Magazines Have Designs on Consumers." MADISON AVENUE 24 (September 1982) : 76+.

How service magazines adapt to audience and social change. HOUSE & GARDEN, ARCHITECTURAL DIGEST, METROPOLITAN HOME, and others cited as examples.

436 Peter, John. "NEW YORK's Evolutionary Redesign." FOLIO 15 (June 1986) : 121-123.

Lots of illustrations show the course of NEW YORK's evolutionary, not revolutionary, redesign.

437 Pool, Gail. "Magazines." WILSON LIBRARY BULLETIN 57 (May 1983) : 780-781.

Why some magazines (e.g., ROLLING STONE, PSYCHOLOGY TODAY, HOUSE & GARDEN) are compelled to revamp and assume new editorial identities. Brief essay on the relationship of identity, life cycle, and revamping in the magazine world.

438 Pool, Gail. "Magazines." WILSON LIBRARY BULLETIN 60 (December 1985) 54-55.

ROLLING STONE changes its image to attract the "right" kind of readers. FORTUNE boasts its readership is affluent and rising professionals. Commentary on magazine demographics, and its importance to magazine profits through advertising.

439 Pool, Gail. "VANITY FAIR." CHRISTIAN SCIENCE MONITOR, 3 March 1983, p. 23.

Negative criticism of the first issue of the new VANITY FAIR. Is its slickness and superficiality a result of aiming for an affluent audience?

440 Powell, Joanna. "Paige Rense. Editor-in-Chief of ARCHITECTUAL DIGEST, BON APPETIT & GEO."

WASHINGTON JOURNALISM REVIEW 5 (May 1983) : 36-41.

Profile of editor who has successfully revived two failing magazines and will try again with a third, GEO. Her redesign turned ARCHITECTURAL DIGEST and BON APPETIT into luxury magazines for monied readers.

441 Randolph, Eleanor. "Changes for MOTHER JONES." WASHINGTON POST, 3 October 1985, p. D1+.

Changes needed at the financially troubled left-wing investigative magazine. Brief article suggests publisher is considering a new editor, a new name, a redesign.

442 Reif, Rita. "New Views for Connoisseurs." NEW YORK TIMES, 5 August 1984, sec. 2, p. H23.

Three magazines, born of the interest in antiques during the 1970s, plan changes for survival in the 1980s.

443 Richter, Paul. "Magazine Leaps into 'Low Culture': SATURDAY REVIEW Changes Image in Effort to Boost Sales." LOS ANGELES TIMES, 5 August 1985, sec. 4, p. 1+.

Sex adorns the cover of the August 1985 issue of SATURDAY REVIEW. Owner-publisher Paul Dietrich tries to boost newsstand sales and acquire advertisers.

444 Rogers, Brian S. "LIFE Burgeons as VANITY FAIR Awaits the Crowds." ADVERTISING AGE 54 (October 17, 1983) : M60.

As VANITY FAIR returns, LIFE celebrates its fifth year back on the newsstand. The new LIFE is edited for the "visually sophisticated baby boomers," VANITY FAIR for the aspiring rich.

445 "ROLLING STONE Going with Magazine Format." ADVERTISING AGE 51 (September 22, 1980) : 112.

Brief news item on format changes at ROLLING STONE. Also noted are increases in ad rates and cover price.

446 "ROLLING STONE Returns to Roots: Expanded Pop Music Coverage, Upgraded Paper Highlight Major Reformatting." FOLIO 14 (April 1985) : 64-65.

447 Romano, Lois. "Vanity's British Import: Editor Tina Brown." WASHINGTON POST, 12 January 1984, p. C1+.

Personality profile of VANITY FAIR's third editor in eleven months. Her plans for the magazine include better writers and more reporting, controversy, and romance.

448 Rowe, David. "Reducing the Danger of Repositioning." FOLIO 13 (July 1983) : 68-69+.

Advice from the editor of a small magazine on repositioning a failing publication to regain lost readers and advertising.

449 Rozen, Leah. "LOOK Cuts ROLLING STONE Ties." ADVERTISING AGE 50 (July 9, 1979) : 1+.

After six weeks, LOOK and Jann Wenner terminate their partnership over disagreements on how much money to spend on the magazine's revival.

450 Rozen, Leah. "New ROLLING STONE Shakes off the Moss." ADVERTISING AGE 52 (January 26, 1981) : 30.

The new ROLLING STONE premiers February 5, 1981. It will have more news and features, more personality profiles and politics along with its change from tabloid to magazine format. RS hopes to decrease its dependence on music advertising.

451 Salmans, Sandra. "Courting the Elite at Conde Nast." NEW YORK TIMES, 6 February 1983, sec. 3, p. 1+.

Conde Nast competes for affluent readers with the rebirth of VANITY FAIR and the redesign of HOUSE & GARDEN.

452 Sansweet, Stephen J. "ARCHITECTURAL DIGEST Becomes a Big Power in the Design World." WALL STREET JOURNAL, 6 August 1976, p. 1+.

How ARCHITECTURAL DIGEST grew from a bland trade magazine to a wide circulation, upscale consumer publication.

453 "SATURDAY REVIEW to Seek Younger Readers, Say New Owners." FOLIO 13 (September 1984) : 57.

Plans of new owners, Paul Dietrich and others, for the magazine.

454 Schardt, Arlie. "LOOK: Dead Again?" NEWSWEEK 94 (July 16, 1979) : 64.

More problems at LOOK magazine despite Jann Wenner (of ROLLING STONE) and his efforts to reestablish LOOK's editorial identity.

455 Schwartz, Tony. "ROLLING STONE's New Trip." NEWSWEEK 90 (October 3, 1977) : 65+.

As it grows older, ROLLING STONE has shifted emphasis from rock stars and political dissidents to show business and political celebrities. Will the change blur its identity and alienate readers?

456 Skipper, John. "Repositioning ROLLING STONE." FOLIO 12 (January 1983) : 90-93+.

When advertising pages decreased in 1980, ROLLING STONE planned changes, including revised editorial focus, redesigned graphics, upgraded paper. After two years, repositioning success is evaluated by comparing 1980 projections with 1982 reality.

457 "Split Personality: A Franco-American LOOK." TIME 113 (February 12, 1979) : 59+.

Revival of LOOK magazine under Daniel Filipacchi combines French designers and American journalists.

458 Steigerwald, Bill. "The New HARPER'S: Cutting its Own Trail Through the Magazine Woods." LOS ANGELES TIMES, 4 April 1984, sec. 5, p. 1+.

HARPER'S has "restructured its look and redefined its editorial purpose." The magazine is targeted to a general audience.

459 Suplee, Curt. "All is VANITY." WASHINGTON POST, 1 March 1983, p. B1+.

VANITY FAIR's first issue did not live up to its promises.

460 Unger, Craig. "Can VANITY FAIR Live Again?" NEW YORK 15 (April 26, 1982) : 28+.

Comparison of the old VANITY FAIR with the new one.

461 Williams, Christian. "New Image for the 80s: Rebirth of Conde Nast's Elite Magazine." WASHINGTON POST, 23 February 1983, p. B1+.

A review of VANITY FAIR's first issue and comments on the expensive promotion to launch its rebirth.

462 "WOMAN'S DAY: Refurbishing the Dynasty." MADISON AVENUE 25 (November 1983) : 114-118+.

WOMAN'S DAY has been graphically redesigned and aggressively promoted on network tv to attract younger readers. The magazine's executives emphasize the strength of their editorial product in relation to increasingly effective advertising.

463 "Women's Service Magazines Adapting for the Eighties." AD FORUM 5 (March 1984) : 57-60.

464 Yovovich, B. G. "Media's Mystery Whiz Kid." ADVERTISING AGE 55 (May 3, 1984) : M6-M7.

Is Jeffrey Gluck really as successful at reviving nearly defunct magazines (and newspapers) as he claims? Some of his acquisitions include SATURDAY REVIEW, MISSOURI LIFE, and FAMILY JOURNAL.

Problems & Deaths

---

465 Alsop, Ronald. "Time Inc.'s TV-CABLE WEEK Said to Fail Because it Neglected Operator Interests." WALL STREET JOURNAL, 19 September 1983, p. 8.

By offering non-cable program listings as well as cable listings, TV-CABLE WEEK lost required support from cable companies. Time's pay cable stations also viewed as possible bias source.

466 Cody, Kevin. "When a Magazine Doesn't Make It." THE PRESS 10 (February 1982) : 17-19.

An economic analysis of problems at SOUTH BAY magazine in Los Angeles. The importance of advertising versus circulation revenue, and the failure of (and others) to reach the rate bases promised.

467 Cooper, David. "Afterword." CENTER 16 (May-June 1983) : 40-42.

The failure of many cultural-intellectual magazines like the SATURDAY REVIEW may be due to the aging of the culturally elite gatekeepers and dislocation of traditional sources of literary power.

468 Cousins, Norman. "SATURDAY REVIEW: Why it Failed --and Succeeded." CHRISTIAN SCIENCE MONITOR, 31 August 1982, p. 23.

Famed and most successful editor of SR laments passing, competition with "peepshow" covers, postal increases. Deplores "annihilation of taste," language.

469 Craig, Jack. "The Life and Death of INSIDE SPORTS Magazine." THE PRESS 10 (February 1982) : 20-21.

Problems at IS included monthly not weekly frequency, less than expected circulation, too low predictions of expected deficits, ad agencies' negative assessment of IS's value. Washington Post Co. may have dumped IS prematurely. An analysis of INSIDE SPORT's failure, and paradoxically positive evaluation of its editorial content and dedication of its staff.

470 "Deaths in the Family." NEWSWEEK 92 (November 27, 1978) : 113+.

Magazines are born and die every year, but constantly increase in number. Deaths of NEW TIMES and VIVA exemplify trouble in the marketplace, although the magazine business is still healthy.

471 "The Demise of a Cable Directory: Heavy Losses and Poor Prospects, Despite Advertising Support." TIME 122 (September 26, 1983) : 75.

Time Inc.'s TV-CABLE WEEK has ceased publication. Cable operators at first welcomed the magazine, but later failed to offer it to subscribers.

472 Diamond, Edwin. "The Unladylike Battle of the Women's Magazines." NEW YORK 7 (May 20, 1974) : 43-46.

Contemporary look at magazine industry problems during the early 1970s. Costs often meant large circulation was a burden. Women's magazines illustrate the problems.

473 Elliott, Stuart J. "CUISINE's Demise to Nourish GOURMET." ADVERTISING AGE 55 (October 8, 1984) : 102.

Despite an in-progress revamp and second place food magazine circulation, CBS' CUISINE was losing money and is ceasing publication. The subscription list will be sold to its competitor, Conde Nast's GOURMET.

474 Elliott, Stuart J. "INSIDE SPORTS is Folded." ADVERTISING AGE 53 (November 8, 1982) : 93.

Lack of advertising and inability to obtain additional financing led to the demise of INSIDE SPORTS.

475 Elliott, Stuart J. "INSIDE SPORTS Still at Bat." ADVERTISING AGE 55 (November 26, 1984) : 72.

Third owner of INSIDE SPORTS is "pleased" despite losses.

476 Emmrich, Stuart. "IS Dilemma: How to Get Advertisers Off the Fence ... " ADVERTISING AGE 53 (July 19, 1982) : 37+.

The new owners of INSIDE SPORTS face problems getting advertiser commitment, even though circulation is good.

477 "The End of the Great Adventure." TIME 100 (December 18, 1972) : 46-50.

Pictorial obituary for LIFE magazine.

478 Ferretti, Fred. "The Short Unhappy Life of SATURDAY REVIEW II." COLUMBIA JOURNALISM REVIEW 12 (July-August 1973) : 23-31.

What happened at SATURDAY REVIEW from the takeover by Charney and Veronis in 1971 until the merger with WORLD in 1973.

479 Friendly, Jonathon. "SATURDAY REVIEW Shuts Down." NEW YORK TIMES, 17 August 1982, p. D1+.

Background of SATURDAY REVIEW's financial troubles 1971 to 1982, and owner Robert Weingarten's plans to cease publication. These plans proved premature.

480 "GEO's Demise: Heavy Costs, Persistent Image Problems Cited." FOLIO 14 (February 1985) : 7.

GEO's circulation of 225,000 would have to double, it's estimated, for magazine to avoid its $500,000 monthly loss. Very brief news item.

481 Gillenson, Lewis W. "The Struggle for Survival by the Last Editor of CORONET." COLUMBIA JOURNALISM REVIEW 1 (Spring 1961) : 34-38.

Reasons for CORONET's decline include dependence on advertising, high cost of subscription fulfillment, race for circulation. Many mass magazines were faced with the same problems in the 1960s and 1970s.

482 Gloede, William F. "GEO Goes Off Without a Niche." ADVERTISING AGE 56 (January 21, 1985) : 2+.

The death of GEO was one of the most expensive failures in the industry's history. GEO tried revamping the magazine and heavy promotion, but never found its niche in the field.

483 "HARPER'S Sinks." ECONOMIST 275 (June 21, 1980) : 34.

Brief but succinct view of HARPER'S problems in the early 1980s. Generalizable to other similar magazines like ATLANTIC and SATURDAY REVIEW.

484 "Here's Good News: GRIT Battles on." NEWSWEEK 100 (September 27, 1982) : 12.

Sales have dropped at GRIT, but the weekly continues to bring good news and upbeat stories to small-town America.

485 Honan, William H. "The Morning After the SATURDAY REVIEW." ESQUIRE 80 (November 1973) : 176-181+.

The demise of SATURDAY REVIEW after Charney and Veronis took over, 1971-1973.

486 "Inside LOOK." NEWSWEEK 76 (September 14, 1970) : 73-74.

Problems at LOOK magazine. Staff cutting, low morale, financial woes lead to speculation about possible folding.

487 "INSIDE SPORTS Suspends Publication." NEW YORK TIMES, 2 November 1982, p. D21.

Even though circulation and advertising were up, the magazine had "no cash and not enough investors" to continue publication.

488 Jacob, Walter. "Double Standards for Second-Class Citizens." WASHINGTON MONTHLY 11 (January 1980) : 37-41.

Red Tag mail service gives priority postal treatment to certain classes of magazines and newspapers for no additional charge, while other magazines get second class treatment. Recent changes render Jacob's critique out-dated, but the article is interesting from a historical perspective. See entry 1082.

489 Jones, Alex S. "GEO Magazine to Stop Publication." NEW YORK TIMES, 16 January 1985, p. D2.

Circulation insufficient for profits. Advertisers concerned about magazine's identity confusion.

490 Kaiser, Charles. "The Last SATURDAY REVIEW." NEWSWEEK 100 (August 30, 1982) : 64.

A brief obituary for SATURDAY REVIEW, a magazine that has been searching for an identity since 1971. This obituary is premature, as SATURDAY REVIEW was subsequently purchased and continued publishing.

491 Kaiser, Charles. "Old Editor, New HARPER'S?" NEWSWEEK 102 (July 25, 1983) : 69.

Change expected at HARPER'S under new editor Lewis Lapham, reappointed after two years absence. The magazine is suffering financial difficulties as advertising revenues slide and circulation is slashed to cut costs.

492 Kaiser, Charles. "Time Inc.'s $47 Million Mistake." NEWSWEEK 102 (September 26, 1983) : 94.

Lavishly-financed TV-CABLE WEEK has become one of the industry's most spectacular disasters. Its worst mistake: the decision to market through cable systems instead of on the newsstand.

493 Kanner, Bernice. "Publish or Perish." NEW YORK 14 (December 7, 1981) : 22+.

Life-threatening problems at some magazines, e.g., GEO, PRIME TIME, INSIDE SPORTS, HARPER'S, PLAYBOY.

494 Kelly, Stephen E. "The Postal Service--Where it's Been and Where it is for U.S. Magazines." ADVERTISING AGE 45 (November 18, 1974) : 169-170+.

Although dated, this article offers an excellent outline of traditional postal service policy towards magazines and analysis of changes made in the early 1970s.

495 Kidder, Rushworth M. "SATURDAY REVIEW Magazine to Fold After Decade of Financial Troubles." CHRISTIAN SCIENCE MONITOR, 18 August 1982, p. B6.

Brief review of the magazine's financial troubles since 1971. Plans of owner Robert Weingarten to cease publication. These plans proved to be premature.

496 Kinkead, Gwen. "Soulful Trouble at Consumers Union." FORTUNE 91 (February 22, 1982) : 119-120.

Non-profit Consumers Union, publisher of CONSUMER REPORTS, operates in the red.

497 Kleinfield, N. R. "CONSUMER REPORTS' Hard Test." NEW YORK TIMES, 2 January 1982, pp. 27-28.

Economic hard times and budget cuts at CONSUMER REPORTS.

498 Kobak, James B. "Curing the Sick Magazine." FOLIO 10 (September 1981) : 67-68+.

Magazine diseases and their symptoms are indicated by circulation, advertising, profit, and competition problems. Suggestions for problem solving although some problems may be fatal.

499 Kobak, James B. "How to Save a Failing Magazine." FOLIO 12 (May 1983) : 71-75.

Isolating the reasons for magazine problems. Examples of how individual magazines have repositioned.

500 Koff, Richard M. "The Compleat Strategist: Forecasting Failure." FOLIO 10 (February 1981) : 74-76.

Charts and graphs said to predict when to fold and when to continue publishing. Self-constructed computer problem-solving models for publishing.

501 "LOOK Magazine Set to be Partly Merged with ROLLING STONE." WALL STREET JOURNAL, 9 May 1979, p. 17.

Management of the magazine and responsibility for a "major overhaul" will rest with ROLLING STONE's Jann Wenner.

502 McFadden. Maureen. "CUISINE: What Happened?" MAGAZINE AGE 6 (January 1985) : 83.

Death of CUISINE demonstrates how appearances can deceive. How four or five magazines aimed at the same million readers can saturate market and kill an apparently healthy publication. Conde Nast buyout of subscription list at rumored $10 million hastened demise.

503 McFadden, Maureen. "What Made GEO a No Go?" MAGAZINE AGE 6 (April 1985) : 42-43.

"Disaffected readership" caused $65 million loss starting with GEO's 1979 birth. Article alleges a key problem was failure to get "prospective subscribers committed" from the beginning. Other problems were identity crisis, lack of editorial focus, translation from original German edition.

504 "Magazines in Jeopardy." TIME 99 (January 10, 1972) : 43.

Rising costs and declining profits are already endangering the magazine industry. Detrimental effect of postal increases could be fatal for some.

505 "Magazines to Drag PO to Court on Costing Concept." EDITOR & PUBLISHER 115 (March 28, 1981) : 25.

MPA Board of Directors voted to oppose U.S. Postal Service plan for distributing overhead costs to certain categories of mail. The social value of magazines implies a lower share of postal costs for them.

506 "MONEY Magazine Profitable for Time Inc." NEW YORK TIMES, 25 October 1982, p. D4+.

Time Inc. shows its ability to get magazines off to a slow start and bring them ultimately to profitability. As with SPORTS ILLUSTRATED in the past, MONEY has finally made for itself what it purports to show its readers--profit.

507 "MORE Magazine Folds." FOLIO 7 (October 1978) : 28.

MORE, a media magazine, folds from lack of readers. COLUMBIA JOURNALISM REVIEW takes over readership. CJR has inherent stability because of university connection and non-profit status.

508 "NEW TIMES, Finding they are Changing, Will Quit Publishing." WALL STREET JOURNAL, 16 November 1978, p. 22.

Declining interest in social issues has led to demise of NEW TIMES.

509 "Poor Market Positioning Spells End for TV-CABLE WEEK." FOLIO 12 (November 1983) : 7.

Reasons and possible reasons for demise of five-month-old Time Inc. venture.

510 "Postal Increases: Publish and/or Perish." TIME 99 (June 19, 1972) : 41.

Arguments for and against postal increases are compared. TIME's position is that the postal service should be efficient and economically run, but still provide a subsidy for readers of magazines.

511 Pruden, Wesley, Jr. "LIFE Quits the Magazine Field it Made." NATIONAL OBSERVER, 16 December 1972, p. 4.

Brief obituary for LIFE, reflecting on its history and final problems.

512 Schardt, Arlie. "HARPER'S: 1850-1980." NEWSWEEK 95 (June 30, 1980) : 71.

Premature obituary for HARPER'S, reflecting on its problems and editorial importance over the years.

513 Schlesinger, Arthur, Jr. "Another Part of the Forest." WALL STREET JOURNAL, 31 January 1974, p. 12.

Schlesinger's editorial regarding the negative effects of proposed postal increases points to the social value of magazines and the reversal of long-standing public policy towards magazines.

514 "A Serious Threat to Magazines." LIFE (August 20, 1971) : 4.

LIFE magazine editorial regarding the negative effects of postal increases on magazines. Proposed increase equals more than twice the industry's 1970 profits.

515 "Time Inc. Cites Television, Postage Rates in Retiring LIFE Magazine After 36 Years." WALL STREET JOURNAL, 11 December 1972, p. 5.

Time Inc.'s financial position at the time of LIFE's demise. Decision to fold LIFE based on revenue loses, rising postal costs, tv competition, changing public tastes. A contemporary look at LIFE's problems.

516 "Time Inc. Folds TV-CABLE WEEK." BUSINESS WEEK (October 3, 1983) : 54.

Brief news item on demise of TV-CABLE WEEK.

517 "Time Strikes the Flag on TV-CABLE WEEK." BROADCASTING 105 (September 19, 1983) : 38.

Although advertiser response was good, TV-CABLE WEEK lost $47 million. Mixed acceptance by cable operators resulted in low circulation.

518 "TV-CABLE WEEK Collapses." DUN'S BUSINESS MONTH (October 1983) : 15.

Brief news item on the failure of Time Inc.'s TV-CABLE WEEK cites severe distribution problems as a cause.

519 Waters, Kenneth Eugene. "Toward the Successful Christian Publication: A Descriptive Analysis of Four Independent Evangelical Christian Periodicals." Ph.D. dissertation, University of Southern California, 1982.

Comparison of two successful and two failed evangelical Christian publications. Successful titles had consistent, well-defined editorial formulas, aggressive advertising departments, good management and planning, adequate financial resources, and mail marketing.

520 Wells, Chris. "Lessons from LIFE." WORLD 2 (February 13, 1973) : 20-23.

Analysis of the factors that killed LIFE.

521 "Why GEO Wasn't Longer for this Earth: Identity Crisis, Say Industry Execs, was Fatal Flaw." FOLIO 14 (March 1985) : 17-18.

Reasons cited for the failure of GEO include unfocused editorial, inflated operating expenses, identity crisis. Direct competition with non-profit SMITHSONIAN and NATIONAL GEOGRAPHIC was not seen as a factor by some analysts.

522 "Will Congress Kill the Magazine Industry?" READER'S DIGEST 104 (January 1974) : 49-53.

Another of many voices speaks against postal increase that will hurt large segments of the magazine industry and contradict long-standing public support for the educational value of magazines.

Chapter 6

AUDIENCE

523 Allen, Richard L., and Bielby, William T. "Blacks' Relationship with the Print Media." JOURNALISM QUARTERLY 56 (Autumn 1979) : 488-496+.

Survey of San Francisco blacks measures their use of and trust in magazines and newspapers, and the relationship of socio-economic factors to media exposure and influence.

524 Andreasen, Margaret, and Steeves, H. Leslie. "Employed Women's Assertiveness and Openness as Shown in Magazine Use." JOURNALISM QUARTERLY 60 (Autumn 1983) : 449-457.

Assertive women read more magazines than non-assertive women, had better-defined ideas of what they needed from magazines, and required less domestic and maternal information.

525 "ARF's Magazine Research Study is Out: Are We Closing in on the Truth." MARKETING & MEDIA DECISIONS 15 (March 1980) : 59-61+.

Audience research firms and their clients offer opinions on the Advertising Research Foundation's study of audience research methodology.

526 Blair, William S. "The Case Against Magazine Audience Measures." JOURNAL OF ADVERTISING RESEARCH 14 (April 1974) : 7-10.

Excerpts from speech to Market Research Council. Highly critical of magazine audience research.

527 Britt, Steuart Henderson; O'Leary, John C.; and Sturges, Ralph R. "The Accuracy of Claimed Subscribership." JOURNAL OF ADVERTISING RESEARCH 13 (December 1973) : 29-32.

Magazine readers both over-report and under-report subscriptions when surveyed.

528 Carter, Virgina, comp. "How to Survey Your Readers." Washington, D.C.: Council for Advancement and Support of Education, 1981.

A brief collection of materials includes papers on the importance of audience surveys, a checklist for conducting your survey, and sample cover letters and survey questionnaires.

529 Childers, Bruce S. "Reach and Frequency Analysis." INDUSTRIAL MARKETING 66 (December 1981) : 60+.

How reach and frequency analysis measures readership and duplication of readers for several publications. How to apply the data when planning an advertising campaign.

530 Clancy, Kevin J.; Ostlund, Lyman E.; and Wynar, Gordon. "False Reporting of Magazine Readership." JOURNAL OF ADVERTISING RESEARCH 19 (August 1979) : 23-29.

Test of reliability of reader response to magazine readership surveys.

531 "DIGEST Ad Causes Stir in Midwest." BROADCASTING 104 (February 28, 1983) : 98.

Using newspaper and trade Magazine ads, READER'S DIGEST released data on Tulsa, Oklahoma studies of television and magazine consumption in cable tv homes. There is television audience erosion but magazine reading is unaffected by cable.

532 Donath, Bob. "ARF Study Aims to Clarify Magazine Research Quandry." ADVERTISING AGE 46 (August 18, 1975) : 20.

Advertising Research Foundation plans research to determine effects of several variables on audience responses. Outlines major problem areas in readership research.

533 Donath, Bob. "New Storm Brews on Simmons Reader

Data." ADVERTISING AGE 48 (October 31, 1977) : 3+.

Simmons and Target Group Index vary on readership data.

534 Dougherty, Philip H. "DIGEST: Remember Tulsa!" NEW YORK TIMES, 3 February 1983, sec. D, p. 17.

Commentary on READER'S DIGEST study of magazine readership in cable tv homes.

535 Durand, Richard M.; Klemmack, David L.; Roff, Lucinda.; and Taylor, James L. "Communicating with the Elderly: Reach of Television and Magazines." PSYCHOLOGICAL REPORTS 46 (June, pt. 2, 1980) : 1235-1242.

General interest magazines reached larger numbers of elderly people than television or other types of magazines.

536 Emmrich, Stuart. "Simmons Out and Surprise! Challenges Fly." ADVERTISING AGE 52 (September 28, 1981) : 1+.

More challenges to Simmons Market Research Bureau's methodology for audience research.

537 Fannin, Rebecca. "Magazine Advertisers Ask: Is the Numbers Game Fading Away?" MARKETING & MEDIA DECISIONS 17 (March 1982) : 66-67+.

While the accuracy of audience research data produced by Simmons Market Research Bureau and Mediamark Research is debated, magazine advertisers are depending on qualitative evaluation to make advertising choices.

538 Grover, Stephen. "Magazine Industry is Jolted by Lawsuits Challenging Audience-Survey Concerns." WALL STREET JOURNAL, 10 March 1975, p. 28.

The importance of audience research data to magazine advertising sales. Some question the accuracy of readership statistics. TIME and ESQUIRE file lawsuits against Simmons.

539 Heller, Karen. "Hot on the Press: Magazines that are Making a Mint." WASHINGTON JOURNALISM REVIEW 6 (April 1984) : 26-27+.

Publishers seeking affluent readers direct their magazines to the baby boomer generation--now aged 20-38, college graduates, professionals. Sophisticated research techniques can pinpoint "market clusters" or geographic areas in which consumer preferences for products as well as magazines have been carefully analyzed.

540 "Industry Moves Toward Verifying Audience Research." FOLIO 14 (December 1985) : 26-27.

The latest on the audience research controversy is a new method called the "Gold

Standard," which reduces reliance on readers' long-term memory and tries to interview them within a day of their reading a magazine.

541 Johnson, J. David. "The Dimensionality of Readership Measures." COMMUNICATION RESEARCH 9 (October 1982) : 607-616.

Comparison of three methods used to measure magazine readership.

542 Johnson, J. David, and Times, Albert R. "Magazine Evaluations and Levels of Readership." JOURNALISM QUARTERLY 58 (Spring 1981) : 96-98.

Analysis of reader reactions to U.S. International Communications Agency magazines points to magazine characteristics that most affected reader evaluations.

543 Katz, Hal. "The Advantages of Narrowcasting." MARKETING & MEDIA DECISIONS 19 (January 1984) : 74+.

Describes trend toward and advantages of narrowcasting in magazines. Narrowcasting refers to targeting a selective, specialized readership.

544 Langschmidt, Wally, and Brown, Michael. "Aspects of Reliability of Response in Readership Research." JOURNAL OF THE MARKET RESEARCH SOCIETY 21 (October 1979) : 228-249.

Comparison of readership research studies in South Africa, 1972-1977. Emphasizes methodological reliability. Was magazine readership measured accurately? Based on the senior author's book, RELIABILITY OF RESPONSE IN READERSHIP RESEARCH.

545 Le Bouef, Robert A., and Matre, Marc. "How Different Readers Perceive Magazine Stories and Characters." JOURNALISM QUARTERLY 54 (Spring 1977) : 50-57.

Age, sex, socio-economic status affect readers' responses to different kinds of magazine fiction.

546 Lechten, Cheryl. "No End in Sight in the Magazine Squabble." MARKETING & MEDIA DECISIONS 15 (November 1980) : 64-65.

The Advertising Research Foundation methodology study has not cleared up the confusion surrounding magazine audience research.

547 Lehnert, Eileen, and Perpich, Mary J. "Attitude Segmentation Study of Supermarket Tabloid Readers." JOURNALISM QUARTERLY 59 (Spring 1982) : 104-111.

Tabloids aim for high reader appeal. Purposive sample of forty readers identifies three types of reader.

548 Lichty, Lawrence W. "Video vs. Print." WILSON QUARTERLY 6 (Special issue 1982) : 49-57.

Survey of Americans shows news is obtained from many sources, including newspapers, television, and magazines. One-third of all adults read one of the three news magazines; one-quarter read READER'S DIGEST.

549 Lieberman Research, Inc. HOW AND WHY PEOPLE BUY MAGAZINES: A NATIONAL STUDY OF THE CONSUMER MARKET FOR MAGAZINES. Port Washington, N.Y.: Publishers Clearinghouse, 1977.

Excellent, simply-presented magazine readership survey. Includes proportion of people reading magazines, why magazines are read, demographic characteristics of heavy readers, magazine reading as it relates to other activities, readership trends.

550 McClintick, David. "Two Firms' Studies Gauging Readership of Periodicals Differ Widely on Results." WALL STREET JOURNAL, 21 October 1977, p. 8.

W. R. Simmons & Associates (now Simmons Market Research Bureau) and Target Group Index varied widely in total audience measurement of the same magazines.

551 McEvoy, George F., and Vincent, Cynthia S. "Who Reads and Why." JOURNAL OF COMMUNICATION 30 (Winter 1980) : 134-140.

Fifty-five percent of the population read books and magazines. Television time does not substitute for reading.

552 "Magazine Challenge: The Search to Validate Readership." MARKETING & MEDIA DECISIONS 18 (September 1983) : 64-65+.

Roundtable discussion of readership research. Two persisting challenges are identified: defining readership and finding a valid measurement of audience.

553 "Magazine Reading Higher by 19% in Cable Homes, MPA Finds in TV Tests." FOLIO 13 (May 1984) : 33.

Magazine Publishers Association replicates earlier READER'S DIGEST studies of magazine reading in cable tv homes.

554 "Magazine Research Controversy: Does MRI have the Answer?" MARKETING & MEDIA DECISIONS 14 (November 1979) : 66-67.

Controversy surrounds magazine audience research data produced by Simmons and Magazine Research Inc. Data collected in 1979 show differences between the two firms.

555 "Magazine Research Maze: What's the Way Out?" MARKETING & MEDIA DECISIONS 14 (December 1979) : 59-63+.

Suggestions for resolving the 1970s controversy over differing audience research data are offered by advertisers, advertising agencies, magazine publishers. More validity and comparability are needed. Magazines dislike paying for research they don't control.

556 "Magazines: Getting a Reading on the Baby Boom." ADVERTISING AGE 55 (October 18, 1984) : 11-50.

A forty-page section featuring articles on magazines' increasing interest in members of the baby boomer generation and the ways in which they are marketing to those readers. Includes articles on ROLLING STONE, MOTHER JONES, NEW YORKER, PSYCHOLOGY TODAY, MONEY, CHANGING TIMES, ESQUIRE, PARENTS, and others.

557 "Magazines to Benefit as They and Agencies Use Psychographics." FOLIO 12 (May 1983) : 16+.

Research can determine psychological and sociological characteristics of audience.

558 "Magazines Versus Television." FOLIO 8 (November 1979) : 77-79.

Summary of Magazine Publishers Association study by Opinion Research Corporation. Findings show adults use magazines more than television or newspapers for information on specific advertised products.

559 Maher, Philip. "Psychographics and Corporate Advertising: Powerful Techniques are Slowly Taking Hold." INDUSTRIAL MARKETING 68 (February 1983) : 64+.

Explanation of various methods used to profile consumer demographics and segment audiences. While no direct references are made to magazines, the concepts are frequently associated with magazine advertising and audiences.

560 Mann, Jim. "Inside SMRB's Insight Retrieval Systems." MAGAZINE AGE 6 (February 1985) : 45-46+.

Outlines system developed by Simmons Market Research Bureau to help users "effectively manipulate millions of facts." Includes ClusterPlus, Prizm, and VALS data.

561 "Most C-Store Shoppers Pre-Plan Magazine Buys, Survey Shows." FOLIO 12 (May 1983) : 13-14.

Convenience store customers differ from other shoppers in magazine purchases. Survey explores the reasons convenience store consumers buy magazines. Covers are an important factor in impulse purchases.

562 Northcott, Kaye. "The Rags of Riches: Magazines Aimed at the Millionaire Market." WASHINGTON JOURNALISM REVIEW 5 (May 1983) : 32-35.

"Only the very-rich are recession-proof enough" to afford what top advertisers sell. Because affluent readers can be located geographically by demographic experts, magazines designed for them are proliferating.

563 Opinion Research Corporation. "A Study of Media Involvement." New York: Magazine Publishers Association, 1979.

Survey to promote magazines as advertising vehicles shows most people get information of all kinds from magazines.

564 Papazian, Ed. "Magazine Audiences: Comparing the Two Methodologies." MARKETING & MEDIA DECISIONS 15 (June 1980) : 16+.

Brief discussion and comparison of two methodologies for audience research: through-the-book and recent reading.

565 Papazian, Ed. "Through the Book Studies Still Seem Valid." MARKETING & MEDIA DECISIONS 15 (December 1980) : 80+.

A brief review of the through-the-book method of audience research, suggesting its validity and commenting on negative criticism.

566 "Reader Research Audits for Business Magazines?" FOLIO 15 (February 1986) : 29-30.

Self-serving "research abuse" cited as necessitating routine surveys of publishers' readership studies.

567 Rentz, Joseph O., and Reynolds, Fred D. "Magazine Readership Patterns." JOURNAL OF ADVERTISING 8 (Spring 1979) : 22-25.

Survey of women's magazine reading habits showed overlapping audiences for groups of magazines. Magazines grouped by common content tended to have the same readers. Media patterns tended to be relatively stable over time.

568 Roberts, John A. "Is Media Research Making Progress?" INDUSTRIAL MARKETING 66 (December 1981) : 54+.

A coherent overview of methodological problems associated with audience research in both consumer and trade magazines.

569 Robinson, John P. "The Changing Reading Habits of the American Public." JOURNAL OF COMMUNICATION 30 (Winter 1980) : 141-152.

Comparison of audience surveys from 1946 to 1977 on reading habits for various age groups. Compares magazine, newspaper, book reading.

570 Rosberg, J. Wesley. "Reader Studies Surge 9% in 80." INDUSTRIAL MARKETING 65 (January 1980) : 75.

Advertising readership studies commissioned by publications are increasing.

571 Rossiter, John R. "Predicting Starch Scores." JOURNAL OF ADVERTISING RESEARCH 21 (October 1981) : 63-68.

Technical discussion of predicting audience recognition and readership of advertising.

572 Rozen, Leah. "New Simmons Report May Stir Research War." ADVERTISING AGE 51 (September 8, 1980) : 20+.

More on the controversy over audience research methodology. The Advertising Research Foundation is highly critical of methods used by Simmons Market Research Bureau.

573 Rozen, Leah. "Reader Data Still Don't Jibe." ADVERTISING AGE 51 (October 6, 1980) : 2+.

Magazine readership data from Simmons Market Research Bureau and MediaMark Research differ greatly. No one can agree on the best methodology to use for measuring readership. New data just released.

574 Schiller, Clark. "Remembered, But Never Read." ADVERTISING AGE 52 (October 26, 1981) : S14-S15.

How magazine audience researchers collect their data from readers, and potential problems with accuracy of the data. Part of AA special section on marketing/advertising research.

575 Simmons Market Research Bureau. ARF COMPARABILITY STUDY: A CONTROLLED FIELD EXPERIMENT COMPARING THREE METHODS OF ESTIMATING MAGAZINE AUDIENCES. New York: Advertising Research Foundation, January 1980.

Compares through-the-book, recent-reading, and mixed recent reading methods of research.

576 Swan, Carroll. "Frank, Tim and Jay Make it a Free-For-All." MARKETING & MEDIA DECISIONS 16 (April 1981) : 70-73+.

Audience research methods used by three research firms: Simmons, Mediamark, and Starch.

577 Taule, Sheldon. "Questioning Pass-Along's Value." MARKETING & MEDIA DECISIONS 17 (January 1982) : 94+.

Pass-along readers may have less value to advertisers than primary readers. Measurement of pass-along readership is imprecise.

578 Tennstadt, Friedrich, and Noelle-Neumann, Elisabeth. "Experiments in the Measurement of Readership." JOURNAL OF THE MARKET RESEARCH SOCIETY 21 (October 1979) : 251-267.

The accuracy of readership research methods. Comparison of several questioning techniques indicates minor variation in the research design may conspicuously change results.

579 Urban, Christine D. "Correlates of Magazine Readership." JOURNAL OF ADVERTISING RESEARCH 20 (August 1980) : 73-80.

Study of demographic, psychographic, and media use factors as determinants of magazine readership. Some positive predictors of general magazine reading included reading news magazines, household income, conservatism. Lengthy bibliography.

580 Venkatesh, Alladi. "Changing Roles of Women--a Life-Style Study Analysis." JOURNAL OF CONSUMER RESEARCH 7 (September 1980) : 189-197.

Three female roles are defined: traditionalist, moderate, and feminist. Study analyzes differences in lifestyle, demographics, magazine readership, perception of female role in advertisements. Excellent bibliography included.

581 Venkatesh, Alladi, and Tankersley, Clint B. "Magazine Readership by Female Segments." JOURNAL OF ADVERTISING RESEARCH 19 (August 1979) : 31-38.

Analysis of reading habits of three types of women: traditionalists, moderates, feminists. MS. and READER'S DIGEST appealed to readers at the extreme ends of the scale.

582 Wells, Chris. "The Numbers Magazines Live By: Careers and Fortunes Depend on the Data, But What if the Data aren't Dependable?" COLUMBIA JOURNALSM REVIEW 14 (September-October 1975) : 22-27.

Excellent overview of syndicated research, its importance to magazines, and the accuracy of data.

583 "What's the Truth?" MARKETING & MEDIA DECISIONS 16 (September 1981) : 70-71+.

Inconsistencies of audience count research.

584 "When Magazine Statistics Come Unstuck." BUSINESS WEEK (January 27, 1975) : 68+.

TIME and ESQUIRE challenge Simmons' total audience data.

585 Wood, Wally. "The Research Battle Rages On." MAGAZINE AGE 1 (January 1980) : 58-60+.

More in the controversy over audience research methods used by Simmons Market Research Bureau and Target Group Index, and the Advertising Research Foundation study of methods. Comparisons between research agencies' data not advised.

586 Wood, Wally. "16 Magazine Research Reports that Agencies Actually Like and Use." MAGAZINE AGE 2 (October 1981) : 25-26+.

Sorting the self-serving from the significant takes work. Seven pages on a variety of audience research reports.

587 "W. R. Simmons Sets a Special Survey of Major Magazines." WALL STREET JOURNAL, 21 July 1975, p. 22.

Study planned to differentiate primary from pass-along readers.

Chapter 7

WRITING

588 Barbieri, Richard. "Writers' Rights." COLUMBIA JOURNALISM REVIEW 22 (July-August 1983) : 16.

National Writers Union signs a contract with MOTHER JONES.

589 Behrens, John C. MAGAZINE WRITER'S WORKBOOK. 3d ed. Holland Patent, N.Y.: Steffen Publishing, 1983.

Focus on magazine article writing. Includes list of markets.

590 Biagi, Shirley. HOW TO WRITE & SELL MAGAZINE ARTICLES. Englewood Cliffs, N.J.: Prentice-Hall, 1981.

A brief book covering magazine articles from idea to marketing. Much information is presented in lists. Overview of law applying to freelancers included.

591 Boggess, Louise. HOW TO WRITE FILLERS AND SHORT FEATURES THAT SELL. 2d ed. New York: Harper and Row, 1981.

A brief book full of ideas for fillers, and tips on writing and marketing them.

592 Brady, John. "The Craft of Interviewing." FOLIO 6 (February 1977): 24-32.

Tips for conducting successful journalistic interviews by author of book of same title.

593 Braunstein, Binnie Syril. "Trials and Joys of Free-Lance Writing." SERIALS LIBRARIAN 7 (Spring 1983) : 57-62.

First person tale of free-lance career. Needed are hard work, creativity, ability to shake off rejection.

594 Burack, Sylvia K., ed. THE WRITER'S HANDBOOK. Boston, Mass.: The Writer, 1986.

Includes reprints of articles from the WRITER magazine, and a list of approximately two thousand markets for free-lanced material. Also covers selling, writing, article ideas, research. Lists what some magazines will not print, significant because it is difficult to learn by reading magazines themselves. A substantial text aimed at somewhat more mature writers than WRITER'S MARKET and WRITER'S DIGEST. Nearly 800 pages.

Despite greater sophistication and depth, this source suffers some of drawbacks of WM/WD. (See WRITER'S MARKET entry, Chapter 2.)

595 Burack, Sylvia K., ed. WRITING AND SELLING FILLERS, LIGHT VERSE, AND SHORT HUMOR. Boston, Mass.: The Writer, 1982.

Writing and selling short pieces to magazines is easiest for beginners. The market for such pieces.

596 Burgett, Gordon. HOW TO SELL 75% OF YOUR FREE-LANCE WRITING. Carpinteria, CALIF.: Write to Sell, 1984.

Selling free-lance work depends on more than good writing. Free-lancing as a business--use of market guides, querying, reselling written material.

597 Burgett, Gordon. THE QUERY BOOK. Carpinteria, Calif.: Write to Sell, 1980.

Details on querying editors for free-lance assignments, including sample letters.

598 Casewit, Curtis W. FREELANCE WRITING: ADVICE FROM THE PROS. Rev. ed. New York: Collier Books, 1985.

Free-lancing both magazine articles and books. How-to advice for the beginner, written in the second person. Includes ideas, marketing, writing, finances, in an easy-to-read style.

599 Cassill, Kay. THE COMPLETE HANDBOOK FOR FREELANCE WRITERS. Cincinnati, Ohio: Writer's Digest Books, 1981.

Lengthy volume on organizing yourself in a free-lance business. Focuses on profits and selling rather than writing.

600 "COLUMBIA JOURNALISM REVIEW Signs with Writers' Union." FOLIO 14 (July 1985) : 26-27.

Union seeks to improve the often poor treatment of free-lancers. Benefits to magazines suggested in this glimpse of the situation.

601 Denniston, Lyle. "When Muckraking Signals Malice." WASHINGTON JOURNALISM REVIEW 7 (June 1985) : 14.

The use of aggressive investigative reporting techniques can work against journalists in libel cases.

602 Emerson, Connie. WRITE ON TARGET. Cincinnati, Ohio: Writer's Digest Books, 1981.

Suggestions for analyzing and selecting markets for free-lanced magazine articles. Tips on style and writing to increase sales. Useful practical handbook.

603 Evans, Glen, ed. THE COMPLETE GUIDE TO WRITING NON-FICTION. Cincinnati, Ohio: Writer's Digest Books, 1983.

Extensive collection of articles by members of the American Society of Authors and Journalists. Covers general topics related to free-lancing from writing to survival, and systematically considers numerous major free-lancing subject specialties.

604 Graham, Betsy P. MAGAZINE ARTICLE WRITING: SUBSTANCE AND STYLE. New York: Holt, Rinehart and Winston, 1980.

A magazine article writing textbook, complete with questions, exercises, and analyzed magazine articles. Emphasis on two complementary principles of a good article: style and content. Covers the topic from ideas through selling, including law, research, and writing.

605 "Grub Street Revisited." TIME 111 (April 10, 1978) : 75+.

Too many free-lance writers are chasing too few magazine publishing opportunites.

606 Gunther, Max. WRITING THE MODERN MAGAZINE ARTICLE. 4th ed. Boston, Mass.: The Writer, 1982.

While usual in many ways, this how-to volume shows the author's quarter century of free-lance experience (including sixteen books), and blends article writing with fiction. Preparation, research, and writing tips, plus extensive case histories. Useful, direct, understandable approach for beginners. No index.

607 Hellyer, Clement David. MAKING MONEY WITH WORDS. Englewood Cliffs, N.J.: Prentice-Hall, 1981.

Not a how-to writing book. Great emphasis on the wide range of outlets for marketing free-lance writing. Book's focus is making money and succeeding as a writer.

608 Hensley, Dennis E. WRITING FOR PROFIT. Nashville, Tenn.: Thomas Nelson Publishers, 1985.

A short overview of free-lancing as a business, including cash, copyrights, ideas, writing style and techniques, marketing strategies.

609 Higgins, Lisa. "Managing Freelancers." FOLIO 12 (November 1983) : 76-77.

Several ideas for editors to save time when dealing with free-lancers: form letters, sending forms on expense policies, tear sheets of a similar article for the first-time free-lancer to emulate, galleys sent to authors.

610 Hoopes, Roy. RALPH INGERSOLL: A BIOGRAPHY. New York: Atheneum, 1985.

Biography of Ingersoll and his contributions to the NEW YORKER, FORTUNE, and LIFE.

611 Howarth, William. "E. B. White at the NEW YORKER." SEWANEE REVIEW 93 (Fall 1985) : 574-583.

The writer E. B. White and his relationship with the NEW YORKER. Comments on the growth and running of the magazine under Harold Ross and William Shawn.

612 Howland, Jennifer. "'Kill' Fees." FOLIO 13 (January 1984) : 49+.

Fees paid when a commissioned article is rejected.

613 Hubbard, J. T. W. "Writing the Personality Profile." FOLIO 12 (September 1983) : 133-134+.

Discusses Robert Ruark's technique for writing a profile. How to use anecdotes effectively for the lead and close; how to select and organize the material.

614 Hudson, Robert V. WRITING GAME: A BIOGRAPHY OF WILL IRWIN. Ames: Iowa State University Press, 1982.

Biography of Will Irwin, 1873-1948, newspaper and magazine journalist.

615 Jacobi, Peter. "The Art of Descriptive Writing." FOLIO 13 (August 1984) : 98-100+.

How to write and edit definitions, identifications, analogies, classifications, statistics, comparisons, etc. Numerous examples illustrate good descriptive writing techniques.

616 Jacobi, Peter. "The Basics of Good Writing." FOLIO 14 (June 1985) : 98-103.

Such items as point of view, worn out words, judicious use of quotes, article focus are illustrated with pithy, pointed examples. Very useful.

617 Jacobi, Peter. "The Editor as Architect." FOLIO 13 (June 1984) : 92-94+.

The best structure for a magazine article depends on the story's purpose. Various structures are defined and liberally illustrated.

618 Jacobi, Peter. "It's a Matter of Focus." FOLIO 12 (DECEMBER 1983) : 94-98+.

How to focus an article subject so it is suitable for the particular slant and audience of a specific magazine.

619 Jacobi, Peter. "Sharpen Your Use of Narrative and Description." FOLIO 13 (November 1984) : 150-154+.

Examples and discussion of narrative storytelling, its uses and how-to's.

620 Jacobi, Peter. "25 Approaches to the Lead." FOLIO 14 (February 1984) : 72-74+.

Advice for the editor on writing effective leads for magazine features. Numerous examples.

621 Jacobi, Peter. "Words." FOLIO 13 (April 1984) : 92-96+.

Word use techniques to improve the editor's writing skills.

622 Kahn, E. J., Jr. ABOUT THE NEW YORKER AND ME. New York: G. P. Putnam's Sons, 1979.

Memoirs of NEW YORKER journalist, presented as a year's diary for 1977.

623 Kall, Bob. "How to Generate Hundreds of Salable Article Ideas." WRITER'S DIGEST 32 (May 1983) : 22-23+.

A system to combine subjects of interest to writers into salable article ideas for magazines.

624 Kubis, Patricia, and Howland, Robert. THE COMPLETE GUIDE TO WRITING FICTION, NONFICTION, AND PUBLISHING. Reston, Va.: Reston Publishing Company, 1985.

Although this volume's strongest emphasis is on fiction and book publishing, magazine article writing is also considered, from the query letter to rewriting. The art of characterizing and interviewing article subjects is a brief but worthy addition.

625 Leary, William. "Jean Stafford, Katharine White, and the NEW YORKER." SEWANEE REVIEW 93 (Fall 1985) : 584-596.

A 1947-1977 friendship between two NEW YORKER correspondents.

626 Lincoln, Melissa Ludtke. "The Free-Lance Life." COLUMBIA JOURNALISM REVIEW 20 (September-October 1981) : 48-54.

The difficulties of being a free-lance magazine writer.

627 MacDougall, A. Kent. "Free-Lance Writers Cite Long List of Woes but Like Independence." WALL STREET JOURNAL, 7 August 1970, p. 1+.

Free-lancers lamented the same problems (e.g., low fees, few markets, rejection, getting in a rut) fifteen years ago as they do today.

628 "Magazine, Newspaper Writing Styles Increasingly Similar." FOLIO 9 (June 1980) : 44.

Differences between newspaper and magazine writing are blurring because magazine writers are trained in newspaper-oriented journalism schools, and newspapers carry more magazine-style features.

629 "McCALL'S Still Top Freelance Market." FOLIO 14 (April 1985) : 40+.

Ranking of top paying free-lance magazine markets.

630 Memmott, A. James. "Wordsworth in the Bleachers: The Baseball Essays of Roger Angell." JOURNAL OF AMERICAN CULTURE 5 (Winter 1982) : 52-56.

Roger Angell is not a sports writer, but he wrote over thirty essays on baseball for the NEW YORKER.

631 Mitford, Jessica. "Investigating Investigative Reporters." MOTHER JONES 10 (January 1985) : 6.

Neatly reviews the point of journalism, which is to affect change, in terms of rightist attack on MOTHER JONES' article "Circle of Poison" (on foreign sale of U.S.-banned pesticides).

632 Mueller, Douglas. "The Fog Index." FOLIO 10 (November 1980) : 67-68+.

Unsurprisingly, the president of the Gunning-Mueller Clear Writing Institute advocates use of the Fog Index to reduce writing complexity and to simplify and make understandable magazine editorial. Useful for those who have not applied the index to their publications. Means of computation given.

633 Peterson, Franklynn, and Kesselman-Turkel, Judi. THE MAGAZINE WRITER'S HANDBOOK. Englewood Cliffs, N.J.: Prentice-Hall, 1982.

How to analyze the magazine marketplace, and select the appropriate vehicle and approach for a magazine article. Authors advise marketing article ideas to editors, not manuscripts. Rules for good magazine writing illustrated with examples. Brief comments on relevant law.

634 Rapoport, Daniel. "Freelancers Exploited." WASHINGTON JOURNALISM REVIEW (October 1977) : 20-24.

Magazine publishers pay free-lancers very little, and are using them more frequently. Reports free-lancers' experiences and policies of specific publications.

635 Rawls, Wendell, Jr. "Interviewing: The Crafty Art." COLUMBIA JOURNALISM REVIEW 21 (November-December 1982) : 46-47.

A few hints from a veteran journalist on interviewing.

636 Rees, Clair. PROFITABLE PART-TIME--FULL-TIME FREELANCING. Cincinnati, Ohio: Writer's Digest Books, 1980.

Another volume on free-lancing, particularly helpful for beginners. Detailed coverage of finances from low rates to delayed payments.

637 "Reporter Tells How He Got the H-Bomb Story." EDITOR & PUBLISHER 112 (April 14, 1979) : 15+.

A recounting of the interviews, tours, and printed sources used by Howard Morland in writing the PROGRESSIVE's H-bomb article.

638 Rivers, William L., and Work, Alison R. FREE-LANCER AND STAFF WRITER: NEWSPAPER FEATURES AND MAGAZINE ARTICLES. 4th ed. Belmont, Calif.: Wadsworth Publishing, 1986.

In addition to covering the standard topics included in most feature writing textbooks (e.g., article ideas, writing techniques, forms), this volume discusses the "magazining of newspapers" and student opportunities for magazine publishing. Varying perspectives of free-lancers, staff writers, and editors are compared. Sample articles with editorial comments in the margin point to elements of good and poor style.

639 Roscow, James P. "It's Taxing to Free-Lance." QUILL 69 (January 1981) : 8-10.

Advice for free-lance journalists on income tax preparation.

640 Rosenbaum, Jean, and Rosenbaum, Veryl. THE WRITER'S SURVIVAL GUIDE. Cincinnati, Ohio: Writer's Digest Books, 1982.

Problems of free-lancing with advice on coping with "rejection, success, and ninety-nine other hangups of the writing life."

641 Sawicki, Stephen. "Muckraking." QUILL 69 (July-August 1981) : 17-19.

Experiences of Mark Dowie, investigative editor and muckraker for MOTHER JONES, "the largest leftest magazine in the U.S."

642 Sayre, Nora. "How Free is the Free-Lance Writer?" MADEMOISELLE 66 (March 1968) : 177+.

Self-discipline is the advice given by a free-lancer to aspiring free-lancers.

643 Schindehette, Susan. "Stills: The Life and Times of Journalism's Middle Child." WASHINGTON JOURNALISM REVIEW 4 (October 1982) : 18-25.

Experiences of magazine photojournalists for TIME, LIFE, NEWSWEEK, PEOPLE, etc. reveal the dangers, difficulties, and emotional involvement.

644 Schonfeld, A. Clay, and Diegmueller, Karen S. EFFECTIVE FEATURE WRITING. New York: Holt, Rinehart and Winston, 1982.

A magazine article writing textbook, including study guide and written assignments. Covers the topic from ideas through writing to selling. Numerous examples illustrate authors' points.

645 Schultz, Terri. "Writers' Equity: The Search for Power in the Marketplace." QUILL 70 (October 1982) : 9-13.

Financial and other problems of free-lancing. Is a national writers' union an answer?

646 Sokolov, Raymond. WAYWARD REPORTER: THE LIFE OF A. J. LIEBLING. New York: Harper & Row, 1980.

Biograpy of Liebling, magazine journalist and press critic, who wrote primarily for the NEW YORKER.

647 Van Til, William. WRITING FOR PROFESSIONAL PUBLICATION. Boston: Allyn and Bacon, 1986.

Covers publishing opportunities from books to professional or scholarly journals, the writer at work, and the editorial function. Use of numerous sample letters (e.g. rejection, query), statements from writers, documents, and bibliographies. Much of the text is written as a conversation between two participants. Lengthy, less prosaic treatment of popular subject.

648 Weir, David, and Noyes, Dan, eds. RAISING HELL: HOW THE CENTER FOR INVESTIGATIVE REPORTING GETS THE STORY. Reading, Mass.: Addison-Wesley Publishing, 1983.

Eight investigative magazine articles are reprinted, followed by comments on how the stories were obtained. Includes four modern muckraking stories from MOTHER JONES.

649 Welles, Chris. "The Craft of Business Reporting." FOLIO 11 (May 1982) : 94+.

Former LIFE and POST business editor, now at Columbia University journalism school, offers excellent how-to-do-it advice, well-founded in a long and successful business reporting career.

650 Zion, Sidney. READ ALL ABOUT IT! New York: Summit Books, 1982.

First person account of background and research for numerous magazine articles written by Zion for HARPER'S, NEW YORK, NEW YORK TIMES MAGAZINE, and others. Text included for some articles.

Chapter 8

PRODUCTION & DESIGN

651 Black, Jim Nelson. "Magazine Design: The Evolution." FOLIO 12 (November 1983) : 80-83+.

A quick history of magazine design as seen through the eyes of several art directors. Coming trends predicted.

652 Bragonier, Reginald, Jr., and Fisher, David J. THE MECHANICS OF A MAGAZINE. New York: Hearst Corporation, 1984.

Promotional volume describes the production of POPULAR MECHANICS, from editorial through circulation. Color illustrations, glossary, index.

653 Callahan, Sean. "PEOPLE." AMERICAN PHOTOGRAPHER 12 (JUNE 1984) : 39-53.

Ten years of the best photos from PEOPLE, with background and how-to notes.

654 Carter, John Mack. "Who Controls the Cover?" FOLIO 12 (July 1983) : 99-101+.

Although selection of subject, art, design, and copy for the cover is usually a cooperative effort, the editor should have the final word.

655 Chapman, Bert. "You Gotta Have a Gimmick." GRAPHIC ARTS MONTHLY 57 (February 1985) : 141-142+.

Demographic and regional editions, innovative advertising gimmicks (e.g., metallic ink, tip-in booklets, gatefolds), and personalized magazines increase complexities of magazine printing.

656 Cohen, Barney. "Silk Threads." AMERICAN PHOTOGRAHPER 14 (February 1985) : 46-59.

Profile and background of sports photographer George Silk, with insights into his days at the old LIFE and since.

657 "Computer Equipped Freelance Writers Aid Publishers." FOLIO 15 (April 1986) : 32.

Typesetting and editing via computer saves publishers time, money. Transmission of copy and corrections via phone line modems.

658 "Covers." NATIONAL REVIEW 32 (December 31,1980) : 1617-1619.

Pictorial essay showing changes in covers of NATIONAL REVIEW from the first issue.

659 Delaney, Rachelle. "How Printers are Planning for Your Future." FOLIO 13 (January 1984) : 72+.

Six-page discussion of present and future technological changes in magazine printing and production. How they affect pre-press, printing, binding, distribution.

660 Dickey, Tom. "John Loengard." AMERICAN PHOTOGRAPER 3 (October 1979) : 60-69.

Interview with photographer John Loengard offers insights into picture editing at the new LIFE compared with the old.

661 Dorn, Raymond. TABLOID DESIGN FOR THE ORGANIZATIONAL PRESS: A COMPENDIUM OF DESIGNS. Chicago: Lawrence Ragan Communications, 1983.

Short volume considers special problems of tabloid design, providing practical assistance in layout.

662 Eckhardt, H. Ted. "Waste Makes Money in the Magazine Publishing Field, Where Voodoo Economics Haunts Wholesalers and Enriches Printers." AMERICAN PRINTER 194 (January 1985) : 30.

The economics of printing more magazines than can be sold.

663 Edwards, Owen. "Living the Life Fantastic." AMERICAN PHOTOGRAHPER 14 (March 1985) : 58-71.

Profile of N.Y.C. magazine photographer, Chris Callis, accompanied by the usual physical descriptions of himself, his studio, and his technique.

664 Epstein, Sue Hoover. "High-Priced Paper: When Quality Counts." FOLIO 14 (December 1985) : 84-89.

Why some publishers use expensive, high-quality paper stock. Reports from such magazines as GOURMET, PERSONNEL JOURNAL, TOWN AND COUNTRY, ARCHITECTURAL DIGEST.

665 Fox, Martin, and Kner, Carol Stevens. PRINT CASEBOOKS: THE BEST IN COVERS AND POSTERS. Bethesda, Md.: RC Publications, 1977-.

An annual series picturing some of the best magazine covers and posters of the year, with descriptive notes about each entry.

666 Garneau, George. "Lasers and Gravure Printing." EDITOR & PUBLISHER 117 (December 1, 1984) : 28.

New printing technology will improve quality of Sunday newspaper magazines.

667 Giffen, Peter. "Three Dimensions in Print." MACLEANS 97 (March 19, 1984) : 59.

Use of holograms on the cover of NATIONAL GEOGRAPHIC.

668 "Going to Press: Webb Co. Exploits a Lucrative Niche in Publishing." BARRON'S 63 (May 16, 1983) : 63.

Webb Co. specializes in long run, four-color magazine printing, including TV GUIDE, and publishes its own special interest magazines.

669 Goodman, Lester. "Computer Graphics: What They Can and Can't Do." FOLIO 13 (November 1984) : 116-121.

Advantages and limitations of computer graphics for magazine production. Includes numerous color illustrations showing computer capabilities.

670 Hattrup, Joseph A. "Programmable Controllers in the Magazine Bindery." GRAPHIC ARTS MONTHLY 57 (June 1985) : 91-92.

Programmable controllers in the bindery can be used for zip code sorting and mailing, inserting loose cards selectively, bundle stacking, defective product tracking and rejecting.

671 Howland, Jennifer. "Users Report: Atex." FOLIO 13 (November 1984) : 143-146+.

Use of Atex text processing and editing system at MEDICAL ECONOMICS and NEWSWEEK.

672 Howland, Jennifer. "Users Report: The CCI 400." FOLIO 13 (August 1984) : 106-108+.

Reports on the pros and cons of the CCI 400 electronic editorial and/or production system from three publishers--Harcourt Brace Jovanovich, Oster Communications, and 13-30 Corporation. Advantages include flexibility and minimal training. Problems include insufficient capacity and lost copy.

673 Hull, Steve. "Production: The Challenge of Change." FOLIO 13 (August 1984) : 69-70+.

How technology is changing production managers' jobs.

674 Hurlburt, Allen. LAYOUT: THE DESIGN OF THE PRINTED PAGE. New York: Watson-Guptill, 1977.

Style, form, content, reader response in relation to layout, from eye movement and optical illusion to art deco and covers. Excellent design is enduring and timeless.

675 "The Importance of Being Rockwell." COLUMBIA JOURNALISM REVIEW 17 (November-December 1979) : 40-42.

Magazine designer Milton Glaser describes Norman Rockwell's talent and ability to capture the spirit of the SATURDAY EVENING POST. Discussion of the function of magazine covers.

676 Jefferson, Robert. "Production Number." MAGAZINE AGE 6 (August 1985) : 70-72+.

Rapid change in production technology, from retouching to halftone gravure and filmless reproduction (digitalizing). Production advances and concerns discussed for most of five pages.

677 Jones, Lauretta, and Phillips, Steve. "The Look You're Looking For." FOLIO 14 (November 1985) : 157-164.

Computer graphics defined as electronic illustration. Five different "looks" in computer graphics defined and illustrated.

678 Kery, Patricia Frantz. GREAT MAGAZINE COVERS OF THE WORLD. New York: Abbeville Press, 1982.

Top quality illustrations of the best U.S. and international magazine covers. Excellent commentary on the history of illustrated magazines and functions of magazine covers. Historical look at such topics as fashion, celebrity caricatures, and humor as they developed through the decades in cover illustrations. Excellent.

679 Kobrin, Sandra. "The Two Faces of Magazine Covers." THE PRESS 9 (December 1981) : 7.

News brief on RUNNER'S WORLD's use of different covers on editions for serious subscribers and casual newsstand buyers.

680 Langford, Bert N. "Applying Micros to Production Management." FOLIO 13 (August 1984) : 79-82+.

Detailed eight-page forecast of how microcomputers are changing production.

681 Learner, Douglas A. "Word Processors Move into Editorial: The New Typesetting Link." FOLIO 11 (June 1982) : 70+.

Manifest technological destiny reviewed, with costs, timetables, transitional suggestions, and alternatives.

682 Lemann, Nicholas. "Whatever Happened to the Family of Man?" WASHINGTON MONTHLY 16 (October 1984) : 12-18.

Documentary photography, once a powerful journalistic influence, has declined with the death of picture magazines. Profile of Diane Arbus, former magazine photographer.

683 Lippold, William A. "Electronic Editing: How It Works." FOLIO 9 (August 1980) : 92+.

Magazines may find electronic editing systems are cost-justifiable.

684 Love, Barbara. "The 1984 Production Trends Survey." FOLIO 13 (January 1984) : 82-83+.

Survey of magazine production managers regarding paper supply, technological changes, future trends.

685 Lukovitz, Karlene. "Color for Connoisseurs: Four Studies in Quality Printing." FOLIO 11 (August 1982) : 68+.

Executives from GEO, GOURMET, NAUTICAL QUARTERLY, and AUDUBON discuss what it takes to get quality, color printing.

686 Lukovitz, Karlene. "The FOLIO Cover Test." FOLIO 11 (July 1982) : 75-60+.

The confusions, complexities, and contradictions of cover design and selection. Need for logo and format continuity from issue to issue reiterated. Those interested in editorial ethics will note the easy confusion of article illustrations with proximate advertising on cover art and art direction offered by David Merrill Design. Consultants compare sales success of covers from competing titles.

687 "Magazine Readers Get Double Coverage." ADVERTISING AGE 55 (July 2, 1984) : 20.

SOUTHERN LIVING's DECORATING & CRAFT IDEAS has two covers, with new and old titles. Draws attention to new name of magazine.

688 "Making a Happy Marriage." GRAPHIC ARTS MONTHLY 55 (August 1983) : 118+.

How printer, W. F. Hall, deals with printing the NATIONAL GEOGRAPHIC.

689 Markus, David. "Great Pages of 1984." AMERICAN PHOTOGRAPHER 14 (March 1985) : 45-57.

Outstanding magazine photos from 1984. How-to and explanatory comments on effective use of photos in magazines.

690 Merrill, David. "Why Covers Fail." FOLIO 9 (March 1980) : 68-73.

Review of basics familiar to anyone who has studied magazine covers. Useful to remind us how little we really know about which covers work and why. Major theme is that cover advertises the magazine and must be efficient.

691 "Moving to Desk Top Publishing." FOLIO 15 (May 1986) : 13-15.

Marriage of computer and typesetter. Outlook: probable success with presently high-cost, high-resolution laser printers. Brief reference to local area networks established to set type from disks. Brief case histories and suggestions.

692 Nelson, Roy Paul. PUBLICATION DESIGN. 3d ed. Dubuque, Iowa: Wm. C. Brown, 1983.

An illustrated text covering all aspects of design. Emphasis on magazines, although books, newspapers, newsletters, etc. are also covered. More text, less flamboyant examples, here than in White's volume on design. Glossary and brief bibliography.

693 "New Equipment Channels Help TV GUIDE Fine Tune Its Publication." AMERICAN PRINTER 191 (September 1983) : 42-43.

TV GUIDE's printing occurs in ten plants throughout the U.S., using some of the most advanced equipment in the printing industry. Description of the equipment and the process.

694 Newcomb, John. THE BOOK OF GRAPHIC PROBLEM SOLVING: HOW TO GET VISUAL IDEAS WHEN YOU NEED THEM. New York: R. R. Bowker, 1984.

Detailed procedure for generating ideas for magazine graphics. Outlined by Art Director of Medical Economics Company, publisher of thirteen health related magazines.

695 "NEWSWEEK Buys Advanced Color Sending System." EDITOR & PUBLISHER 116 (September 3, 1983) : 30.

What InfoCOLOR-2 production package will do to increase the magazine's prepress production capabilities and high-quality color.

696 "An Overview of Penta's Editorial System." PUBLISHER'S WEEKLY 226 (December 7, 1984) : 37-38+.

What the Penta Systems International computerized editorial system can do for magazine and book publishers.

697 Paolucci, Bert. "Where to Cut Production Costs." FOLIO 15 (January 1986) : 126-130.

Options for production cost reduction reviewed by production consultant, former employee of Time Inc. and American Heritage turned writer-lecturer.

698 Parnau, Jeffery. "The Editorial/Typesetting/ Paste-Up Loop." FOLIO 15 (February 1986) : 132+.

Production problems and their causes. Suggestions to reduce time, frustration, cost in the "loop." Good for beginners and experienced practitioners.

699 Parnau, Jeffery R. "In-House Prep: New Techniques Save Time and Money." FOLIO 12 (January 1983) : 75-78+.

Pre-press production techniques for the publisher to do in-house. Options discussed.

700 Parnau, Jeffery R. "Printing: The New Technology

Comes of Age." FOLIO 9 (February 1980) : 34-35+.

Somewhat abstract but thoughtful look at technological change. Why it has, will, and in part may not take place in the pressroom.

701 Parnau, Jeffery R. "Production Trends: The Next Five Years." FOLIO 11 (January 1982) : 57-58+.

Technological advances in printing and production, from page preparation to binding.

702 Paul, Greg. "Great Design on a Tight Budget." FOLIO 12 (February 1983) : 73-75+.

Tips on magazine design and illustration for publishers on low budgets. Illustrated.

703 Peter, John. "Breaking the Rules and Winning." FOLIO 14 (January 1985) : 124.

Unique NEW YORKER covers do not relate to inside editorial.

704 Peter, John. "The Cover Story." FOLIO 7 (August 1978) : 44-48.

Rules for good covers. They should reflect the magazine's identity and content, allow recognition by readers, and cause consumers to act (buy and read the magazine).

705 Peter, John. "The 'Electronic' Art Director." FOLIO 12 (February 1983) : 83.

How electronic equipment is changing the process of art direction and magazine appearance.

706 Powers, Jack. "Good-By Paste-Up." FOLIO 15 (March 1986) : 99-105.

Electronic page make-up reviewed and discussed extensively.

707 Powers, Jack. "Pre-Press Equipment Changing Rapidly." FOLIO 14 (August 1985) : 85-86+.

Typesetting, pagination, and image processing systems are growing less expensive and easier to use. Composition systems seeking to eliminate manual paste-up, interactive image processing workstations, cost, efficiency aspects are discussed.

708 Powers, Jack, and Rabidoux, Lisa. "Computer Graphics Systems Review." FOLIO 15 (May 1986) : 92-97.

New software is changing the way images are created. Sample high-resolution four-color and black-and-white drawings and photos computer-produced from 35 mm slides. Substantial discussion.

709 Raloff, Janet. "Holographic Eagles Wing Across

Country." SCIENCE NEWS 125 (February 25, 1984) : 119.

Brief note on NATIONAL GEOGRAPHIC's use of holograms on magazine covers.

710 Reed, Christopher. "How to Make a Magazine." HARVARD MAGAZINE 79 (March-April 1977) : 65-71.

Printing and production functions in producing a magazine.

711 "Retouching Poses Ethical Questions." FOLIO 14 (March 1985) : 19-20.

Computerized photo retouching and alteration means photography may not reflect reality.

712 Sanders, Norman. GRAPHIC DESIGNER'S PRODUCTION HANDBOOK. New York: Hastings House, 1982.

Guide to printing and graphic design.

713 Scala, Ted. "What's Good Design?" FOLIO 14 (November 1985) : 146-153.

Interviews with five top designers on how to create designs which communicate editorial ideas.

714 Stark, Hilmer. "The 1983 Paper Primer." FOLIO 12 (January 1983) : 83-84+.

Types and prices of paper, including a glossary of terms.

715 Walfish, Andrew. "Sex is In, Politics is Out." MORE 7 (September 1977) : 25-30.

Comments on magazive covers from best-selling and worst-selling issues of 1976. Worthwhile summary of cover characteristics that attract or turn away newsstand buyers.

716 White, Jan V. "Considerate Typography." FOLIO 13 (March 1984) : 97-99+.

Typography basics. How to make graphics work towards easier transfer of total content to readers. Understandable breakdown of complex, artistic subject.

717 White Jan V. "Crystal-Clear Communication." FOLIO 14 (December 1985) : 97-100.

Breaks down and illustrates key elements in creating unity between design and body copy.

718 White, Jan V. DESIGNING FOR MAGAZINES: COMMON PROBLEMS, REALISTIC SOLUTIONS. 2d ed. New York: R. R. Bowker, 1982.

A companion book to EDITING BY DESIGN, this volume offers specific ideas for practical application of White's philosophy. Reiterates the basic theme that visual form is inseparable from editorial. Each chapter considers one part of a magazine, including covers, contents, departments, editorials, openers. Chapters begin with written material regarding purpose and basic rules, and end with numerous visual examples.

719 White, Jan V. EDITING BY DESIGN. 2d ed. New York: R. R. Bowker, 1982.

A how-to book of magazine design, emphasizing the interrelationship of two often separated functions, editing and design. Layout techniques related to how readers use magazines. Verbal descriptions brief and pithy. Concepts and principles well-illustrated with diagrams, drawings, and photos. Use of grids and typography, with heavy emphasis on use and selection of pictures and illustrations.

720 White, Jan V. GRAPHIC IDEA NOTEBOOK: INVENTIVE TECHNIQUES FOR DESIGNING PRINTED PAGES. New York: Watson-Guptill Publications, 1980.

Noted graphics expert designed this volume as a ready reference manual for publication editors and designers seeking new approaches to graphic dilemmas. Pictorial ideas often explained with handwritten notes, addressing such objectives as getting attention, breaking up text, preparation of charts, using mugshots and maps. Very brief index. Stylized visual presentation and briefness of explanatory notes may make this a difficult tool to use. Parts of this book appear as articles in FOLIO magazine.

721 White, Jan V. "Grids." FOLIO 10 (June 1981) : 85-91+.

Examples of page/spread layout ideas using familiar system.

722 White, Jan V. MASTERING GRAPHICS: DESIGN AND PRODUCTION MADE EASY. New York: R. R. Bowker, 1983.

Basics of graphic design for all types of publications from magazines to newsletters and tabloids. Compares types of publications. Clearly written text illustrated with some 480 graphic examples. Coverage ranges from selection of logo to choice of paper, from typography to printing and binding. Emphasis on creating, selecting, and displaying photographs and illustrations to enhance a publication's editorial content.

723 White, Jan V. "Visual Persuasion." FOLIO 13 (October 1984) : 97-101+.

Examples and discussion of visual vocabulary, including optical illusion as a technique of distortion and persuasion. Numerous examples and their effects.

724 White, Jan V. "Words and Pictures." FOLIO 12 (February 1983) : 65-70.

How design relates to editorial content.

725 Yovovich, B. G. "The Right Type Commands Newsstand Respect." ADVERTISING AGE 54 (October 17, 1983) : M48.

Increasing importance of cover lines.

Chapter 9

HISTORY

726 Alexander, J. Heywood. "Brainerd's (Western) Musical World." NOTES 36 (March 1980) : 601-614.

Notes on the history of American music periodicals since 1786, with emphasis on editor Charles Brainerd's founding of the WESTERN MUSICAL WORLD in 1884.

727 Alpert, Hollis. "What Killed COLLIER'S?" SATURDAY REVIEW 40 (May 11, 1957) : 9-11+.

The rise and fall of COLLIER'S may represent a significant pattern for the magazine industry. A look at COLLIER's history, financial problems, management, lack of editorial identity, circulation.

728 Appel, John J. "Jews in American Caricature: 1820-1914." AMERICAN JEWISH HISTORY 71 (September 1981) : 103-133.

Stereotyping cartoons of Jews and other ethnic minoritites in American magazines since the nineteenth century, with particular emphasis on PUCK.

729 "The Art of the Cover." AMERICAN PRINTER 192 (October 1983) : 135-138.

The INLAND PRINTER (now AMERICAN PRINTER) was the first magazine to offer different covers on each issue during the 1890s. Description of some early covers and the effect of changing covers on the printing and publishing industry.

730 Baker, Howard. "The GYROSCOPE." SOUTHERN REVIEW 17 (October 1981) : 735-757.

Story of the GYROSCOPE, a literary magazine published 1929-1930. Includes references to other similar magazines of the period.

731 Bakker, Jan. "Another Dilemma of an Intellectual in the Old South: Caroline Gilman, the Peculiar Institution, and Greater Rights for Women in the Rose Magazines." SOUTHERN LITERARY JOURNAL 17 (Fall 1984) : 12-25.

Gilman's literary fame as the best known Southern female author in the antebellum period rested on the national distribution of her popular youth magazines, 1832-1839. An analysis of her writing points to a pattern of feminism and rebellion against the submissive female role.

732 Barrett, William. "Portrait of the Radical as an Aging Man." COMMENTARY 67 (May 1979) : 40-47.

The philosophy and writings of Philip Rahv, a founder of PARTISAN REVIEW, 1934.

733 Bart, Peter. "Giants On Uneasy Footing." COLUMBIA JOURNALISM REVIEW 1 (Spring 1962) : 32-33.

Outlines major problems for mass circulation magazines during the 1960s.

734 Beasley, Maurine. "The Muckrakers and Lynching: A Case Study in Racism." JOURNALISM HISTORY 9 (Autumn-Winter 1982-1983) : 86-91.

Coverage of lynching in five muckraking magazines, 1902-1912. When there was little consensus on "fact", muckrakers failed to stimulate reform.

735 Berkove, Lawrence I. "Man With the Burning Pen: Ambrose Bierce as Journalist." JOURNAL OF POPULAR CULTURE 15 (Fall 1981) : 34-40.

Biographical essay on newspaper and magazine journalist whose career spanned the years 1867-1909.

736 Best, James J. "The Brandywine School and Magazine Illustration: HARPER'S, SCRIBNER'S and

CENTURY, 1906-1910." JOURNAL OF AMERICAN CULTURE 3 (Spring 1980) : 128-144.

Magazine illustration in the early days before photography was used. Emphasis on the work of illustrator Howard Pyle and his influence on the field.

737 Bidwell, John. "The ENGRAVER AND PRINTER, A Boston Trade Journal of the Eighteen Nineties." PAPERS OF THE BIBLIOGRAPHICAL SOCIETY OF AMERICA 71 (January-March 1977) : 29-48.

The editorial concept and content of the ENGRAVER AND PRINTER, influential Boston trade journal. Publication spanned brief period of great change in printing and technology, 1891-1896.

738 Blanton, Lynne. "The Agrarian Myth in Eighteenth and Nineteenth Century American Magazines." Ph.D. dissertation, University of Illinois, 1979.

Comparison of general interest magazine content, 1780-1800, 1830-1850, 1880-1900, dealing with farmers, agriculture, nature, country living. Rhetoric praising farmer was constant, but there was "erosion of the foundations of the agrarian myth" over the period of the study as industrialization of America occurred.

739 Bogart, Leo. "Magazines Since the Rise of Tele-

vision." JOURNALISM QUARTERLY 33 (Spring 1956) : 153-166.

Magazine industry trends in 1956 showed increased circulation, increased specialization, changing emphasis in editorial content, decreased advertising dollars. Influential factors are the impact of television, changing demographics, increased education, and home ownership.

740 Bold, Christine. "Voice of the Fiction Factory in Dime and Pulp Westerns." JOURNAL OF AMERICAN STUDIES 17 (April 1983) : 29-46.

Analysis of the pulp western novel and magazines from the late nineteenth century.

741 Bow, James. "TIME's Financial Markets Column in the Period Around the 1929 Crash." JOURNALISM QUARTERLY 57 (Autumn 1980) : 447-450+.

TIME did not predict the 1929 crash. Column was more often optimistic than pessimistic.

742 Brady, Kathleen. IDA TARBELL: PORTRAIT OF A MUCKRAKER. New York: Seaview/Putnam, 1984.

A biography of Ida Tarbell, from childhood to her death in 1944. Details her career as an investigative journalist for McCLURE'S.

743 Bridges, Lamar W. "George Kibbe Turner of

McCLURE'S MAGAZINE." JOURNALISM QUARTERLY 61 (Spring 1984) :178-182.

Analysis of the work of a little-known, but leading staff writer at McCLURE'S MAGAZINE, 1906-1916.

744 Brier Stephen. "The Career of Richard L. Davis Reconsidered: Unpublished Correspondence from the NATIONAL LABOR TRIBUNE." LABOR HISTORY 21 (Summer 1980) : 420-429.

Davis, first black member of the National Board of the UMW, 1891-1896, served as intermediary between white labor management and black workers. Analysis of his journal writings illustrates use of published materials to study history.

745 Budrys, Algis. "Paradise Charted." TRIQUARTERLY no. 49 (Fall 1980) : 5-75.

Relationship of commercial science fiction to literature, with emphasis on publishing science fiction magazines from the 1920s to the 1970s.

746 Bullock, Penelope L. THE AFRO-AMERICAN PERIODICAL PRESS, 1838-1909. Baton Rouge: Louisiana State University Press, 1981.

History of black magazines in the U.S. until 1909 with brief sketches of individual titles.

Focus on historical and cultural influences on the black press.

747 Cardozo, Arlene Rossen. "American Magazine Coverage of the Nazi Death Era." JOURNALISM QUARTERLY 60 (Winter 1983): 717-718.

Analysis of sixty-four READER'S GUIDE listings from 1941-1944 showed opinion magazines carried more Nazi stories than news and feature magazines combined. The NATION and NEW REPUBLIC carried nearly half the articles.

748 Cater, Douglass. "Max Ascoli, of the REPORTER." ENCOUNTER 50 (April 1978) : 49-52.

Biography and personal reminiscences of the author on the death of Max Ascoli, creator, editor, publisher, owner of the REPORTER. Published from 1949-1968, the REPORTER began as an opponent of McCarthyism.

749 "CELEBRITIES: The Sad Story of a Magazine Born Eighty Years too Soon." AMERICAN HERITAGE 33 (February-March 1982) : 64-67.

CELEBRITIES MONTHLY, the PEOPLE magazine of the 1890s, was unsuccesfully published between 1895 and 1897.

750 "A Century of the CENTURY." CHRISTIAN CENTURY 101 (1984).

Multi-part series tracing the history of the CHRISTIAN CENTURY. Each part individually titled and authored:

1916-1922 (March 7, 1984) : 243-246.
1923-1929 (June 6, 1984) : 595-600.
1930-1937 (August 29, 1984) : 795-799.
1938-1945 (September 26, 1984) : 867-871.
1946-1952 (October 24, 1984) : 979-983.
1953-1961 (November 21, 1984) : 1091-1095.
1962-1971 (December 12, 1984) : 1170-1173.

751 Cohen, Paul E. "Barrett Wendell and the Harvard Literary Revival." NEW ENGLAND QUARTERLY 52 (December 1979) : 483-499.

HARVARD MONTHLY, literary journal published 1885-1921, began as a mouthpiece for a "club-like group" of undergraduates, and developed into a serious literary journal as famous Harvard alumni were persuaded to contribute.

752 Coll, Gary. "Noah Webster, Magazine Editor and Publisher." JOURNALISM HISTORY 11 (Spring-Summer 1984) : 26-31.

Noah Webster's contributions as publisher of AMERICAN MAGAZINE, founded in New York City in 1788 and surviving only a year. Analysis of his reasons for publishing, the magazine's content, and later attempts to revive it.

753 Cooney, Terry A. "Cosmopolitan Values and the Identification of Reaction: PARTISAN REVIEW in the 1930s." JOURNAL OF AMERICAN HISTORY 68 (December 1981) : 580-598.

The cultural and political stance of PARTISAN REVIEW during the 1930s. How the magazine changed from an alliance with the communist party prior to 1937 to anti-Stalinist afterwards.

754 Cote, Joseph A. "Clarence Hamilton Poe: The Farmers Voice. 1899-1964." AGRICULTURAL HISTORY 53 (January 1979) : 30-41.

The success and contributions of PROGRESSIVE FARMER founded 1899 and still published. The article deals with the magazine and its content during Poe's editorship, 1899-1964.

755 Cox, Richard W. "Art Young: Cartoonist from the Middle Border." WISCONSIN MAGAZINE OF HISTORY 61 (Autumn 1977) : 32-58.

Best known for political cartoons in the radical magazine, THE MASSES, his work appeared in numerous other magazines and newspapers, 1880s to 1940s, including the SATURDAY EVENING POST.

756 Curtis, Bruce. "Sinclair and Sumner: The Private Background of a Public Confrontation." MID-AMERICA 60 (October 1978) : 185-190.

Summary and comparison of opposing articles on socialism by Upton Sinclair and William Graham Sumner, published in COLLIERS WEEKLY October 29, 1904.

757 Daniel, Walter C. "Langston Hughes' Introduction to ESQUIRE Magazine." JOURNAL OF POPULAR CULTURE 12 (Spring 1979) : 620-623.

Contributions to ESQUIRE, 1934-1936, of Langston Hughes, "brilliant young Negro author".

758 Davis, Stephen. "'A Matter of Sensational Interest': The CENTURY 'Battles and Leaders' Series." CIVIL WAR HISTORY 27 (December 1981) : 338-349.

The historical value of CENTURY MAGAZINE's 1880s series on the Civil War.

759 Dennis, Everette E., and Allen, Christopher. "PUCK, the Comic Weekly." JOURNALISM HISTORY 6 (Spring 1979) : 2-7+.

The reasons for PUCK's success, 1877-1918, included skilled lithographers and artists, group journalism, and the right editorial concept at the right time.

760 Dinan, John A. THE PULP WESTERN: A POPULAR HISTORY OF THE WESTERN FICTION MAGAZINE IN AMERICA. San Bernardino, Calif.: Borgo, 1983.

History of pulp western magazines emphasizes the writers, editors, and artists of the genre.

761 Douglas, George H. "Edmund Wilson: The Man of

Letters as a Journalist." JOURNAL OF POPULAR CULTURE 15 (Fall 1981) : 78-85.

Biographical article on journalist Edmund Wilson's career, which included editing for the NEW YORKER, NEW REPUBLIC, and VANITY FAIR.

762 Edkins, Diana. "Pioneers of Commercial Color: Bruehl, Keppler, Muray, Outerbridge, Steichen." MODERN PHOTOGRAPHY 42 (September 1978) : 104-109+.

Discussion of color photography in magazines from the 1910 NATIONAL GEOGRAPHIC through the 1930s when improved color reproduction techniques introduced a new era in magazine publishing. Focuses on five photographers, their publications, camera equipment, and technology.

763 Endres, Fred F. "Pre-Muckraking Days of McCLURE'S MAGAZINE, 1893-1901." JOURNALISM QUARTERLY 55 (Spring 1978) : 154-157.

Articles on successful people and ventures dominated the magazine's content.

764 Endres, Kathleen L. "The Women's Press in the Civil War: A Portrait of Patriotism, Propaganda, and Prodding." CIVIL WAR HISTORY 30 (March 1984) : 31-53.

Analysis of nine women's magazines published in the North during the Civil War.

765 Evans, John Whitney. "John LaFarge, AMERICA, and the Newman Movement." CATHOLIC HISTORICAL REVIEW 64 (October 1978) : 614-643.

Primary focus on the history of the Catholic Newman movement, with references to articles published in AMERICA magazine during the 1920s and 1930s about the movement.

766 Faderman, Lillian. "Lesbian Magazine Fiction in the Early Twentieth Century." JOURNAL OF POPULAR CULTURE 11 (Spring 1978) : 800-817.

Lesbian relationships were treated naturally and without belief they were immoral in the nineteenth century and first two decades of the twentieth century, appearing in fiction of such magazines as LADIES' HOME JOURNAL and HARPER'S.

767 Felchner, William J. "Early Science Fiction Magazines." HOBBIES 90 (May 1985) : 62-66.

Heavily illustrated history and description of science fiction magazines, particularly the pulps published from the 1920s through the 1950s. Although written for the magazine collector, the article has relevance for the magazine student.

768 Fienberg, Lorne. "Colonel Noland of the SPIRIT: The Voices of a Gentleman in Southwest Humor." AMERICAN LITERATURE 53 (May 1981) : 232-245.

Discussion of Charles Noland's contributions

to the SPIRIT OF THE TIMES during the 1830s and 1840s. The magazine's mission was to "cultivate the qualities of the ideal gentleman".

769 Fishbein, Leslie. REBELS IN BOHEMIA: THE RADICALS OF THE MASSES, 1911-1917. Chapel Hill, N.C.: University of North Carolina Press, 1982.

The writers and editors of the MASSES, a socialist magazine banned during World War I.

770 Foley, Martha. THE STORY OF STORY MAGAZINE. New York: Norton, 1980.

Memoirs of the founder and editor of STORY magazine, a publication devoted wholly to short stories.

771 Fowler, Bridget. "'True to Me Always': An Analysis of Women's Magazine Fiction." BRITISH JOURNAL OF SOCIOLOGY 30 (March 1979) : 91-119.

Qualitative analysis of fiction in cheap British women's magazines in the 1920s and 1930s. Noted are recurring themes, sex roles, images of society. Work is the way to success. Heroines are unobtrusive, functional adornments with no personalities.

772 Gabler, William G. "The Evolution of American Advertising in the Nineteenth Century."

JOURNAL OF POPULAR CULTURE 11 (Spring 1978) : 763-771.

Illustrated history of the artistic and typographical evolution of magazine and newspaper advertising 1790-1890. Development of advertising reflects technological and economic change in U.S.

773 Garcia, Hazel. "Of Punctilios Among the Fair Sex: Colonial American Magazines, 1741-1776." JOURNALISM HISTORY 3 (Summer 1976) : 48-52+.

Only a small portion of colonial magazine content concerned women; most references to women were related to love and marriage.

774 Garrison, Bruce L. "Robert Walsh's AMERICAN REVIEW: America's First Quarterly." JOURNALISM HISTORY 8 (Spring 1981) : 14-17.

Walsh founded the AMERICAN REVIEW in 1811 as an outlet for his own political writing.

775 Gilhooley, Leonard. "Brownson, the American Idea, and the Early Civil War." THOUGHT 53 (March 1978) : 55-69.

Civil War topics dominated the pages of BROWNSON'S QUARTERLY REVIEW, 1860-1864.

776 "Government, Writers & Media Cooperated in WW II

to Expand Job Options for Women." MEDIA REPORT TO WOMEN 9 (April 1, 1981) : 4-5.

How magazine fiction was used as a propaganda tool during World War II to encourage women to work outside the home. SATURDAY EVENING POST and TRUE STORY played major roles. Article is composed of quoted passages from paper and book by Maureen Honey. See entries 783-786.

777 Gressley, Gene M. "Mr. Raine, Mammon and the Western." ARIZONA AND THE WEST 25 (Winter 1983-1984) : 313-328.

Biographical article on William MacLeod Raine, magazine journalist and writer of western stories in the 1920s.

778 Grobman, Alex. "What did They Know? The American Jewish Press and the Holocaust, 1 September 1939--17 December 1942." AMERICAN JEWISH HISTORY 68 (March 1979) : 327-352.

Study of twenty Jewish periodicals in America, 1939-1942, reveals that atrocities were reported, and American Jews were criticized for their lack of protest against them.

779 Hamovitch, Mitzi Berger. "Hunting for the HOUND & HORN." AMERICAN SCHOLAR 51 (Autumn 1982) : 543-549.

History and content of the HOUND & HORN, an elegant little magazine published 1927-1934.

780 Harlan, Louis R. "Booker T. Washington and the VOICE OF THE NEGRO, 1904-1907." JOURNAL OF SOUTHERN HISTORY 45 (February 1979) : 45-62.

The most promising black magazine to appear in the early twentieth century. Washington tried first to influence and then to silence it.

781 Heller, Steven. "The Art of Sensationalism." PRINT 38 (March-April 1984) : 58-65.

An illustrated history of sensationalism in U.S. and European magazines and tabloids. Examples from the sixteenth, nineteenth, and twentieth centuries show today's tabloids are part of an old tradition.

782 Heller, Steven. "Photojournalism's Golden Age." PRINT 38 (September-October 1984) : 68-79.

An illustrated essay on picture magazines of the 1920s and 1930s. Includes European as well as American titles.

783 Honey, Maureen. CREATING ROSIE THE RIVETER: CLASS, GENDER, AND PROPAGANDA DURING WORLD WAR II. Amherst, Mass.: University of Massachusetts Press, 1984.

Documentation of the propaganda campaign that established the myth of the female war worker as a patriotic homemaker thrust into the workforce. Composition of the myth as illustrated in magazine advertising and fiction in TRUE STORY and SATURDAY EVENING POST 1941-1946. War-time females were portrayed as stronger, more dependable, and more compassionate than pre-war females. In reality, war work offered already employed working class women an opportunity for higher paying jobs.

784 Honey, Maureen. "Images of Women in the SATURDAY EVENING POST, 1931-36." JOURNAL OF POPULAR CULTURE 10 (Fall 1976) : 352-358.

SATURDAY EVENING POST fiction 1931-1936 depicts white middle-class women as interested in careers and respected for their intelligence.

785 Honey, Maureen. "Recruiting Women for War Work: OWI and the Magazine Industry During World War II." JOURNAL OF AMERICAN CULTURE 3 (Spring 1980) : 47-52.

Publication of the MAGAZINE WAR GUIDE 1942-1945 by the Office of War Information. Distributed to writers and free-lancers of magazine fiction, the GUIDE recommended ways to use propaganda in formula fiction to encourage women to enter war production.

786 Honey, Maureen. "The Working-Class Woman and Recruitment Propaganda During World War II: Class Differences in the Portrayal of War Work." SIGNS 8 (Summer 1983) : 672-687.

SATURDAY EVENING POST and TRUE STORY compared.

POST heroines were strong women, while TRUE STORY heroines failed to show leadership.

787 Hook, Sidney. "The Radical Comedians: Inside PARTISAN REVIEW." AMERICAN SCHOLAR 54 (Winter 1984-1985) : 45-61.

Analysis of the PARTISAN REVIEW and its editors since 1940. Suggests that the magazine has not been a political influence but "a forum for non-sectarian writing during a highly sectarian period."

788 Hoopes, Roy. "Birth of a Great Magazine." AMERICAN HISTORY ILLUSTRATED 20 (September 1985) : 34-41.

Account of the birth of LIFE magazine that differs from the conventional account by illustrating the important role played by Ralph Ingersoll, then general manager of Time Inc.

789 Hounshell, David A. "Public Relations or Public Understanding? The American Industry Series in SCIENTIFIC AMERICAN." TECHNOLOGY AND CULTURE 21 (October 1980) : 589-593.

Origin and authorship of American Industry Series which appeared in SCIENTIFIC AMERICAN 1879-1882. The series is of value to historians of American technology although the articles were really front-page advertisements purchased by the companies featured.

790 Hunter, Doreen. "Fredric Henry Hedge, What Say You? " AMERICAN QUARTERLY 32 (Summer 1980) : 186-201.

The transcendental philosophy of Hedge, and his relationship to THE DIAL magazine under the editorship of Emerson in the 1840s.

791 Hynes, Terry. "Magazine Portrayals of Women, 1911-1930." JOURNALISM MONOGRAPH, no. 7. Lexington, Ky.: Association for Education in Journalism, 1981.

After study of ATLANTIC, COSMOPOLITAN, LADIES' HOME JOURNAL, and SATURDAY EVENING POST, the author concludes content encouraged greater freedom for women.

792 Jackman, S. W. "Tribulations of an Editor: Benjamin Silliman and the Early Days of the American Journal of Science ond the Arts." NEW ENGLAND QUARTERLY 52 (March 1979) : 99-106.

1820s correspondence from the founder of the JOURNAL regarding the difficulties of publishing.

793 John, Arthur W. THE BEST YEARS OF THE CENTURY: RICHARD WATSON GILDER, SCRIBNER'S MONTHLY, AND CENTURY MAGAZINE, 1870-1909. Champaign, Ill.: University of Illinois Press, 1981.

A history of CENTURY, a "great American magazine in its greatest years," and of the man largely responsible for shaping it. Of particular note are the changes which occurred in magazines at the turn of the century, when advertising was first accepted and mass circulation publications appealed to readers outside the cultured upper and middle classes.

794 Johnson, Abby Arthur, and Johnson, Ronald MaBerry. PROPAGANDA AND AESTHETICS: THE LITERARY POLITICS OF AFRO-AMERICAN MAGAZINES IN THE TWENTIETH CENTURY. Amherst, Mass.: University of Massachusetts Press, 1979.

Black cultural, political, and literary magazines and journals as platforms for social and political expression. A chronological analysis of content trends.

795 Jones, David Lloyd. "Measuring and Mobilizing the Media, 1939-1945." MIDWEST QUARTERLY 26 (Autumn 1984) : 35-43.

During World War II, government bureaus analyzed media editorial content, and used data to influence their information policy. Offices of War Information primarily relied on voluntary cooperation from all media, magazines to radio, to further government propaganda.

796 Jones, Nancy Baker. "A Forgotten Feminist: The Early Writings of Ida Husted Harper, 1878-1894.: INDIANA MAGAZINE OF HISTORY 73 (June 1977) : 79-101.

HARPER'S magazine and newspaper articles show her to be a feminist, recognizing the injustices even though accepting the advantages of femininity.

797 Kedro, M. James. "Literary Boosterism." COLORADO MAGAZINE 52 (Summer 1975) : 200-224.

Founded in 1889, GREAT DIVIDE was a Colorado magazine featuring local-color fiction, biographies of prominent Colorado people, and boosterism. Analysis of nineteenth century content illustrates the blending of cultural promotionalism with popular literature and advertisement.

798 Keller, Mark. "Big Bear of--Maine??? Toward the the Development of American Humor." NEW ENGLAND QUARTERLY 51 (December 1978) : 565-574.

Pre-Civil War humor in the SPIRIT OF THE TIMES is illustrated by analysis of an 1852 story, "A Bear Fight in Maine".

799 Kelly, R. Gordon. MOTHER WAS A LADY: SELF AND SOCIETY IN SELECTED AMERICAN CHILDREN'S PERIODICALS, 1865-1890. Westport, Conn.: Greenwood Press, 1974.

Notes on nineteenth century publishing. Qualitative content analysis of children's periodicals reviews common content themes. Magazines viewed as agents of socialization and reflectors of popular culture.

800 Kennedy, George A. "Gildersleeve, the JOURNAL, and Philology in America." AMERICAN JOURNAL OF PHILOLOGY 101 (Spring 1980) : 1-11.

The development of the AMERICAN JOURNAL OF PHILOLOGY on its 100th anniversary.

801 Kern, Donna Rose Casella. "Sentimental Short Fictio[n] Women Writers in LESLIE'S POPULAR MONTHLY." JOURNAL OF AMERICAN CULTURE 3 (Spring 1980) : 113-127.

Changes in formula fiction published for women 1876-1900 in LESLIE'S POPULAR MONTHLY. Economic and social changes after 1885 were related to increased adventure themes and more complex plots. A non-quantitative description.

802 Kessler, Lauren. "Against the Grain: The Lonely Voice of POLITICS Magazine 1944-1949." JOURNALISM HISTORY 9 (Summer 1982) : 49-52+.

POLITICS magazine, and its editorial opposition to rising trends of consumerism, suburbanization, and cold war politics following World War II.

803 Kronick, David A. A HISTORY OF SCIENTIFIC & TECHNICAL PERIODICALS. 2d ed. Metuchen, N.J.: Scarecrow Press, 1976.

A scholarly international history of the scientific and technical press, 1665-1790. Extensive bibliography.

804 Leverette, William E., Jr., and Shi, David E. "Herbert Agar and FREE AMERICA: A Jeffersonian Alternative to the New Deal." JOURNAL OF AMERICAN STUDIES 16 (April 1982) : 189-206.

From 1937 to 1947, the journal FREE AMERICA served to promote the decentralization of government and industry in America.

805 Lewis, David Levering. "Dr. Johnson's Friends: Civil Rights by Copyright During Harlem's Mid-Twenties." MASSACHUSETTS REVIEW 20 (Autumn 1979) : 501-519.

Contributions of editor Charles S. Johnson and the Urban League's OPPORTUNITY magazine to the cultural life of New York City's Harlem in the 1920s.

806 Lichtenstein, Nelson. "Authorial Professionalism and the Literary Marketplace 1885-1900." AMERICAN STUDIES 19 (Spring 1978) : 35-53.

Opportunities for literary publishing increased after the Civil War, with development of syndicated fiction and cheap, mass magazines. An analysis of publishing complexities of the 1880s and 1890s, with emphasis on the factors promoting growth of the magazine industry.

807 Lichtenwanger, William. "When NOTES was Young: 1945-1960." NOTES 39 (September 1982) : 7-30.

Early history and development of NOTES, the journal of the Music Library Association.

808 Luker, Ralph E. "Lost World of Garry Wills." SOUTH ATLANTIC QUARTERLY 79 (Winter 1980) : 1-16.

The 1960s writing and philosophy of Garry Wills, one-time writer for the conservative NATIONAL REVIEW.

809 McClary, Andrew. "Germs are Everywhere: The Germ Threat as Seen in Magazine Articles 1890-1920." JOURNAL OF AMERICAN CULTURE 3 (Spring 1980) : 33-46.

Non-quantitative discussion of magazine coverage of germs, 1890-1920. Did the "germ scare" in magazines affect the decline of infectious disease since the turn of the century?

810 McClary, Andrew. "Sunning for Health: Heliotherapy as Seen by Professionals and Popularizers, 1920-1940." JOURNAL OF AMERICAN CULTURE 5 (Spring 1982) : 65-68.

Differing evaluations of heliotherapy as a cure in the JOURNAL OF AMERICAN MEDICAL ASSOCIATION and HYGEIA, 1920-1940. How the publication's mission determined its message.

811 McDonald, Susan Waugh. "Edward Gardner Lewis:

Entrepreneur, Publisher, American of the Gilded Age. MISSOURI HISTORICAL SOCIETY 35 (April 1979) : 154-163.

Lewis' WOMAN'S MAGAZINE was a successful imitation of Bok's LADIES' HOME JOURNAL.

812 McDonald, Susan Waugh. "From Kipling to Kitsch: Two Popular Editors of the Gilded Age: Mass Culture, Magazines and Correspondence Universities." JOURNAL OF POPULAR CULTURE 15 (Fall 1981) : 50-61.

Growth of American magazines in the 1890s, with particular emphasis on COSMOPOLITAN, THE WOMAN'S MAGAZINE, and their role as promoters of mass culture.

813 "The McWilliams Years." NATION 227 (December 2, 1978) : 593-622.

Special issue recognizing the accomplishments and issues tackled in the NATION under the editorship of Carey McWilliams 1926-1976.

814 Marcaccio, Michael D. "Did a Business Conspiracy End Muckraking? A Reexamination." HISTORIAN 47 (November 1984) : 58-71.

Analysis of muckraking magazines suggests that they were not financially sound, and the hostilities between the magazines and business have been overstated. Their demise is most likely the result of business problems, and not a business conspiracy to be rid of them.

815 Margolis, John D. JOSEPH WOOD KRUTCH: A WRITER'S LIFE. Knoxville, Tenn.: University of Tennessee Press, 1980.

Biography of Krutch, who wrote for various magazines in the 1930s and 1940s.

816 Marks, Patricia. "Mrs. Wettin Meets a Chum: LIFE's View of Victoria, 1883-1901." JOURNAL OF AMERICAN CULTURE 3 (Spring 1980) : 80-94.

LIFE, a short-lived turn of the century American humor magazine, published numerous caricatures, satires, parodies about Queen Victoria. An illustrated essay.

817 Marti, Donald B. "Agricultural Journalism and the Diffusion of Knowledge: The First Half Century in America." AGRICULTURAL HISTORY 54 (January 1980) : 28-37.

Early development of farm journals, 1800-1850, influenced present character of the genre.

818 Masel-Walters, Lynne. "To Hustle with the Rowdies: The Organization and Functions of the American Woman Suffrage Press." JOURNAL OF AMERICAN CULTURE 3 (Spring 1980) : 167-183.

A fifty-two-year history of women's suffrage journals, their development, death, editorial efforts, and audience reactions to them. Also considered is coverage of the suffrage cause in the contemporary popular press.

819 Mather, Anne. "A History of Feminist Periodicals; Part I." JOURNALISM HISTORY 1 (Autumn 1974) : 82-88.

Titles, descriptions, and contents of feminist periodicals from the nineteenth century to the 1960s.

820 Mather, Anne. "A History of Feminist Periodicals; Part II." JOURNALISM HISTORY 1 (Winter 1974-1975) : 108-111.

Feminist periodicals in the 1960s.

821 Mather, Anne. "A History of Feminist Periodicals; Part III." JOURNALISM HISTORY 2 (Spring 1975) : 19-23+.

Feminist periodicals from 1970.

822 Mead, Rita H. "Cowell, Ives and NEW MUSIC." MUSIC QUARTERLY 66 (October 1980) : 538-559.

Henry Cowells, promoter of "ultra-modern" music and founder of the journal NEW MUSIC QUARTERLY in 1927, described the publication as a "circulating music library via a magazine of unsalable scores."

823 Meservey, Anne Farmer. "The role of Art in American Life: Critics' Views of Native Art and Literature, 1830-1865." AMERICAN ART JOURNAL 10 (May 1978) : 72-88.

Description of art criticism in leading intellectual magazines of the nineteenth century.

824 Miller, Tice L. "Identifying the Dramatic Writers for Wilkes's SPIRIT OF THE TIMES, 1859-1902." THEATRE SURVEY 20 (May 1979) : 130-133.

Chronicle of the drama reviewers who wrote for the SPIRIT OF THE TIMES.

825 Miller, William. DOROTHY DAY: A BIOGRAPHY. San Francisco, Calif.: Harper & Row, 1982.

Biography of Dorothy Day, founder of the Catholic Worker Movement and the CATHOLIC WORKER.

826 Morace, Robert A. "The Writer and his Middle Class Audience: Frank Norris, a Case in Point." JOURNAL OF AMERICAN CULTURE 3 (Spring 1980) : 105-112.

Analysis of Frank Norris' writings for the San Francisco WAVE, 1896-1897. How Norris successfully used his understanding of his audience to adapt his own artistic purposes to his readers' needs and vaues.

827 Moran, John C. "F. Marion Crawford and his Essay 'Treasures of the Vatican'." PAPERS OF THE BIBLIOGRAPHICAL SOCIETY OF AMERICA 74 (April-June 1980) : 75-76.

The magazine contributions of Crawford, 1881-1909, particularly his essay in EVERYBODY'S MAGAZINE.

828 Moss, William M. "Vindicator of Southern Intellect and Institutions: The SOUTHERN QUARTERLY REVIEW." SOUTHERN LITERARY JOURNAL 13 (Fall 1980) : 72-108.

History of the SOUTHERN QUARTERLY REVIEW, founded 1841, pro-slavery, antebellum, Southern periodical. Problems were engendered by its openly partisan editorial policy which denied the magazine broad-based readership.

829 Moulton, Elizabeth. "Remembering George Davis." VIRGINIA QUARTERLY REVIEW 55 (Spring 1979) : 284-295.

Chatty remembrance of author's editorial training days under George Davis at MADEMOISELLE during the 1940s.

830 Murray, Randall L. "Edwin Lawrence Godkin: Unbending Editor in Times of Change." JOURNALISM HISTORY 1 (Autumn 1974) : 77-81+.

The writings of Godkin, founder and editor of the NATION from 1865-1881.

831 Murray, Will. THE DUENDE HISTORY OF THE SHADOW MAGAZINE. Greenwood, Mass.: Odyssey Publications, 1980.

832 Myerson, Joel. THE NEW ENGLAND TRANSCENDENTALISTS AND THE DIAL. Rutherford, N.J.: Fairleigh Dickinson University Press, 1980.

A history of the DIAL magazine, 1840-1844, and biographical sketches with portraits of major contributors.

833 Neugeboren, Jay. "STORY." AMERICAN SCHOLAR 52 (Summer 1983) : 396-400+.

More than a review of Martha Foley's memoirs, THE STORY OF STORY, this article summarizes the history of STORY magazine from its 1931 founding.

834 Nuhn, Marilyn. "Old Television Magazines." HOBBIES 88 (October 1983) : 102-105.

Description of 1950s television magazines, such as TV GUIDE, INSIDE TV, RADIO STARS AND TELEVISION. Written for the collector, the article has noteworthy photographs and brief historical comments for the magazine student.

835 Ogles, Robert M., and Howard, Herbert H. "Father Coughlin in the Periodical Press 1931-1942." JOURNALISM QUARTERLY 61 (Summer 1984) : 280-286+.

Analysis of articles indexed in the READERS' GUIDE, 1931-1942, about Father Coughlin, the "radio priest," shows magazine attention paralleled the rise and fall of his career.

836 Paul, John J. "The Great Chicago Fire as a National Event." AMERICAN QUARTERLY 36 (Winter 1984) : 668-683.

Newspapers, magazines, and trade publications focused attention on the Chicago fire turning it into a national event.

837 Peterson, Theodore. "Successive Threats Peril Magazines; Editorial Values Keep Medium Vital." ADVERTISING AGE 51 (April 30, 1980) : 166-170+.

A capsule history of magazine trends and problems by a notable magazine scholar. Part of a special AA issue detailing the relationship between advertising and society.

838 Piott, Stephen L. "The Lesson of the Immigrant: Views of Immigrants in Muckraking Magazines

1900-1909." AMERICAN STUDIES 19 (Spring 1978) : 21-33.

Comparison of non-fiction reform writers' portrayal of the immigrant with that of fiction writers. Fiction writers attacked prejudice and recognized immigrants' contributions to America. Reform writers portrayed immigrants as innocent victims of capitalism.

839 Pitcher, E. W. "COLUMBIAN MAGAZINE and Lane's Annual Novelist (1786)." NOTES & QUERIES 25 (June 1978) : 209-211.

Early issues of the COLUMBIAN MAGAZINE failed to attract original fiction, and so reprinted it from other sources.

840 Pitcher, E. W. "Fiction in the BOSTON MAGAZINE (1783-1786): A Checklist with Notes on Sources." WILLIAM AND MARY QUARTERLY 37 (July 1980) : 473-483.

Brief history of the literary publication BOSTON MAGAZINE, and an annotated bibliography of the fiction it published.

841 Pitcher, E. W. "The Philadelphia LITERARY MISCELLANY of 1795: Magazine or Serial Anthology?" PAPERS OF THE AMERICAN BIBLIOGRAPHIC SOCIETY 77 (no. 3, 1983) : 333-335.

Description of LITERARY MISCELLANY as a serial anthology, complementing but not a part of the history of the American magazine.

842 Pitcher, Edward W. "CHRISTIAN DISCIPLE: From Prospectus to Publication in 1813." AMERICAN NOTES AND QUERIES 20 (Novenber-December 1981) : 48-50.

Discussion of CHRISTIAN DISCIPLES's initial editorial philosophy. Also known as CHRISTIAN EXAMINER, 1824-1869.

843 Porter, Jack Nusan. "Rosa Sonnenschein and THE AMERICAN JEWESS: The First Independent English Language Jewish Women's Journal in the United States." AMERICAN JEWISH HISTORY 68 (September 1978) : 57-63.

Brief history and description of the AMERICAN JEWESS, published 1895-1899.

844 Prior-Miller, Marcia R. "VOGUE 1929-1942: A Graphic Profile." M.A. thesis, University of Missouri, 1981.

VOGUE magazine was a leader in technology, photography, design in the 1930s. Methodology is a combination of historical review, qualitative content analysis, and interviews.

845 Raitz, Karl B., and Brunn, Stanley D. "Geographic Patterns in the Historical Development of Farm

Publications." JOURNALISM HISTORY 6 (Spring 1979) : 14-15+.

Growth and geographical distribution of farm magazines since 1840. Trend toward regional specialization.

846 Range, Jane, and Vinovskis, Maris A. "Images of Elderly in Popular Magazines: A Content Analysis of LITTELL'S LIVING AGE, 1845-1882." SOCIAL SCIENCE HISTORY 5 (Spring 1981) : 123-170.

The elderly were portrayed positively as "remarkably healthy, sane, and independent of their children and society" and affectionately treated.

847 Rao, S. Sreenivas. "Why CORONET Failed." JOURNALISM QUARTERLY 42 (Spring 1965) : 271-272.

Reasons for CORONET's failure suggest advertisers prefered specialized magazines. High circulation not necessarily a sign of strength.

848 Ray, Cora Corkill. "A Descriptive Comparison of the War-Related Content of GOOD HOUSEKEEPING During World War I and World War II." M.S. thesis, University of Kansas, 1980.

Common themes in World War I issues were patriotism, duty, democracy, while World War II issues were more concerned with housing, food shortages, victory gardens, comfort of the armed forces.

849 Reaves, Shiela. "How Radical were the Muckrakers? Socialist Press Views, 1902-1906." JOURNALISM QUARTERLY 61 (Winter 1984) : 763-770.

Socialist reaction to muckrakers as reported in five journals. Muckrakers were moralists, reaching mass audiences with reports of facts and scandals--not ideology.

850 Rees, Thomas. "Harris Merton Lyon: A Neglected American Master of the Short Story." JOURNAL OF AMERICAN CULTURE 3 (Spring 1980) : 145-153.

Analysis of the magazine fiction of a popular writer in the early twentieth century.

851 Reuss, Carol. "BETTER HOMES AND GARDENS: Consistent Key to Long Life." JOURNALISM QUARTERLY 51 (Summer 1974) : 292-296.

History of BETTER HOMES AND GARDENS from its 1922 founding through the 1960s.

852 Reynolds, Robert D., Jr. "The 1906 Campaign to Sway Muckraking Periodicals." JOURNALISM QUARTERLY 56 (Autumn 1979) : 513-520+.

Economic pressures applied by big business may have overcome the "journalistic integrity" of some muckraking magazines.

853 Richards, David A. "America Conquers Britain: Anglo-American Conflict in the Popular Media During the 1920s." JOURNAL OF AMERICAN CULTURE 3 (Spring 1980) : 95-103.

Popular magazines in the 1920s reflected and shaped popular attitudes towards Britain. Americans saw Britain falling to second place as a world power, a situation Britain refused to accept, resulting in deteriorating Anglo-American relations.

854 Roberts, Nancy L. DOROTHY DAY AND THE CATHOLIC WORKER. Albany: State University of New York Press, 1984.

855 Roberts, Nancy L. "Journalism for Justice: Dorothy Day and the CATHOLIC WORKER." JOURNALISM HISTORY 10 (Spring-Summer 1983) : 2-9.

Since 1933, Dorothy Day's tabloid-sized publication has been protesting social injustice and advocating reform. A leader in interpretive reporting, the journal is associated with Catholic Worker Houses for the poor.

856 Robinson, Phyllis C. "Mr. McClure and Willa." AMERICAN HERITAGE 34 (August-September 1983) : 26-31.

Biographical article describing the working relationship of Willa Cather and S. S. McClure of McCLURE'S magazine in the early twentieth century.

857 Roff, Sandra Shoiock. "A Feminine Expression: Ladies Periodicals in the New York Historical Society Collection." JOURNALISM HISTORY 9 (Autumn-Winter 1982-1983) : 92-99.

The aims and content of a variety of nineteenth century women's magazines.

858 Rollins, Peter C. "The Context and Rhetorical Strategy of Will Rogers' 'Letters From a Self-Made Diplomat to his President (1926)'." JOURNAL OF AMERICAN CULTURE 3 (Spring 1980) : 70-79.

Description of a SATURDAY EVENING POST series by Will Rogers about his European trip 1926.

859 Ross, Robert W. SO IT WAS TRUE: THE AMERICAN PROTESTANT PRESS AND THE NAZI PERSECUTION OF THE JEWS. Minneapolis, Minn.: University of Minnesota Press, 1980.

U.S. religious publications failed to report the holocaust even though aware of the facts.

860 Rothberg, Morey D. "To Set a Standard of Workmanship and Compel Men to Conform to it: John Franklin Jameson as Editor of the AMERICAN

HISTORICAL REVIEW." AMERICAN HISTORICAL REVIEW 89 (October 1984) : 957-975.

The founding of the AMERICAN HISTORICAL REVIEW in 1895. Its development, goals, and editorial policies under its first editor in the first quarter of the twentieth century.

861 Schell, Ernest. "Edward Bok and the LADIES' HOME JOURNAL." AMERICAN HISTORY ILLUSTRATED 16 (February 1982) : 16-23.

The success of the LADIES' HOME JOURNAL rested on Bok's ability to anticipate readers' needs. Also discussed are the magazines' content, promotion, growth, influence under Bok.

862 Schell, Ernest. "Portfolio: Edward Bok's LADIES' HOME JOURNAL." AMERICAN HISTORY ILLUSTRATED (February 1982) : 25-29.

Color illustrations from early editions of the LADIES' HOME JOURNAL.

863 Schmidt, Dorothy. "Magazines, Technology, and American Culture." JOURNAL OF AMERICAN CULTURE 3 (Spring 1980) : 3-16.

Historical look at the role and achievements of magazines in American culture. The influence of technology and advertising on the development of modern magazines.

864 Schofield, Ann. "Rebel Girls and Union Maids: The Woman Question in the Journals of the AFL and IWW, 1905-1920." FEMINIST STUDIES 9 (Summer 1983) : 335-358.

Women are portrayed in the journals of the American labor movement, 1905-1920, as one of two types--Rebel Girl or Union Maid.

865 Schofield, Mary Anne. "Wordsworth and the Philadelphia PORT FOLIO." ENGLISH LANGUAGE NOTES 18 (March 1981) : 186-191.

William Wordsworth's publishing in American periodicals of the early nineteenth century. His early positive reception and later criticism as the PORT FOLIO became more American in tone.

866 Scholnick, Robert J. "THE GALAXY and American Democratic Cutlure, 1861-1878." JOURNAL OF AMERICAN STUDIES 16 (April 1982) : 69-80.

Portrait of a literary magazine, 1866-1878. Unlike its contemporaries, GALAXY emphasized American not European culture, and reflected all social classes, regions, practical aspects of life.

867 Sealander, Judith. "Antebellum Black Press Images of Women." WESTERN JOURNAL OF BLACK STUDIES 6 (Fall 1982) : 159-165.

Antebellum black magazines were underfunded, often missed publication, and contained primarily digest material from other sources rather than local news. A non-quantitative content analysis of the black female role shows dual image: sympathetic, domestic wife and courageous, wily slave, neither meek nor mild. Often black editors copied stereotypes for white women.

868 Searles, Patricia, and Mickish, Janet. "'A Thoroughbred Girl' Images of Female Gender Role in Turn-of-the-Century Mass Media." WOMEN'S STUDIES 10 (no. 3, 1984) : 261-281.

Qualitative analysis of 1905 LADIES' HOME JOURNAL fiction, with particular emphasis on heroines and gender-relevant themes. Conservative message probably helped readers to cope with changing female role. Fiction defined appropriate attitudes and behavior for women.

869 Sedgwick, Ellery III. "Fireworks: Amy Lowell and and the ATLANTIC MONTHLY." NEW ENGLAND QUARTERLY 51 (December 1978) : 489-508.

Correspondence between poet Amy Lowell and ATLANTIC MONTHLY editor Ellery Sedgwick, 1910-1925, concerning the acceptability of her writing for the magazine.

870 Servos, John W. "Disciplinary Program that Failed: Wilder D. Bancroft and the JOURNAL OF PHYSICAL CHEMISTRY, 1896-1933." ISIS 73 (June 1982) : 207-232.

Bancroft's editorship of the JOURNAL, his career at Cornell, and his use of the JOURNAL as a platform for his views about the study of chemistry.

871 Shi, David E. "POLITICOS: A Modern Look at a Muckraking Classic." SOUTH ATLANTIC QUARTERLY 80 (Summer 1981) : 289-304.

Review of present-day criticism of 1938 muckraking magazine, POLITICOS.

872 Slezak, Mary. "The History of Charlton Press, Inc. and its Song Lyric Periodicals." JOURNAL OF AMERICAN CULTURE 3 (Spring 1980) : 184-194.

The story of Charlton Press, the largest publisher of music magazines and the only U.S. publisher of song lyric periodicals. Discusses various titles, editorial procedures, copyright, audience.

873 Smith, Cynthia Zoe. "Emigre Photography in America: Contributions of German Photojournalism from Black Star Picture Agency to LIFE Magazine, 1933-1938." Ph.D. dissertation, University of Iowa, 1983.

How innovations in German mass-circulation picture magazines were transferred to the U.S. LIFE magazine was an American example of the new style of photojournalism. Methodology included oral history and archival research.

874 Snyder, Robert E. "Margaret Bourke-White and the Communist Witch Hunt." JOURNAL OF AMERICAN STUDIES 19 (April 1985) : 5-25.

Although a target of McCarthyism in the 1950s after a photo essay in LIFE magazine on SAC headquarters, Margaret-Bourke White's career was undamaged.

875 Socolofsky, Homer E. "The Capper Farm Press Experience in Western Agricultural Journalism." JOURNAL OF THE WEST 19 (April 1980) : 22-29.

The development and use of farm journals in the west, with particular attention to those published by Arthur Capper. Covers 1880-1978, with greatest emphasis on 1900-1920,

876 Southard, Bruce. "Language of Science-Fiction Fan Magazines." AMERICAN SPEECH 57 (Spring 1982) : 19-31.

Brief description of first "fanzines" in mid-1930s, with glossary of words coined in science fiction fan magazines to the present.

877 Steinberg, Salme Harju. REFORMER IN THE MARKETPLACE. Baton Rouge, La.: Louisiana State University Press, 1979.

A history of LADIES' HOME JOURNAL, with emphasis on Edward Bok, Cyrus Curtis, and their roles in developing LHJ's editorial and business excellence.

878 Steiner, Linda. "Finding Community in Nineteenth-Century Suffrage Periodicals." AMERICAN JOURNALISM 1 (Summer 1983) : 1-15.

Women's suffrage periodicals, 1850-1870, united advocates for a common cause and brought meaning to their lives.

879 Stinson, Robert. "Ida M. Tarbell and the Ambiguities of Feminism." PENNSYLVANIA MAGAZINE OF HISTORY AND BIOGRAPHY 101 (April 1977) : 217-239.

After 1909, Ida Tarbell's writing for AMERICAN MAGAZINE and other publications defended the nineteenth century image of women as wives and mothers, not political participators.

880 Stinson, Robert. LINCOLN STEFFENS. New York: Frederick Ungar, 1979.

The muckraker's work and his autobiography are discussed and analyzed. Steffen's roles as student, teacher, reporter, muckraker, mediator, and autobiographer are examined.

881 Sullivan, Paul W. "G. D. Crain Jr. and the Founding of ADVERTISING AGE." JOURNALISM HISTORY 1 (Autumn 1974) : 94-95.

Founded in 1930, ADVERTISING AGE was unlike other trade journals because it focused on hard news, investigative reporting, information, and editorial integrity.

882 Taft, William H. "Bernarr Macfadden: One of a Kind." JOURNALISM QUARTERLY 45 (Winter 1968) : 627-633.

Uniqueness of the physical culturist on journalism reviewed 13 years after his death by caring, thorough journalistic historian.

Career highlights and magazine foundings reviewed.

883 Tebbel, John. THE AMERICAN MAGAZINE: A COMPACT HISTORY. New York: Hawthorn, 1969.

Classic, often-cited, compact history of magazines by noted historian. Covers 1741-1969. Offers useful insights into the times and conditions faced by the industry, and how magazines adapted over two centuries.

884 Terkel, Studs. "The Decisive Decade." AMERICAN PHOTOGRAPHER 14 (December 1984) : 39-59.

How LIFE covered 1946-1955.

885 Thomas, Samuel J. "Portraits of a 'Rebel' Priest: Edward McGlynn in Caricature, 1886-1893." JOURNAL OF AMERICAN CULTURE 7 (Winter 1984) : 19-32.

Caricatures of social activist priest Edward McGlynn, 1886-1893, from American magazines. Emphasis on PUCK. Includes illustrations with analysis of eleven caricatures.

886 Tinling, Marion. "Hermione Day and THE HESPERIAN." CALIFORNIA HISTORY 59 (Winter 1980) : 282-289.

Edited by Hermoine Day, 1858-1862, the HESPERIAN was a San Francisco based women's magazine, carrying traditional home and fashion stories as well as essays on social issues and science. Day used the magazine to promote women's equality.

887 Topping, Gary. "ARIZONA HIGHWAYS: A Half-Century of Southwestern Journalism." JOURNAL OF THE WEST 19 (April 1980) : 71-80.

History of ARIZONA HIGHWAYS, founded in 1925. Its forerunners, use of photographs, and national appeal.

888 Tucker, Edward L. "Two Young Brothers and Their ORION." SOUTHERN LITERARY JOURNAL 11 (Fall 1978) : 64-80.

Development and content of ORION, 1842-1844, a Southern literary magazine founded by two sons of a Baptist minister. Its content reflects the romanticism and sentimentality of the era, while its uniqueness lies in its humorous tone.

889 Vaughn, Stephen. "'To Create a Nation of Noble Men': Public Education, National Unity, and the NATIONAL SCHOOL SERVICE, 1918-1919." HISTORIAN 41 (May 1979) : 429-449.

Story of a government bulletin, distributed to schools, to emphasize the obligations of citizenship. It has been described as an expression of wartime propaganda.

890 Wainwright, Loudon. "Life Begins: The Birth of the Late, Great Picture Magazine." ATLANTIC MONTHLY 241 (May 1978) : 56-73.

Lengthy history of the founding of LIFE magazine. How the picture magazine concept evolved, how LIFE got its name. Notes on the people involved in its design and birth, particularly Henry Luce.

891 Wassmuth, Birgit Luise Johanna. "Art Movements and American Print Advertising: A Study of Magazine Advertising Graphics." Ph.D. dissertation, University of Minnesota, 1983.

How, to what extent, and why the art movement, Art Deco, is reflected in American magazine advertising 1915-1935. Includes historical background from secondary sources and content analysis of LADIES'S HOME JOURNAL, VOGUE, and SATURDAY EVENING POST.

892 Weingarten, Irving. "The Image of the Jew in the American Periodical Press, 1881-1921." Ph.D. dissertation, New York University, 1980.

Periodical press coverage of Jews during the mass immigration of East European Jews between

1881-1921. Overall a negative Jewish stereotype was perpetuated, although approximately one-third of the analyzed articles were positive.

893 Wellborn, Charles. "Brann vs the Baptists: Violence and Southern Religion." RELIGION IN LIFE 47 (Summer 1978) : 220-229.

A history of William Cowper Brann's 1890s magazine, THE ICONOCLAST--a large circulation "monthly compendium of personal philosophy, invective, and comment" against "the contemporary political, social, and religious scene."

894 Whalen, Matthew D., and Tobin, Mary F. "Periodicals and the Popularization of Science in American Culture, 1860-1910." JOURNAL OF AMERICAN CULTURE 3 (Spring 1980) : 195-203.

Popular science coverage in mass magazines, 1860-1910. Considers the types of readers and the magazines that developed to serve them.

895 Whitfield, Stephen J. "Dwight MacDonald's POLITICS Magazine, 1944-1949." JOURNALISM HISTORY 3 (Autumn 1976) : 86-88+.

MacDonald's philosophy as contained in POLITICS magazine is relevant even after the magazine's death.

896 Wilcox, Gary B., and Moriarty, Sandra E. "Humorous Advertising in the POST, 1920-1939." JOURNALISM QUARTERLY 61 (Summer 1984) : 436-439.

More humorous ads and fewer ads were found in the 1930s than the 1920s.

897 Wilson, Charles R. "Radical Reservations: Indians and Blacks in American Magazines, 1865-1900." JOURNAL OF POPULAR CULTURE 10 (Summer 1976) : 70-79.

Blacks and Indians were treated similarly and poorly, both conceptualized in racial terms. Non-quantitative comparison.

898 Wilson, Christopher P. "The Era of the Reporter Reconsidered: The Case of Lincoln Steffens." JOURNAL OF POPULAR CULTURE 15 (Fall 1981) : 41-49.

Emphasis on the earlier training years of Steffen's career, prior to his working at McCLURE'S MAGAZINE.

899 Wilson, Janice Crabtree. "The GENERAL MAGAZINE AND IMPARTIAL REVIEW: A Southern Magazine in the Eighteenth Century." SOUTHERN LITERARY REVIEW 11 (Spring 1979) : 66-77.

Brief overview of Southern periodicals in the eighteenth century, with in-depth discussion of the two extant issues of the GENERAL MAGAZINE, 1798, printed in Baltimore.

Chapter 10

PUBLISHING AND PUBLISHERS

900 Alexander, Charles P. "EBONY'S Man: John Johnson Keeps Running." TIME 126 (December 9, 1985) : 68.

Millionaire publisher of EBONY has launched a magazine of fashionable living for black men, EM: EBONY MAN. Comments on Johnson's syndicated tv show, his management style, and the founding of EBONY.

901 Alter, Jennifer, and Merrion, Paul. "Can New Hefner Rebuild Empire?" ADVERTISING AGE 53 (May 3, 1982) : 2+.

Christie Hefner assumes presidency of Playboy Enterprises.

902 Alter, Stewart. "Will Magazines Stand the Tests of Time Inc?" MAGAZINE AGE 2 (August 1981) : 52+.

Vice president for magazines at Time Inc.

offers four pages of salient facts about launches and motivations, reader orientation, etc.

903 Beam, Alex. "A Publisher Who Craves a World Beat." BUSINESS WEEK (January 14, 1985) : 32.

Bernard Goldhirsh, founder of numerous magazines based on his own personal interests and experiences, has acquired WORLD EXECUTIVE'S DIGEST. Brief description of Goldhirsh Group and plans for the new acquisition.

904 Blyskal, Jeff. "A Divorce Made in Heaven." FORBES 133 (May 21, 1984) : 80-81.

Time Inc.'s divestiture of Temple-Inland forest products company was a move to decrease Time's vulnerability to unfriendly corporate takeover.

905 Byron, Christopher. THE FANCIEST DIVE. New York: W. W. Norton, 1986.

Money and management at Time Inc., its mistakes, behind-the-scenes rivalries and ambitions, executive weaknesses. Company is described as "$2.8 billion collection of only vaguely related businesses." Editor-in-chief Henry Grunwald has criticized DIVE as untrue, distorted, invention-filled.

906 Canape, Charlene. "New Moneymakers at Hearst." NEW YORK TIMES, 6 March 1983, sec. 3, p. F1+.

Magazines now dominate Hearst Corporation, a major shift in corporate strategy during the past five years. Other enterprises include newspapers, book companies, television stations.

907 Chaney, Lindsay, and Cieply, Michael. THE HEARSTS: FAMILY AND EMPIRE--THE LATER YEARS. New York: Simon & Schuster, 1981.

Family biography from the death of William Randolph Hearst, 1951, to present. Brief references throughout to Hearst Magazines. Index.

908 "Charter to Shed Magazine, End Publishing Work." WALL STREET JOURNAL, 9 July 1982, p. 18.

Charter Co. has sold its last magazine, LADIES' HOME JOURNAL, to Family Media Inc. Other publishing interests sold to Time Inc. and McCall Publishing.

909 Cook, Edward Earl. "13-30 Corporation: A Case Study in Innovative Magazine Publishing." M.A. thesis, University of Tennessee, 1983.

History, growth, development of 13-30 Corporation, and its role in American magazine publishing. Based on interviews with corporate personnel. Early success depended on founders' knowledge of college market and that market's receptiveness.

910 Cooney, John. THE ANNENBERGS: THE SALVAGING OF A

TAINTED DYNASTY. New York: Simon & Schuster, 1982.

From unsavory beginnings created by his father, Walter Annenberg's rise to power and renewed wealth via TV GUIDE and SEVENTEEN are chronicled.

911 Danzig, Fred. "Hearst's Top Team Shapes Goals for Next 25 Years." ADVERTISING AGE 47 (February 16, 1976 : 3+.

Hearst management objectives will focus on profits more than ever. Biographical profiles of top executives.

912 Dougherty, Philip. "CBS Seeks Magazine Culture." NEW YORK TIMES, 10 October 1985, p. D19.

Summary of speech by CBS Magazines' president Peter Diamandis. He describes management changes in the organization, and the establishment of a College of Magazine Publishing for employees.

913 Ebert, Larry Kai. "Meredith at 75: Multi-Media Expansion." ADVERTISING AGE 48 (October 31, 1977) : 3+.

Profile of Meredith Corporation, with a strong historical emphasis.

914 Elliott, Stuart J. "Annenberg: At 76, He Remains Ahead of the Game." ADVERTISING AGE 55 (December 13, 1984) : 3+.

Biographical article on Triangle Publications' president-chief executive officer, Walter Annenberg.

915 Elliott, Stuart J. "CBS, Ziff in Magazine Tiff." ADVERTISING AGE 56 (May 20, 1985); 103.

CBS seeks financial damages from Ziff Corporation, claiming "financial misrepresentation" led to overpayment on CBS' recent purchase of twelve consumer magazines.

916 Elliott, Stuart J. "Diamandis Likes 'Challenge' at CBS Mag." ADVERTISING AGE 57 (February 3, 1986) : 35.

Peter Diamandis' management of CBS Magazines, including new titles recently purchased from Ziff. Lawsuit against Ziff dismissed December 1985.

917 Elliott, Stuart J. "Goldhirsh: The Entrepreneur's Entrepreneur." ADVERTISING AGE 56 (April 8, 1985) : 4+.

The Goldhirsh Group stresses small business and high technology magazine publishing. Brief review of several Goldhirsh titles.

918 Elliott, Stuart J. "NEW YORKER: It Won't Ever Be a Conglomerate." ADVERTISING AGE 53 (December 6, 1982) : 4.

Even though the New Yorker Magazine Inc. has acquired some new titles, the corporation will always center around the NEW YORKER, according to company president. A prophecy interesting in light of the NEW YORKER's 1985 acquisition by Newhouse.

919 Elliott, Stuart. "Rodale Press Getting in Shape for the 80s." ADVERTISING AGE 55 (December 24, 1984) : 4+.

Rodale Press' corporate philosophy emphasizing health, physical fitness, self-sufficiency comes in and out of the mainstream. Recent changes focus on reaching the young, urban professional in an effort to attract more national advertising and move into the mainstream.

920 Elliott, Stuart J. "Time Heads South for a Winner." ADVERTISING AGE 56 (February 25, 1985) : 1+.

Time Inc. buys Southern Progress Corporation, publisher of SOUTHERN LIVING.

921 Elliott, Stuart J. "Whittle, Moffitt Split 13-30, EMG." ADVERTISING AGE 57 (April 17, 1986) : 3+.

Phillip Moffitt will run Esquire Magazine Group, and Christopher Whittle will head 13-30 Corporation. Parting is described as amicable.

922 Emmrich, Stuart. "In Business to Stay: CBS Publications." ADVERTISING AGE 53 (March 22, 1982) : 54+.

Despite recent personnel and management changes at CBS, the company is committed to a future in publishing. Plans are underway for the revitalization and promotion of WOMAN'S DAY.

923 Emmrich, Stuart. "New Projects Stretch Time Inc." ADVERTISING AGE 54 (January 17, 1983) : 10+.

New projects, such as launching TV-CABLE WEEK, are raising Time Inc.'s debt to more than half a billion dollars.

924 Emmrich, Stuart. "On-the-Rise Goldhirsh Looks to High-Tech, Too." ADVERTISING AGE 54 (March 28, 1983) : 3+.

Brief recount of Goldhirsh Group's magazine publishing success. Plans for launch of a technology magazine.

925 Emmrich, Stuart, and Spillman, Susan. "Blending Risk-Taking with a 'Family' Atmosphere: The Combination Has Been Successful at Time Inc. --Usually." ADVERTISING AGE 53 (November 29, 1982) : M4-M5+.

Profile of Time Inc's management, with complementary piece on business assets and revenue.

926 English, Mary McCabe. "At Rodale, They Practice What They Preach." ADVERTISING AGE 54 (July 18, 1983) : M18-M19.

Rodale Press offers physical fitness programs and success incentives to employees.

927 English, Mary McCabe. "A Word Factory Runs its Message to the People." ADVERTISING AGE 55 (March 26, 1984) : M32-M33.

Profile of Rodale Press. Its special interest magazines have a direct and gimmick-free approach.

928 Fabrikant, Geraldine. "A Media Giant Loses its Swagger: Time." NEW YORK TIMES, 1 December 1985, sec. 3, p. F1+.

A corporate profile of Time Inc., with emphasis on its waning spirit of independence and risk-taking, and its nervousness in these times of corporate takeovers. Time Inc. develops new magazines on a reduced scale, and has begun buying existing titles. Time's top management for the present and future considered.

929 "Faces: Phillip Moffitt and Christopher Whittle." FOLIO 10 (August 1981) : 60+.

Profiles of Whittle and Moffitt, 13-30 Corporation executives, and their successful revitalization of ESQUIRE.

930 Fannin, Rebecca. "The Hotshots." MARKETING & MEDIA DECISIONS 19 (May 1984) : 62-65+.

Christopher Whittle and Phillip Moffitt of 13-30 Corporation, and their success in reviving ESQUIRE.

931 "A First at Time Inc." BUSINESS WEEK (March 11, 1985) : 46.

News brief on Time Inc's purchase of Southern Progress Corporation, and its foremost title SOUTHERN LIVING, the first magazine Time has bought.

932 "Fortune 500: Publishing is Best Total Return on Investment Industry." FOLIO 14 (July 1985) : 22-23.

Brief comparison of top eleven companies by 1983 and 1984 dollar sales and Fortune 500 rank. Indicates a 27.1 percent return on investment.

933 Gelman, David. "Success Story." NEWSWEEK 86 (November 10, 1975) : 54.

Profile of John H. Johnson, founder and publisher of EBONY magazine.

934 Gralla, Lawrence. "The Inside Story of the Gralla Sale." FOLIO 14 (November 1985) : 180-184+.

Gralla believes growth has accelerated but the business is otherwise little changed after buyout by United Newspapers of London. Details on planning, stock handling, pricing, employee and officer management over time. Thoughtful if rosy view of buyout.

935 Greenberg, Jonathon. "It's a Miracle." FORBES 130 (December 20, 1982) : 104+.

Personality profile of John H. Johnson, publisher and owner of EBONY.

936 Greenwald, John. "Auditing the Grand Acquisitor." TIME 122 (October 24, 1983) : 72+.

The IRS audits the Newhouse empire.

937 Grigsby, Jefferson. "Newhouse, after Newhouse." FORBES 124 (October 29, 1979) : 110+.

Corporate profile of the Newhouse family holdings, a $1 billion enterprise. With the senior Newhouse dead, how will the two chief executives (Si and Donald) handle the business?

938 Gutis, Philip S. "Turning Superheroes into Super Sales." NEW YORK TIMES, 6 January 1985, sec. 3, p. F6.

Profile of Jenette Kahn, founder of several magazines and now publisher of DC COMICS.

939 Hall, Carol. "Home to Work & Homes Working for You." MARKETING & MEDIA DECISIONS 21 (April 1986) : 24.

Time Inc. tries publishing controlled circulation magazines. Offers less risk, lower start-up and promotion costs.

940 Howard, Scott G., and Newton, Catherine K. "Hiring the Best People." FOLIO 14 (December 1985) : 90-95.

Three publishing companies explain their techniques for hiring better people more often. Cahners, Cardiff, and Hart suggest standardization of questioning, screening resumes against criteria of existing successful employees, checking references, and follow-up to verify performance of employees vis-a-vis procedures used.

941 Hoyt, Michael, and Schoonmaker, Mary Ellen. "Onward--and Upward?--with the Newhouse Boys." COLUMBIA JOURNALISM REVIEW 24 (July-August 1985) : 37-39+.

Lengthy background article on the Newhouse family and its publishing empire. Heavily oriented towards newspapers, some reference is made to the NEW YORKER and VANITY FAIR.

942 "Humbled and More Cautious Time Inc. Marches On." BUSINESS WEEK (February 13, 1984) : 62-63+.

Recent failures for Time Inc. include TV-CABLE WEEK, WASHINGTON STAR, teletext, and subscription tv. For the future, the forecast is for slow but steady growth, fewer risks, possible acquisitions of magazines, more specialized magazines. Lengthy corporate profile.

943 "Hutch Trouble: The Playboy Pays for Perks." TIME 115 (February 25, 1980) : 81.

Brief news item on the Securities and Exchange Commission's inquiry into PLAYBOY executives' compensation.

944 Janos, Leo. "Porn Publisher Larry Flynt Beats Drugs but Remains Unashamedly Hooked on Sleaze." PEOPLE WEEKLY 20 (August 1, 1983) : 30-32+.

Personality profile on publisher of HUSTLER magazine.

945 Kanner, Bernice. "More Expansion in Hearst Plans." ADVERTISING AGE 50 (October 8, 1979) : 2+.

Hearst Corporation plans growth in consumer magazine division. The magazine development unit often tests new titles by publishing them first as annual off-shoots of successful magazines.

946 Kanner, Bernice. "Rodale Patiently Waiting for World to Catch up With It." ADVERTISING AGE 51 (July 21, 1980) : 64+.

Rodale Press, the unconventional publisher, tries to attract mainstream advertisers. What makes Rodale different.

947 Kinkead, Gwen. "Mort Zuckerman, Media's New Mogul." FORTUNE 112 (October 14, 1985) : 190-192+.

Personality profile of real estate developer who bought ATLANTIC and U.S. NEWS.

948 Klein, F. C., and Laing, J. R. "Hotel Losses, Decline in Circulation Weaken Hugh Hefner's Empire." WALL STREET JOURNAL, 13 April 1976, p. 1+.

Playboy Enterprise's financial problems include competition from imitators of PLAYBOY, impulsive management, poor hotel investment.

949 Kleinfield, N. R. "The Big Magazine Auction." NEW YORK TIMES, 16 November 1984, p. D1+.

Sale of Ziff-Davis' twenty-four magazines.

950 Landro, Laura. "A Proposed Spin Off, Canceled Projects Mark New Era at Time, Inc." WALL STREET JOURNAL, 6 December 1983, p. 1.

Failure of TV-CABLE WEEK, cancelation of teletext, spin-off of Temple-Inland indicate management challenges for Time Inc. Vulnerability to takeover and pressure for profits prompt a move toward more centralized management.

951 Lee, Richard. "Many Faces of Mort Zuckerman." WASHINGTONIAN 20 (March 1985) : 140-145.

Personality profile of Mortimer Zuckerman, owner of the ATLANTIC and U.S. NEWS & WORLD REPORT. Speculation on his role in publishing the news magazine.

952 Lipman, Joanne. "Mort Zuckerman Seeks to Influence Opinion, Not Just Own Land." WALL STREET JOURNAL, 27 September 1985, p. 1+.

Profile of millionaire Mortimer Zuckerman, his business acumen and intention to become a journalist and opinion shaper. As new owner of U.S. NEWS he has named himself editor in chief.

953 Lukovitz, Karlene. "Publishing Management Structures." FOLIO 12 (May 1983) : 57-60+.

How six different publishing companies are run: Time Inc., Forbes, Gralla Publications, CBS Publications, MOTHER JONES, Bill Communications.

954 McClintick, David. "Reserved, Soft-Spoken Murdoch is Antithesis of the Papers He Owns." WALL STREET JOURNAL, 7 January 1977, p. 1+.

Profile of Rupert Murdoch, and commentary on

his planned takeover of NEW YORK magazine.

955 McManus, Kevin. "Two Crains in a Candy Store." FORBES 133 (February 27, 1984) : 94-96.

Crain Communications, publishers of ADVERTISING AGE and AUTOMOTIVE NEWS, has an opportunistic business philosophy that some say lacks long-term strategy. Brief paragraphs on major publications with emphasis on corporate management style.

956 Marcial, Gene G. "Are the Raiders Marching on Time Inc.?" BUSINESS WEEK (September 23, 1985) : 99.

Time Inc. executives say no, but others think Time Inc. is a takeover target. Some financial reasons why a takeover is possible.

957 Marich, Bob, and Levin, Gary M. "Hefner Eases Grasp on PLAYBOY Helm." ADVERTISING AGE 56 (April 8, 1985) : 6.

Following a stroke, Hugh Hefner will take a less active role in management of Playboy Enterprises, yielding to daughter, Christie.

958 Marshall, Christy. "Inventive Goldhirsh Finds a Profitable Formula." ADVERTISING AGE 51 (November 10, 1980) : 90.

Two new science magazines from Goldhirsh,

TECHNOLOGY (for readers interested in practical application) and HIGH TECHNOLOGY (for scientists).

959 "Meredith Corp." WALL STREET JOURNAL, 22 November 1985, p. 24.

Very brief news item: Meredith Corporation has agreed in principle to purchase LADIES' HOME JOURNAL and HEALTH from Family Media Inc.

960 "Mike Levy, Publisher of TEXAS MONTHLY and NEW WEST." FOLIO 10 (March 1981) : 55-56.

This lawyer-publisher is depicted as surrounding himself and running his magazine with "tough, mean, aggressive counsel." Personality profile of lawyer Levy and his successful publishing career.

961 Moore, Mike. "Time Inc. Takes a Dive." QUILL 74 (April 1986) : 30-32.

Management and money at Time Inc. Is the company "adrift ... on a sea of dollars," as suggested by Christopher Byron in his new book, THE FANCIEST DIVE.

962 Moore, Thomas. "Trouble and Strife in the Cowles Empire." FORTUNE 107 (APRIL 4, 1983) : 156-158+.

Cowles' financial decline is complicated by lawsuits and family disagreements. Known as found-

of LOOK magazine, Cowles currently owns newspapers and broadcasting stations.

963 Peter, John. "13-30 Corp." FOLIO 7 (September 1978) : 37+.

Pre-Esquire days of 13-30 Corporation, successful magazine publishing house formed by two students to publish youth magazines.

964 Potts, Mark. "A Media Empire in Trouble." WASHINGTON POST, 20 March 1983, pp. G1-G3.

Rise and fall of the Cowles family, owners of a loose confederation of companies, once a communication giant. Former owners of LOOK magazine, major holdings are now newspapers.

965 Prendergast, Curtis, with Colvin, Geoffrey. THE WORLD OF TIME INC.: THE INTIMATE HISTORY OF A CHANGING ENTERPRISE. Vol. 3, 1960-1980. New York: Atheneum, 1986.

Fact-filled, recent history of Time Inc. by twenty-three-year staffer covers a complicated period in the company's history. Time's response to the impact of television, climbing postal and paper rates, Luce's death, upheavals within their magazines including discrimination suits and a strike.

966 "The Pros Shrug Off Time Inc. Takeover Talk." BUSINESS WEEK (October 8, 1984) : 154.

Rumor of a takeover resulted in price increase for Time Inc.'s stock. Financial analysts were unimpressed by Time's prospects, and stock fell as rumors quieted.

967 "Publishing Hall of Fame Inducts 14 New Members." FOLIO 15 (January 1986) : 49-50.

Folio Educational Trust Inc. honors John Tebbel, Henry Luce, Robert E. Kenyon Jr., Bennett Cerf, and other magazine and book publishers in its second annual awards program.

968 Reichley, A. James. "How John Johnson Made It." FORTUNE 77 (January 1968) : 152-153+.

The success story of John Johnson, publisher of EBONY magazine. The article's style is dated, even when considering its 1968 publication date, but the information on Johnson and the civil rights role of EBONY are relevant from a historical viewpoint.

969 Richman, John. "What Business are You Really In? Lamco Communications Inc." INC. 5 (August 1983) : 80+.

Grit Publishing's transformation from a single-publication company to a growing diversified communications company.

970 Richter, Paul. "Jitters Mar Celebration at Time

Inc." LOS ANGELES TIMES, 4 November 1984 sec. 6, pp. 1-2+.

Time Inc.'s current financial picture. Magazine and book revenue at an all-time high, but HBO faces slow growth, new magazine ventures are risky, and depressed stock prices bring fears of takeover.

971 Ricklefs, Roger. "Emphasis on Efficiency at Time Inc. has Many Shaking in their Boots." WALL STREET JOURNAL, 12 February 1973, p. 1+.

The effects of LIFE's demise on LIFE staffers and other Time Inc. employees. Relevant from a historical viewpoint and as one of few articles written from the perspective of employees in a major magazine publishing firm.

972 Robinson, Gail. "The Guild of VOGUE." COLUMBIA JOURNALISM REVIEW 21 (November-December 1982) : 10-11.

Disgruntled Conde Nast employees call in the Newspaper Guild, and management responds with improved benefits.

973 "Rodale Reaches Out for the Mainstream." BUSINESS WEEK (October 27, 1980) : 85+.

PREVENTION and ORGANIC GARDENING have one million plus circulations, and Rodale is launching an aggressive campaign to attract big name national advertisers. Long-standing policy of refusing ads for processed food, alcohol, tobacco, and chemical insecticides will be upheld.

974 Rosenberg, Hilary. "Playboy Worn Out at 30?" FINANCIAL WORLD 152 (June 30, 1983) : 40-42.

Playboy's corporate problems include lost legal battles and "fading glory" of PLAYBOY magazine. While the magazine is still the mainstay of the corporation, the Hefners have high hopes for the cable-tv channel.

975 Rowan, Roy. "Intrigue Behind the Ivy at READER'S DIGEST." FORTUNE 109 (June 25, 1984) : 64-67.

Edward T. Thompson, READER'S DIGEST editor-in-chief, is fired in power play as death of owner Lila Wallace approaches. Deteriorating profits precipitated the takeover by publisher George V. Grune.

976 Salmans, Sandra. "Profits Again at a Shrunken PLAYBOY." NEW YORK TIMES, 25 March 1984, sec. 3, p. F1+.

Christie Hefner is turning PLAYBOY around, although revenues are only half what they once were. The magazine is still the focal point of Playboy Enterprises. Discussion of management strategies and revenue sources.

977 "School's in at CBS Magazines." ADVERTISING AGE 55 (May 7, 1984) : 76.

CBS College of Magazine Publishing is newly created to teach the staff of CBS Magazines.

978 Schwartz, Tony. "Four O'Clock Scholar." NEW YORK 17 (December 24, 1984) : 66-67.

Personality profile of S. I. Newhouse, director of Conde Nast Magazines, a part of the huge conglomerate owned by the Newhouse family.

979 Seebohm, Caroline. THE MAN WHO WAS VOGUE: THE LIFE AND TIMES OF CONDE NAST. New York: Viking, 1982.

Biography of publisher Conde Nast, founder of VOGUE, VANITY FAIR, HOUSE & GARDEN, and a portrait of the fashionably wealthy circles in which he moved.

980 "Selling Off a Magazine Empire." TIME 124 (December 3, 1984) : 62-63.

Sale of Ziff-Davis publications to CBS and Rupert Murdoch.

981 Seneker, Harold. "Where's the Growth?" FORBES 134 (December 31, 1984) : 30-31.

CBS will try to recoup losses in its overpayment to Ziff-Davis by depreciating intangible assets, particularly subscription lists, on its tax return. Slow growth in most of CBS' major businesses explains the interest in the Ziff-Davis magazines, viewed as profitable specialized titles, of interest to advertisers in reaching specific target audiences.

982 Sloan, Pat. "Fairchild Legend Wears Well." ADVERTISING AGE 55 July 19, 1984 : 3+.

Profile of Fairchild Publications and its magazines, purchased by Capital Cities Communications in 1968.

983 Smith, Desmond. "Thompson: Media's Quiet Giant." ADVERTISING AGE 55 (May 14, 1984) : 4+.

American newspaper and magazine holdings of Thompson Newspapers Ltd., Toronto.

984 Sonenclar, Robert. "Despite its Troubles, TIME Still Marches On." FINANCIAL WORLD 153 (November 28, 1984) : 14-15+.

Economic commentary on Time Inc. includes the divestiture of its forestry products business, problems at HBO, TV-CABLE WEEK's failure, lagging revenues at DISCOVER. Problems are balanced with increased ad revenue and profits, and new leadership of the magazine development group.

985 Spectorsky, A. C. "13 Steps to Publishing a Successful Magazine." FOLIO 6 (October 1977) : 50+.

A list of thirteen rules for successful magazine publishing from PLAYBOY executive. Includes primacy of the reader, ethical publishing, leadership, flexibility, editorial excellence.

986 "Stalking the Captive Audience." SALES & MARKETING MANAGEMENT 124 (February 4, 1980) : 14-15.

Brief overview of expansion plans proposed by 13-30 group, a publishing house best known for special-interest student publications. Plans include purchase of ESQUIRE and publication of industry-sponsored magazines.

987 "A Switch in Partners for ESQUIRE's Owner." BUSINESS WEEK (January 14, 1980) : 32.

Foreign financial backers of 13-30 Corporation purchase of ESQUIRE magazine.

988 "Time Covers the Big One." NATION 240 (June 22, 1985) : 758-759.

Civil defense plans drawn up by Time Inc. in 1950 for the protection of employees and reconstruction of the business in the event of nuclear war.

989 "Time's Troubles." FINANCIAL WORLD 154 (November 13, 1985) : 8.

Problems for Time Inc. include declining HBO, poor reception from advertisers and consumers for the proposed PICTURE WEEK, an overhaul of DISCOVER to attract upscale readers.

990 Trachtenberg, Jeffrey A. "Nobody Reads the White Space." FORBES 133 (May 21, 1984) : 110+.

Brief profile of Syd Silverman and VARIETY, trade journal of the entertainment industry

991 "The Ups and Downs of Media's Big Time." ADVERTISING AGE 54 (June 27, 1983) : M10+.

A multi-page directory of the hundred largest U.S. media companies, with narrative and list of holdings. Includes many magazine publishers.

992 Vespa, Mary, and Wohlfert-Wohlberg, Lee. "Talk of the Town." PEOPLE 23 (March 25, 1985) : 87-88.

Personality profile of S. I. Newhouse on the occasion of his purchase of the NEW YORKER.

993 "WASHINGTON POST: New Ventures Get Off to an Uncertain Start." BUSINESS WEEK (September 22, 1980) : 64+.

Profile of the Washington Post Co., with mention of its failed magazine INSIDE SPORTS, its proposed magazine FOCUS, and NEWSWEEK.

994 Weisberg, Louis. "Peterson's Aim is Right on Target." ADVERTISING AGE 55 (July 26, 1984) : 13.

Profile of Peterson Publishing. Circulation for its fifteen specialized titles (e.g., HOT ROD TEEN, MOTOR TREND) focuses on newsstand sales.

995 "Why Does George Holmes Keep Winning Awards?: Jewelers' Circular-Keystone Editor-in-Chief Holds a Record." FOLIO 14 (March 1985) : 61-63+.

This magazine is interested in covering crucial issues in the jewelry business instead of pleasing advertisers. Editor Holmes offers readers thorough, informative journalism.

996 Williams, Winston. "EBONY Publisher Rebuilds Empire." NEW YORK TIMES, 4 December 1982, p. 35+.

Financial problems for John H. Johnson, EBONY publisher, seem resolved. Further diversification planned.

997 Zoglin, Richard. "New Additions, Southern Style." TIME 125 (March 4, 1985) : 72.

Time Inc. buys SOUTHERN LIVING magazine.

Chapter 11

BUSINESS OF MAGAZINES

998 "Adding Regional Flavor." ADVERTISING AGE 54 (May 2, 1983) : M22.

SOUTHERN LIVING's traveling cooking school is its most successful promotion technique.

999 "Advertisers Do Not Subsidize Lower Prices." USA TODAY 3 (August 1982) : 14.

Brief summary of Vincent Norris' study of the relation between cover prices and advertising pages. Published in JOURNALISM QUARTERLY 1982. See entry 1080.

1000 Alter, Jennifer. "4 A's Joins Quest for Demographic Audit." ADVERTISING AGE 52 (November 9, 1981) : 2+.

Coalition of advertising agencies press for ABC audit of demographic editions.

1001 Angelo, Jean. "Ad Sales Directors' Average Earnings: $81,287." FOLIO 15 (April 1986) : 86-94.

Extensive survey analysis of ad sales compensation.

1002 Angelo, Jean. "1986 Editorial Salary Survey." FOLIO 15 (May 1986) : 76-82+.

Editors average salary $52,000+. Detailed breakdown covers ten pages.

1003 Butrick, Frank M. "Managing the Privately-Owned Magazine." FOLIO 10 (August 1981) : 94+.

How to develop with, manage, and maintain a privately-owned magazine publishing company.

1004 Carlson, Walter. "Budgeting: A Matter of Style." FOLIO 13 (July 1984) : 56-58+.

Publishers and consultants discuss budgeting in the magazine business. Includes various approaches and the steps taken in the budgeting process, without specific, complete examples.

1005 Carlson, Walter. "Single-Copy Options for Small Magazines." FOLIO 13 (July 1984) : 81-82+.

Experiences of seven small magazines in creating distribution routes for single-copy sales.

1006 Chase, Dennis. "Overseas Licensing Growing." ADVERTISING AGE 55 (April 23, 1984) : 55-56.

In the face of dwindling U.S. magazine profitability, many consumer magazine publishers are selling overseas.

1007 Cleaver, Joanne. "Magazines Rack Up Newsstand Sales." ADVERTISING AGE 55 (March 26, 1984) : M38-M39.

Special interest publishers are trying to break into single-copy sales. Chain bookstores and stores selling products related to the magazine's subject provide attractive outlets.

1008 Compaine, Benjamin M. THE BUSINESS OF CONSUMER MAGAZINES. White Plains, N.Y.: Knowledge Industry Publications, 1982.

One of the best books available on the business of magazines. Concise and heavily documented with statistical evidence and examples. Covers all phases of magazine publishing, from circulation to audience research, from group ownership to the size and structure of the industry, from advertising to production. Compares special interest and general interest magazines. Appendix includes profiles of major publishing houses.

1009 Cox, Meg. "ESQUIRE Magazine Principals will End their Partnership." WALL STREET JOURNAL, 4 April 1986, p. 18.

Whittle and Moffitt end their partnership amicably. Moffitt will remain ESQUIRE's chief executive officer and editor in chief, while Whittle will take over 13-30 Corporation.

1010 "Distribution Tests of Magazines Show U.S. Mail Costs Less." WALL STREET JOURNAL, 22 August 1975, p. 4.

In response to rising postal rates, magazines experiment with alternate delivery. Methods work fine, but cost more than mail service.

1011 Dougherty, Philip H. "New Color in LIFE's Campaign." NEW YORK TIMES, 24 December 1982, p. D4.

LIFE plans an advertising campaign to attract advertisers.

1012 Elliott, Stuart J. "It's in the Cards and the Cards and the Cards." ADVERTISING AGE 55 (April 9, 1984) : 14+.

Humorous article about magazine blow-in cards by AA'S magazine reporter.

1013 Elliott, Stuart J. "Magazines React to Single-Copy Sales Slump." ADVERTISING AGE 56 (March 4, 1985) : 66.

Commentary on 1984 circulation statistics from the Audit Bureau of Circulations.

1014 Elliott, Stuart J. "Pressure Finally Gets to SCIENTIFIC AMERICAN." ADVERTISING AGE 57 (April 7, 1986) : 79.

SCIENTIFIC AMERICAN is up for sale due to decreased advertising, business-side turnover. Seeks to avoid unfriendly takeover. As of July 1986, the German firm, Verlagsguppe Georg von Holtzbrinck, had agreed to buy it for $52.6 million. See also NEW YORK TIMES, 4 July 1986, p. 31+.

1015 "Experts Say Strategy for WOMAN'S WORLD Could Work--With $$$." FOLIO 10 (April 1981) : 8.

WOMAN'S WORLD is relying on newsstand sales not advertising sales as its initial revenue source.

1016 Fabrikant, Geraldine. "Magazine Madness: The Story Behind the Buyout Binge." BUSINESS WEEK (March 18, 1985) : 149-150.

Some of the reasons why magazine properties are popular corporate acquisitions.

1017 Farrar, Ray. "Understanding Single-Copy Distribution." FOLIO 13 (July 1984) : 64-67+.

Explanation of how the newsstand distribution system works from the viewpoint of the national distributor.

1018 Fischer, Jim. "Exploring In-House Fulfillment." FOLIO 12 (September 1983) : 102+.

The pros and cons for the magazine publisher on handling fulfillment within the company or hiring an outside firm.

1019 FOLIO: THE MAGAZINE FOR MAGAZINE MANAGEMENT. THE HANDBOOK FOR MAGAZINE PUBLISHING. 2d ed. New Canaan, Conn.: Folio Publishing Corp., 1983.

Unlike the loose-leaf first edition, the second edition is hardcover and bound. An exhaustive 790-page volume of reprinted articles selected from the magazine, 1972-1983. Subdivided into thirteen sections including advertising, printing, management, editorial. Each section contains from one to three dozen reprints. Also includes brief biographies of contributors.

1020 Forsyth, David P. "A Basic Guide to Magazine Research." FOLIO 10 (February 1981) : 44-46+.

Excellent, lengthy outline of the types and uses of magazine research. Includes advertising, audience, circulation, editorial, and new publication feasibility research.

1021 Foster, David H. "Circulation Battle Plan." FOLIO 13 (June 1984) : 66+.

Circulation strategies are important in determining a magazine's success and failure. Lengthy overview of circulation includes the pros and cons of large circulations, challenge of mature magazines, and the relationship between circulation and advertising.

1022 Foster, David H. "Circulation Pricing Strategies." FOLIO 12 (September 1983) : 89-90+.

Excellent discussion of magazine pricing. Importance of balancing price in relation to subscribers, single-copy buyers, advertisers, and company profit requirements.

1023 Foster, David H. "Setting Circulation Goals." FOLIO 12 (March 1983) : 135-140.

Various approaches to setting financial and marketing goals for magazine circulation. An important consideration is the magazine's position along its life cycle continuum.

1024 Galante, Steven P. "European Publishers See U.S. Magazine Industry as a Growth Market, but a Tricky One to Conquer." WALL STREET JOURNAL, 13 June 1985, p. 35.

European publishers are interested in the U.S. magazine market, but face problems getting their publications on the shelves.

1025 Gloede, William. "Media Properties Hot Items." ADVERTISING AGE 55 (July 23, 1984) : 6.

Media broker discusses trend in sales of media

companies. Magazine properties are in demand, especially those aimed at specialized audiences.

1026 Goodwin, Betty. "L.A.'s Newsstands Cater to a Wordly Appetite." LOS ANGELES TIMES, 6 July 1984, sec. 5, p. 1+.

Newsstands offer magazines, in a wide variety of topics, reflecting the growing sophistication of readers.

1027 Grossman, Gordon. "Circulation Management: An Art or a Science?" DIRECT MARKETING 45 (September 1982) : 68+.

Circulation management is both art and science. Its art is salesmanship and simplification. Its science is understanding of statistics. Categories and techniques of different circulation approaches listed.

1028 Hall, Lee Boaz. "Foreign Editions: Look Before You License." FOLIO 11 (April 1982) : 85-87.

Pros and cons of selling American magazines abroad.

1029 Hall, Peter. "Media Madness." FINANCIAL WORLD (April 17-30, 1985) : 12-18+.

Lengthy, corporation by corporation analysis of the wave of media mergers and acquisitions in the communications industry. CBS and Time Inc. are major magazine publishers mentioned.

1030 Helming, Ann. "Advice--For a Price." ADVERTISING AGE 53 (October 25, 1982) : M32+.

Advantages and duties of magazine consultants.

1031 Herrera, Frank. "The Shifting Single-Copy Market-Place." FOLIO 11 (July 1982) : 83-87.

Trends in single-copy sales. Charts illustrating sales by retail outlet type and single-copy expenses included.

1032 Hoffman, Jerome. "The Third Way: Combining In-House and Outside Fulfillment." FOLIO 13 (February 1984) : 64+.

How to best handle fulfillment--servicing customer requests and getting magazines to subscribers on time.

1033 Howland, Jennifer. "National Distributors: Scanning the Future." FOLIO 14 (February 1985) : 69-76.

Lengthy discussion of magazine distribution covers the roles of national distributors and publishers, marketplace trends, technological advances.

1034 "Independent Booksellers Rate Magazines." FOLIO 12 (February 1983) : 33.

PUBLISHERS WEEKLY survey reports booksellers' attitudes about sale of magazines in bookstores.

1035 Jones, Alex S. "Circulation Bureau Under Fire." NEW YORK TIMES, 27 December 1983, sec D, pp. 1-2.

Current problems and criticism of ABC range from faked circulation reports to demand for broader audience analysis.

1036 Kanabayashi, Masayoshi. "U.S.-Supported Magazine Ventures Try to Crack Tough Japanese Market." WALL STREET JOURNAL, 10 October 1984, p. 36.

NEWSWEEK begins Japanese edition, and ASPECT, U.S.-backed spinoff of INC., will also enter the Japanese market.

1037 Kanner, Bernice. "Inside a Deal: Brokering a Magazine." NEW YORK 17 (June 4, 1984) : 20+.

How a broker handles the negotiations for the sale of a magazine publishing company.

1038 Kanner, Bernice. "Magazine Land." NEW YORK 18 (January 28, 1985) : 19-21.

Where to find 2500-3000 magazine titles for sale in one place--the Pan Am Building off Grand

Central Station in New York City. Description of the 1200-square-foot newsstand, how many and which titles it sells.

1039 Kaufman, Lionel. "Are Our Print Media Going Global?" MARKETING & MEDIA DECISIONS 19 (December 1984) : 70+.

Overseas editions of American magazines primarily aim for affluent audiences.

1040 Kaufman, Lionel. "1984's Magazine Circulation Picture." MARKETING & MEDIA DECISIONS 19 (October 1984) : 148+.

1984 circulation trends for leading consumer and special interest magazines.

1041 Kleiner, Art. "The Secret World of Magazine Mailing Lists." CO-EVOLUTION QUARTERLY 33 (Spring 1982) : 143-144.

Approximately 95 percent of U.S. magazines rent their subscriber lists. Informal survey reviews some which do and some which don't rent their lists, to whom, and for how much.

1042 Kleinfield, N. R. "Busy Pan Am Newsstand." NEW YORK TIMES, 18 June 1984, sec. D, p. 1+.

Newsstand in New York City Pan Am Building, centered in the advertising world, is busy and sensitive to national trends.

1043 Klingel, John D. "Circulation Reporting Methods." FOLIO 11 (March 1982) : 94-97+.

Maintaining control of financial and physical distribution operations. Trend-spotting and the finalities of report preparation. Examples.

1044 Klingel, John D. "The Long-Range Profits in Single-Copy Sales." FOLIO 13 (August 1984) : 126-127.

Maximizing profits from newsstand sales allows decreasing expenses to obtain new subscriptions. When planning circulation, consider the net cost of obtaining each reader.

1045 Knoll, Erwin. "Some Call it Junk." PROGRESSIVE 48 (December 1984) : 4.

Editorial explaining the importance of direct-mail solicitations (otherwise known as junk) to magazines like the PROGRESSIVE.

1046 Kobak, James B. "Economics of Magazine Circulation." MARKETING & MEDIA DECISIONS 17 (Fall 1982) : 57-58+.

Methods and costs of obtaining subscriptions and the relationship of advertising rates to circulation.

1047 Kobak, James B. "Getting the Most from Outside

Professionals." FOLIO SUPPLIERS 12 (May 1983) : 207-208+.

Types of consultants available to magazine staff, and how their services can be used.

1048 Kobak, James B. "1984: A Billion Dollar Year for Acquisitions." FOLIO 14 (April 1985) : 82-95.

Magazine consultant discusses current high prices for magazine properties, the difficulties of valuing them, and the influence of the "glamour factor." Individual magazine sales of 1984 are analyzed, including the Ziff-Davis and U.S. NEWS & WORLD REPORT sales.

1049 Kobak, James B. "Subscriptions vs. Single Copy Sales." FOLIO 7 (November 1978) : 42-44.

Major factors to consider when determining where to sell magazines.

1050 Kobak, James B. "What's So Bad About Conglomerates, Anyway?" FOLIO 9 (May 1980) : 72-74.

Item by item rebuttal to BUSINESS WEEK editor's attack on the growth of conglomerates.

1051 Koff, Richard M. "The Compleat Strategist: Balancing Revenue Streams." FOLIO 8 (December 1979) : 53-57.

The interrelationships between newsstand, subscription, and advertising revenues.

1052 Lande, Melissa. "Choosing a National Distributor." FOLIO SUPPLIERS 12 (May 1983) : 199-200+.

The role of the national distributor and what a publisher should look for in choosing one. Reprinted from FOLIO 9 (July 1980) : 56+.

1053 Lande, Melissa. "Striving for Efficiency in Single Copy Sales." FOLIO 10 (July 1981) : 53-54+.

Problems and waste in single-copy sales.

1054 LeRoux, Margaret. "Magazines Coax Subscribers with Contests." ADVERTISING AGE 54 (May 2, 1983) : M20+.

Direct mail promotions are often used to increase magazine circulation. Many use contests and prizes as lures.

1055 Love, Barbara. "The FOLIO Editorial Salary Survey." FOLIO 11 (August 1982) : 88-90+.

Ten-page review of editorial salaries. Interesting definitions of tasks as assigned by titles. Covers business and consumer magazines, art directors, top editors of several levels.

Useful for comparison with other FOLIO salary surveys. See also entries 1002 and 1062.

1056 Love, Barbara. "FOLIO Survey of Magazine Research." FOLIO 10 (February 1981) : 54+.

Survey report based on 583 responses. FOLIO found business magazines spend more on marketing and media research than their consumer siblings (70 percent to 6C percent). The average spent was 2 percent of gross income. Eight-page article consists mostly of charts, graphs, and statistics on costs, percentages, and responses. Eleven common research problems, and fourteen research types are listed.

1057 Love, Barbara. "Lessons from the '82 Recession." FOLIO 11 (December 1982) : 59-62+.

Management revisited with a recession twist since 1982 was a recession year. Covers all aspects from personnel and circulation to paper and printing contracts. Offers strategies for dealing with management problems during a recession and planning for the growth period to follow.

1058 Love, Barbara. "1981 FOLIO Subscription Sales Survey." FOLIO 10 (October 1981) : 63-66.

Offers statistics and graphs on varied circulation aspects. Suggests premiums as "very good," and itemizes fourteen problem areas circulation executives encounter.

1059 Love, Barbara. "Production: Who Gets Paid How Much." FOLIO 14 (January 1985) : 76-86+.

Survey of production executives and staff revealed those most highly paid were employed in the Northeast on large circulation magazines. Analysis of production jobs and salaries considers type of magazine, level of responsibility, circulation, job title, gender. Numerous statistical tables.

1060 Love, Barbara, ed. THE HANDBOOK OF CIRCULATION MANAGEMENT. New Canaan, Conn.: FOLIO Publishing Corp., 1980.

Chapters written by magazine experts and circulation personnel. Covers the basics of circulation management. Includes glossary.

1061 Love, Barbara, and Angelo, Jean. "FOLIO's First Circulation Salary Survey Reveals Circulation Director's Average Salary 68% Higher than Manager's." FOLIO 14 (October 1985) : 100-105.

Directors average $38,226; managers average $22,763. High salaries correlate with males employed on high circulation, audited magazines. Highest salaries also correlated with other factors such as region, bonuses, number of employees supervised.

1062 Love, Barbara, and Angelo, Jean. "1985 Editorial Salary Survey--Editor's Average Salary: $34,623." FOLIO 14 (July 1985) : 69-74+.

Offers salary averages and ranges by job title for editors (managing, executive, senior, associate, copy) and art directors. Breaks down data by gender, number of pages, consumer v. business, geographic region.

1063 Lukovitz, Karlene. "Cashing in on Renting Out Your List." FOLIO 14 (October 1985) : 106-114.

Mailing list rentals as a source of income. Four list managers discuss the problems and solutions to list management.

1064 Lukovitz, Karlene. "In-Store Service: Where does the Buck Stop?" FOLIO 12 (March 1983) : 143-147.

Although servicing in-store magazine racks is important for increasing sales, there is conflict over whose job it is.

1065 Lukovitz, Karlene. "Magazine Suppliers Look at the Eighties." FOLIO 11 (November 1982) : 131-132+.

Interviews with magazine suppliers of circulation fulfillment, computerized management systems, paper, direct mail marketing, and printing forecast industry trends.

1066 Lukovitz, Karlene. "RDAs: Who's Watching the Stores?" FOLIO 9 (July 1980) : 67-68+.

Lengthy report on the status of Retail Display Allowance (RDA) programs. Monitoring of displays is nearly non-existent, while retail display allowances are increasing. Records are vague about who's paying what to whom.

1067 MacKay-Smith, Anne. "Some Youths Who Hit Road to Sell Magazines Come Back Embittered." WALL STREET JOURNAL, 17 September 1984, p. 1.

Traveling magazine sales crew members report long hours, poor living conditions, pressure to perform, little money. Legal action against agencies hiring young people has been unsuccessful.

1068 "'Magazine Availability Crisis' at Airports: MPA." ADVERTISING AGE 55 (April 23, 1984) : 120.

Airport concessions are handling fewer magazines to make space for more expensive goods. MPA is fighting this move.

1069 "Magazine Merger Mania." ECONOMIST 294 (March 9, 1985) : 71-72.

Increase in sales of magazine properties in U.S. Forest product companies are being sold to pay for new magazine acquisitions. As magazine ad revenue increases, so do prices of magazines.

1070 "Magazine Publishers Go Where the Money Is." BUSINESS WEEK (October 5, 1981) : 31+.

ARCHITECTURAL DIGEST, TOWN & COUNTRY, VOGUE head the list of magazines aiming for affluent readers. More publishers are seeking high-income audiences.

1071 "Magazine Publishers' Romance with MBAs: Is it Fading?" FOLIO 12 (May 1983) : 6-8.

MBAs need not only business expertise but artistic feeling for magazines as well.

1072 "Magazine Sales Climb as More Supermarkets Include Bookstores." FOLIO 13 (April 1984) : 50-51.

Bookstores within supermarkets increase magazine sales.

1073 "Magazine Selling Chain Needs Restoration of 'Mom & Pop' Stores." FOLIO 13 (September 1984) : 44.

Magazines may be forced out of large chain stores and need new outlets. Director of Distribution for Hearst Magazines laments the passing of "mom and pop" retail stores.

1074 "The Magazines' Counter Attack." BUSINESS WEEK (March 29, 1982) : 170.

Magazines vy with each other and other products for the prime space near supermarket checkout stands.

1075 Marshall, Christy. "ABC Rejects Proposal for Demo Audits." ADVERTISING AGE 52 (March 16, 1981) : 6.

Audit Bureau of Circulations does not audit demographic editions. Controversy between publishers and ad agencies.

1076 "Mergers and Acquisitions Gaining New Attention as Publishers Seek to Expand." FOLIO 13 (November 1984) : 11-12.

As magazine profits expand, more publishers seek growth through acquisition of new titles.

1077 Milner, Rosemary. "Editorial Offers Increase Sales for Women's Magazines." DIRECT MARKETING 46 (October 1983) : 82+.

Magazine revenues may be substantially increased by selling carefully selected merchandise in the editorial pages of women's magazines. Tips for successfully using this practice are outlined by London-based Hearst Corporation subsidiary, publishers of GOOD HOUSEKEEPING, COSMOPOLITAN, and others.

1078 Montgomery, Philip G. "Preparing for In-House Fulfillment." FOLIO 15 (April 1986) : 110-115.

A step-by-step plan for selecting and implementing an in-house subscription fulfillment system. Considers changes needed in existing organizational structure and physical plant as well as training staff and testing new system.

1079 Morton, John. "The Price is Right (Through the Roof)." WASHINGTON JOURNALISM REVIEW 7 (April 1985) : 60.

Brief commentary on the prices for media properties, especially magazines.

1080 Norris, Vincent P. "Consumer Magazine Prices and the Mythical Advertising Subsidy." JOURNALISM QUARTERLY 59 (Summer 1982) : 205-211+.

Comparing cover prices and advertising pages shows advertising does not underwrite magazine production costs. Excellent analysis.

1081 Norris, Vincent P. "MAD Economics: An Analysis of an Adless Magazine." JOURNAL OF COMMUNICATION 34 (Winter 1984) : 44-61.

Detailed economic analysis of MAD magazine, based on publisher-supplied data, shows how a magazine survives without advertising revenue.

1082 Pace, Charles. "Second Class Mail Merger: Sorting Out the Facts." FOLIO 13 (June 1984) : 86-90.

Answers about the Postal Service's decision to

handle all second class mail in the preferential mail network.

1083 Park, Edwards. "Around the Mall and Beyond." SMITHSONIAN 13 (November 1982) : 29+.

A first person account of a tour of the subscription fulfillment facilities for SMITHSONIAN magazine, handled by Neodata in Boulder, Colorado.

1084 Pinto, Leonard F. "Short-Run Paper Buying." FOLIO 13 (January 1984) : 84-87.

Advice on buying paper, for publishers of small and medium-sized magazines.

1085 "Publishers Sort Out Ways to Bypass the Mails." BUSINESS WEEK (August 4, 1975) : 64-65.

Describes alternate distribution methods for magazines.

1086 Rankin, William Parkman. "The Evolution of the Business Management of Selected General Consumer Magazines in the United States from 1900 through 1975." Ph.D. dissertation, New York University, 1979.

Review of business management in selected eighteenth and early nineteenth century magazines. Changes in magazines circa 1900. Emphasis on business management of BETTER HOMES & GARDENS, LIFE,

SATURDAY EVENING POST, NEWSWEEK, THIS WEEK to the present. Dissertation later formed basis for book. See entry 1087.

1087 Rankin, W. Parkman, and Waggaman, Eugene Sauve, Jr. BUSINESS MANAGEMENT OF GENERAL CONSUMER MAGAZINES. 2d. ed. New York: Praeger, 1984.

Updated version of the 1980 volume which was based on Rankin's doctoral dissertation. The history, people, management, financial and business organization of five consumer magazines--SATURDAY EVENING POST, BETTER HOMES & GARDENS, NEWSWEEK, THIS WEEK, LIFE. Includes short general chapters dealing with early magazine development, corporate structure, management philosophy, sales, and marketing.

1088 "READER'S DIGEST Decides to Quit the Numbers Game." FOLIO 14 (November 1985) : 36-37.

READER'S DIGEST will trim 1.5 million "unprofitable" subscriptions from its rate base. Ad agencies said to approve. Drop to continue from 17.75 million monthly, yielding per issue circulation supremacy to TV GUIDE at 17 million.

1089 Reed, Robert. "Audit Bureau Makes the Numbers Count: But Some Question the Worth of What Prints Out." ADVERTISING AGE 55 (January 9, 1984) : M4-M5.

Audit Bureau of Circulations is seen by many as the foremost authority on magazine and newspaper circulation data. Recent allegations against the seventy-year-old organization contend poorly trained auditors allowed false circulation data to be accepted as truth.

1090 Reese, Diane. "Alternate Routes to Single-Copy Sales." FOLIO 15 (June 1986) : 86-93.

Some small and special interest magazines can't get the newsstand exposure they need through the traditional distributor-wholesaler system. Success comes by going directly to local wholesalers and retailers. Examples of magazines that have successfully created individualized alternate distribution mechanisms.

1091 Reese, Diane. "The Paper Chase." FOLIO 13 (December 1984) : 68-76.

Publishers discuss creative planning to deal with paper shortages, such as new sources of paper, trends in prices.

1092 Reese, Diane. "Revitalizing Single-Copy Sales." FOLIO 15 (February 1986) : 84-93.

How to improve lagging newsstand sales. Reasons for the slump include competition for reader time with growing popularity of VCR's and the pursuit of physical fitness, cut-rate subscription offers, competition for chain store space from other non-food products. Methods to improve newsstand sales include cultivating retailers, working with wholesalers, adapting covers to draw buyers, cutting prices, tv promotion, better retail display. Numerous examples.

1093 "Refund Offer is Seen as Good Way to Boost Newsstand Sales." FOLIO 13 (April 1984) : 48-49.

Discount coupons offered to buyers of GEO.

1094 Rhoads, Geraldine. "How to Sell a Magazine One Issue at a Time." SATURDAY REVIEW 54 (September 11, 1971) : 61-63.

Editor of WOMAN'S DAY discusses the importance of covers and other factors in single-copy sales.

1095 Richter, Paul. "Magazines Concerned as Store Sales Decline." LOS ANGELES TIMES, 22 July 1985, sec. 4, p. 1+.

The declining newsstand sales and high returns of unsold magazines that characterized 1984 continue into 1985. Publishers ship more magazines than they can sell to get better newsstand display even though it is wasteful.

1096 Riipa, Karole. "How IDs Assess Their Bookstore Business." PUBLISHERS WEEKLY 224 (December 2, 1983) : 48-49+.

Survey of local independent magazine distributors yields advice on selling magazines in bookstores.

1097 "Rock Magazine Pops out of a Vending Machine." FOLIO 13 (November 1984) : 66.

An innovative way to sell magazines.

1098 "ROLLING STONE: Direct Sales, Well-Managed, Pay in Specialty Outlets." FOLIO 9 (April 1980) : 32+.

Success of ROLLING STONE in selling direct to retailers, by-passing the normal distribution channels.

1099 Rossant, John. "Exporting a Racy Esprit to the U.S. Magazine Market." BUSINESS WEEK (December 10, 1984) : 60+.

French publisher Daniel Filipacchi is planning expansion to the U.S. He has terminated a contract with Playboy Enterprises and made a deal with Bob Guccione of PENTHOUSE.

1100 Schein, Eliot DeY. "Inside INSIDE SPORTS." FOLIO 11 (June 1982) : 126-128.

Direct mail promotion campaigns under two owners of INSIDE SPORTS (NEWSWEEK and Active Markets, Inc.).

1101 Scott, Ron. "Single-Copy Sales Decline: Is Editorial at Fault." FOLIO 15 (April 1986) : 129-130.

Reversing a decline in newsstand sales may depend more on revitalizing editorial than on devising new circulation strategies.

1102 Scott, Ron. "Why Single Copies Aren't Selling." FOLIO 14 (October 1985) : 187-188.

Lack of distribution control and fixed pricing are cited as cause of three-decade decline in single-copy (newsstand) sales.

1103 Scott, Ronald. "Selling Direct: Why Publishers Hesitate." FOLIO 13 (August 1984) : 114-115.

Disadvantages for publishers selling direct to retailers instead of using national distributors.

1104 Scott, Ronald T. "Short-Sighted Circulation Managers." FOLIO 14 (September 1984) : 114.

Balance needed between single-copy and subscription sales. Action on one side affects numbers on the other.

1105 Sherrid, Pamela. "An Out-of-Focus Image." FORBES 136 (September 23, 1985) : 181.

ROLLING STONE's image problem is not with

readers but advertisers. RS's new marketing campaign is trying to change advertiser perception of its average reader from "an aging hippie" to a "dapper yuppie." As music industry ads shrink, RS seeks auto, clothing, tobacco, liquor ads.

1106 Smith, Edward J., and Fowler, Gilbert L., Jr. "The Status of Magazine Group Ownership." JOURNALISM QUARTERLY 56 (Fall 1979) : 572-576.

A statistical description of magazine group ownership. A large portion of the magazine industry is controlled by groups, with 102 magazine ownership groups controlling 480 magazines.

1107 Solomon, Debbie. "Magazine Advertising Expenditures." MARKETING & MEDIA DECISIONS 20 (January 1985) : 76-77.

Discussion of how much money magazines spend to advertise themselves.

1108 Solomon, Deborah. "Foreign Circulation." MEDIA & MARKETING DECISIONS 13 (June 1984) : 100-102.

Listing of magazines with greatest foreign circulation.

1109 Strong, William. "Managing Non-Paid Circulation: Theory and Craft." FOLIO 11 (September 1982) : 125-127.

Useful and unusual look at circulation manager's job, and perceptions relating to non-paid circulation magazines. Discusses goals, efficiency, economy, sources, plans.

1110 Suhler, John S., and Lamb, David C. "Financial Performance Review: How Magazine Publishing Stacks Up." FOLIO 15 (February 1986) : 110-114.

Investment bankers analyze magazine profitability and growth over first half of the 1980s.

1111 Tebbel, John. "Time to Change Your Page Size." SATURDAY REVIEW 54 (October 9, 1971) : 68-70.

In 1971, magazines were decreasing page size to deal with increasing postal and production costs.

1112 "Technology Available to Commingle Magazines." FOLIO 14 (November 1985) : 27-28.

Postal savings may be possible by mixing titles in single bundles.

1113 "TV GUIDE to Expand its Role as Distributor." ADVERTISING AGE 55 (June 4, 1984) : 4.

TV GUIDE seeks single-copy distribution accounts.

1114 "Walden Bookstores are Finding Profits in Magazine Sales." FOLIO 13 (April 1984) : 47.

Selling magazines not only increases customer traffic, it makes money for the Walden chain.

1115 "Wholesaler Anti-Trust Questions." FOLIO 14 (March 1985) : 22-23.

Connecticut and Massachusetts are investigating single-copy distribution as possible violation of anti-trust laws.

1116 Wolaner, Robin. "The MOTHER JONES Renewals Mystery." FOLIO 12 (April 1983) : 92-94+.

Subscription circulation strategy at MOTHER JONES.

1117 Wood, Wally. "Circulation Marketing: Let Your Magazine do the Selling." FOLIO 14 (June 1985) : 78-86.

Using blow-in cards and other ad devices within the magazine itself to boost circulation. Techniques, goals, response rates, and graphics which pull in readers.

1118 Wood, Wally. "When the Magazine is the Client." MAGAZINE AGE 6 (April 1985) : 55-56.

Having the magazine INC. as an ad buying

client offers benefits and some problems for the agency.

1119 Zotti, Ed. "Sagging Sales No Laughing Matter." ADVERTISING AGE 53 (October 25, 1983) : M19+.

Falling circulation a problem for two humor magazines, MAD and NATIONAL LAMPOON.

Chapter 12

ADVERTISING

1120 Abbott, William. "Magazines in the Media Mix." FOLIO 13 (April 1984) : 137+.

Advantages of magazine advertising compared to advertising in other media. Campaigns of airline and cosmetics industries cited as examples.

1121 "'Advertorials' Gain in Share at FORTUNE, SCIENTIFIC AMERICAN." FOLIO 13 (April 1984) : 39.

Advertorials are increasing in importance as sources of magazine ad revenue.

1122 "Advertorials Secure New Advertisers, Attract Better Response." FOLIO 8 (September 1979) : 7-9.

Advantages of advertorials, ads that look like

magazine editorial material. READER'S DIGEST and WOMAN'S DAY are two magazines selling advertorials.

1123 "Advocacy Ad Seeks Direct Response." FOLIO 14 (June 1985) : 30.

READER'S DIGEST will carry advocacy ads which champion causes and attempt to influence public opinion. Up to one million readers are expected to return detachable postage paid cards supporting the ad's stance. Respondents' names and addresses will be sent to appropriate Congressmen.

1124 "Advocacy Pages: New Ad Sales Opportunity." FOLIO 11 (November 1982) : 34.

Advertisers may discuss public policy issues in magazines in advocacy pages, bought at advertising rates. Prediction that much future corporate advertising will take this form. NEWSWEEK offers an advocacy page.

1125 "Agency Studies Effects of Ad Clutter on Magazine Readers." FOLIO 9 (May 1980) : 8+.

Ad agency suggests clutter may reduce ad effectiveness.

1126 Alter, Stewart. "Leo Burnett's Pointed Views on Demographic Editions, Newsweeklies, and City Magazines." MAGAZINE AGE 2 (October 1981) : 36+.

More information about demographic editions and city magazines is being generated for advertisers than is being scrutinized. Cautions advertisers about possible "uncertain audience at premium prices." Five pages of discussion and statistics.

1127 Alter, Stewart. "Networking: One Way to Maximize Efficiency." MAGAZINE AGE 3 (September 1982) : 30-31+.

Magazine networks sell ads for several publications as a package. Networks vary, and may be composed of magazines from a single publisher (e.g., CBS Magazine Network) or of a single type (e.g., East/West Network of in-flight magazines). Discounts usually offered to benefit advertisers.

1128 Alter, Stewart. "Research on Eye Movement Shows Editorial Environment DOES Affect Ad Readership." MAGAZINE AGE 3 (October 1982) : 42+.

Report on Perception Services' readership research on ad effectiveness in COSMOPOLITAN, SPORTS ILLUSTRATED, PLAYBOY, PEOPLE. Editorial environment affects ad readership--best position is next to a dull page. Readership of different magazines and product ads varies.

1129 Alter, Stewart. "Shop Talk from WORKING WOMAN and the ATLANTIC." MAGAZINE AGE 4 (September 1983) : 76-77.

WORKING WOMAN accepts advertising for a catalog section through which products may be ordered via telephone. The ATLANTIC allows readers to order fashion catalogs.

1130 Anderson, Richard C. "Buy Magazines for their Heavy Readers." MARKETING & MEDIA DECISIONS 18 (March 1983) : 84+.

Advertisers should buy magazine space for the heavy, primary readers of the book, and direct their ads to this group.

1131 Anderson, Richard C. "Primary Readers are Better Customers." FOLIO 13 (February 1984) : 50-51.

Advertisers look at magazines as products. The buyer or primary reader, not the pass-along, is what most interests those advertisers.

1132 "Back to the Limelight." MAGAZINE AGE 6 (August 1985) : 8-9.

Editors review five years of highlight reports on the state of magazine advertising and offer forecasts. Varied, sometimes opposing, viewpoints.

1133 Baer, Laurel. "Changing Lifestyles, Changing Media." MARKETING & MEDIA DECISIONS 17 (August 1982) : 62-63+.

Tips for advertisers on reaching new life-style markets. The challenge is to relate people's life-style changes to their new magazine consumption habits.

1134 Barest, Bonnie. "Advertorially Speaking." MARKETING AND MEDIA DECISIONS 21 (January 1986) : 90-91.

The pros and cons of advertising supplements are briefly commented on from three perspectives: the magazine's advertising department, the editorial department, and the advertiser.

1135 "The Battle Over Positioning." MARKETING & MEDIA DECISIONS 15 (June 1980) : 66-67+.

Magazines are changing formats and adding good editorial to the back of the book, but advertisers still fight over forward position.

1136 Beardon, William; Teel, Jesse E.; Durand, Richard M.; and Williams, Robert H. "Consumer Magazines--An Efficient Medium for Reaching Organizational Buyers." JOURNAL OF ADVERTISING 8 (Spring 1979) : 8-16.

Comparison of effectiveness of television, consumer magazines, and trade magazines in reaching purchasers for organizations. Consumer magazines were found most efficient.

1137 Berzweig, Jay. "Magazines: Know Thy Reader." MADISON AVENUE 26 (January 1984) : 120-122.

The most important factors in the competition to attract advertising are editorial excellence and targeted readership. Advertisers select magazines related to their product area as well as for the lifestyles the magazines represent.

1138 Blann, Robert L. "The Influence of Background Photographs Upon the Evaluation of Magazine Advertisements." Ph.D. dissertation, Ohio University, 1978.

Comparison of advertising with and without product-related photographic backgrounds. Most highly rated were ads with non-related photographic backgrounds.

1139 Bohn, Joseph, and Maher, Philip. "Merchandising: A Way Around the Rate Card?" BUSINESS MARKETING 68 (May 1983) : 8+.

Controversy over Chevrolet's request for magazines to develop competitive merchandising plans to win their advertising business. Merchandising consists of sales support to advertisers beyond the advertising itself.

1140 Bray, Thomas J. "More Magazines Offer a Chance to Aim Ads at Specific Groups." WALL STREET JOURNAL, 17 March 1970, p. 1+.

In 1970, demographic advertising was a relatively new technique. Ads targeted to specific occupational and/or income groups appeared only in special editions sent to subscribers in those groups.

1141 Brown, John. "Affluenza: An American Epidemic Sweeping Upscale Magazine Advertising." MAGAZINE AGE 4 (July 1983) : 16+.

Tongue-in-cheek commentary on the trend towards advertising to an affluent market. "Seven stages of affluenza" defined and illustrated by seven upscale magazine ads.

1142 Campanella, Donna. "One Bad Sales Call Too Many!" MARKETING & MEDIA DECISIONS 20 (May 1985) : 106+.

Advice for sales representatives from magazines on their advertising sales calls.

1143 Campanella, Donna. "You Deserve a (Rate) Break Today?" MARKETING & MEDIA DECISIONS 20 (February 1985) : 110-112.

Magazine publishers tendency to negotiate ad rates without sticking to the rate card.

1144 "Catalogs Bloom in Magazines." FOLIO 14 (January 1985) : 21.

Pre-printed catalog inserts are a new source of advertising revenue for magazines.

1145 "Catalogs in Magazines: A Significant Trend? Answer a Firm 'Maybe'." FOLIO 13 (November 1984) : 75-76.

Insertion of preprinted catalogs in magazines.

1146 Chook, P. H. A. "A Continuing Study of Magazine Environment, Frequency and Advertising Performance." JOURNAL OF ADVERTISING RESEARCH 25 (August-September 1985) : 23-33.

Survey of two hundred companies on magazine research priorities by the Advertising Research Foundation.

1147 Coen, Robert J. "Price Increases to Moderate in 1985." ADVERTISING AGE 55 (November 29, 1984) : 11-13.

Forecast by McCann Erickson executive on advertising rates for all media. Magazines are discussed on p. 12.

1148 "Copy-Intrusive Ads an Act of Piracy." ADVERTISING AGE 56 (October 28, 1985) : 18.

Editorial from AA offers negative reactions to irregularly-shaped magazine ads. Editorial copy winds around and jumps over these "copy-intrusive ads." While advertising should be innovative, it should not damage a magazine's editorial credibility.

1149 Cunningham, Mary Ann. "Consumer Magazines and the Tobacco Habit." MARKETING & MEDIA DECISIONS 21 (March 1986) : 86+.

Banning tobacco advertising could force some magazines out of business. Includes statistical data on individual magazines' tobacco industry ad revenue.

1150 Dimond, Robert E. "Selling Special Sections." FOLIO 11 (April 1982) : 73-76.

Advertising supplements, advertorials, and section twos are special sections on one subject or advertising client. Emphasis on their profitability, and how to do it from ad salesman's point of view. Types of interested corporate advertisers listed along with twenty reasons for their interest. Editorial ethicists, "gangway!"

1151 Donath, Bob. "Researchers Put Old Numbers in New Packages." INDUSTRIAL MARKETING 66 (April 1981) : 84.

Computer services will allow advertisers access to years of ad readership data for predicting success of new ads and determining problems with old ones. See also p. 4 of this issue of INDUSTRIAL MARKETING.

1152 Donath, Bob. "Revenue Picture Bright, but Selling Against TV Still a Prime Challenge." ADVERTISING AGE 48 (January 31, 1977) : 22+.

Compares selling advertising in tv and magazines.

1153 Dougherty, Philip H. "Regional Magazine Optimism." NEW YORK TIMES, 19 April 1983, p. D19.

The City and Regional Magazine Association forms plan to offer group discount to advertisers.

1154 "East/West Network: Up in the Air?" FOLIO 15 (June 1986) : 67.

East/West Network currently publishes eleven in-flight magazines for airlines. Mergers and acquisitions with the airline industry could have a negative impact.

1155 Edelson, Alfred. "Advocacy Advertising: Issue Ads are Better, but There's Still Room for Improvement." ADVERTISING AGE 52 (March 30, 1981) : 47-48.

Corporate advertising campaigns improve advocacy ads. Some recent examples from magazines.

1156 Elliott, Stuart J. "Advertorials: Straddling a Fine Line in Print." ADVERTISING AGE 55 (April 30, 1984) : 3+.

The controversy, criticism, and appeal of advertorials. Advantages for advertisers are numerous, including high reader attention, removal of ad from magazine clutter, long life. Criticisms by noted media scholars are briefly quoted.

1157 Elliott, Stuart, and Levin, Gary. "Rate-Break Charges Shake Seven Sisters." ADVERTISING AGE 56 (August 19, 1985) : 2+.

BETTER HOMES & GARDENS allows discount ad rates in response to decline in ad pages, and faces criticism from other magazines.

1158 "Emerging Lifestyles: Give Them the Simple Life." MARKETING & MEDIA DECISIONS 15 (January 1980) : 74-76+.

Suggestions for advertisers on selling products to magazine readers who are trying to reduce their materialism and establish a simple life. List of magazines edited for the "voluntary simplicity segment" of American readership.

1159 Emmrich, Stuart. "Seven Sisters Pitch for Ads in Concert." ADVERTISING AGE 53 (January 25, 1982) : 2+.

Seven women's magazines will approach top package goods advertisers with a joint presentation designed to switch advertising dollars from tv to women's magazines.

1160 Endicott, Craig. "NEW YORK TIMES MAGAZINE Not Resting on Laurels." ADVERTISING AGE 56 (January 24, 1985) : 34.

NEW YORK TIMES MAGAZINE is redesigning back pages, adding a Part 2 magazine, allowing inserts and gatefolds to attract more advertising.

1161 Fannin, Rebecca. "Advertiser Sponsored Magazines: Custom Designed Targeting." MARKETING & MEDIA DECISIONS 17 (November 1982) : 66-67+.

Advertisers are distributing free high-quality magazines that subtly disguise their promotional objectives. Advantages are creating favorable corporate image, encouraging activities yielding greater sales, reaching best audiences.

1162 Fannin, Rebecca. "Consumer Magazines Ask for 7% Rate Hike." MARKETING & MEDIA DECISIONS 19 (Fall 1984 Special) : 59-60+.

Magazine ad rate increases for 1985 are less than expected. Considers the place of ad rates in the total picture of magazine economics.

1163 Fannin, Rebecca. "Magazine Blockbusters." MARKETING & MEDIA DECISIONS 17 (June 1982) : 66-67+.

Magazine blockbusters or multi-page advertising sections (including catalogs) have been successful as an alternative to television specials. They may be used to build company prestige, introduce new products, target specific audiences. Numerous examples.

1164 Fannin, Rebecca. "When Once is Not Enough." MARKETING & MEDIA DECISIONS 19 (February 1984) : 62-63+.

Some uses of multi-page ads and tip-in inserts. They avoid clutter and allow ads to stand out from competing messages. Aimed at advertisers seeking more effective use of magazines.

1165 Fannin Rebecca, and Poltrak, Terence. "The Magazine Rate Card: Build up or Break Down?" MARKETING & MEDIA DECISIONS 20 (April 1985) : 42-45+.

Lengthy discussion of rate cards and negotiating magazine advertising rates. Media buyers and publishers comment on pros and cons.

1166 Feldman, Sidney. "Advertorials: Impact at a Premium." MAGAZINE AGE 1 (May 1980) : 26-30+.

Definition and types of advertorials. Sources quoted believe advertorials do not debase a magazine's editorial product. Numerous examples.

1167 Green, Michelle. "Marketing: Magazines; Single-Sponsor Publications." MADISON AVENUE 26 (February 1984) : 68+.

Corporate-sponsored magazines offer an uncluttered advertising medium and a targeted audience. Some corporations publish their own magazines. Others hire publishers like 13-30 Corporation to do it for them.

1168 Grossman, Morton E. "Accurate Ad Sales Forecasting." FOLIO 13 (July 1984) : 75-76+.

Forecasting ad sales using background data and knowledge of economic trends.

1169 Grossman, Morton E. "Developing Research to Support Marketing Goals." FOLIO 14 (March 1985) : 95-102.

Research ideas and techniques outlined for magazine ad sales and marketing staff. Research is necessary for strategic marketing and ad sales. "You don't do research to LEARN something, you do it to PROVE something."

1170 Grossman, Morton E. "Making Your Research Into a Sales Tool." FOLIO 14 (April 1985) : 105-112.

Lengthy article on interpreting magazine readership data. How to use research as a tool in selling ads.

1171 Haugh, Louis J. "Magazine Merchandising is Sporting a New Look." ADVERTISING AGE 51 (November 24, 1980) : 44.

Fearful of losing advertising, more magazines are offering product promotion and merchandising, ranging from product endorsements to sweepstakes.

1172 Holland, Robin. "One Book ... One Advertiser." MAGAZINE AGE 1 (July 1980) : 28+.

13-30's single-advertiser magazines, designed to target specific hard-to-reach audiences. Editorial independence is considered important by 13-30 Corporation, as readers know "when they're being conned," and articles designed only to serve advertisers would not be read.

1173 Kanner, Bernice. "WOMAN'S DAY Offers Advertorial." ADVERTISING AGE 50 (June 4, 1979) : 8.

To regain lost ad pages, WOMAN'S DAY is offering an advertorial section. One critic asks: Are the ads properly labeled or will they be confused with editorial copy?

1174 Kaufman, Lionel. "How Effective are Advertorials?" MARKETING & MEDIA DECISIONS 19 (March 1984) : 70-71+.

BUSINESS WEEK is offering non-adjacent advertising space in special issues carrying staff-written editorial sections on computers. Professionals offer opinions of effectiveness of advertorials.

1175 Kelly, J. Steven. "Subliminal Embeds in Print Advertising: A Challenge to Advertising Ethics." JOURNAL OF ADVERTISING 8 (Summer 1979) : 20-24.

Experiment on the impact of subliminal mesages. Public news media are beginning to observe and report various types of subliminal techniques used in magazine advertising. Suggests lack of advertising ethics detrimental to ad community.

1176 Kessler, Ellen Terry. "Social Conscience or Self-Interest?" MAGAZINE AGE 1 (June 1980) : 26+.

Advocacy advertising by corporations in magazines grows more popular. Some examples.

1177 Kesler, Lori. "Little Guys Find Strength in Numbers." ADVERTISING AGE 55 (March 26, 1984) : 39-41.

Small magazines form a network to sell ads as a group.

1178 Kilbourne, William E.; Painton, Scott; and Ridley, Danny. "The Effect of Sexual Embedding on Responses to Magazine Advertisements." JOURNAL OF ADVERTISING 14 (no. 2, 1985) : 48-56.

Effectiveness of ads with and without sexual embeds (hidden pictures masked by distortions) produced inconsistent results. The male embed in a cigarette ad was ineffective while the female embed in a liquor ad was effective. Useful bibliography on subliminal embeds. W. B. Key's pioneering book is notable in said bibliography.

1179 Kobak, James B. "Rate Setting for Magazines." MARKETING & MEDIA DECISIONS 17 (Fall 1982) : 41-44+.

Magazine consultant lists and discusses the factors that determine ad rates and what publishers are doing to fight cost increases. Includes statistics showing magazine trends in number of titles, circulation, advertising.

1180 Laitin, Julie A. "Creating Persuasive Sales Presentations." FOLIO 13 (April 1984) : 76-81.

How to create an effective presentation combining your magazine's unique benefits with the special needs of the advertiser.

1181 Lehmkuhl, David C. "The Invalid World of Cost Per Thousand." MARKETING & MEDIA DECISIONS 17 (August 1982) : 92.

Another attack on the stereotype that CPM (cost per thousand) equals cost/profit efficiency. Such variables as long reading time, pass-along readers, and at-home reading are important in selection of magazines for advertising.

1182 Lieberman, Milton. "Edit/Ad: What's in a Ratio?" ADVERTISING AGE 52 (June 8, 1981) : 54.

Thoughts on the ratio of editorial to advertising copy in a magazine. Does it relate to the effectiveness of the advertising message or to the publication's relationship with its readers?

1183 Longshore, Spencer H. III. "Special Interest Magazines CAN Sell National Accounts. Part I: Laying the Groundwork." FOLIO 13 (April 1984) : 82-83+.

To sell limited circulation special interest magazines to national advertisers, sales staff must analyze the magazine, define the audience, understand the magazine's editorial position, and carefully select national advertiser(s) to approach.

1184 Longshore, Spencer H. III. "Special Interest Magazines CAN Sell National Accounts." Part II: The Presentation." FOLIO 13 (May 1984): 112-114+.

Factors to consider when planning and presenting a magazine to a potential advertiser.

1185 Love, Barbara. "Merchandising: 37 Creative Approaches." FOLIO 12 (September 1983) : 118+.

Lengthy discussion of merchandising as a way to increase ad sales by enhancing the value of the advertising page for the advertiser. Numerous examples of specific magazines' merchandising approaches.

1186 "Loyalty of Readers to Magazine Linked to Ad Effectiveness." FOLIO 13 (May 1984) : 33-34.

Reader interest in a magazine contributes to effectiveness of ads, say the results of Doyle Dane Bernbach study.

1187 MacDougall, A. Kent. "For Kraft Cheese, How About a Cow?" MORE 1 (November 1971) : n.a.

Description of various types of attention-getting ads.

1188 McFadden, Maureen. "BETTER HOMES AND GARDENS Serves Up an Advertorial that Cooks." MAGAZINE AGE 4 (September 1983) : 75.

Food advertisements offering recipes and photos simulate BH&G's cookbook format.

1189 McGann, Anthony; Russell, Judith F.; and Russell, J. Thomas. "Variable Pricing in Advertising Space for Regional and Metro Magazines." JOURNALISM QUARTERLY 60 (Summer 1983) : 269-274.

Investigation of pricing structures for advertising in metro or regional editions of national magazines found no pricing equilibrium within the industry.

1190 Madden, Thomas J., and Weinberger, Marc G. "The Effects of Humor on Attention in Magazine Advertising." JOURNAL OF ADVERTISING 11 (no. 3, 1982) : 8-14.

There is a positive relationship between humor and attention in advertising, but it is not independent of respondent's race and sex. Authors conclude that "audience effects confound the impact of humor."

1191 Maneloveg, Herb. "How Service Magazines Might Serve Themselves--and Their Advertisers." MARKETING & MEDIA DECISIONS 17 (May 1982) : 82+.

Criticism of the joint advertising presentation of the seven traditional women's service magazines.

1192 Mazzenga, Isabel Burk. "Single-Sponsor Issues--When are they Right for Business to Business Advertisers." MAGAZINE AGE 6 (June 1985) : 40-41.

Seven individuals offer opinions, problems, and solutions on sponsoring single issues.

1193 Meskil, John. "Long-Term Prediction for Magazines --Up." MARKETING & MEDIA DECISIONS 18 (May 1983) : 88+.

Magazine advertising is up because of target marketing, increased television rates, better magazine product, better magazine ads.

1194 Meskil, John. "Magazines: Taking a Hard Look Beyond the Numbers." MARKETING & MEDIA DECISIONS 17 (December 1982) : 83+.

Advice for the magazine advertiser on how to get the most for the money includes: establishing a closer relationship between editorial and advertiser, dominating without buying a two-page spread, using new publications.

1195 "More Magazine Ads Despite Newsstand Ills." BUSINESS WEEK (November 12, 1979) : 40-42.

A contradiction in the magazine industry--newsstand sales decline while advertisers increase magazine budgets.

1196 Moriarty, Susan Ernst. "Novelty vs. Practicality in Advertising Typography." JOURNALISM QUARTERLY 61 (Spring 1984) : 188-190.

Need for novelty in magazine advertising overrides need for legibility in attracting readers.

1197 "The NATION's Ad Policy." NATION 228 (January 27, 1979) : 68-69.

The NATION will accept advertising although views expressed are repugnant to those of editors. Advertising that impedes use of editorial columns will be rejected. Examples.

1198 Neher, Jacques. "Magalogs Latest Vehicle for Advertisers." ADVERTISING AGE 51 (November 3, 1980) : 10.

Department store retailers experiment with magalogs, a cross between a magazine and a catalog. Includes description of YOU, a slick fashion quarterly published for Des Moines, Iowa department store by Meredith Corporation, publisher of BETTER HOMES.

1199 Norris, Eileen. "Network the Bait to Lure National Advertisers." ADVERTISING AGE 56 (January 17, 1985) : 20-21.

Details of the City and Regional Magazine Association's Network Discount Media Plan.

1200 Norris, Vincent P. "Consumer Valuation of National Ads." JOURNALISM QUARTERLY 60 (Summer 1983) : 262-268.

Consumers place little value on the informational function of magazine advertising.

1201 "One-Sponsor Issues Attracting Magazines." NEW YORK TIMES, 29 January 1985, p. D1+.

TIME and NEWSWEEK, like many specialized magazines, find single-sponsor issues profitable. Difficult to avoid impression that the issue promotes a product and is advertising in editorial shoes.

1202 Orlow, David. "Before You Change Ad Rates ... " FOLIO 13 (April 1984) : 68-72.

How to set or change ad rates. What rate cards should look like.

1203 Orlow, David, and Grossman, Morton. "Secondary Research: Fast, Effective and Cheap." FOLIO 12 (April 1983) : 81-85+.

How to use research done by others for their purposes in selling your own magazine advertising.

1204 Ostheimer, Richard H. "Magazine Advertising During Recessions." JOURNAL OF ADVERTISING RESEARCH 20 (December 1980) : 11-16.

Reviews familiar theme that advertisers cut ad expenditures during recessions, and lag behind in raising outgo once profits improve again.

1205 Paskowski, Marianne. "Buying Media: How Valuable is VALS?" MADISON AVENUE 24 (October 1982) : 104+.

Values and Lifestyles Systems (VALS) segments consumers into types based on lifestyles and values. Simmons Market Research Bureau as of 1982 VALS-coded respondents in its magazine research report. Paskowski discusses how this data can be used by advertising buyers, its advantages and disadvantages.

1206 "Personalized Ads: A Trend in the Making?" FOLIO 14 (April 1985) : 21-22.

Personalized magazine ads that address subscribers individually appeared for the first time in recent issues of FARM INDUSTRY NEWS. Opinions of publishers and ad executives on this gimmick.

1207 "Picks Magazines to Bypass the Biggies." MARKETING & MEDIA DECISIONS 16 (September 1981) : 112+.

How advertising agency picks specific magazines to match individual needs, budgets, and character of advertiser.

1208 Pierce, Thurman. "New Values in Print." MARKETING & MEDIA DECISIONS 18 (March 1983) : 121-132.

Advertising executive assesses the value of consumer magazines and newspapers as advertising media. An overview of the print industry, suggesting it has never been healthier and detailing current trends.

1209 Rehm, Jack, and Rice, Roger D. "Magazines vs. Television." MADISON AVENUE 27 (September 1985) : 92-94.

A pair of articles debating the advantages of magazines and television as advertising media by

Magazine Publisher's Association and Television Bureau of Advertising presidents.

1210 Reid, Leonard N.; Rotfeld, Herbert J.; and Barnes, James H. "Attention to Magazine Ads as Function of Layout Design." JOURNALISM QUARTERLY 61 (Summer 1984) : 439-441.

Magazine ads which de-emphasize illustrations attract less reader attention.

1211 Reid, Leonard N., and Soley, Lawrence C. "Decorative Models and the Readership of Magazine Ads." JOURNAL OF ADVERTISING RESEARCH 23 (April-May 1983) : 27-32.

Academic study found male readers noted ads with female models more often than ads with male models.

1212 Rivinus, Willis M. "Ad Inserts: Where the Hidden Money is." FOLIO 14 (January 1985) : 110-116.

Profits accompany magazine use of advertiser-supplied inserts, such as catalogs or self-service booklets. Discussion of costs involved, profit potential, and how they are used.

1213 Roberts, Johnnie L. "Faster to Read: Magazines Carry Fewer Ad Pages." WALL STREET JOURNAL, 11 September 1985, p. 33.

Decline in magazine advertising pages is attributed to economic uncertainty, comparison with 1984 (a big year due to the Olympics), refusal of magazines to negotiate rates.

1214 Rosen, Marcella. "Rethinking an Old Medium." MARKETING & MEDIA DECISIONS 17 (April 1982) : 97-98.

Mass magazines are fighting to win share of advertising using regional editions and networks.

1215 Rotfeld, Herbert J.; Reid, Leonard N.; and Wilcox, Gary B. "Effects of Age Models in Print Ads on Evaluation of Product and Sponsor." JOURNALISM QUARTERLY 59 (Autumn 1982) : 374-381.

Age of models in ads did not affect consumer's product evaluation.

1216 Rotfeld, Herbert J., and Rotzoll, Kim B. "Is Advertising Puffery Believed?" JOURNAL OF ADVERTISING 9 (no. 3, 1980) : 16-20.

Subjects exposed to magazine ads with puffery retained more information. Forty percent believed the claims true.

1217 Schultz, Louis M., and Ephron, Michael. "Is Off-Card on Target?" MARKETING & MEDIA DECISIONS 21 (April 1986) : 146-147.

Opposing views on magazine advertising rate cards--should they be sacred or negotiable? Poll of M&MD readers (advertising and media buyers generally) favors negotiated rates.

1218 Shuptrine, F. Kelly, and McVicker, Daniel D. "Readability Levels of Magazine Ads." JOURNAL OF ADVERTISING RESEARCH 21 (October 1981) : 45-51.

Use of the Fog Index to measure ad readability in nine magazines, including SCIENTIFIC AMERICAN and FORTUNE. Ads in NATIONAL ENQUIRER and TRUE CONFESSIONS rated higher than ads in NEWSWEEK, NEW YORKER, and PEOPLE. No ads ranked higher than junior high level. Authors conclude advertisers do not adapt ads to readers' educational levels.

1219 Siegal, Sherry. "Research, Marketing Short-Changed." ADVERTISING AGE 56 (January 17, 1985) : 16+.

City magazine advertising network lacks believable audience research.

1220 Sloan, Bernard. "Did Apple's Big Bite of NEWSWEEK Pay Off?" MAGAZINE AGE 6 (June 1985) : 43.

Did "election-extra" issue sell MacIntosh for Apple? Answer, "maybe." Ins and outs of buying and creating advertising for an entire, extended-sale, special issue.

1221 Sobczynski, Anna. "Industry Experts Read Between the Lines: (Or, How to Assess a Magazine in 2500 Words or Less)." ADVERTISING AGE 55 (March 26, 1984) : M27-M29.

Advice from a panel of media executives on evaluating magazines for advertising placement. Deals with supporting new magazines, subscriber quality, negotiating ad rates, appraising ad performance.

1222 Stidger, Ruth W. "How to Evaluate Magazine Editorial When You Don't Have Time to Read." MAGAZINE AGE 6 (March 1985) : 51.

Formula for questionnaire alleged to allow advertisers to evaluate editorial without reading it. Useful rudiments pointed out. Take salt.

1223 Stoller, David. "What 15 Media Directors Say About Editorial Environment." MAGAZINE AGE 2 (April 1981) : 72+.

How some ad industry experts judge the context in which their ads might appear. Half-page sidebar on Bloom Agency experiment in such evaluation.

1224 Strickland, Donald E., and Finn, T. Andrew. "Targeting of Magazine Alcohol Beverage Advertisements." JOURNAL OF DRUG ISSUES 14 (Summer 1984) : 449-467.

Study of magazine advertisements, with attention to targeted audiences. Highest incidence of alcohol advertising in black, men's, and science magazines; lowest in women's and youth magazines.

1225 "'Subliminal Synergism' Attracts Advertisers to NEW WOMAN." FOLIO 11 (September 1982) : 34-35.

NEW WOMAN manager creates technique to attract readers to ad copy and ultimately sell more color ads. Involves harmonizing color schemes of ad page and adjacent editorial copy.

1226 Suhler, John S., and Lamb, David C. "Ad-Supported Media Grow More Robust." ADVERTISING AGE 55 (November 29, 1984) : 22+.

Assesses all ad-supported media, including magazines and business press, with data on revenue, income, and assets.

1227 "The Sunday Magazine Network." MADISON AVENUE 26 February 1984) : 102-106.

Executives of the Metropolitan Sunday Newspaper Network offer sales presentation to prospective advertisers. Network benefits stressed. Research indicates high reader involvement and advertising effectiveness in Sunday supplements.

1228 "Sunday Magazine Network Starts $1 Million Ad Campaign." EDITOR & PUBLISHER 116 (October 15, 1983) : 4.

Marketing plan unites Sunday magazines to convince advertisers they can reach 48 percent of adults in top fifty markets by using Sunday supplements.

1229 "Swapping Ad Space for Travel." FOLIO 14 (April 1985) : 27.

Bartering is a way to increase magazine advertising and cut publishing costs.

1230 Teicher, Jon. "Media Imperatives: What Is It?" FOLIO 5 (December 1976) : 35-37.

Description of media imperatives as a planning tool for advertisers, emphasizing the importance of advertising in both magazines and tv. Imperatives suggest heavy users of one medium are heavy users of other media.

1231 Thompson, Gene. "Business Media Can be Fun." MARKETING & MEDIA DECISIONS 17 (April 1982) : 98.

Buying ad space in consumer magazines is a different skill compared with media buying in business magazines.

1232 Vallence, Karla. "Does 'Subliminal Synergism' Trick Readers?" CHRISTIAN SCIENCE MONITOR, 28 October 1982, p. 6.

NEW WOMAN ties advertising to editorial through use of color, a new technique known as subliminal synergism.

1233 VandenBergh, Bruce G., and Bartlett, Nan. "Puffery and Readership of Magazine Ads." JOURNALISM QUARTERLY 59 (Winter 1982) : 645-648.

Reader attention unaffected by puffery in automobile ads from TIME, NEWSWEEK, and SPORTS ILLUSTRATED. Recognition increases as size increases.

1234 VandenBergh, Bruce, and Reid, Leonard N. "Effect of Product Puffery in Response to Print Ads." In CURRENT ISSUES AND RESEARCH IN ADVERTISING, pp. 123-234. Edited by James H. Leigh and Claude R. Martin Jr. Ann Arbor, Mich.: University of Michigan, 1980.

Overstated magazine ads yielded dissatisfaction with tried products. Understated ads yielded the opposite.

1235 VandenBergh, Bruce G., and Reid, Leonard N. "Puffery and Magazine Ad Readership." JOURNAL OF MARKETING 44 (Spring 1980) : 78-81.

Puffery and non-puffery ads did not differ in readability.

1236 Waring, Priscilla Alex. "Impact Without Impecunity: How to Boost Corporate Print Ad Effectiveness and Save Money." INDUSTRIAL MARKETING 66 (March 1981) : 50-52+.

Improving magazine advertising effectiveness. How the message is presented is more important than the information given. Effectiveness increased by using color, telegraphic illustrations, specific headlines, readable copy.

1237 "What's New in Magazine Advertising." ADVERTISING AGE 45 (November 18, 1974) : 108.

A description of various ad units and types.

1238 Wood, Wally. "Create a Medium." MAGAZINE AGE 6 (October 1985) : 46-47+.

With 150,000 prospective buyers for paint spray equipment, and largest magazine for painters at 14,000 circulation, ad agency creates magazine to reach target audience.

1239 Woodside, Arch G., and Ronkainen, Ilkka A. "Travel Advertising: Newspaper Versus Magazines." JOURNAL OF ADVERTISING RESEARCH 22 (June-July 1982) : 39-43.

Comparison of effectiveness of black and white newspaper ads with color magazine ads for North Carolina tourism. More readers of newspaper ads visited the state.

1240 Yardley, Jonathon. "Consuming Interest: CU Takes Umbrage at Ads." WASHINGTON POST, 6 February 1984, p. C1+.

CONSUMER REPORTS argues against use of their high ratings as endorsements in product advertising. An interpretation of Consumers Union motives.

1241 "Ziff-Davis Explains How its Network Works." MADISON AVENUE 25 (March 1983) : 116-123.

Ziff-Davis offers a sales presentation to prospective advertisers, stressing advantages of advertising in several of their seven male-oriented special interest publications. Ziff-Davis has since sold its magazines to CBS and Rupert Murdoch.

Chapter 13

LAW, ETHICS & CENSORSHIP

Law

1242 Abrams, Bill. "CBS-Ziff Battle is More than a Fight Over Money." WALL STREET JOURNAL, 23 May 1985, p. 6.

Disagreement and lawsuit over whether Ziff misrepresented the profits of twelve consumer magazines sold to CBS. For William Ziff, the issue is his personal honor.

1243 Aharoni, Dov. GENERAL SHARON'S WAR AGAINST TIME MAGAZINE: HIS TRIAL AND VINDICATION. New York: Steimatzky Publications, 1985.

Account of the trial, with careful review of TIME's reporting and writing method. Author feels trial's outcome vindication for Sharon.

1244 Alter, Jonathan. "'Between the Lines' at TIME." NEWSWEEK 104 (December 10, 1984) : 79.

Testimony in the TIME-Sharon libel suit raises questions about the editorial research and writing procedures used by news magazines.

1245 "Appeals Court Overturns Judgment Against PENTHOUSE." PUBLISHER'S WEEKLY 222 (November 26, 1982) : 9.

Brief news item on PENTHOUSE libel case. Though not labeled fiction, published article was too fantastic too refer to real person, hence no libel against the real "Miss Nebraska." Decision notable for its protection of fiction.

1246 "A Bad Case Makes Worse Law." TIME 109 (February 21, 1977) : 51-52.

Brief commentary on Larry Flynt, HUSTLER magazine, and the Cincinnati ruling against him in 1977.

1247 "Bad Day at Black Rock." TIME 125 (May 27, 1985) : 62.

CBS sues Ziff-Davis for misrepresentation of financial data in the sale of twelve consumer magazines.

1248 Bodine, Laurence. "Libel Suits: Their Effect on

Newsmagazine Editors." EDITOR & PUBLISHER 118 (March 16, 1985) : 48+.

Libel suits have increased editorial caution in sensitive stories, amounting to intimidation. Court cases have also focused attention on news magazine editing practices.

1249 Brody, Michael. "Landmark Press Decision Upheld; Court Affirms Award for Bad-Faith Suit Against BARRON'S." BARRON'S 63 (March 28, 1983) : 37.

Appeals court affirms bad-faith suit for BARRON'S in case of Nemeroff v. Abelson. Case sets legal precedent--financial journalists' routine industry contacts do not equal collusion.

1250 Burstein, Daniel. "I Dreamed I Saw Pol Pot Last Night." QUILL 70 (May 1982) : 17-19.

Unsatisfactory responses from the NEW YORK TIMES MAGAZINE on plagiarism charges against free-lanced story on Cambodia.

1251 Carley, William M. "CONSUMER REPORTS Libel Case Worries Publishers, Who Fear Another Setback by the Supreme Court." WALL STREET JOURNAL, 24 January 1983, p. 46.

Summary to 1983 of Bose v. Consumers Union. Bose Corporation sued CONSUMER REPORTS for its negative rating of Bose's loudspeakers.

1252 Carley, William M. "Ruling in CONSUMER REPORTS Case is Seen Providing Significant Protection to Press." WALL STREET JOURNAL, 12 November 1982, p. 39.

Appeals court overturned lower court decision against CONSUMER REPORTS. The magazine may have been guilty of imprecise language but not actual malice.

1253 Chapnick, Howard. "PENTHOUSE vs. Kodak: The Still-Open Case of Confiscated Color Slides." POPULAR PHOTOGRAPHY 87 (September 1980) : 83+.

Legal issues involved in PENTHOUSE's lawsuit against Kodak for refusal to return sexually explicit transparencies.

1254 Cohen, Barbara, and Rubin, David M. "Rancho La Costa: A Resort the Press Can't Touch." MORE 7 (November 1977) : 30-32+."

Background on the as yet (1977) unresolved libel suit brought against PENTHOUSE by La Costa Resort.

1255 Colford, Steven W. "The Pain of Libel Premiums: Small Magazines Hurt the Most." WASHINGTON JOURNALISM REVIEW 8 (May 1986) : 16-17.

As premiums and deductibility for libel insurance increase, so does editorial caution, especially on small magazines. The result is a "chilling" of magazine journalism. Magazines without insurance will become more timid.

1256 "Consumers' Union Wins Libel Appeal Against Bose Corp." WALL STREET JOURNAL, 5 November 1982, p. 10.

1257 "Courts Decision Protects CU's Research and Sources." CONSUMER REPORTS 45 (October 1980) : 587-588.

CONSUMER REPORTS not forced to testify about its editorial research in lawsuit between chiropractors and American Medical Association.

1258 Denniston, Lyle. "The Color of Your Money." WASHINGTON JOURNALISM REVIEW 6 (September 1984) : 19.

In Regan v. TIME, the Court upheld the law making it a criminal offense to print an exact reproduction of currency. Discussion of First Amendment implications of the decision.

1259 Denniston, Lyle. "In the Shadow of Sharon." WASHINGTON JOURNALISM REVIEW 7 (March 1985) : 52.

Thoughts on the Sharon libel case against TIME magazine.

1260 Denniston, Lyle. "Supreme Vindication." WASHINGTON JOURNALISM REVIEW 6 (July-August 1984) : 14.

Discussion of Supreme Court verdict in Bose v. Consumers Union, and the implications for future libel verdicts.

1261 "Disputed Ad Promo Upheld by Fla. Judge." EDITOR & PUBLISHER 115 (August 23, 1980) : 18.

Doctrine of fair use permits display of TV GUIDE cover in comparative advertising by competitor.

1262 Elliott, Stuart J. "TIME Fights Malice in Blunderland Image." ADVERTISING AGE 56 (February 4, 1985) : 3+.

Time Inc. may have won the libel suit brought by Ariel Sharon, but has its journalistic reputaation been damaged?

1263 Fields, Howard. "High Court Sides with Media in Libel Case." PUBLISHERS WEEKLY 225 (May 18, 1984) : 38.

Brief review of the Supreme Court decision in Bose Corporation's libel suit against CONSUMER REPORTS.

1264 "Free-Lancers Gain Wide Support to Eliminate

Work-For-Hire Contracts." FOLIO 12 (August 1983) : 37-38.

Under the work-for-hire provision in copyright law, free-lancers lose all rights and royalties for their work in favor of the party commissioning it.

1265 Goldfarb, Ronald L. "Does an Article have a Legal Right to Life?" COLUMBIA JOURNALISM REVIEW 17 (May-June 1978) : 57.

Does a writer's employer have a legal right to kill an article? An attorney's interpretation of the issue, which has not yet been decided by the courts.

1266 Gordon, R. L. "READER'S DIGEST Promotion Draws $1.75 Million Fine." ADVERTISING AGE 51 (July 7, 1980) : 1+.

READER'S DIGEST receives penalty for violation of FTC order against using simulated checks and currency in promotional mailings.

1267 Gould, Peter C., and Gross, Stephen H. LEGAL AND BUSINESS ASPECTS OF THE MAGAZINE INDUSTRY 1984. New York: Practicing Law Institute, 1984.

Update of 1979 volume. Covers printing contracts, circulation and distribution, advertising, trademarking of titles, acquisitions.

1268 Greenhouse, Linda. "High Court Sustains Ford Memoir Copyright." NEW YORK TIMES, 21 May 1985, p. 1+.

In using Ford's actual words not historical information, the NATION went beyond reporting and infringed copyright. Includes excerpts from the decision and news analysis.

1269 Gross, Stephen H., and Smith, Edward L. LEGAL AND BUSINESS ASPECTS OF THE MAGAZINE INDUSTRY 1979. New York: Practicing Law Institute, 1979.

Handbook for seminar offered for attorneys in the magazine industry. Assorted articles on various aspects of the industry, and background on applicable law. For most recent edition, see entry 1267.

1270 "High Court Vote for Press Rights." NEWSWEEK 103 (May 14, 1984) : 81.

Brief item on the Supreme Court's finding for CONSUMER REPORTS in Bose v. Consumers' Union.

1271 "In the Wake of Sharon vs. TIME." FOLIO 14 (April 1985) : 21+.

Analysis of the TIME-Sharon verdict and discussion of TIME's questionable editorial policies.

1272 "Is Your Magazine Title Protected?" FOLIO 12 (November 1983) : 7-8.

Trademark search is important before launching a new magazine. Trademark filing and first use of trademarked title also of prime importance, even above formal registration with government.

1273 Johnston, Harry III. "Libel and the Magazine Publisher." FOLIO 5 (December 1976) : 31-32.

Overview of libel law with reference to precedent-setting cases.

1274 Jakobson, Cathryn. "BARRON's Bad Boy." COLUMBIA JOURNALISM REVIEW 22 (January-February 1984) : 13-14.

Brief overview of lawsuits against BARRON's columnist Alan Abelson.

1275 Kretchmer, Arthur. "Justice for HUSTLER." NEWSWEEK 89 (February 28, 1977) : 13.

PLAYBOY editorial director Arthur Kretchmer may be offended by HUSTLER, but believes Larry Flynt's obscenity conviction ill-founded. This editorial is critical of the "community standards" doctrine in obscenity law.

1276 Kupferberg, Seth. "Libel Fever: Seven-Figure Awards are Giving Editors the Chills--With no Relief in Sight." COLUMBIA JOURNALISM REVIEW 20 (September-October 1981) : 36-40.

Deals primarily with newspaper libel cases, mentioning magazine cases only in passing. Discusses historical background of libel law, recent cases, and the "killing" effect they have on journalism.

1277 Landes, Robert N., and Roome, Katherine A Davis. "Magazine Acquisitions: A Legal Checklist." FOLIO 11 (November 1982) : 120+.

Aimed at large corporate buyers and sellers with the probable effect of increasing inquiries (and fees) to the legal community. Useful as a primer for uninitiated.

1278 Lankenau, John C. "Living with the Risk of Libel." FOLIO 14 (November 1985) : 170-176.

Protection against libel includes stringent in-house fact-checking, review by counsel, and libel insurance.

1279 "Libel: 'Megaverdicts' Have the Media on the Defensive." BUSINESS WEEK (October 29, 1984) : 129-130.

Analysis of recent libel cases against magazines, newspapers, books and consideration of the reasons why there are so many suits.

1280 Lubasch, Arnold H. "Magazine's Use of Book by Ford Upheld in Court." NEW YORK TIMES, 18 November 1983, p. 1+.

This decision in favor of the NATION was overturned by the Supreme Court in May 1985. See entries 1268, 1286.

1281 McGrath, Peter. "Absence of Malice." NEWSWEEK 105 (February 4, 1985) : 52-58.

Lengthy coverage of TIME's victory over Ariel Sharon. Discussion of the verdict, its implications for the press, and libel law in general.

1282 Margolick, David. "The NATION Ruling: News and the Public Domain." NEW YORK TIMES, 18 November 1983, p. 84.

This early decision for the NATION that copyright had not been violated was later overturned by Supreme Court May 1985. See entries 1268, 1286.

1283 Metcalf, Slade R. "Acquiring Rights." FOLIO 13 (May 1984) : 107-109.

Explication of various legal and financial rights for free-lancers, publishers, and employed writers. Work-for-hire agreements likely to diminish because they severely limit journalists' rights.

1284 Metcalf, Slade R. "Courts Getting Tough on Editorial Opinion." FOLIO 13 (October 1984) : 217+.

Review of court decisions on libel emphasizing the recent trend towards limiting writer's expression of opinion without fear of recrimination.

1285 Metcalf, Slade R. "Libel: Staying out of Trouble." FOLIO 12 (November 1983) : 70+.

Large 1983 libel awards have chilled reporters and editors as well as publishers and writers. The attorney-author argues that guidelines are needed.

1286 Navasky, Victor. "Now Courts are in the News Business." NEW YORK TIMES, 2 July 1985, p. 29.

Editor of the NATION comments on the Supreme Court's decision in the copyright case over Ford's memoirs. The Court ruled the NATION violated copyright law.

1287 "New Writers' Union Signs Contract With MOTHER JONES." FOLIO 12 (August 1983) : 38.

National Writers Union, founded Spring 1983, signed contract with its first magazine, MOTHER JONES, for protection of free-lancers.

1288 Phelan, James. "The Rising Price of Profs." COLUMBIA JOURNALISM REVIEW 21 (July-August 1982) : 16.

Journalism professors, called as expert witness for both sides in PENTHOUSE magazine libel lawsuit, gave contradictory testimony regarding the magazine's use of accepted journalistic procedures.

1289 "Publishing Attorneys Laud Supreme Court Ruling in Libel Case." FOLIO 13 (July 1984) : 5-6.

Supreme Court upholds Court of Appeals decision in favor of CONSUMER REPORTS. Appellate review in libel cases is essential in safeguarding First Amendment rights.

1290 Radolf, Andrew. "Hats Off to the Judge." EDITOR & PUBLISHER 118 (February 2, 1985) : 9+.

Libel attorneys praise verdict in Sharon v. TIME because it was delivered in three parts. The verdict established Sharon had proved only two parts of the standard--TIME's language was defamatory and factually false. Sharon did not prove TIME acted "with knowing falsity or in reckless disregard of the truth."

1291 Reid, Allyson. "Hispanics Find DIGEST Hard to Swallow." COLUMBIA JOURNALISM REVIEW 21 (November-December 1982) : 11.

Brief news item. League of United Latin American citizens charges the READER'S DIGEST with "defamation" and "benign neglect."

1292 Riley, Sam G. "Fighting Back: What Redress Media Have Against Frivolous Libel suits." JOURNALISM QUARTERLY 59 (Winter 1982) : 566-572.

The court's finding of bad faith and lack of basis for suit in Nemeroff v. Abelson, libel case won by BARRON'S WEEKLY, suggests ways for the media to fight against unfounded libel suits.

1293 Roberts, Eugene L., Jr. "On Collision Course." QUILL 73 (April 1985) : cover, 14-19.

Libel suits and their inhibiting effect on freedom of expression.

1294 Roper, James E. "Supreme Court Rules on Libel." EDITOR & PUBLISHER 117 (May 5, 1984) : 15.

In Bose v. Consumers Union, the Supreme Court ruled appeals court must consider issues of fact as well as law. CONSUMER REPORTS' victory is considered a significant libel ruling and a victory for the press.

1295 Rose, Robert L. "Investment Adviser Alleges Newsletter was Copied Illicitly." WALL STREET JOURNAL, 22 July 1985, p. 5.

Copyright infringement is the primary problem facing newsletters.

1296 Rosentiel, Thomas B. "Part of Sharon Story in Error, TIME Concedes." LOS ANGELES TIMES, 10 January 1985, p. 1+.

On Sharon's libel suit against TIME.

1297 Rosenstiel, Thomas B. "Sharon Loses Suit as Jury Finds No Malice." LOS ANGELES TIMES, 25 January 1985, sec. 1, p. 1+.

TIME won its case when the jury decided Sharon had failed to prove that anyone at TIME knew the story was false when it was published.

1298 Schardt, Arlie. "Who Owns the News?" NEWSWEEK 95 (March 10, 1980) : 86.

The NATION magazine is sued for copyright infringement in the early publication of Ford's memoirs.

1299 Schrieber, Norman. "The Copyright War Between Editors and Writers." WRITER'S DIGEST 58 (January 1978) : 18-21.

How free-lancers should handle editors in copyright questions.

1300 Schultz-Brooks, Terri. "The Copyright Con." COLUMBIA JOURNALISM REVIEW 22 (January-February 1984) : 33-36.

Free-lance writers need to beware of the way some publishers use copyright laws.

1301 Serrill, Michael. "When a Scoop is 'Piracy': The Supreme Court Balances Copyright Against Press Rights."

Review of Supreme Court decision that the NATION had violated copyright laws in publishing Ford's memoirs.

1302 "Sharon Case: TIME's Bittersweet Victory." U.S. NEWS & WORLD REPORT 98 (February 4, 1985) : 10.

Even though TIME won its libel suit, its credibility has been damaged.

1303 Stein, M. L. "Penthouse Victory Seen as Libel Claim Deterrent." EDITOR & PUBLISHER 115 (May 22, 1982) : 26.

In the longest libel trial in American legal history, a jury found PENTHOUSE had not libeled La Costa Resort in an article alleging connections between the resort and organized crime.

1304 Stevens, George E. "Legal Protection for a Magaazine Article Idea." JOURNALISM QUARTERLY 61 (Autumn 1984) : 679-682.

Analysis of Welin v. READER'S DIGEST, and its implications for writers who believe their article ideas have been stolen by editors.

1305 Stevens, George E. "Unauthorized Use of a Newspaper's Name." JOURNALISM QUARTERLY 61 (Summer 1984) : 426-429.

Discussion of trademark infringement with reference to the WASHINGTON POST, ESQUIRE, and Time Inc.

1306 Stonecipher, Harry W. "Protection for the Editorial Function: Is First Amendment Right Being Eroded?" JOURNALISM QUARTERLY 58 (Autumn 1981) : 363-370.

Discussion of First Amendment legal precedents, primarily oriented to newspapers but with relevance for magazine journalism as well.

1307 Swan, Jon. "On the Libel Front: The Little Guy in the Big Suit." COLUMBIA JOURNALISM REVIEW 21 (January-February 1983) : 42-43.

Financial problems for a small publisher forced to fight a libel suit against a big corporation. Case of THE MILKWEED, a monthly tabloid published in Madison, Wisconsin.

1308 Walsh, Edward, and Denton, Herbert H. "Jury Clears TIME of Malice, Ending Sharon Libel Case." WASHINGTON POST, 25 January 1985, p. A1.

TIME employees were nonetheless chastised as having acted "negligently and carelessly," and Sharon is regarded as having won political and public relations battles at home.

1309 "When Personal Memoirs are News: Press Freedom Outweighs an Ex-President's Copyright." TIME 122 (November 28, 1983) : 68-69.

News account of the 1983 Federal Appeals Court decision overturning a 1979 District Court ruling. The appeals court ruled that NATION magazine's use of Ford's memoirs did not violate copyright law. This 1983 decision overturned by the Supreme Court in 1985.

1310 Yoakum, Robert. "The Great HUSTLER Debate." COLUMBIA JOURNALISM REVIEW 16 (May-June 1977) : 53-56+.

Comparison of obscenity cases against HUSTLER and SCREW magazines. While the SCREW case received little media attention, the HUSTLER case excited much comment.

1311 Yoakum, Robert. "An Obscene, Lewd, Lascivious, Indecent, Filthy, and Vile Tabloid entitled SCREW." COLUMBIA JOURNALISM REVIEW 15 (March-April 1977) : 38-39+.

Were SCREW and SMUT convicted of U.S. Postal Service violations because of their political rather than pornographic content? Lengthy analysis of the legal issues and political overtones of the case tried in 1975.

Ethics

1312 Abbott, William. "The Editorial Connection." FOLIO 12 (September 1983) : 203+.

Conflict between advertising department desire to make editorial product profitable and attractive to advertisers and editorial department desire for reader service and independence.

1313 "Ad Opportunities Found in Editorial Catering to Readers' 'Audience'." FOLIO 11 (August 1982) : 8+.

Creating editorial material to attract second-level audiences and additional advertisers.

1314 "Advertising Meets Editorial." COLUMBIA JOURNALISM REVIEW 1 (Fall 1962) : 14-22.

Pictorial examples from magazines of advertiser influence on editorial copy.

1315 "An Award for Non-Advertising." MARKETING & MEDIA DECISIONS 18 (April 1983) : 36.

Awards offered by the American Lung Association to forty-two magazines that refuse cigarette advertising.

1316 Bagdikian, Ben H. THE MEDIA MONOPOLY. Boston: Beacon Press, 1983.

While this is not a book about magazines per se, there are many references to magazines. Of particular interest are comments on the impact of advertising on magazines, corporate ownership, muckraking, and coverage of smoking and health by magazines.

1317 Bonafede, Dom. "Hitting the Ground Rules Running." WASHINGTON JOURNALISM REVIEW 4 (January-February 1982) : 41-45

Anatomy of December 1981 ATLANTIC article on David Stockman raises questions about the practice of journalism in Washington, particularly on-the-record and off-the-record rules and the relationship between the reporter and his sources.

1318 Clark, Roy Peter. "The Unoriginal Sin: How Plagiarism Poisons the Press." WASHINGTON JOURNALISM REVIEW 5 (March 1983) : 42-47.

Plagiarism in magazines and newspapers may

take many forms: robbing newspaper morgues; using material from wire services, other media and press releases without attribution or under another by-line; recycling already-used stories.

1319 Cockburn, Alexander. "Chewng More than He's Bitten Off." NATION 241 (July 20, 1985) : 39.

Debate over an anti-abortion advertisement in the PROGRESSIVE. Includes brief mention of anti-cigarette article killed by editor of the NEW REPUBLIC--a magazine that accepts cigarette ads.

1320 Cummins, Ken. "The Cigarette Makers: How They Get Away With Murder ... With the Press as an Accessory." WASHINGTON MONTHLY 16 (April 1984) : 14-22.

Trends in cigarette advertising with an ethical slant. Only the last two pages refer to magazine and other media advertising.

1321 Dale, Kristan C. "ACSH Survey: Which Magazines Report the Hazards of Smoking?" ACSH NEWS & Views 3 (May-June 1982) : 1+.

Content analysis shows magazines with no cigarette ads contain more information about smoking dangers than magazines with cigarette ads. Survey conducted by the American Council on Science and Health (ACSH).

1322 Ernster, Virginia L. "Mixed Messages for Women: A Social History of Cigarette Smoking and Advertising." NEW YORK STATE JOURNAL OF MEDICINE 85 (July 1985) : 335-340.

Details of cigarette advertising campaigns directed at women since 1900, with emphasis on magazine advertising.

1323 "Exodus of QUEST." TIME 117 (January 12, 1981) : 57.

Editor and religious publisher of a secular magazine, QUEST, clash over non-publication of an article. In protest, editor and five others resign.

1324 Fedler, Fred; Meeske, Mike; and Hall, Joe. "TIME Magazine Revisited: Presidential Stereotypes Persist." JOURNALISM QUARTERLY 56 (Summer 1979) : 353-359

Replication of a 1965 study by John Merrill shows TIME magazine still carries a Republican bias.

1325 Fischer, John. "The Perils of Publishing: How to Tell When You Are Being Corrupted." HARPER'S 236 (May 1968) : 13-14+.

Publishing ethics and the pressure brought to bear on an editor. In the author's experience, advertisers rarely dictate editorial policy.

Greater dangers of corruption lie in the editor's power as gatekeeper and the potential conflicts between the magazine's business and editorial functions.

1326 Fitzgerald, Mark. "Pleasing the Advertiser?" EDITOR & PUBLISHER 117 (March 24, 1984) : 18-19.

News director of the JOURNAL OF THE AMERICAN MEDICAL ASSOCIATION (JAMA) is fired after confirming publication of an article to appease a drug company that had pulled advertising to protest an earlier story. Questions how much influence drug advertisers have on editorial content of medical journals, both profit and non-profit.

1327 Gloede, William. "RJR Sees Impact of Issue Ads." ADVERTISING AGE 55 (July 9, 1984) : 52.

Controversial campaign by R. J. Reynolds Tobacco Co. on the issue of smoking. Some ads say company doesn't advertise to children.

1328 Gralla, Milton. "8 Ways to Fight 'Puff'." FOLIO 7 (April 1978) : 37-38.

How to avoid using unwanted public relations releases from advertisers. How editors should handle pressure from advertisers and ad sales staff. Should be retitled "8 Ways to Accept Puff While Denying You Do So."

1329 Greenburg, Peter S. "Star Wars." NEW TIMES 10 (February 6, 1978) : 39-45.

As demand for celebrity coverage increases, magazines barter space, covers, and editorial control for interviews.

1330 Griffith, Thomas. "Get Your Balance Elsewhere." TIME 21 (February 14, 1983) : 63.

No one set of standards applies to all areas of journalism. Newspapers and network tv news may have an obligation to be objective, but no one can expect the same of specialized magazines.

1331 Grover, Stephen. "Aided by Cigarette Ads, Magazine Industry Rebounds but Still Loses Ground to TV." WALL STREET JOURNAL, 7 December 1972, p. 48.

The television ban on cigarette advertising was been one factor in advertising gains for magazines circa 1970, although competition with tv for advertising dollars was still strong. Brief commentary and cautious optimism for the general health of magazines in the early 1970s.

1332 Guyon, Janet. "Do Publications Avoid Anti-Cigarette Stories to Protect Ad Dollars." WALL STREET JOURNAL, 22 November 1982, p. 1+.

Article suggests cigarette advertisers exert much influence on magazine editorial.

1333 Henry, Nancy. "Women's Magazines: The Chic Sell." NATION 214 (June 5, 1972) : 710-712.

A "soft" advertising-editorial policy has kept women's magazines viable.

1334 Hinckle, Warren. "The Adman Who Hated Advertising: The Gospel According to Howard Gossage." ATLANTIC 233 (March 1974) : 61-72.

Lightly written commentary on the history of advertising and its detrimental effects on magazines and press freedom. Summary of ideas of Howard Gossage.

1335 Hochschild, Adam. "Hatchet Job in the Pressroom." MOTHER JONES 5 (June 1980) : 5.

Editorial concerning censorship at the COLUMBIA JOURNALISM REVIEW. Hochschild suggests new editor Manoff was fired because he printed too many articles too critical of important media.

1336 Holcomb, Betty. "Grounded at HARPERS." COLUMBIA JOURNALISM REVIEW 21 (November-December 1982) : 7-8

Editor Michael Kinsley disagrees with Chairman Donald Petrie over the wisdom of touring Lebanon at Israeli government expense.

1337 Kessler, Ronald. "Cigarette Ads May Soon Begin Fading Away in Papers, Magazines, as well as on TV." WALL STREET JOURNAL, 5 September 1969, p. 4.

Magazines and newspapers were taking sides in 1969. Some planned to require health warnings or ban cigarette ads. Others planned to allow them as usual. Background material for the controversy over cigarette advertising in magazines.

1338 Kurtzer, Steve. "Magazines: The Next Decade." MARKETING & MEDIA DECISIONS 20 (June 1985) : 142+.

Magazine forecast from the advertiser perspective. Advertising will become increasingly connected to editorial as consumers demand more product information.

1339 Labarbera, Priscilla A. "Shame of Magazine Advertising." JOURNAL OF ADVERTISING 10 (no. 1, 1981) : 31-37.

Discussion of deceptive back-of-the-book magazine ads from viewpoints of editors and industry/government groups. Study includes ten magazines, mostly women's magazines, and recommends ending the use of such ads. Offers interesting insights.

1340 Lehmkuhl, David C. "Serving Two Masters." MARKETING & MEDIA DECISIONS 18 (September 1983) : 94+.

Magazines must serve both readers and advertisers. Suggestions for coping offered from advertiser perspective.

1341 MacDougall, A. Kent. "Blandness, Bias Mar Many Trade Journals, Press Critics Contend: Ads are Presented as News; Companies' Views Echoed; Editors Help to Sell Space." WALL STREET JOURNAL, 13 January 1971, p. 1+.

1342 Mall, Janice. "Cigarette Ads Zero in on Women." LOS ANGELES TIMES, 25 April 1982, sec. 4, p. 9.

Reports study by Virginia Ernster of cigarette ads in women's magazines from 1920s to present. See entry 1322.

1343 Malloy, Michael T. "Journalistic Ethics: Not Black, Not White, but ... a Rainbow of Gray." NATIONAL OBSERVER, 26 July 1975, p. 1+.

Stress on newspaper ethics, but some references to magazines.

1344 Mannes, Marya. "The Intruders." REPORTER 27 (August 16, 1962) : 50-52+.

As early as 1962, the clutter and intrusion of magazine advertising was noted. Mannes explores the ways advertising impinges on editorial content with references to LIFE and LOOK magazines.

1345 Papazian, E. "Must Advertisers Cave in to Pressure Groups?" AD FORUM 5 (April 1984) : 16.

1346 Perlez, Jane. "Deadlines and Politics Cause Firing of Editor." WASHINGTON JOURNALISM REVIEW 2 (April 1980) : 5-6.

COLUMBIA JOURNALISM REVIEW editor Robert Manoff, responsible for "enlivening" the magazine, is fired. Was it because his editorial policy was disapproved by publisher Edward W. Barrett?

1347 Perry, Susan. "A Tough Habit to Kick." COLUMBIA JOURNALISM REVIEW 21 (July-August 1982) : 8-9.

Cigarette advertiser effect on editorial copy. Minneapolis writer fired for anti-smoking copy published in TWIN CITIES READER.

1348 "Press Reacts to Article in NEW TIMES Claiming Celebs Control Editors." FOLIO 7 (April 1978) : 16+.

Summary of NEW TIMES magazine article that claims celebrities are controlling editorial comment about them in US, ROLLING STONE, TIME. See entry 1329.

1349 Rosen, Jane. "Magazines Cater to Package Goods Marketers." ADVERTISING AGE 55 (March 14, 1985) : 24.

Men's magazines add traditionally female-oriented editorial to attract new advertising.

1350 Rosenstiel, Thomas B. "NEWSWEEK Political 'Extra' Fuels Debate on News Embargoes." LOS ANGELES TIMES, 9 November 1984, part 1, p. 19.

NEWSWEEK reports administration's tax plans after the election, having agreed to withhold publication of the story until then.

1351 Rotzoll, Kim B. "Gossage Revisited." JOURNAL OF ADVERTISING 9 (no. 4, 1980) : 6-14.

Academic review of Howard L. Gossage's criticism of advertising practice. He called advertising "overkill, tasteless, irrelevant messages." Article connects his earlier criticism to current concerns.

1352 Rowse, Arthur. "It Must be Legitimate, Thelma, They Advertise in the WALL STREET JOURNAL." WASHINGTON MONTHLY 16 (June 1984) : 37-38+.

Although claiming to screen them, respectable financial magazines and newspapers publish investment ads from unscrupulous firms that cheat investors.

1353 Ruffel, Charles. "Uncle Tom's Cabin." COLUMBIA JOURNALISM REVIEW 22 (March-April 1984) : 7-8+.

Black writer-apprentice charges TIME magazine with racial discrimination in his dismissal. Comments on the writer-apprenticeship program at TIME.

1354 Sadler, Shelby. "List Prices." WASHINGTON JOURNALISM REVIEW 6 (December 1984) : 11.

Magazines rent their subscriber lists to political campaigners.

1355 Schardt, Arlie. "Quitting on the Upbeat." NEWSWEEK 97 (January 12, 1981) : 87.

Founding editor Robert Shnayerson and five top staffers quit QUEST magazine following a dispute with the magazine's sponsor, Worldwide Church of God, over its editorial independence.

1356 Smith, Anthony. "Is Objectivity Obsolete?" COLUMBIA JOURNALISM REVIEW 19 (May-June 1980) : 61-65.

The development of journalistic objectivity, the New Journalism, and a comparison of newspaper and magazine practices.

1357 Smith, R. C. "The Magazines' Smoking Habit." COLUMBIA JOURNALISM REVIEW 16 (January-February 1978) : 29-31.

While accepting increasing amounts of cigarette advertising, magazines have not reported dangers of tobacco to health. Often quoted, early statement on this subject.

1358 Sommer, Robert, and Pilisuk, Tammy. "Pesticide Advertising in Farm Journals." JOURNAL OF COMMUNICATION 32 (Winter 1982) : 37-42.

Financial dominance of pesticide advertising in farm journals leaves farmers with no trustworthy information on pest control. Content analysis of four journals from 1977-1979.

1359 "Status Symbol: HARVARD BUSINESS REVIEW Looks Great in an Attache Case, but can you Trust a Magazine that Plugs its Authors' Services?" SAVVY 4 (November 1983) : 14.

1360 Stein, Robert. "Norman Cousins vs. the Promoters." NEW YORK 5 (June 19, 1972) : 46-50.

Details of the conflicts between SATURDAY REVIEW editor Norman Cousins and investors Charney and Veronis who took over the magazine in 1971. Dated but of historical interest.

1361 "This Sporting Life." TIME 104 (November 4, 1974) : 56.

FIELD AND STREAM fires outspoken columnist for angering politicians.

1362 "TIME Magazine to Start Statue of Liberty Ads." NEW YORK TIMES, 28 June 1985, p. 41.

Brief news clip on TIME's provision of free space for public service ads donated by ad agencies for the Statue of Liberty.

1363 "Trade Magazines Today Afraid to Criticize the Industries They Serve." FOLIO 9 (March 1980) : 30+.

Opinion of retiring executive of Young & Rubicam advertising agency, William Marsteller.

1364 Van Gelder, Lindsy. "PLAYBOY's Charity: Is it Reparations or Rip-Off?" MS. (June 1983) : 78-81.

The Playboy Foundation's support for feminist causes has divided feminists. Some of the reasons why relate to the questions: does pornography exploit women? and is there a difference between the Foundation and the magazine?

1365 Welles, Chris. "Business Journalism's Glittering Prizes." COLUMBIA JOURNALISM REVIEW 17 (March 1979) : 43-45.

Are prizes for magazine and newspaper business journalists really public relations boosters for their sponsors?

1366 Whelan, Elizabeth M. "When NEWSWEEK and TIME Filtered Cigarette Copy." WALL STREET JOURNAL, 1 November 1984, p. 30.

Cigarette advertisers influence magazines to downplay health dangers of smoking. Author is director of American Council on Science and Health.

1367 Whiteside, Thomas. "Cigarette Ads in the Magazines: Selling Death." NEW REPUBLIC 164 (March 27, 1971) : 15-17.

Magazines increased revenue by accepting cigarette ads after tv ban.

1368 "Who'll Watch the Media Watcher?" NEWSWEEK 95 (March 3, 1980) : 49.

Robert Manoff fired as editor of COLUMBIA JOURNALISM REVIEW. Many believed he stepped on too many influential toes.

Free Press & Censorship

1369 Abrams, Garry. "Sex Magazine Sales Spark Free-Speech Debate." LOS ANGELES TIMES, 23 December 1984, sec. 6, p. 1.

Drive to ban sex magazines at the university bookstore, Cal State Northridge.

1370 Alpern, David M. "Churches, Politics and the Tax Man." NEWSWEEK 96 (October 6, 1980) : 46.

Non-profit churches (and their magazines, e.g., TODAY'S CATHOLIC) are subject to IRS rules which prohibit endorsement of political candidates.

1371 "Anti-Life Movement." NEWSWEEK 97 (March 2, 1981) : 83.

News capsule about Washington D.C. retailers' refusal to sell the February 1981 LIFE magazine, because it carried family photographs of an accused murderer, purchased by LIFE for $8000.

1372 Baldwin, William. "Those 'Nonprofit' Profits." FORBES 126 (September 1, 1980) : 98.

Non-profit magazines do not mean poverty; non-profit postage costs taxpayers big money.

1373 "Big Mama v. Big Brother." NATION 231 (November 29, 1980) : 564-565.

Discussion of Big Mama Rag Inc., non-profit magazine publisher, and its successful suit against the IRS when its non-profit status was questioned.

1374 "A Bill to Curb Legitimate Publications." NEW YORK TIMES, 5 July 1984, sec. A, p. 14.

Letter to the editor from Thomas Stoddard, N.Y. Civil Liberties Union, regarding proposed state legislation of "minor's display bill."

1375 Caneff, Dennis. "The Auditor as Editor." QUILL 73 (April 1985) : 20-23+.

IRS rulings and court cases on BIG MAMA RAG, MOTHER JONES, and others. Does the IRS question non-profit status of controversial magazines because their content is objectionable?

1376 "Censorship Seen to Have Increased Over Past Year." FOLIO 10 (December 1981) : 51+.

Publishers report censorship of magazines other than men's entertainment titles.

1377 Condo, Jerry. "Is PLAYBOY Magazine Suitable for Blind Readers." THE PRESS 9 (May 1981) : 7.

Conservative congressman rails at Library of Congress' inclusion of PLAYBOY on its list of Braille-reproduced publications sent free to requesting blind persons,

1378 Consoli, John. "The PROGRESSIVE Triumphs in H-Bomb Case." EDITOR & PUBLISHER 112 (September 22, 1979) : 9+.

Justice Department abandons court battle against the PROGRESSIVE after newspaper publishes letter to a senator which outlines information on H-bomb construction obtained through unclassified sources.

1379 Consoli, John. "Secret Opinion Stirs New Controversy in Bomb Case." EDITOR & PUBLISHER 112 (June 16, 1979) : 12.

Legal briefs and opinions in the case against the PROGRESSIVE are secret, even from PROGRESSIVE editors.

1380 Denniston, Lyle. "The SEC Power-Grab." QUILL 72 (September 1984) : 21-24+.

How the SEC is challenging First Amendment freedom of the press in regulating business and financial journalism.

1381 "THE DIAL gets Nonprofit Status." BROADCASTING 100 (January 12, 1981) : 64.

Philip Merrill, publisher of the WASHINGTONIAN, unsuccessfully challenged THE DIAL's nonprofit status. He believes it puts the government in the publishing business, is a threat to press independence, and is unfair competition. THE DIAL is a program guide for public television.

1382 English, Dierdre. "IRS to MJ: 'Never Mind'." MOTHER JONES 8 (December 1983) : 5.

MOTHER JONES has mixed reactions to its victory over the IRS. The ruling cannot be a precedent and therefore will be of no help to other small non-profit organizations.

1383 English, Dierdre. "Journalism: The Little Chill." MOTHER JONES 9 (November 1984) : 6.

Restriction on the freedom of the non-profit press. An editorial.

1384 Fannin, Rebecca. "PO Wallops Non-Profit Magazines." MARKETING & MEDIA DECISIONS 17 (April 1982) : 68-69+.

How 100 percent increase in second class mailing costs will affect non-profit magazines.

1385 Frame, Randy. "Citizens Battle a Booming Pornography Business." CHRISTIANITY TODAY 28 (September 7, 1984) : 72-73.

Groups picket 7-Eleven convenience stores to protest their policy on selling men's magazines--PLAYBOY, PENTHOUSE, and FORUM. Author believes pornography is not only increasing but changing in tone.

1386 Friedman, Robert. "The United States v. THE

PROGRESSIVE." COLUMBIA JOURNALISM REVIEW 18 (July-August 1979) : 27-35.

THE PROGRESSIVE magazine has been enjoined on national security grounds from writing about the hydrogen bomb.

1387 Ingersoll, Bruce. "Financial Newsletters Face Growing Pressure to Register with SEC." WALL STREET JOURNAL, 15 November 1984, p. 1+.

Newsletters required to register as investment advisers; publishers contend First Amendment rights are being violated.

1388 Ingersoll, Bruce. "Investment Letter Publisher Charged Over Stock Articles." WALL STREET JOURNAL, 1 October 1985, p. 20.

SEC sues publisher for recommending readers invest in three companies not yet registered with the SEC.

1389 Ingersoll, Bruce. "SEC Charges PENNY STOCK Publisher with Taking Money for Favorable Stories." WALL STREET JOURNAL, 20 December 1984, p. 5.

1390 Ingersoll, Bruce. "U.S. Judge Bars Financial Newsletter, Publisher From Violating Adviser's Act." WALL STREET JOURNAL, 25 April 1985, p. 12.

A major victory for the SEC as federal judge requires INVESTMENT INTELLIGENCE, a weekly newsletter from Financial News Associates, to register as an investment adviser. Although a setback for newsletter publishers, ethical questions are raised about newsletter claims.

1391 "Inside: IRS." WASHINGTON POST, 10 January 1983, p. A1.

IRS has begun an attempt to take away the non-profit status of MOTHER JONES magazine, an act which the magazine says is politically motivated.

1392 Kilpatrick, James. "U.S. Censor." WASHINGTON POST, 14 August 1984, p. A19.

Editorial on the SEC as censor of stock market newsletter. First amendment violation claimed.

1393 "Largest Texas Prison Bans EBONY's KKK story." JET 57 (November 1, 1979) : 28.

Huntsville prison bans EBONY issue containing article on KKK that prison officials judged racially inflammatory.

1394 Mackenzie, Angus. "Sabotaging the Dissident Press." COLUMBIA JOURNALISM REVIEW 19 (March-April 1981) : 57+.

Government tactics to silence anti-war publication involve the CIA, FBI, army, the IRS.

1395 MacKenzie, Angus. "When Auditors Turn Editors: The IRS and the Nonprofit Press." COLUMBIA JOURNALISM REVIEW 19 (November-December 1981) : 29-34.

The future of non-profit magazines may be decided by the IRS, as exemplified by the IRS confrontations with MOTHER JONES and BIG MAMA RAG. Religious periodicals protest restrictions as interfering with free speech. Non-profit press may not carry on propaganda or influence legislation.

1396 "Men's Entertainment Magazines Target of 'Vigilante Groups'." FOLIO 13 (November 1984) : 65.

Right-wing and religious groups try to intimidate retailers to stop selling men's magazines they consider pornographic.

1397 Millecam, Melissa; Palomo, Juan; and Long, Charles. "Blowup at Baylor." QUILL 68 (May 1980) : 23-28.

Student rights and press freedom challenged at Baylor University as PLAYBOY magazine arrives to photograph co-eds.

1398 "MOTHER JONES Wins IRS Judgment." WASHINGTON POST, 10 November 1983, p. C4.

After a three-and-a-half-year battle with the IRS, MOTHER JONES has been declared a legitimate tax-exempt enterprise.

1399 "MS.'s New Tax Status Piques Interest of Other Publishers." FOLIO 8 (December 1979) : 4+.

MS.'s new non-profit status brings advantages and disadvantages.

1400 "Newsletter Publisher Censured for Failure to Disclose Payments." WALL STREET JOURNAL, 27 January 1983, p. 41.

Securities and Exchange Commission censures publisher of NORTHWEST INVESTMENT REVIEW for not disclosing payment received from companies it had written about.

1401 "Non-Profit Magazines Pressured by IRS?" FOLIO 11 (March 1982) : 6-7.

IRS audit of MOTHER JONES prompted FOLIO to question non-profit publishers. Most report no harassment by the IRS.

1402 Peterzell, Jay. "Can You Name that Agent? A Look at How the Intelligence Identities Protection Act Works." COLUMBIA JOURNALISM REVIEW 23 (November-December 1985) : 46-47.

When the law was passed in 1982, many viewed it as a violation of the First Amendment. Magazines and newspapers have paid little attention to it and have not been prosecuted.

1403 "Power to Destroy." NATION 237 (November 19, 1983) : 485.

Was the IRS audit of MOTHER JONES political harassment?

1404 "Pretoria Bans Issue of NEWSWEEK While Expelling its Correspondent." NEW YORK TIMES, 13 September 1985, p. A10.

NEWSWEEK issue featuring a cover story on South Africa and co-author of the article are banned from that country.

1405 "Resolution Used by County to Curb HIGH TIMES Sales." FOLIO 11 (November 1982) : 16.

County requests local merchants not sell HIGH TIMES magazine.

1406 "Retail Chains Cutting Number of 'Entertainment' Titles they Carry." FOLIO 13 (July 1984) : 21+.

Some retail chains refuse to sell some or all men's entertainment magazines.

1407 Reynolds, Richard. "MJ: Banned in Texas." MOTHER JONES 9 (November 1984) : 11.

Half-page description of inability of Texas legislator to obtain taxpayer-paid subscription to MOTHER JONES because of the magazine's "political nature." Another case of censorship.

1408 Revett, John. "Magazines Seen Next Censor Target." ADVERTISING AGE 52 (October 26, 1982) : 3+.

Publishers bracing themselves for censorship activity from the Moral Majority. Initial complaints against lingerie ads in mainstream magazines in high school libraries.

1409 "The Right War." NATION 241 (July 6, 1985) : 4-5.

Commonsense Unlimited founded in northeast Mississippi to protest Morality in America's censorship of skin magazines and sleazy comic books.

1410 Rivinus, Willis M. "Not-For-Profit Magazines Needn't be Losers." FOLIO 11 (August 1982) : 103-105.

Revenue losses in non-profit magazines highlight other problems; ten areas to examine to determine the health of a non-profit magazine.

1411 "SEC Says Magazine Published Advice in Violation of Law." WALL STREET JOURNAL, 21 July 1982, p. 21.

STOCK MARKET magazine illegally gives investment advice according to SEC.

1412 "SEC Says Publisher of Financial Letter Broke Securities Law." WALL STREET JOURNAL, 1 May 1985, p. 5.

In a "reaffirmation of its regulatory authority over investment newsletters," SEC files suit against F.X.C. Investors Corporation newsletter.

1413 Shapiro, Harvey D. "Unfair Shares: Writers who Profit from Wall Street's Pipeline." WASHINGTON JOURNALISM REVIEW 6 (July-August 1984) : 34-36+.

Business and financial journalists for newspapers and magazines have access to inside information. SEC favors restrictions on journalists similar to those for investment advisers.

1414 "Should the DIAL be Turned Off?" TIME 116 (September 15, 1980) : 84.

The controversy over government subsidy for non-profit publishing ventures like DIAL in competition with commercial magazines.

1415 Stevens, William K. "Priest in Texas Defies Ruling by IRS that Bars Stand on Political Issues." NEW YORK TIMES, 22 June 1980, sec. 1, p. 24.

Editor of TODAY'S CATHOLIC openly challenges IRS ruling that non-profit publications may not endorse political candidates by endorsing Reagan's candidacy. Will the IRS challenge TODAY'S CATHOLIC and force a court battle? Apparently not.

1416 Stevenson, Tom. "The Profitable Nonprofit Press." FOLIO 5 (October 1976) : 38-42+.

Questions the fairness of government subsidizing of the non-profit press. Should non-profit magazines compete with commercial publications?

1417 Swain, Bruce M. "The PROGRESSIVE, the Bomb and the Papers." JOURNALISM MONOGRAPHS, no. 76. Association for Education in Journalism, May 1982.

In March 1979, the government filed suit in federal court to prevent the PROGRESSIVE from publishing an article on the hydrogen bomb, the first injunction against publication of a magazine article. Swain's monograph deals with the events of the case, journalistic coverage of it, and the support-nonsupport the PROGRESSIVE received from the journalistic profession.

1418 "Thou Shalt Not Sell Skin Magazines." WALL STREET JOURNAL, 1 November 1985, p. 33.

News brief states policy of United Dairy Farmers, convenience store chain. PENTHOUSE, PLAYBOY, and other adult titles will not be sold by this chain.

1419 Wall, James W. "Don't Say 'Nuts' to the IRS." CHRISTIAN CENTURY, 97 (July 16, 1980) : 723-724.

Critical comments on TODAY'S CATHOLIC's advocating political stance in opposition to IRS conditions for tax-exempt publications.

1420 Wermiel, Stephen. "High Court Rules Certain Newsletters are Exempt from Regulation by SEC." WALL STREET JOURNAL, 11 June 1985, p. 3.

Court decides the Securities and Exchange Commission cannot regulate financial newsletters published independently of brokerage firms.

1421 Witt, Matt. "Venture in Union Journalism." COLUMBIA JOURNALISM REVIEW 17 (July-August 1978) : 50-52.

In the 1970s the UNITED MINE WORKERS JOURNAL attempted to become a true voice of reform for union members, but pressure from national and district union officials forced its editor to retreat to its traditional format.

1422 Wynter, Leon E. "Financial Periodical Said to Act Illegally in Company Profiles." WALL STREET JOURNAL, 17 July 1984, p. 44.

STOCK MARKET magazine ordered by judge to register with the SEC as an investment adviser. Some companies supplied copy to magazine and some directly or indirectly paid for stories.

Chapter 14

ANCILLARY BUSINESSES & ELECTRONIC PUBLISHING

1423 "Advertising Agencies Link Ads, Editorial in Electronic Publications." FOLIO 13 (April 1984) : 6+.

Advertising agencies venture into electronic publishing, with publications that contain editorial and ads on one subject.

1424 Ahl, David H. "Magazines of the Future." CREATIVE COMPUTING 8 (January 1982) : 14.

Ahl offers his opinion that printed magazines are here to stay, although opportunities exist in publication of electronic magazines for special interest groups, such as financiers, coin collectors, astronomers, etc.

1425 "American Baby Inc. Tests New Film Series for Hospitals." FOLIO 13 (September 1984) : 8-9.

AMERICAN BABY is publishing advertiser-supported, educational films for new mothers.

1426 "Banking on BETTER HOMES." BUSINESS WEEK (June 7, 1982) : 81+.

Meredith Corporation introduces its first videodisc.

1427 Cook, David T. "Even Without the Magazine, ESQUIRE is a Savvy Business." CHRISTIAN SCIENCE MONITOR, 21 July 1982, p. 11.

ESQUIRE, founded to publish a clothing journal, has many other business activities.

1428 "Diversification is the News at U.S. NEWS." BUSINESS WEEK (August 16, 1982) : 32.

U.S. NEWS is diversifying into computer-based publishing services, a satellite transmission network, and real estate.

1429 Elliott, Stuart J. "PLAYBOY Guides May Go Paid." ADVERTISING AGE 53 (October 18, 1982) : 79.

PLAYBOY is testing conversion of its guides to paid from free circulation.

1430 Gaffner, Haines B. "Database & Software Opportunities: Finally the Time is Right." FOLIO 13 (January 1984) : 63-65+.

Databases and software offer publishing opportunities for magazines. Publishers are advised to become involved during a "two-year window" of opportunity.

1431 "Get Ready for the Video Publishing Explosion." MARKETING & MEDIA DECISIONS 16 (APRIL 1981) : 59-63.

Opportunites open to publishers in teletext, cable tv, video cassettes, databases. What companies are getting involved?

1432 "Individual Magazines' Database Opportunities Seen as Limited." FOLIO 10 (August 1981) : 4.

Incompleteness of information limits possibilities for database publishing of individual magazines, according to Jerome D. Luntz, president of the Center for Business Information. He suggests magazines license their database material to a database publisher who combines like information from all periodicals in the particular field.

1433 Love, Barbara. "Keeping up With Database Publishing." FOLIO 9 (August 1980) : 86-91+.

Role of magazines in database publishing. Profit-making opportunities are increased through reuse of information.

1434 McFadden, Maureen. "The NEW YORKER's Hidden Holdings." MAGAZINE AGE 6 (May 1985) : 50+.

NEW YORKER is involved in numerous other businesses--paper products, computers, books, COOK'S MAGAZINE, HORTICULTURE magazine, Tribune Star Publishing, U.S. edition of ELLE, office furniture, and printing.

1435 Mandel, Charles. "Don't Ignore Video Options." FOLIO 13 (March 1984) : 60-61+.

Advice and opportunities for publishers seeking entry to video publishing.

1436 "NEWSTRACK, a Cassette Magazine, Covers the Business World." FOLIO 10 (March 1981) : 8.

NEWSTRACK carries articles from print magazine pages on audio tapes.

1437 Norris, Eileen. "PLAYBOY-Licensed Products Proliferate." ADVERTISING AGE 57 (March 6, 1986) : 39-40.

A run-down on PLAYBOY'S non-magazine products and business ventures from 1953 onward.

1438 "PLAYBOY Making Profit on Guides, Despite Large Non-Paid Circulation." FOLIO 10 (July 1981) : 26+.

Ad-supported PLAYBOY guides, distributed free with the intention of later converting recipients into paying customers, are among Christie Hefner's efforts to broaden PLAYBOY'S interests and profit sources.

1439 Pollack, Andrew. "Computerizing Magazines." NEW YORK TIMES, 25 August 1983, sec. D, p. 2.

Magazines will someday have floppy disks accompanying printed articles.

1440 "Publisher Starts Videotex Info Service." FOLIO 14 (March 1985) : 46.

Oster Communications gives investors instant access to news on futures via personal computers.

1441 Salmans, Sandra. "Beyond MOTHER EARTH NEWS." NEW YORK TIMES, 9 August 1983, p. D1+.

Increased revenue and circulation prompt MOTHER EARTH NEWS owners to investigate new ventures. Possibilities include licensing the MOTHER EARTH name, publishing single-sponsor magazines, starting a culture magazine.

1442 "SUCCESSFUL FARMING Grosses $75,000 on Software Products." FOLIO 12 (August 1983): 7+.

Magazine sells computer software management programs for farmers.

1443 "13-30 Profits From Posters." FOLIO 14 (March 1985) : 41-42.

13-30 Corporation markets ad-carrying, informational posters, part magazine and part billboard, to attract readers' attention in places where magazines don't.

1444 "Tips on Tape: Cassette Magazines Arrive." TIME 119 (June 14, 1982) : 78.

Trade, not consumer, magazines may be profitable on videotapes.

1445 "Videos: A Natural Magazine Spin-Off." FOLIO 14 (August 1985) : 38-39.

Magazines, types of content, and markets for existing expertise in video form--both sales and rentals.

1446 "Videotaped 'Magazine' Produced by Owner of OCEAN REALM." FOLIO 11 (May 1982) : 53.

Video magazine for serious divers, based on a quarterly, print counterpart.

1447 "Videotext to Give Magazines 'Substantial Competition' by 1990." FOLIO 10 (March 1981) : 15+.

Delivering computer-stored information to consumers via telephone or cable tv presents a competitive threat to magazines.

Chapter 15

TELEVISION CONNECTION

1448 Alter, Stewart. "Weekly Magazines: Substitute for TV?" MAGAZINE AGE 4 (December 1983) : 32-34+.

Audience erosion and rising tv costs are leading advertisers to consider magazines as part of their media mix--not as a tv substitute. Weekly magazines offer immediacy, more frequent running of ads, and fast audience accumulation. They are closest to providing what tv offers.

1449 Bettner, Jill. "After the Centerfold." FORBES 133 (March 26,1984) : 43-44.

PLAYBOY magazine is still the center of Playboy Enterprises' business operation, although the video ventures look promising.

1450 Birnbaum, Bob. "Diminishing Cable Opportunities." FOLIO 13 (July 1984) : 124+.

Magazine publishers need to take advantage of

the opportunities for them in cable television programming.

1451 Birnbaum, Bob. "The Future: Short- and Long-Term." FOLIO 14 (February 1985) : 111.

Interview with GOOD HOUSEKEEPING editor on the future of electronic publishing.

1452 "Cable TV Market 'Wide Open' to Joint Ventures." FOLIO 10 (March 1981) : 15+.

Cable television networks are eager for joint ventures in programming with special interest and consumer magazines.

1453 Christopher, Maurine. "Hearst and ABC Tell Cable Plan." ADVERTISING AGE 52 (February 2, 1981) : 2+.

Hearst and ABC form partnership for cable tv programming using Hearst magazines, such as COSMOPOLITAN and GOOD HOUSEKEEPING as content sources.

1454 Condon, Ed. "Don't Overlook TV Sub Sales." FOLIO 12 (February 1983) : 45-46.

Playboy executive discusses the pros and cons of using television advertising for magazines, citing PLAYBOY'S experience.

1455 Dougherty, Philip H. "Cable may be Helping Magazines." NEW YORK TIMES, 29 February 1984, sec. D, p. 20.

Network television audience erosion makes magazines a good advertising alternative, says the Magazine Publishers Association.

1456 Dougherty, Philip H. "Magazines and Papers Try TV." NEW YORK TIMES, 20 October 1982, sec. D, p.18.

Magazines use tv to advertise themselves.

1457 Elsner, David M. "Magazines Get a Boost as Advertisers Try to Beat Increasing Television-Time Costs." WALL STREET JOURNAL, 6 December 1977, p.48.

As cost of tv time increases, major name-brand advertisers turn to magazines. Some advertisers complain that editorial copy is not expanding in relation to advertising, and some magazines look too much like catalogs.

1458 "Gannett's Film Unit Eyes TV Magazines." EDITOR & PUBLISHER 115 (February 6, 1982) : 28.

Gannett's Gateway Productions turns print magazines into television magazines.

1459 Greenberg, Joseph. "Reasons For Concern."

MARKETING & MEDIA DECISIONS 16 (January 1981) : 92+.

Another comparison of magazines and cable televison, with the pros and cons of each medium for the advertiser.

1460 Halliday, David Graham. "Magazines: The Net TV Alternative?" MARKETING & MEDIA DECISIONS 18 (August 1983) : 54-55+.

Magazine Publishers Association campaign to attract more advertising to magazines.

1461 Knoll, Steve. "Translating Magazines Into Programs." NEW YORK TIMES, 29 July 1984, sec. 2, p. H22.

Magazine-based programming on cable tv amounts to "a marriage of convenience."

1462 Learner, Douglas A. "Moving into Cable TV." FOLIO 11 (May 1982) : 103-108.

Advice for magazine publishers planning to expand into cable tv programming. Focus on choosing a network, participation in joint ventures with tv producers, finding a production company, making money.

1463 Lehmkuhl, David C. "New Ally: Cable." MARKETING & MEDIA DECISIONS 18 (April 1983) : 96+.

One effect of cable is network audience erosion which leads to increased magazine advertising. Reference to READER'S DIGEST's Tulsa, Oklahoma survey of cable and non-cable tv homes.

In cable homes, network tv audiences declined but magazine reading stayed the same.

1464 Levine, Harold. "Working Both Sides of the Street." FOLIO 11 (May 1982) : 75+.

Many magazine publishers are getting into broadcasting. What problems will they face? Brief opinion piece by advertising executive.

1465 Levine, Suzanne. "Getting into Cable." FOLIO 11 (March 1982) : 60-61.

MS. magazine produces a television show.

1466 Love, Barbara. "The Cable TV Connection." FOLIO 10 (May 1981) : 70-74.

The potential for links between cable tv and magazines, along with some possible problems. Accumulated magazine editorial may not be as important as an understanding of techniques which make presentation on a tv screen work.

1467 Macdonald, Katharine. "From Mags to Riches." COLUMBIA JOURNALISM REVIEW 19 (May-June 1980) : 9+.

Magazine articles sold to movie and television producers.

1468 "Need Cable & Mags War?" VARIETY (May 27, 1981) : 86.

Advertising executive's opinion that magazine and cable television could complement each other. Magazines need not be negatively affected by cable television.

1469 Neher, Jacques. "Meredith Taking its Franchise to Cable." ADVERTISING AGE 52 (February 9, 1981) : 70+.

Publisher of BETTER HOMES & GARDENS investigates video publishing using editorial borrowed from its magazines.

1470 Pool, Gail. "Can Magazines Find Happiness With Cable?" COLUMBIA JOURNALISM REVIEW 21 (January-February 1983) : 47+.

Magazines are getting involved in cable television. A look at what cable and magazines can do for each other.

1471 Pool, Gail. "Magazines." WILSON LIBRARY BULLETIN 56 (June 1982) : 779-780.

Magazine involvement in television, with some specific examples. Author suggests magazines are becoming involved because they are afraid not to.

1472 Reiss, Craig. "Video Publishing Explorers." MARKETING & MEDIA DECISIONS 17 (February 1982) : 68-69+.

Four magazine publishers discuss ventures into cable television programming. Some see entry into cable as a promotional tool. Others view it as another profitable way to apply their editorial expertise.

1473 Rosen, Marcella. "End the Battle Against TV." FOLIO 13 (January 1984) : 58-60.

Even though audience erosion of network television is benefitting magazine ad sales, the trend may not last. Magazines need to work with instead of compete against television.

1474 Rosen, Marcella. "A Plethora of Platitudes." MARKETING & MEDIA DECISIONS 16 (April 1981) : 90+.

Compares special interest print magazines with cable tv. Print can compete with cable because of regional and demographic edition fexibility.

1475 Salmans, Sandra. "Video is Drawing Publishers." NEW YORK TIMES, 18 April 1983, sec. D, p. 1+.

Magazines are becoming involved in television ventures, particularly women's and general interest magazines.

1476 Scott, Ronald T. "Competing With TV." FOLIO 10 (April 1981) : 66.

Brief account of magazine industry response to television since the 1950s, with thoughts on the future.

1477 "Time Inc.'s Video Profits Overtaking Publishing Profits." FOLIO 11 (August 1982) : 40.

Review of Time Inc. stockholders report 1982 points to success of electronic publishing although it still lags behind magazine and book publishing.

1478 Yovovich, B. G. "The Siren Call of Video Entices Many: Being Informative is No Longer Enough; Entertainment is the Key." ADVERTISING AGE 53 (October 25, 1982) : M44+.

Publishers are attracted to television programming. Experts offer advice on the differences between magazines and tv and some of the pitfalls.

Chapter 16

BUSINESS PRESS

Trade Journals & Business Press Management

1479 "Agency, Ad Execs Critical of Magazine Trade Ad Content." FOLIO 12 (January 1983) : 6+.

Criticism of poor trade magazine ad content with presumably ineffective results.

1480 Allen, Tom. "Business Press Hit by Inflation; But Ad Schedules Hold or Rise." ADVERTISING AGE 45 (November 18, 1974) : 88+.

Specialized magazines, particularly in the business press, were thriving in the early 1970s when many mass circulation magazines floundered. Magazine problems included rising paper costs and shortages, postal increases, inflation.

1481 Anderson, Russell F. "Relaunching the Faltering

Magazine." FOLIO 7 (March 1978) : 47-49.

McGraw Hill's total revamp of the faltering magazine CONSTRUCTION METHODS AND EQUIPMENT.

1482 Bernstein, S. R., and Sawyer, Howard G. "Progress in a Primitive Art: Industrial Advertising." INDUSTRIAL MARKETING 66 (May 1981) : 80-82+.

The past and future in business press advertising.

1483 Bertrand, Kate. "Acquisitions, Startups Enliven Business Press." ADVERTISING AGE 56 (April 25, 1985) : 28.

Today's business press is characterized by increasing group ownership and competition.

1484 "Business Advertising." ADVERTISING AGE 50 (June 25, 1979) : S2-S31.

This special section on business advertising also includes articles on the business press with strong emphasis on the trend toward mergers, acquisitions, and diversification.

1485 "Business Magazines' Annual Growth Rate Over Five Years: 11%." FOLIO 13 (April 1984) : 10.

Revenue and operating incomes of major business publishers 1978-1982 compared.

1486 "Business Press." ADVERTISING AGE 52 (May 11, 1981) : S1-S23.

Special section on specialized business magazines emphasizes their increasing diversity and usefulness as marketing and advertising tools.

1487 "Business Press." ADVERTISING AGE 53 (May 10, 1982) : M7-M40.

Lead article in this special report discusses the function of the business press in delivering information to industry management, and factors leading to the growth and sophistication of the business press. Many other articles are of a general nature dealing with such subjects as database publishing, circulation, how business magazines narrowcast their markets, and advertising in the business press.

1488 "Business Press." ADVERTISING AGE 54 (May 16, 1983) : M9-M44.

This special report includes forecasts for the industry, statistics on the fastest growing business magazines, computer magazines, and articles on specific publishing companies such as Cahners, Thompson.

1489 "Business Press." ADVERTISING AGE 55 (April 26, 1984) : M15-M50.

Lead article notes the business press has been called the "healthiest segment of journalism."

Numerous profiles of specific trade journals, discussion of the Business Publications Audit, industry overview.

1490 "Business Press." ADVERTISING AGE 56 (April 25, 1985) : 13-35.

Articles included in this special report cover group ownership in the business press, publication redesign, diversification, promotion, acquisitions, relationship between a business magazine and the industry it covers, profiles of specific titles and publishing companies.

1491 "Business Press." ADVERTISING AGE 57 (April 21, 1986) : S1-S12.

Special report on the business press. Lead article suggests business magazines narrow focus to target smaller, more demographically defined audiences. Individual articles look at specialized publications in the following areas: computers, architecture, metal industry, children's retailing, medicine, farm.

1492 "Capital Reading: NATIONAL JOURNAL Tells All." TIME 114 (August 27, 1979) : 71-72.

Description of NATIONAL JOURNAL, difficult-to-read, sophisticated monthly trade magazine aimed at businessmen, lobbyists, legislators, bureaucrats who deal with the federal government daily.

1493 Crooke, Robert. "Travel Business Magazines: Too Much of a Good Thing." MAGAZINE AGE 1 (June 1980) : 51-52+.

Business magazines for travel agencies. Agents criticize them for "editorial softness," although editorial integrity and individuality are major publisher concerns. Examples.

1494 "Designs For a War or Just Some More Doodling?" INDUSTRIAL MARKETING 66 (March 1981) : 96-98+.

Critique of new business ads in DESIGN NEWS. Are they efficiently communicating new technologies?

1495 Donahue, Christine. "Farmer's Market." FORBES 133 (June 18, 1984) : 36.

Webb Co. of St. Paul publishes small magazines and prints others, like TV GUIDE, for large publishers. Some notable successes are failing magazines, bought cheap and revitalized.

1496 Donath, Bob. "Postal Costs Worry ABP." INDUSTRIAL MARKETING 65 (June 1980) : 18.

Annual ABP conference attendees are concerned about climbing postal rates.

1497 Donovan, Alicia. "Awareness of Trade-Press

Advertising." JOURNAL OF ADVERTISING RESEARCH 19 (April 1979) : 33-35.

MODERN PLASTICS subscriber survey reveals trade publication advertising increases recognition of new products among influential people in target markets.

1498 Edel, Richard. "FOLIO Builds a Portfolio of Publishing Information." ADVERTISING AGE 55 (April 26, 1984) : M46-M48.

The growth and development of FOLIO, a trade journal that serves the magazine publishing industry. Mentions conferences sponsored by FOLIO, special issues like the FOLIO 400, and launch of related publications like CATALOG AGE.

1499 Edel, Richard. "Magazines Draw on Redesigns For Shot in the Arm." ADVERTISING AGE 56 (April 25, 1985) : 14-15.

Redesign of business press titles may be most effective if done at a magazine's peak of profitability rather than on its down swing.

1500 Forsyth, David P. "Total Audience is Measured." ADVERTISING AGE 51 (October 20, 1980) : S29-S31.

A list of nine ways to approach total audience measurement for business publications and related problems. Part of an AA magazine special section on research.

1501 Garino, David P. "MILLING & BAKING NEWS Thrives by Exclusivity and Spotting Trends." WALL STREET JOURNAL, 12 December 1973, p. 1+.

1973 profile of an unusual trade magazine that doesn't hustle advertisers or fill pages with public relations articles.

1502 Gervasi, Tom. "The Doomsday Beat." COLUMBIA JOURNALISM REVIEW 18 (May-June 1979) : 34-40.

McGraw Hill's defense community trade magazine, AVIATION WEEK, exercises influence at all levels of government worldwide.

1503 Goldstrom, Don. "Goldstrom's Media Spin-Offs." MARKETING & MEDIA DECISIONS 15 (July 1980) : 70-71+.

Armstrong Cork has produced its own consumer magazine since the mid-1970s. GOOD IDEAS FOR DECORATING is not a house organ or give-away, but a retail consumer magazine with the company name on the cover. Its decorating theme allows its products to be appreciated and builds awareness of them in consumers.

1504 Gulotta, Charlie. "Merchandising in the Business Press." MADISON AVENUE 25 (May 1983) : 74+.

Many business magazines offer advertisers a variety of services, such as ad reprints, direct mail letters, market research, training films and courses. Grouped together, these services are called merchandising. Examples.

1505 Gussow, Don. "The Leadership Function of the Specialized Business Press." MAGAZINE AGE 1 (January 1980) : 82+.

Function of the business press is to provide news, information, and leadership in shaping the direction of industries served. Leadership offered by creating new industries, changing old ones, conducting seminars, recognizing achievements, founding technical associations. Examples.

1506 Gussow, Don. THE NEW BUSINESS JOURNALISM: AN INSIDER'S LOOK AT THE WORKING OF AMERICA'S BUSINESS PRESS. San Diego, Calif.: Harcourt Brace Jovanovich, 1984.

Written for would-be and junior journalists. History, functions, and structure of the business press are covered. Growth, advertising, public relations for and merchandising of magazines explained. Bibliography, glossary, and partial list of colleges offering business journalism. Basic, useful.

1507 Hartmen, Thomas. "Reporting For Service: The Big Guns of the Military Press." WASHINGTON JOURNALISM REVIEW 6 (July-August 1984) : 28-32.

The military press consists of independent publications dealing with defense issues. Examples are AVIATION WEEK & SPACE TECHNOLOGY, ARMY TIMES, DEFENSE WEEK.

1508 Hulin-Salkin, Belinda. "Media Giants Muscle In As Revenues Rise." ADVERTISING AGE 56 (April 25, 1985) : 13+.

1984 was a good year for the business press.

1509 Jereski, Laura Konrad. "Booming Business Press Plans Small Cost Push." MARKETING & MEDIA DECISIONS 19 (Fall 1984 special) : 73-74+.

Economic review points to a healthy business press. Predictions for industry growth, increased advertising rates and pages.

1510 Kimbrell, Wendy. "Cahners Steps on Fast Track For Growth." ADVERTISING AGE 56 (April 25, 1985) : 26-27.

Cahners reflects changes in the business press with stepped-up advertising campaign, desire for new magazines, growth.

1511 King, Thomas H. "The Business Press: Success For the Right Reasons." FOLIO 400 11 (October 1982) : 360.

Praise for the business press from the president of the ABP (now Association of Business Press Publishers).

1512 King, Thomas H. "Competing In the Shifting Marketplace." FOLIO 400 12 (October 1983) : 522.

Even in the face of competition from cable tv, the business press will remain successful because of editorial leadership, says ABP president.

1513 McGuire, Jack. "Business of the Business Press." ADVERTISING AGE 51 (June 9, 1980) : S20-S23.

Profiles of three business publishers who found their niches in three different ways: by expanding and acquiring titles, by concentrating on a specific editorial focus, by developing a single-advertiser magazine.

1514 Maher, Philip. "IRON AGE Develops Reach and Frequency Service." INDUSTRIAL MARKETING 67 (December 1982) : 25-26.

Reach and frequency analysis tells advertisers which and how many people see their ads, and how often they see them. Used by consumer magazines, it is now available for trade journals.

1515 "Major Magazine Publisher Updates its System to Keep Pace With Growth." COMMUNICATIONS NEWS 17 (July 1980) : 66-67.

Internal computerized telephone communication network at Harcourt Brace Jovanovich.

1516 "Meridian Publishing Company Offers Packaged Communiçations." INLAND PRINTER/AMERICAN LITHOGRAPHER 179 (September 1977) : 70-72.

This publisher offers nine different magazines dealing with home and general interest subjects that may be purchased by businesses for use as internal or external house organs.

1517 Mill, Charles S. "Acquisitions Change Face of Business Press." ADVERTISING AGE 50 (June 25, 1979) : S1+.

Current trends in the business press, with particular emphasis on the effects of mergers and acquisitions, conversion to offset printing, growth of business-to-business advertising, and spin-off publications.

1518 Mill, Charles S. "Business Papers Visualize Multimedia Moves In '80s." ADVERTISTNG AGE 51 (April 30, 1980) : 181-184.

Capsule history of the business press and brief forecast for the future. Part of a special AA issue on the relationship between advertising and society.

1519 Moyer, Ronald S. "Techniques For Converting From Free To Paid." FOLIO 14 (June 1985) : 93-97.

Systematic approaches and tips for converting from free to paid circulation. List of key considerations for determining whether to convert.

1520 Mulholland, James S., Jr. "Business Press Adds New Services To Increase Revenues and Profits." ADVERTISING AGE 45 (November 18, 1974) : 99.

Rising costs and ways to increase revenue in the business press.

1521 Neher, Jacques. "Magazines Feast On Industry Growth." ADVERTISING AGE 50 (August 13, 1979) : S12-S13.

The wide variety of specialized business magazines for the food service industry.

1522 Oliver, Belinda J. "SMRB's New Study: A Taste of What May Come?" MAGAZINE AGE 6 (January 1985) : 65+.

Simmon's market study for RESTAURANTS & INSTITUTIONS is called its first for a specialized business magazine. Description and methodology for the "reach and frequency" study. Implied utility of such study for other specialized business publications.

1523 Owen, David. "The Fifth Estate: Eavesdropping On American Business Talking To Itself." ATLANTIC 256 (July 1985) : 80-84.

A look at a variety of trade magazines. Most are little known, not sold on newsstands, but very profitable. Emphasis on content, new product news, public relations releases. Influence of these publications not based on numbers of readers but on who they are.

1524 Paskowski, Marianne. "Business Press Report: Mixed Reviews for the Medium." INDUSTRIAL MARKETING 65 (December 1980) : 30-32+.

Mixed predictions about the business press' declining share of advertising dollars.

1525 Patterson, Perry. "81's Hot Trade Magazines: Good Year Expected For Publishers." INDUSTRIAL MARKETING 67 (March 1982) : 99-100.

Forecast for advertising gains in business publications.

1526 Pool, Gail. "Magazines." WILSON LIBRARY BULLETIN 57 (September 1982) : 67-68.

Overview of the business press, including news coverage of industry, advertising, puffery, and the commercial value and ethics of advertorials. Trade publications can be critical of industries they serve by raising issues and openly criticizing major companies.

1527 Pool, Gail. "Magazines." WILSON LIBRARY BULLETIN 58 (January 1984) : 364-365.

Magazines for the small businessman or entrepreneur, with particular emphasis on INC.

1528 Pool, Gail. "Magazines." WILSON LIBRARY BULLETIN 58 (June 1984) : 748-749.

Advertising receives little coverage in the general press. ADVERTISING AGE, a trade publication for advertising "insiders," provides good understanding of the field. A favorable review of AA.

1529 Stevenson, Richard W. "The Battle of Two Ad Magazines." NEW YORK TIMES, 14 October 1985, p. D1+.

ADWEEK is offering competition to ADVERTISING AGE. As ADWEEK increases its circulation, ADVERTISING AGE publishes twice a week, offering a special "Thursday" magazine.

1530 "Trade Magazines Use Catalog Sections as Merchandising Aids." FOLIO 13 (March 1984) : 26-27.

Trade magazines offer advertising opportunities in special brochure sections similar to catalogs.

1531 "Trade Publications Suffer or Thrive Along With the Market They Cover." WALL STREET JOURNAL, 2 September 1982, p. 1.

Brief news item provides several examples.

1532 Wall, Wendy L. "ADVERTISING AGE's Editor Quits as Plan to Expand Proceeds: Shake-up is Seen as Weekly Prepares to Take on Rival and Print Twice a Week." WALL STREET JOURNAL, 2 April 1984, p. 26.

Changes in direction for ADVERTISING AGE as it competes with ADVERTISING WEEK may be forthcoming.

1533 "What's New in Green Thumbs and Big Blue." MAGAZINE AGE 6 (May 1985) : 48-49.

A round-up of research on specialized magazines offers glimpses of fascinating information found in specialized business magazines.

1534 Wood, Wally. "Comparing Apples to Apples." MAGAZINE AGE 6 (April 1985) : 59-61.

Half BPA's one thousand audited publications agree with media buyers on common definition of audience and questionnaire used to measure individuals against that definition. Result is alleged comparability within 101 magazine markets.

1535 Wood, Wally. "Notice of Censure." MAGAZINE AGE 6 (July 1985) : 46-47.

What it means to advertisers when BPA censures magazines. Three levels of action against magazines are censure, probation, and expulsion. How to seek meaning behind these labels.

1536 Wood, Wally. "Through-the-Book for the Metalworking Market." MARKETING & MEDIA DECISIONS 21 (April 1986) : 150+.

Simmons Market Research Bureau conducts first readership study of an industrial market using through-the-book methodology. Paid for by IRON AGE. Brief methodological notes, and criticism of study from AMERICAN MACHINIST.

House Organs

1537 Barrus, Robert J. "Champion Closes the Gap World-Wide." INDUSTRIAL MARKETING 64 (October 1979) : 68+.

Champion Spark Plug's external house organ, MOTOR MAIL, is printed in eleven languages.

1538 Boushay, James M. "Company 'House Organs' Offer Treasure Chest of Journalistic Ideas." QUILL AND SCROLL 51 (October-November 1976) : 4-7.

House organs provide content and format ideas for school publication editors. Includes a list of representative company publications.

1539 Cheney, George. "Rhetoric of Identification and the Study of Organizational Communication." QUARTERLY JOURNAL OF SPEECH 69 (May 1983) : 143-158.

Study of ten corporate magazines from 1979 isolated strategies used to promote identification between employees and the corporation.

1540 "Company Publications." CPA JOURNAL 50 (December 1980) : 91-94.

Excerpt from SMALL BUSINESS REPORT on company publications--goal, editorial content, newsletters, and response testing.

1541 D'aprix, Roger M. "The Believable House Organ." MANAGEMENT REVIEW 68 (February 1979) : 23-28.

The role of the corporate communicator, management objectives for house organs, and the need to bridge the "credibility gap" between employees and management.

1542 "Focusing on Publishing or Perishing." NATIONAL UNDERWRITER (Property Edition) 84 (July 11, 1980) : 45+.

Advice on typography and graphics for editors of external house organs published for insurance agents.

1543 Fossage, Neal. "What to Know Before Starting a Corporate Magazine ... and Why Selling ads in Them Presents a Gamble." BUSINESS MARKETING 64 (December 1984) : 98+.

Economics, format, editorial, graphics, audience, marketing/image objectives when launching a corporate magazine.

1544 Grover, Stephen. "Most Firms' House Organs Emphasize Employee News and Avoid Controversy." WALL STREET JOURNAL, 17 November 1978, p. 19.

Company publications present an image of management's benevolence, emphasizing employees' work and play. An overview with examples.

1545 Hall, Trish. "Philip Morris Co. Magazine Promotes Pro-Smoking Issues." WALL STREET JOURNAL, 24 July 1985, p.12.

Quarterly publication designed for smokers promotes the cigarette industry.

1546 Hargreaves, Thomas G. "The Manager as Editor." MANAGEMENT WORLD 7 (June 1978) : 12-16.

Tips for the manager on beginning, financing, editing, and managing a company magazine. Suggests the editor does not need to be an expert.

1547 "How Amex Employees Learn What's Happening." MANAGEMENT REVIEW 69 (February 1980) : 48-49.

A new employee communication system at American Express features a quarterly magazine, videotape magazine, and newsletters.

1548 Howard, Elizabeth. "More Than a Bulletin Board." PUBLIC RELATIONS JOURNAL 38 (July 1982) : 34-35.

Suggestions for improving content and design objectives of company magazines.

1549 Jeffers, Dennis W., and Bateman, David N. "Redefining the Role of the Company Magazine." PUBLIC RELATIONS REVIEW 6 (Summer 1980) : 11-29.

Proposed model for setting goals and measuring effectiveness of company publications. House organs need to become part of management decision-making and evaluation.

1550 Mann, Jim. "Is Your House Organ a Vital Organ?" PERSONNEL JOURNAL 56 (September 1977) : 461-462.

For an effective company magazine, management needs to determine the purpose and audience of the publication and evaluate whether the cost is worth the potential achievement.

1551 Mehren, Elizabeth. "Smokers You're Not Alone." LOS ANGELES TIMES, 26 July 1985, sec. 5, p. 1+.

PHILIP MORRIS MAGAZINE, with controlled circulation of 150,000, is a consumer-sized four-color quarterly. It covers smoking positively, with topics such as coping with militant non-smokers and growing tobacco.

1552 Mills, David. "Publications at No Charge are Subtle Ads." WALL STREET JOURNAL, 5 August 1983, p. 23.

Corporate-sponsored magazines serve advertising purposes.

1553 Neuman, Jackie Stillwell. "IMPACT Readership Survey." M.A. thesis, University of Texas, 1983.

Readership of employee magazine, IMPACT. Frequency and amount of reading was related to length of employment and type of work performed.

1554 "Never Underestimate the Employee Newsletter." TRAINING AND DEVELOPMENT JOURNAL 38 (February 1984) : 7.

Goals of the successful house organ.

1555 Orser, Frank. "Selling Readership: An Approach to the Production of the Company-Sponsored Magazine." SERIALS REVIEW 7 (October-December 1981) : 43-45.

External house organs may be produced in-house or by specialized communications firms like Webb Co. Some considerations and advantages for companies wishing to sponsor a magazine.

1556 Pool, Gail. "Magazines." WILSON LIBRARY BULLETIN 58 (February 1984) : 445-446.

Company-sponsored magazines are usually distributed free, and few have outside advertising. Many avoid ethical conflicts by emphasizing editorial unrelated to the company's products.

1557 Pool, Gail. "Marketers Use Custom Magazines to Toot Their Own Horns." AD FORUM 4 (September 1983) : 41+.

1558 Rosen, M. Daniel. "An Editorial Snapshot of 15 Customer Magazines." COMMUNICATION WORLD (March 1985) : 15-17.

Descriptions of 15 external house organs representing different formats, companies, editorial approaches, etc.

1559 Salmans, Sandra. "Getting Employees to Read the Company Newsletter." INTERNATIONAL MANAGEMENT 32 (June 1977) : 48-50.

Employee newsletter needs balanced treatment of good and bad corporate news.

1560 Sloan, Pat. "Bloomies' Book Adds Ads; Will Editorial Come Next?" ADVERTISING AGE 56 (July 29, 1985) : 3.

Bloomingdale's catalog carries paid advertising. Will it add editorial copy and become a magazine?

1561 "Stores Try Publishing Their Own Magazines." BUSINESS WEEK (July 27, 1981) : 34.

Department store magazines aimed at customers are external house organs.

1562 Wells, Hugh. "Comforting Dialogue for a Corporate Editor." PUBLIC RELATIONS JOURNAL 39 (August 1983) : 35.

Lightly written editorial about the role of a house organ editor.

1563 Winski, Joseph M. "Giving House Organ a Quality Image is a Tough Road to Hoe." WALL STREET JOURNAL, 12 November 1974, p. 1+.

Profile of Deere & Co.'s house organ, THE FURROW.

Chapter 17

TYPES OF MAGAZINES

General Interest Magazines

1564 Alter, Jonathan. "Just Like a Rolling Stone." NEWSWEEK 105 (June 17, 1985) : 63.

ROLLING STONE publisher, Jann Wenner, caters to his enjoyment of celebrity journalism with his acquisition of US. How the revamped US will face its competition, PEOPLE.

1565 Alter, Jonathan. "Trying to Buy a Legend." NEWSWEEK 105 (February 25, 1985) : 90-91.

Following S. I. Newhouse's offer to buy the NEW YORKER, there is much speculation into his reasons and his plans for the magazine.

1566 Bagdikian, Ben H. "The Wrong Kind of Readers: The Rise and Fall of the NEW YORKER." PROGRESSIVE

47 (May 1983) : 52-54.

Problems for the NEW YORKER can be traced to the magazine's editorial stand against the Viet Nam War. Readership increased on college campuses, but advertisers withdrew their business because the magazine attracted the "wrong kind of reader." By the early 1980s, its high-quality demographics (i.e., affluent readers) had recovered.

1567 Baker, Ross K. "Taking Off, Putting On." AMERICAN DEMOGRAPHICS 5 (August 1983) : 52.

Tongue-in-cheek comment on the decline of nudity in the NATIONAL GEOGRAPHIC. With alternative magazines offering nudity, growing lack of nude models in natural environments to photograph, and high advertising costs, the magazine is facing financial difficulties.

1568 Barber, Simon. "The Boss Don't Like Robbery, Make It Swindle: Inside the NATIONAL ENQUIRER." WASHINGTON JOURNALISM REVIEW 4 (July-August 1982) : 46-49.

Readable first person account of what it's like to work for the NATIONAL ENQUIRER. How story ideas are conceived, written, and researched.

1569 Beem, Edgar Allen. "If You're in Maine, You Advertise in the NEW YORKER." THE PRESS 10 (October 1982) : 9-10.

NEW YORKER has a relatively small circulation, but excellent demographics. Readers are 95 percent college educated with average annual household income over $61,000. Thirty-four Maine businesses advertised in the NEW YORKER in 1981.

1570 Beinstock, Michael E. "Gossip Lives." MARKETING & MEDIA DECISIONS 20 (October 1985) : 100+.

Magazines respond to readers' "unquenchable desire for knowledge" about celebrities. Some gossip magazines upgrade graphics, paper, and appearance to attract younger, upscale readers.

1571 Benzel, Jan. "People's Choice." WASHINGTON JOURNALISM REVIEW 6 (December 1984) : 34-37.

Profile of PEOPLE magazine's managing editor, Pat Ryan.

1572 Berg, Eric N. "Newhouse Purchasing the NEW YORKER." NEW YORK TIMES, 9 March 1985, p. 1+.

Sale marks the first time the NEW YORKER has changed hands since its 1924 founding. Newhouse promises independence for the magazine.

1573 Bernard, George. INSIDE THE NATIONAL ENQUIRER ... CONFESSIONS OF AN UNDERCOVER REPORTER. Port Washington, N.Y.: Ashley Books, 1977.

Former NATIONAL ENQUIRER reporter gives first

person account of his experiences reporting for the tabloid.

1574 Block, Bernard. "Romance and High Purpose: The NATIONAL GEOGRAPHIC." WILSON LIBRARY BULLETIN 58 (January 1984) : 333.

Profile of the NATIONAL GEOGRAPHIC from the early twentieth century.

1575 Brockway, Brian. "Always on Sunday." MADISON AVENUE 27 (February 1985) : 92+.

The new look in Sunday magazines and general comments on the genre. Recent problems include competition from free-standing advertising inserts and undefined image.

1576 Brookhiser, Richard. "Evil of Banality." NATIONAL REVIEW 37 (October 4, 1985) : 47-49.

Scathing criticism of the NEW YORKER. Praise for editor Shawn, cartoons, and the magazine's accuracy seems insignificant when compared to the magazine's alleged sterility, confusion, irrelevancies, and poor reviews.

1577 Buffum, Charles. "Sunday Best: Newspaper Magazines and a Parade of Weekend Reading." WASHINGTON JOURNALISM REVIEW 5 (October 1983) : 32-35.

Locally-edited Sunday newspaper magazines offer wide variety in format and are a healthy segment of the magazine and newspaper industries.

1578 Carney, Thomas. "They Only Laughed When It Hurt." NEW TIMES 11 (August 21, 1978) : 48-55.

Profile and problems of the NATIONAL LAMPOON, founded 1969.

1579 "CHANGING TIMES Happy with Ad Move." ADVERTISING AGE 53 (June 14, 1982) : 37.

Although profitable, CHANGING TIMES needed a new revenue source, so began accepting advertising.

1580 Christenson, Reo M. "Report on the READER'S DIGEST." COLUMBIA JOURNALISM REVIEW 3 (Winter 1965) : 30-36.

Analysis of READER'S DIGEST public affairs content, with emphasis on two specific articles.

1581 Conaway, James. "All the World to See: The Globe Trotting Journalists of the NATIONAL GEOGRAPH-IC." WASHINGTON POST, 20 December 1984, p. B1+.

Brief human interest recount of the strange interests and unusual lifestyles of NATIONAL GEOGRAPHIC photograhers.

1582 Conroy, Sarah Booth. "The NEW YORKER ain't Broke ... " WASHINGTON POST, 22 September 1985, p. C5.

WASHINGTON POST commentary on the lamentable condition of the NEW YORKER. Clearly the paper feels such change unthinkable. An American institution has been lost.

1583 Corkery, P. J. "The NATIONAL ENQUIRER." ROLLING STONE (June 11, 1981) : 18-21+.

First person account of life as an editor and reporter on the NATIONAL ENQUIRER.

1584 Cote, Kevin. "DIGEST Wrestles with Local Image." ADVERTISING AGE 55 (December 3, 1984) : 56-57.

Problems in attracting advertisers for READER'S DIGEST international editions.

1585 Cowan, Wayne. "Digesting the DIGEST." CHRISTIANITY AND CRISIS 43 (March 21, 1983) : 94-98.

READER'S DIGEST philosophy and biases as perceived by a religious critic.

1586 Diamond, Edwin. "Celebrating Celebrity." NEW YORK 18 (May 13, 1985) : 22+.

The market for gossipy, celebrity magazines is expanding. Includes old, new, and redesigned titles--PICTURE WEEK, US, ET (Entertainment Tonight), PEOPLE. Comments on why celebrity magazines are so popular.

1587 Diamond, Edwin. "The Talk of the NEW YORKER." NEW YORK 18 (March 25, 1985) : 14.

What will life be like at the NEW YORKER after William Shawn's retirement and takeover by S. I Newhouse? Mention of rarefied atmosphere to date, political maneuverings of staff and editor. Another useful look at the NEW YORKER phenomenon.

1588 Elliott, Stuart J. "Eustace Moving to a Newhouse?" ADVERTISING AGE 56 (February 18, 1985) : 2+.

Problems at the NEW YORKER, and the potential benefits of a possible purchase by Newhouse.

1589 Elliott, Stuart J. "First Fallout at NEW YORKER." ADVERTISING AGE 56 (May 27, 1985) : 1+.

Retirement of J. Kennard Bosee, president of the NEW YORKER MAGAZINE Inc., following disagreements with new owner Newhouse of Advance Publications. NEW YORKER executives said to be concerned over Advanced Publication's involvement in NEW YORKER business operations.

1590 Elliott, Stuart J. "New LIFE Turning Corner to Profitability." ADVERTISING AGE 54 (September 26, 1983) : 82.

LIFE's profitability is increasing as its new identity takes root.

1591 Elliott, Stuart J. "NEW YORKER Looks 'Up' to 86." ADVERTISING AGE 56 (September 30, 1985) : 92.

Under new publisher Steven Florio, NEW YORKER plans costly tv promotional campaign to build circulation and increase advertising pages. Other changes include revised advertising policy to allow more formats.

1592 Elliott, Stuart J. "Personality Journalism Develops Sunny Disposition: Popular PEOPLE Makes Friends, Influences Rivals." ADVERTISING AGE 56 (October 3, 1985) : 27.

Profiles of some celebrity magazines that meet growing public interest in personality journalism. Comparison of PEOPLE, US, STAR, ET (a spin-off of television's Entertainment Tonight).

1593 Elliott, Stuart J. "Steve Florio: The Best and the Brashest at the NEW YORKER." ADVERTISING AGE 56 (July 11, 1985) : 4-5.

Career profile of the new man in charge of the NEW YORKER. New publisher's background includes ESQUIRE and GENTLEMAN'S QUARTERLY.

1594 Elliott, Stuart J. "VANITY FAIR Feels Time Will Tell Its Success." ADVERTISING AGE 57 (March 31, 1986) : 36.

Circulation and advertising increase. Success related to editor Tina Brown's creation of consistent identity for VF, blending famous literary figures, trendy fun, social commentary, and chic celebrities.

1595 Elsner, David. "SATURDAY EVENING POST, 1970s Model, Attracts Readers but not Ads." WALL STREET JOURNAL, 2 November 1977, 1+.

The new POST, a nostalgia magazine, doesn't need advertising to survive.

1596 Elzey, Wayne. "The Most Unforgettable Magazine I've Ever Read: Religion and Social Hygiene in the READER'S DIGEST." JOURNAL OF POPULAR CULTURE 10 (SUMMER 1976) : 181-190.

The READER'S DIGEST offers a "social cosmology" or clear, practical, and consistent scheme for interpreting the world. A non-quantitative analysis of DIGEST content.

1597 "ENQUIRER Loses Round." ADVERTISING AGE 52 (March 23, 1981) : 2.

In libel suit against the NATIONAL ENQUIRER, judge rules the tabloid is a magazine not a newspaper.

1598 Fabrikant, Geraldine. "VANITY FAIR's Slick Formula; New Success for Magazine." NEW YORK TIMES, 26 August 1985, p. D1+.

The troubled VANITY FAIR has improved circulation and increased advertising pages, although it is still losing money. Editorial primarily covers lifestyles of the rich and powerful.

1599 Gage, Theodore J. "Inside Info: ENQUIRER Tells All. Can a Readership of 20 Million Be Bad?" ADVERTISING AGE 53 (December 6, 1982) : M34-M35.

Although audience demographics are low, circulation is high. NATIONAL ENQUIRER wants to sell itself to skeptics in the advertising business.

1600 Garment, Suzanne "READER'S DIGEST Continues to Chase Big Stories." WALL STREET JOURNAL, 7 January 1983, p. 16.

The READER'S DIGEST editorial policy includes hard-hitting investigative stories.

1601 "The GEOGRAPHIC Maps its Route to a Rebound." BUSINESS WEEK (July 19, 1982) : 60.

Financial problems possible for the non-profit NATIONAL GEOGRAPHIC, as the magazine faces circulation loss. Even though the publication loses money, the Society has healthy revenues of $272 million annually.

1602 Gloede, William F. "CBS Sells Off FAMILY WEEKLY." ADVERTISING AGE 56 (February 25, 1985) : 1+.

Gannett agrees to buy FAMILY WEEKLY, an ailing magazine CBS has been unable to make profitable.

1603 Gloede, William. "Defections to PARADE Rain on USA WEEKEND." ADVERTISING AGE 56 (July 29, 1985) : 1+.

Many newspapers are switching to PARADE from the revised FAMILY WEEKLY (now USA WEEKEND since its revamp and purchase by Gannett). Circulation increases for PARADE will change the market and cast doubt on the future of the Sunday Magazine Network.

1604 Gloede, William. "Sunday Magazine Warfare Winds Down." ADVERTISING AGE 56 (October 21, 1985) : 56.

Competition between PARADE and USA WEEKEND cools off.

1605 Gloede, William. "Sunday Magazines Feel Ad Pinch." ADVERTISING AGE 56 (January 24, 1985) : 28+.

Sunday magazines are losing ad pages. Some problems are high cost of advertising, weak editorial, incompatibility of the medium with advertisers' goals.

1606 Gloede, William F. "USA WEEKEND Rolls South, West." ADVERTISING AGE 56 (August 5, 1985) : 64.

Brief update on the circulation competition between PARADE and USA WEEKEND (formerly FAMILY WEEKLY). See also AA, 26 August 1985, p. 42.

1607 Goldman, John J., and Mehren, Elizabeth. "Inside the NEW YORKER: Fear and Trembling." LOS ANGELES TIMES, 27 March 1985, sec. 5, p. 1+.

Since its birth, the NEW YORKER has had only one owner and two editors. Proposed sale to Newhouse leaves unrest. Will the unique magazine change under corporate ownership? Many comments by eminent press critic Ben Bagdikian.

1608 Gourlay, Jay. "'I Killed Gig Young!' and Other Confessions from Inside the NATIONAL ENQUIRER." WASHINGTON MONTHLY 13 (September 1981) : 32-38.

Contest stimulates story-idea gathering at the NATIONAL ENQUIRER.

1609 Green, Joey. "Last Laughs." ROLLING STONE (September 29, 1983) : 74+.

Lengthy historical review of the NATIONAL LAMPOON from its 1970 founding. Emphasis on the personalities that created and shaped it. Formerly a top humor magazine, this critic finds it "low on gags."

1610 Griffith, Thomas. "Trouble in Paradise. Yes,

Trouble." TIME 117 (January 12, 1981) : 58-59.

The NEW YORKER is receiving mixed reviews from critics. Some feel admiration, others betrayal at its lack of inspiration and growing boredom. As long-time editor William Shawn approaches retirement, the staff is unsettled about the future.

1611 Griffin, George. "The Gospel According to Tabloids." GRAPHIC ARTS MONTHLY 55 (August 1983) : 130+.

How the tabloids use graphics to provoke reader involvement.

1612 Grover, Stephen. "Grocery-Day Gossip is Ringing up Profit at PEOPLE Magazine." WALL STREET JOURNAL, 6 May 1976 p. 1+.

PEOPLE magazine is selling successfully at supermarket check-out counters.

1613 Hayes, John P. "Newspaper-Sponsored Magazines as a Market for Freelancers." JOURNALISM QUARTERLY 56 (Autumn 1979) : 586-589.

Survey of Sunday supplements reveals their high use of free-lance material.

1614 Hayes, John P. "Sunday Newspaper Magazines: Good Market for Students." JOURNALISM EDUCATOR 34 (July 1979) : 48-50.

Surveyed newspaper-sponsored magazines report 50 percent free-lance editorial content. Yet magazines receive few queries.

1615 Holder, Stephen. "The Family Magazine and the American People." JOURNAL OF POPULAR CULTURE 7 (Fall 1973) : 264-279.

The role of family magazines, such as COLLIER'S and SATURDAY EVENING POST. How they interacted with the audience to provide information, entertainment, escape, assistance in forming opinion, reinforcement of values, and a consumer's showcase.

1616 Hornblower, Margot. "It's New! It's Old! It's US." WASHINGTON POST, 17 June 1985, p. D1+.

Profile of US under Jann Wenner's brand new leadership. Pictures magazine as continuingly fluffy, insignificant Hollywood-oriented pap.

1617 Hornblower, Margot. "New Face at the NEW YORKER: from Steve Florio, a Marketing Revolution." WASHINGTON POST, 19 September 1985, p. C1.

The loosening up of the sixty-year-old magazine after Newhouse purchase, including television appearances and perfume ads featuring nudes.

1618 Hynds, Ernest C. "Survey Examines Status of Newspapers' Magazines." EDITOR & PUBLISHER 112 (July 7, 1979) : 32-33.

Editorial policies, objectives, content, staff, and planned changes on locally-edited Sunday magazines.

1619 Jones, Alex S. "At READER'S DIGEST, A Fight Over Philosophy." NEW YORK TIMES, 1 June 1984, p. A1+.

Shake-up in top management at the READER'S DIGEST. Editor-in-chief Ed Thompson is fired.

1620 Jones, Alex S. "Newhouse is Purchasing the NEW YORKER for $142 Million." NEW YORK TIMES, 9 March 1985, p. 31.

Article focuses briefly on the vast communications holdings of the Newhouse family.

1621 Kaiser, Charles. "The Talk of the NEW YORKER." NEWSWEEK 101 (March 14, 1983) : 67-68.

As the "resident genius" of the NEW YORKER, editor William Shawn, nears retirement, speculation about the future of the magazine runs high. Many believe Shawn's choice of successor a poor one.

1622 Kelly, James. "Changing the Guard at 60: Media Baron Samuel I. Newhouse will Buy the NEW YORKER." TIME 125 (March 18, 1985) : 65.

S. I. Newhouse acquires the NEW YORKER. Although he promises to "preserve the quality of the magazine," many staff members lack confidence in his promises.

1623 Kessler, Ellen Terry. "Always on Sunday: Big Numbers for National Advertisers." MAGAZINE AGE 1 (March 1980) : 22-24.

Popularity of Sunday magazines. Detailed comparison for advertisers of nationally-syndicated and individually-published magazines. Many are changing their images and marketing themselves aggressively as magazines not newspaper supplements.

1624 Kobel, Peter. "NEW AGE Strives for a New Image". ADVERTISING AGE 57 (February 17, 1986) : 46.

Profile of NEW AGE, a general interest magazine with a specific audience--an upscale readership with a social conscience. NEW AGE accepts no tobacco advertising.

1625 Lacob, Miriam. "Drama in Real Life at READER'S DIGEST." FOLIO 14 (February 1985) : 88-92.

The controversy behind Edward T. Thompson's firing from READER'S DIGEST editorship. Were declining profitability and waning editorial strength involved?

1626 Lacob, Miriam. "READER'S DIGEST: Who's in Charge?" COLUMBIA JOURNALISM REVIEW 23 (July-August 1984) : 41-43.

The reasons why READER'S DIGEST's editor-in-chief was forced into early retirement.

1627 "LOS ANGELES TIMES MAGAZINE." MADISON AVE 27 (June 1985) : 86-91.

A new concept in Sunday magazines will be introduced by the LOS ANGELES TIMES. The consumer format publication is touted by its staff as having numerous readership advantages for prospective advertisers.

1628 Lowenstein, Roger. "NATIONAL ENQUIRER Softening its Image in Bid for New Advertisers and Readers." WALL STREET JOURNAL, 25 October 1985, p. 33.

NATIONAL ENQUIRER attracts more advertising as service articles such as recipes and "how-to" pieces are added. Although celebrity journalism is still the publication's mainstay, it faces a lot of competition from other celebrity magazines. Revenues are climbing, but circulation is down.

1629 MacDougall, A. Kent. "READER'S DIGEST Posts Top Publishing Success Since the Scriptures." WALL STREET JOURNAL, 17 March 1966, p. 1.

Timeless commentary on DIGEST philosophy and content.

1630 McFadden, Maureen. "The Sunday Magazines: Advertisers View Changes Warily." MAGAZINE AGE 4 (September 1983) : 48-49.

Sunday supplements charge high ad rates, anticipate some format changes and improved editorial, and seek (but have been unsuccessful) recognition as national magazines from the MPA. Note the full-page advertisement for the Sunday Magazine Network within this article.

1631 Machalaba, Daniel. "More Papers Publish Sunday Magazines, Gaining Prestige and Challenging PARADE." WALL STREET JOURNAL, 1 June 1982, p. 30.

Many Sunday newspapers are starting magazine supplements, using a formula that works--local personality cover stories, celebrity question and answer features, puzzle pages, and home decorating articles. PARADE responds by offering a special edition with local features and advertising.

1632 Meyers, Janet. "POST Time for Revamped Sunday Book." ADVERTISING AGE 57 (April 21, 1986) : 35.

Redesign for WASHINGTON POST SUNDAY MAGAZINE follows lead by other Sunday supplements for a down-sized book with upscale editorial to attract affluent readers.

1633 Miller, Annetta. "Going Straight: THE NATIONAL ENQUIRER has an Identity Crisis." FLORIDA TREND (July 1985) : 52.

1634 Mitchell, Henry. "Keeping the Change at the NEW YORKER." WASHINGTON POST, 20 September 1985, p. B2.

Critical commentary on change at the seemingly unchangeable NEW YORKER. One of a series of editorials in the POST lamenting linguistic and attitudinal changes since the Newhouse purchase.

1635 "The NEW YORKER's New Owner." BUSINESS WEEK (March 25, 1985) : 36.

News brief on Samuel I. Newhouse Jr. and his purchase of the NEW YORKER.

1636 "Newspapers." ADVERTISING AGE 56 (January 24, 1985) : 13-43.

The special report on newspapers deals with Sunday editions, and has several articles on Sunday supplement magazines (pp. 28-38).

1637 "Now the Story can be Told! How Tabloids Survived the Recession." BUSINESS WEEK (November 7, 1983) : 145+.

The four major tabloids (NATIONAL ENQUIRER, STAR, GLOBE, NATIONAL EXAMINER) were unaffected by the recession, and had the greatest increase in newsstand sales of all magazines in 1982. Sophisticated marketing, public interest in celebrities, cheap cover prices contribute to their success.

1638 Pendleton, Jennifer, and Cuneo, Alice Z. "Good Start for Two Sunday Magazines." ADVERTISING AGE 56 (October 21, 1985) : 54.

Innovative, slick Sunday magazines from the LOS ANGELES TIMES and SAN FRANCISCO CHRONICLE AND EXAMINER are well-received.

1639 Peter, John. "Learning from LIFE--Old and New." FOLIO 15 (January 1986) : 142-144.

The new LIFE is no longer a news-oriented weekly but a more colorful monthly photo feature magazine. Pictorial essay illustrates some differences in page layouts and covers.

1640 Peter, John. "Sunday Supplements Now Real Magazines." FOLIO 14 (September 1985) : 115-117.

Sunday supplements are becoming recognized as controlled circulation magazines. Layout illustrations show their superior designs which are not always matched by superior editorial content. Only a few supplements are of magazine quality.

1641 Radolf, Andrew. "Metro Sunday Newspapers Predict Turnaround." EDITOR & PUBLISHER 116 (December 10, 1983) : 12-13.

Sunday magazine ad revenues down. Suggestions for selling space by convincing advertisers "their ads work better when directly associated with editorial columns."

1642 Randall, Michael H. "Tabloids." SERIALS REVIEW 11 (Summer 1985) : 31-35.

Popularity, credibility, content, reporting networks of tabloids. Comparative reviews of four titles--that may "err on the side of charity." Includes the GLOBE, NATIONAL ENQUIRER, NATIONAL EXAMINER, SUN.

1643 Ranly, Don. "A Look at Editors, Content and Future of the Sunday Newspaper Magazine." JOURNALISM QUARTERLY 58 (Summer 1981) : 279-285.

Survey of Sunday newspaper magazine editors finds job contentment, little previous magazine experience, disagreement about best content, and popularity of the publications.

1644 Rogers, Brian. "A Cut--a Large Cut--Above the Rest." ADVERTISING AGE 52 (November 23, 1981) : S44-S45+.

Uniqueness of the award-winning Sunday NEW YORK TIMES MAGAZINE.

1645 Rovit, Earl. "Modernism and Three Magazines: An Editorial Revolution." SEWANEE REVIEW 93 (Fall 1985) : 540-553.

TIME, READER'S DIGEST, and the NEW YORKER, cultural products of the late 1920s. As consumer products, they are "masterpieces of design."

Their optimism and adherence to the American Dream parallel messages from Hollywood and Madison Avenue.

1646 Rozen, Leah. "DIGEST to Avoid Change." ADVERTISING AGE 52 (April 20, 1981) : 28.

READER'S DIGEST editor-in-chief, Edward T. Thompson, announces there are no planned changes in policy or personnel with the recent death of founder Dewitt Wallace.

1647 Rowse, Arthur, and Stillman, Don. "Two DIGEST Cases." COLUMBIA JOURNALISM REVIEW 6 (Winter 1967-1968) : 24-27.

Two brief articles on READER'S DIGEST. The first criticizes use of advertorials nearly indistinguishable from editorial copy. The second criticizes a DIGEST series on diminishing social security resources that is alleged to present "highly debatable conclusions" as "factual analysis."

1648 Ruth, Marcia. "Sunday Magazines." PRESSTIME 8 (April 1986) : 12-14.

New competition among nationally distributed Sunday magazines, and changing format among locally produced supplements. Despite vast differences among titles, many believe they should unite to sell advertising space.

1649 Schwartz, Tony. "The GEOGRAPHIC Faces Life." NEWSWEEK 83 (September 12, 1977) : 111.

Dispute over the GEOGRAPHIC's editorial direction and the publication of controversial articles.

1650 Shenon, Philip. "GEOGRAPHIC's Troubled World." NEW YORK TIMES, 16 December 1982, p. F10.

Financial problems at the National Geographic Society.

1651 Shloss, Carol. "Privilege of Perception." VIRGINIA QUARTERLY REVIEW 56 (Autumn 1980) : 596-611.

James Agee's perceptions of Margaret Bourke-White, photojournalist for LIFE magazine.

1652 Span, Paula. "In the Picture: The First Decade of PEOPLE Magazine." WASHINGTON POST, 3 March 1984, p. C1+.

PEOPLE owes its success to "personality journalism" and photography. Celebrities' unwillingness to pose for photographs and the negotiations involved are briefly discussed.

1653 Stein, Jeff. "An Optimist for CHANGING TIMES." MAINLINER (MARCH 1980) : 62+.

Profile of Austin Kiplinger, founder of CHANGING TIMES and other publications.

1654 "Supps Busting Out All Over." MARKETING & MEDIA DECISIONS 15 (April 1980) : 62-63+.

Lengthy report on Sunday newspaper supplements, such as PARADE and FAMILY WEEKLY. New titles for mass targets and special interest audiences are published. Newspapers grow more popular as part of the magazine distribution system.

1655 "Switching from Newpaper to Magazine Mentality." FOLIO 15 (January 1986) : 26-28.

Newly introduced LOS ANGELES TIMES MAGAZINE seeks magazine professional advice to overcome early criticism. The magazine lacks focus and direction, and fails to target its audience. Basic problem--newspaper mentality differs from magazine mentality.

1656 "The TIMES Decided We are Not US." NEWSWEEK 95 (March 17, 1980) : 86.

The New York Times Co. sells US to the Macfadden Women's Group.

1657 Unger, Craig. "Murmuring at the NEW YORKER." NEW YORK 16 (November 28, 1983) : 28-33+.

As seventy-six-year-old editor William Shawn approaches retirement, questions are raised about his successor. A quick look at past editors, and an in-depth look at Shawn.

1658 "VANITY FAIR." MADISON AVENUE 27 (October 1985) : 109-116.

VANITY FAIR executives explain benefits to advertisers of a "livelier, focused" VANITY FAIR. A sales presentation in roundtable format.

1659 Wallach, Van. "NATIONAL GEOGRAPHIC in Unusual Position." ADVERTISING AGE 56 (October 3, 1985) : 30.

Even with 86 per cent editorial content, NATIONAL GEOGRAPHIC has difficulty selling ad space because it can't guarantee positioning next to editorial and away from competitors.

1660 Weber, Ronald. "Letting Subjects Grow: Literary Nonfiction from the NEW YORKER." ANTIOCH REVIEW 36 (Fall 1978) : 486-499.

Discussion of factual or literary nonfiction in the NEW YORKER, and the influential role of that magazine in developing the form.

1661 Yardley, Jonathon. "Living in the Past: At the NEW YORKER, the Good Old Days are Gone." WASHINGTON POST, 25 June 1984, p. B1+.

Skeptical comment on the chances of reviving SATURDAY REVIEW to its old glory. Critical review of WALL STREET JOURNAL article on NEW YORKER accuracy. Is the use of composite scenes and characters deserving of such rebuke?

1662 Yenckel, James T. "Have Magazine; Will Travel." WASHINGTON POST, 15 February 1984, p. D6.

Description of TRAVEL magazine, NATIONAL GEOGRAPHIC'S one-year-old off-spring.

Women's Magazines

1663 "Baker's Dozen in Women's Magazines." MARKETING & MEDIA DECISIONS 14 (October 1979) : 64-65+.

Six new women's magazines, edited for the contemporary woman, augment the seven traditional titles. Descriptions of the new titles, with pertinent advertiser information, are included. New titles focus on lifestyle rather than special subject areas.

1664 Beckman, Jody, and Lentini, Cecelia. "From the Old ... to the New." ADVERTISING AGE 53 (July 26, 1982) : M30+.

A pair of articles on the long-published, traditional "seven sisters" of women's magazines, and the newer titles created for working women.

1665 "Big Vogue." FORTUNE 110 (October 29, 1984) : 8+.

News brief on VOGUE's record-setting large size issues.

1666 Biggs, Mary. "Women's Literary Journals." LIBRARY QUARTERLY 53 (January 1983) : 1-25.

Questionnaire survey of literary magazines edited by and for women. Similar to most literary magazines in their independence, financial problems, low circulation. Editing styles vary, content has strong identification with feminism, priority given to female writers. Discussion of editorial organization, selection procedures, financial concerns.

1667 "BRIDE'S." MADISON AVENUE 27 (March 1985) : 94-99.

Another sales presentation for prospective advertisers--this time from BRIDE'S. Considers the magazine's readership and product sales potential.

1668 Cantor, Muriel G., and Jones, Elizabeth. "Creating Fiction for Women." COMMUNICATION RESEARCH 10 (January 1983) : 111-137.

Magazine analysis and interviews with fiction writers and editors for REDBOOK and TRUE STORY suggest how the magazines' content differs, how fiction is selected, how the writers fit into the commercial system. Magazine fiction is a cultural form and an economic commodity.

1669 Carmody, Deirdre. "Women's Magazines are More than Fashionable." NEW YORK TIMES, 15 February 1978, sec. 2, p. 1.

Those who forecast doom for women's magazines because of the women's movement were wrong. Traditional magazines have not suffered circulation losses. The women's movement created a need for a new type of magazine for women.

1670 Cleaver, Joanne. "The Sisters Get Older, Wiser and Tougher." ADVERTISING AGE 54 (October 17, 1983) : M34+.

Content changes in women's magazines diminish the differences between them--militant magazines include fashion and food; service magazines include investigative reporting.

1671 Collins, Lisa. "A Beauty Lesson: After May be Nicer, but Before is Forever." WALL STREET JOURNAL, 4 September 1985, p. 1+.

Reporter reports her experience being "made over" by NEW WOMAN magazine.

1672 Cooper, Nancy. "Feminist Periodicals." MASS COMM REVIEW 3 (Summer 1977) : 15-22.

Feminist periodicals are "produced by, for and about women and are outgrowths of the women's liberation movement." Not generally available on newsstands (with the exception of MS.), they are widely varied. Five titles are described and compared, with additional references to MS.

1673 Dreyfus, Joel, and Rogers, Michael. "ELLE makes a U.S. Curtsy." FORTUNE 112 (September 16, 1985) : 8-9.

Brief news item on ELLE's arrival on U.S. newsstands. Refers to other foreign magazine publishers entering the U.S. market.

1674 Ellenthal, Ira. "REDBOOK Redux." FOLIO 12 (September 1983) : 142+.

Under new management by Hearst, REDBOOK is focusing on a broader audience, aged 25 to 44.

1675 Elliott, Stuart J. "McCALL's Goes Out for a Livelier Product." ADVERTISING AGE 57 (February 10, 1986) : 30.

McCALL'S controversial new editor will shorten articles and create busier pages and covers, resulting in a "contemporary newsy format." Editorial will still be a mix of service and celebrities.

1676 Elliott, Stuart J. "MADEMOISELLE Lights no Candles for 50th." ADVERTISING AGE 56 (February 18, 1985) : 56.

Profile of MADEMOISELLE on its 50th birthday.

1677 Elliott, Stuart J. "No COSMO Clone, Says NEW WOMAN." ADVERTISING AGE 57 (January 6, 1986) : S4.

How NEW WOMAN defines its niche in the market. Is it really different from the competition? A few details on its editorial and economics.

1678 Elliott, Stuart J. "Record Issue Marks 100 Years of HOUSEKEEPING." ADVERTISING AGE 56 (May 13, 1985) : 106.

GOOD HOUSEKEEPING celebrates 100 years of publication, presenting a modern approach to women's service for an audience aged 25 to 40.

1679 Elliott, Stuart J. "SELF, Near 5, Still Fights Skeptics." ADVERTISING AGE 54 (September 26, 1983) : 41.

SELF, a trend-setting women's physical fitness magazine, keeps alert for needed changes to maintain its success.

1680 Elliott, Stuart J. "Women's Books Drop Combined Pitch: 7 Sisters Act Breaks Up." ADVERTISING AGE 54 (January 10, 1983) : 1+.

Reasons for the demise of the women's magazine advertising network.

1681 Elliott, Stuart J. "Yup! They're Yummies: RED-

BOOK Coins Slogan for Moms." ADVERTISING AGE 56 (May 23, 1985) : 51.

REDBOOK coins the word "yummy," an acronym for young upwardly mobile mommy. REDBOOK seeks an affluent market, aged 25 to 44, the baby-boomers.

1682 Emmrich, Stuart. "The Daughters of MS." ADVERTISING AGE 53 (September 13, 1982) : M2-M3.

Many women have initiated careers in the male dominated business side of magazine publishing after beginning on MS. MS. has also been the leader in a new category of women's magazines.

1683 Emmrich, Stuart. "WORKING WOMAN Enters 7 Sisters' Turf." ADVERTISING AGE 53 (April 19, 1982) : 24.

WORKING WOMAN's rise to success from an ailing position four years ago depended on successfully reaching the target audience, not as easy as it seemed.

1684 Fannin, Rebecca. "Women's Editors View Their 'Implosion.'" MARKETING & MEDIA DECISIONS 17 (October 1982) : 59-61+.

Women's changing social roles have fragmented women's magazine publishing, producing very specialized publications. Editors of sixteen women's magazines discuss the success of their diverse approaches, efforts to reshape identities, and the future.

1685 "Fashion Magazines." ADVERTISING AGE 56 (April 4, 1985) : 17-31.

Special section on fashion magazines includes articles on specific fashion magazine titles (e.g., HARPER'S BAZAAR), individual publishers (e.g., Conde Nast), over-all health of the industry, European fashion magazines, and men's fashion magazines.

1686 Fenn, Donna. "Fashion Magazines: 99 Ways to Increase Your Insecurity." WASHINGTON MONTHLY 13 (April 1981) : 28-31.

Popularity and effects of fashion magazines. How they've changed since the 1950s.

1687 Ferguson, Marjorie. FOREVER FEMININE: WOMEN'S MAGAZINES AND THE CULT OF FEMINITY. London: Heinemann, 1983.

Excellent sociological study of women's magazines as a social institution. Although British, some American magazines and editors were included in the study. Methodology combines historical research, content analysis from 1949 to present, extensive interviews with editors. Author concludes women's magazines "promote a cult of femininity" by providing public platforms from which to instruct and socialize women in the "appropriate attitudes, rituals and purchases" necessary to play chosen roles. Magazines defined as socialization agents and value promoters.

1688 Ferguson, Marjorie. "The Women's Magazine Cover Photograph." In THE SOCIOLOGY OF JOURNALISM AND THE PRESS, pp. 219-238. Edited by Harry Christian. Sociological Review Monograph, no. 29. University of Keele, Great Britain, 1980.

Although based on a study of British women's magazine covers, Ferguson's findings are relevant to U.S. women's publications. Discussion of the role, significance, and sociological implications of cover photos. See also entry 107.

1689 Folse, Lynn. "Magazines Join the Movement." ADVERTISING AGE 56 (September 12, 1985) : 36+.

Changes in women's magazines in response to the women's movement include new titles and revamping traditional titles.

1690 Green, Laura. "SAVVY Magazine: Success for a Scaled Down Time." THE PRESS 10 (February 1982) : 6-7.

SAVVY represents a new trend, the women's "sophisticated magazine" field, another claim made for the fastest growing segment of the magazine industry. In comparison with traditional service books, magazines for sophisticated working women have small circulations. Comparison of SAVVY with SELF and MS.

1691 Hirschfeld, Neal. "WORKING WOMAN Caters to the Career-Minded." ADVERTISING AGE 55 (April 2, 1984) : M22.

WORKING WOMAN has narrowed its original audience from employed women to women in management. Statistics illustrate readership by age, occupation, income.

1692 Kastor, Elizabeth. "Giving Them ELLE, After a Fashion: A Magazine for America's Nouvelle Woman." WASHINGTON POST, 23 August 1985, p. B1.

Typical explanation of whom ELLE claims its readers to be and some comments about its formal introduction to U.S. market.

1693 Kastor, Elizabeth. "Focus: The Renaissance of 'Women's Magazines'." WASHINGTON POST, 7 May 1984, p. C5.

Changes in and surprising stability of "seven sisters" and other women's magazines. Changes include more articles for working women in traditional magazines, and new titles specifically for career women.

1694 McCracken, Ellen. "Demystifying COSMOPOLITAN: Five Critical Methods." JOURNAL OF POPULAR CULTURE 16 (Fall 1982) : 30-42.

COSMOPOLITAN is subjected to study by five different analytical approaches. The usefulness of each method is discussed.

1695 MacDougall, A. Kent. "LADIES' HOME JOURNAL, McCALL'S Fight it Out with Sugar and Spice." WALL STREET JOURNAL, 3 August 1970, p. 1+.

How LADIES' HOME JOURNAL and McCALL'S struggled with competition in the 1970s. Historically illustrates the nature of the conflict between the two publications.

1696 McFadden, Maureen. "Sibling Rivalry: How the Seven Sisters are Making it Through the 80s." MAGAZINE AGE 3 (January 1982) : 48-53+.

Despite rumors that the traditional seven women's service magazines have failed to adapt to changing women's lifestyles, they continue to have great strength. Problems include competition from special-interest women's books, inflation, editorial identity crisis, declining editorial to advertising ratio.

1697 "Magazines Targeted at the Working Woman." BUSINESS WEEK (February 18, 1980) : 150+.

A new class of women's magazines is emerging.

1698 "Magazines that Mirror Women's Success." BUSINESS WEEK (January 11, 1982) : 39-40.

SAVVY and WORKING WOMAN magazines focus on executive and professional women.

1699 Marshall, Christy. "New Women's Magazine Aims Big." ADVERTISING AGE 52 (March 3, 1981) : 40.

Lane Bryant, retailer of women's fashions in large sizes, backs new magazine for big women.

1700 Marshall, Christy. "Wholesalers Balk over WOMAN'S WORLD." ADVERTISING AGE 52 (February 9, 1981) : 82.

Wholesalers unhappy over marketing conditions set by WOMAN'S WORLD publisher, which includes a smaller discount for the wholesaler than is customary.

1701 "The New Woman." WALL STREET JOURNAL, 10 January 1979, p. 22.

Conde Nast's newest venture is SELF magazine. Brief commentary on evolution of women's magazines and SELF's special niche in the field.

1702 Nobile, Philip. "Worry Lines at the Women's Magazines." NEW YORK 14 (May 18, 1981) : 19-20.

Decrease in advertising pages at women's magazines indicates trouble. LADIES' HOME JOURNAL has a new editor to revitalize the magazine's content.

1703 Peter, John. "Women's Magazines: A Survey of the Field." FOLIO 6 (April 1977) : 74-79.

Overview of women's magazine publishing. Discussion of "supermarket prosperers," lifestyle magazines, fashion magazines, new arrivals, magazines that have repositioned. References to the role of magazines such as MS. in dramatizing the changing female role.

1704 Pfaff, Fred. "Fashion Fever." MARKETING & MEDIA DECISIONS 21 (March 1986) : 72-74+.

Market is crowded with slick, targeted, upscale women's magazines. Almost all are changing to appeal to modern women. Almost all pursue lifestyle themes. For the media buyer, they are difficult to tell apart.

1705 Polakov, Alexander. "Fairchild's W Provides a Guide to the Good Life." ADVERTISING AGE 56 (April 4, 1985) : 28.

The weekly publication W combines newspaper reporting techniques with gloss and color of a magazine to create a fashion magazine targeted at an elite, affluent audience.

1706 Polakov, Alexander. "Manhattan Magazine Details Alternatives." ADVERTISING AGE 56 (April 4, 1985) : 30.

DETAILS, a trendy fashion magazine, has a sexually nonexclusive editorial position.

1707 Pool, Gail. "Magazines." WILSON LIBRARY BULLETIN 56 (May 1982) : 696-697.

Reviews of new women's magazines for the "so-called new woman." Emphasizes individual perspectives of such titles as SELF, NEW WOMAN, WORKING WOMAN, SAVVY, MS.

1708 Pool, Gail. "Women's Publications: Some Issues." MASSACHUSETTS REVIEW 24 (Summer 1983) : 467-473.

A brief look at some less familiar women's magazines and journals, e.g., APHRA, SOUJOURNER, SIGNS, CHRYSALIS.

1709 Randall, Michael H. "Bridal Magazines." SERIALS REVIEW 8 (Summer 1982) : 29-31.

Comparative review of content and audiences of BRIDE'S and MODERN BRIDE.

1710 "REDBOOK Zeroes in on Women of the 80s." MADISON AVENUE 25 (September 1983) : 108-112+.

REDBOOK executives offer sales presentation for prospective advertisers. Emphasis on combination with other Hearst publications, the repositioning of REDBOOK from a traditional women's service magazine to one for the total woman aged 25 to 44.

1711 Rozen, Leah. "MS. Plans to Stay on Leading Edge of Change." ADVERTISING AGE 51 (September 22, 1980) : 20+.

MS. publisher Patricia Carbine offers plans for the future and reports on the advantages of the magazine's non-profit status.

1712 Sanguinetti, Mary Alice. "Indexing of Feminist Periodicals." SERIALS LIBRARIAN 8 (Summer 1984) : 21-33.

Review and extensive list of indexes to feminist periodicals. Includes a list of feminist periodical titles with addresses.

1713 "SELF's Winning Pitch for Women Readers." BUSINESS WEEK (June 8, 1981) : 64.

Success of SELF magazine in increasing advertising revenue and making a profit when other women's magazines are losing advertising.

1714 Sobczynski, Anna. "Cautious Moves Propel Magazine Pioneers." ADVERTISING AGE 54 (October 3, 1983) : M34+.

Glossy, colorful, local magazines for women are "publishing's latest phenomenon."

1715 Sobczynski, Anna. "HARPER'S BAZAAR Fashions Success on Newsstand." ADVERTISING AGE 56 (April 4, 1985) : 20.

Brief history and current financial success of HARPER'S BAZAAR.

1716 Stineman, Esther. "Women's Magazines: Serving Up the 'New Woman' in the Same Old Ways." SERIALS REVIEW 5 (October-December 1979) : 25-29.

Changing content in women's magazines such as REDBOOK. Some say women's magazine content serves as a "social barometer" of trends and the impact of social movements. Reference to new magazines spawned by the women's movement. Other articles in this issue of SERIALS REVIEW deal with feminist periodicals and include numerous reviews of titles.

1717 Suplee, Curt. "Woman Magazine: Panning for Gold." WASHINGTON POST, 25 February 1984, p. C4.

Critique of a new magazine, WASHINGTON WOMAN.

1718 Sweet, Neesa. "Service Books Keep Step with the New Housewife: Women's Magazines Change Their Pitch--Slowly--to Readers." ADVERTISING AGE 54 (October 3, 1983) : M38.

The ads magazines use to sell themselves reflect their changing editorial concepts.

1719 Talese, Gay. "Vogueland, Oshkosh it Wasn't." ESQUIRE 99 (June 1983) : 214-216+.

VOGUE's sophistication shines in its models, its staff, its language, its readers. Lengthy characterization of the magazine, with passing references to its hierarchical ranking in relation to other women's fashion magazines.

1720 Trager, Cara S. "Conde Nast Publications Design Varying Styles." ADVERTISING AGE 56 (April 4, 1985) : 26.

Comparison of GLAMOUR, MADEMOISELLE, and VOGUE. Although once narrowly defined as fashion magazines, editorial scope has widened to include nutrition, fitness, travel, entertainment, etc.

1721 Uihlein-Fellars, Reven. "Department Store Books Don New Look." ADVERTISING AGE 56 (April 4, 1985) : 28.

Department store catalogs are becoming fashion magazines.

1722 Williamson, Jane. "Feminist Periodicals: A Beginner's Guide." SERIALS LIBRARIAN 8 (Summer 1984) : 13-20.

Reviews of feminist periodicals from the offbeat to the academic. Also lists a few directories of women's media.

1723 Williamson, Jane. "Sister Publications--Record of a Decade." MS. 11 (July-August 1982) : 50.

Overview of the feminist press, with names and addresses of specific publications.

1724 "Women's Magazines Lose Pep." BUSINESS WEEK (August 30, 1982) : 72-73.

Women's service magazines, with decreasing circulation and advertising pages, "face a crisis triggered by social change" and recession.

Men's Magazines

1725 Brady, James. "Deja Vu over ESQUIRE." ADVERTISING AGE 50 (May 7, 1979) : 100.

Flip and critical review of interview with 13-30 Corporation's Whittle and Moffitt regarding their purchase of ESQUIRE.

1726 Canape, Charlene. "Refashioning the Male Marketplace." MARKETING & MEDIA DECISIONS 20 (March 1985) : 84-86+.

ESQUIRE, GENTLEMEN'S QUARTERLY, and M flourish as lifestyle magazines for the successful male of the 1980s. How the three contrast rather than compete with each other.

1727 "Dreams of Glory." ECONOMIST 296 (September 28, 1985) : 30.

Brief news item on the SOLDIER OF FORTUNE yearly convention. The magazine supports anti-communist activities worldwide.

1728 Ehrenreich, Barbara, and English, Deirdre. "The Male Revolt: Feminists Were Not the First to Flee the Family." MOTHER JONES 8 (April 1983) : 25-31.

Selections from Ehrenreich's book, THE HEARTS OF MEN (1983) and introductory comments by MJ editor English. Selections deal with PLAYBOY and its relation to the male mentality 1950s through 1970s, the battle of the sexes, and the revolt against traditional sex roles. While emphasis is on PLAYBOY, other magazines are referred to.

1729 Elliott, Stuart J. "GQ Definitely is Dressed for Success." ADVERTISING AGE 53 (October 11, 1982) : 38+.

Brief commentary on GENTLEMEN'S QUARTERLY's market position and growth.

1730 Elliott, Stuart J. "Guides Killed so PLAYBOY May Prosper." ADVERTISING AGE 54 (April 25, 1983) : 34.

Separate subject guides on fashion and electronic entertainment will now be bound into PLAYBOY magazine to broaden its editorial content. Changes stem from Playboy Enterprise's financial difficulties.

1731 Elliott, Stuart J. "Men's Magazines Addressing Segments." ADVERTISING AGE 56 (April 4, 1985) : 30.

Trend in the late 1970s towards fashion and lifestyle magazines for men.

1732 Elliott, Stuart J. "PENTHOUSE to Cut Ads." ADVERTISING AGE 55 (May 10, 1984) : 3+.

PENTHOUSE reducing ad pages because competition for advertising sales has given advertisers too much voice in the magazine's editorial content.

1733 Ellis, James E. "Now Even PLAYBOY is Bracing for a Midlife Crisis." BUSINESS WEEK (April 15, 1985) : 66+.

The rebuilding of Playboy Enterprises into a smaller but more profitable leisure company. Changing attitudes towards sex and increased competition require redefinition of PLAYBOY from a skin magazine to a men's lifestyle magazine.

1734 Emmrich, Stuart. "PENTHOUSE Playing Tough." ADVERTISING AGE 53 (July 5, 1982) : 30.

Competition between PLAYBOY and PENTHOUSE heats up with PENTHOUSE ad accusing PLAYBOY of "stretching the truth."

1735 "ESQUIRE Magazine Owner Negotiating to Sell the Biweekly." WALL STREET JOURNAL, 27 April 1979, p. 41.

ESQUIRE losing money since Esquire Inc. sold the magazine in 1977. 13-30 Corporation rumored to be new buyer.

1736 "For Magazines a Strong Readership." NEW YORK TIMES, 17 October 1982, sec. 3, p. F23.

Male adventure magazines, such as SOLDIER OF FORTUNE, are doing very well.

1737 Gerson, Walter M., and Lund, Sander H. "PLAYBOY Magazine: Sophisticated Smut or Social Revolution?" JOURNAL OF POPULAR CULTURE 1 (Winter 1967) : 218-227.

A circular relationship exists between increasing popular interest in sexuality and the success of PLAYBOY in the late 1960s. A sociological analysis of PLAYBOY's main function, socialization. Readers learn how to imitate the morality and behavior of the "PLAYBOY stereotype."

1738 "GQ Fashions a Style of Life." MADISON AVENUE 25 (January 1983) : 132-137+.

Sales presentation from GQ includes brief history of its development, competition, audience and editorial concept. Emphasis on reader demographics and what the magazine offers prospective advertisers.

1739 "GQ to Extend Quality Beyond Fashion." ADVERTISING AGE 54 (October 10, 1983) : 36.

GQ's new editor plans more sophisticated, wittier, provocative editorial.

1740 Griffith, Thomas. "Merchants of Raunchiness." TIME 110 (July 4, 1977) : 69+.

Once the undisputed skin magazine leader, PLAYBOY faces loss of readers and much competition. Comparison of PLAYBOY, PENTHOUSE, HUSTLER, and OUI.

1741 Griffith, Thomas. "Stuck with a Magazine's Genes." TIME 114 (August 13, 1979) : 63.

Brief essay on ESQUIRE. How its editorial concept has evolved since 1933, and what changes are likely under its new owners Moffitt and Whittle.

1742 Grover, Stephen. "Esquire Inc. to Sell its Monthly Magazine to Group Featuring Felker, 2 Associates." WALL STREET JOURNAL, 29 August 1977, p. 4.

Announcement of Clay Felker's purchase of ESQUIRE. Interesting only because it reports another of the several recent owners of ESQUIRE, and another of Clay Felker's briefly owned publications.

1743 Harrigan, Susan. "Can Southern Lads Keep ESQUIRE Afloat?" WALL STREET JOURNAL, 3 March 1980, p. 1+.

Profile of ESQUIRE's new owners, Christopher Whittle and Phillip Moffitt, and the problems they face in making ESQUIRE profitable again.

1744 Hefner, Christie. "PLAYBOY: The Right Idea, at the Right Time, Right Place." DIRECT MARKETING 45 (April 1983) : 24+.

The PLAYBOY editorial concept and purpose is described by the president of Playboy Enterprises. The magazine's purpose is not to be the best skin magazine but a multifaceted lifestyle magazine, a tastemaker and trendsetter for the upwardly mobile, leisure oriented young adult. Also discussed are PLAYBOY spin-offs and marketing strategy.

1745 Henry, William A. "ESQUIRE at Mid-Century." TIME 122 (November 21, 1983) : 54.

Brief comments about ESQUIRE's changing styles since its 1933 founding.

1746 Hicks, Jonathon P. "For Black Men on the Way Up." NEW YORK TIMES, 7 November 1985, p. D1+.

Johnson Publishing introduces EBONY MAN, a monthly for upwardly mobile black men, offering editorial on fashion, fitness, personal finance.

Brief look at the company's financial situation.

1747 "Is this the Real Message of Pornography." HARPER'S 269 (November 1984) : 35.

A HUSTLER magazine cover strengthens the organization Women Against Pornography. Brief item is part of larger article on roundtable discussion of pornography.

1748 Kaiser, Charles. "ESQUIRE's Happy BIRTHDAY." NEWSWEEK 102 (November 21, 1983) : 77.

Under ownership of Whittle and Moffitt, ESQUIRE is again making a profit, due to their perception of changing tastes among men's magazine readers.

1749 Kanner, Bernice. "Peacock Alley: Life-Style Magazines for Men." NEW YORK 16 (September 26, 1983) : 24+.

The "coming of age" of men's fashion and lifestyle magazines is exemplified by M, ESQUIRE, GQ. Strong competition for the older, sophisticated, affluent male reader. Are there enough readers and advertisers to sustain these magazines?

1750 Kelly, James. "Quiche Eaters Read no Further: SOLDIER OF FORTUNE, Ten Years Old, Wants Only the Macho." TIME 126 (August 19, 1985) : 54.

Profile of SOLDIER OF FORTUNE and its new style of participatory journalism: raising money and training teams of soldiers in Afghanistan, El Salvador, Nicaragua.

1751 Klein, Frederick C. "HUSTLER Magazine is Gaining in Battle for Male Readership." WALL STREET JOURNAL, 26 December 1975, p. 1+.

Optimistic Larry Flynt believed HUSTLER would surpass PLAYBOY and PENTHOUSE in circulation by 1976. How Flynt got into publishing through a newsletter for his night club customers.

1752 Klein, Jeffrey. "Born Again Porn." MOTHER JONES 3 (February-March 1978) : 12-14+.

Fluffy article detailing MOTHER JONES' interview with Larry Flynt, publisher of HUSTLER. A few worthwhile paragraphs about Flynt's purpose and perception for the magazine and its hard-to-categorize audience.

1753 Koten, John, and Johnson, Robert. "As Men's Values Shift, PLAYBOY Seeks a Way to Still Seem Exciting." WALL STREET JOURNAL, 12 September 1985, p. 1+.

Finding itself out-of-touch with today, PLAYBOY is working on a new image.

1754 Langway, Lynn. "Courting the Clothes Hound." NEWSWEEK 102 (October 3, 1983) : 92.

Magazines featuring men's fashions include M and GENTLEMEN'S QUARTERLY.

1755 Levin, Gary. "Johnson's EBONY MAN to Debut." ADVERTISING AGE 56 (August 19, 1985) : 70.

A new entry to the men's fashion magazine category.

1756 Levin, Gary. "Men's Sophisticate Titles Feel Circulation Pinch." ADVERTISING AGE 56 (October 3, 1985) : 52-53.

PLAYBOY and PENTHOUSE blame a more conservative social climate and competition for circulation losses.

1757 Love, Robert. "The Retreat of the Skin Mags." WASHINGTON JOURNALISM REVIEW 3 (November 1981) : 33-35.

After 1970s growth, 1980s skin magazines are losing circulation and profits. The baby boom generation which financed the publishing sexual revolution has grown up and lost interest.

1758 Lownes, Victor. THE DAY THE BUNNY DIED. Secaucus, N.J.: L. Stuart, 1983.

First person account of PLAYBOY's rise and "catastrophic fall" after the investment in London casinos. Told by former PLAYBOY executive.

1759 MacDougall, A. Kent. "ESQUIRE Keeps Thriving by Deflating Heroes, Backing the Unpopular." WALL STREET JOURNAL, 8 May 1968, p. 1+.

In 1968, ESQUIRE showed rising profits, advertising, and circulation. Profile of ESQUIRE twenty years ago makes an interesting comparison to ESQUIRE today.

1760 Maddox, Sam. "Armchair Intrigue Targeted to Gung-ho Readers." ADVERTISING AGE 53 (October 25, 1982) : M51+.

Magazines for bold adventurers: SOLDIER OF FORTUNE, NEW BREED, GUNG-HO, and EAGLE.

1761 Margolis, Richard J. "Funding Feminists." NEW LEADER 66 (May 30, 1983) : 10-11.

Playboy Foundation is based on importance of individual rights in a free society. Grants made to groups supporting civil rights, sex law reform, abortion rights, and feminist causes. Feminist organizations have viewed the foundation with hostility.

1762 Migneault, Robert LaLiberte. "Marketing Macho Adventure." SERIALS REVIEW 10 (Spring 1984) : 11-26.

Lengthy article profiles the history, function, content, audience of men's military adventure magazines, such as SOLDIER OF FORTUNE, GUNG-

HO, and others. Compares and reviews titles. Includes bibliography.

1763 Miller, Russell. BUNNY: THE REAL STORY OF PLAYBOY. London: Michael Joseph, 1984.

An account of PLAYBOY magazine's beginnings, its rivalry with PENTHOUSE and HUSTLER, and the current business problems confronting Playboy Enterprises.

1764 Morgenthaler, Eric. "SOLDIER OF FORTUNE is for Readers Aspiring to be Exactly That." WALL STREET JOURNAL, 15 September 1981, p. 1+.

A most unusual special interest magazine for "professional adventurers," with information on guerrilla warfare, shooting laser weapons, blowing up railroads.

1765 Nelson, Sara. "The Male Market Defined with a Capital M." ADVERTISING AGE 54 (September 5, 1983) : M28.

Brief description of men's lifestyle magazine, M, with 30 percent fashion for men.

1766 Overton, Tom. "Oh, You Kid!." QUILL 70 (December 1982) : 30-31.

About PLAYBOY's "Sex on Campus, 1982" survey.

1767 Pace, Eric. "Spurning Macho Past, ESQUIRE Finds Success." NEW YORK TIMES, 17 September 1984, p. D1.

ESQUIRE's success under 13-30 Corporation. Its readers are "a new breed of upscale American male--and female." Promotion techniques to attract new readers and advertisers.

1768 Piantadosi, Roger. "ESQUIRE's Whittle & Moffitt." WASHINGTON JOURNALISM REVIEW 3 (November 1981) : 38-41.

13-30 Corporation founders comment on themselves, each other, and their new acquisition, ESQUIRE. Part of a special report: "Magazines in the 80s."

1769 "PLAYBOY Puts a Glint in the Admen's Eyes." BUSINESS WEEK (June 28, 1969) : 142-144+.

A late 1960s view of PLAYBOY's successful formula.

1770 "PLAYBOY vs. PENTHOUSE." BUSINESS WEEK (December 6, 1982) : 106-107.

Two soft porn magazines lose readers. Some of the reasons include video competition and rivalry between PLAYBOY and PENTHOUSE for advertisers. PLAYBOY is trying to reposition itself as a men's lifestyle magazine, but PENTHOUSE is leaving its editorial policy unchanged.

1771 Reed, Cecelia. "ESQUIRE Edits a Strong COLLECTION." ADVERTISING AGE 54 (September 5, 1983) : M28.

Brief comment on ESQUIRE's semiannual men's fashion magazine.

1772 Reed, Robert. "PLAYBOY Faces Turnaround Fight." ADVERTISING AGE 54 (August 1, 1983) : 1+.

Critics attribute PLAYBOY's financial problems to the magazine's failure to change in response to changes in "men, society and the publishing climate."

1773 Rose, Val. "Paying the Wages of War." MACLEAN'S 96 (April 11, 1983) : 62-63.

Increasing popularity of male adventure magazines, such as SOLDIER OF FORTUNE and its imitators. Brief comment on trends from the 1960s decline of male adventure magazines (e.g., TRUE, ARGOSY), the 1970s demand for soft pornography, and the rising interest in military adventure magazines.

1774 Runde, Robert. "Fortunes from Scratch: The Wages of Skin." MONEY 9 (February 1980) : 68-70+.

Bob Guccione started PENTHOUSE in London in 1965, moving it to the U.S. in 1969. Other business ventures have included magazine spin-offs such as VIVA, FORUM, OMNI, films, and a casino.

1775 Schwartz, Tony. "PLAYBOY's Quarter Century." NEWSWEEK 93 (January 1, 1979) : 68.

The once-daring PLAYBOY magazine has become an institution, a no-longer daring guide to good living. Comparison of PLAYBOY to its competitors.

1776 "Sex Magazines and Feminism." HUMANIST 38 (November-December 1978) : 44-51.

Four opinions on sexual magazines. Pornographic magazines may have a legitimate social function.

1777 Smilby, F. STOLEN SWEETS: THE COVER GIRLS OF YESTERYEAR, THEIR ELEGANCE, CHARM AND SEX APPEAL. New York: Playboy Press, 1981.

1778 Solomon, Debbie. "ESQUIRE Registers Young Achievers." ADVERTISING AGE 55 (October 18, 1984) : 32.

Special ESQUIRE issue recognizes achievements of three hundred Americans under age forty. Recent history of ESQUIRE since purchase by 13-30 Corporation, and how the magazine changed to meet the needs of the baby boom generation.

1779 Thomas, Bill. "What Does a Man Want? Four Magazines that are Trying to Provide it." WASHINGTON JOURNALISM REVIEW 6 (December 1984) : 21-23.

Changing images and new popularity for men's magazines. ESQUIRE, GENTLEMEN'S QUARTERLY, and M aim at different population segments, from rising to established executive. PLAYBOY is deemphasizing sex.

1780 Ward, Robert. "Grossing Out with Publishing's Hottest Hustler." NEW TIMES 6 (January 9, 1976) : 43-46+.

Profile of Larry Flynt and HUSTLER magazine.

1781 Wolfe, Alan. "Magazine Merchants of Death." NATION 233 (July 4, 1981) : 1+

At least a dozen gun and mercenary publications are available on magazine racks, e.g., SHOOTING TIMES and SOLDIER OF FORTUNE. Do these reflect our culture?

Business & Finance Magazines

1782 Alter, Jonathan. "Boom in the Business Press." NEWSWEEK 105 (January 7, 1985) : 66.

Some argue that the fastest growing new journalistc medium is the city-regional business publication. There is much competition between titles and with national business magazines for advertising revenue.

1783 Bonner, George R. "FACT Challenges MONEY for Personal-Finance Readership." CHRISTIAN SCIENCE MONITOR, 2 September 1982, p. 10.

New ad-carrying magazine, FACT, from publishers of the Value Line Investment Survey, challenges MONEY magazine. Both seem to be doing well.

1784 Canape, Charlene. "An 'Elitist' Journal Makes New Inroads." ADVERTISING AGE 53 (November 22, 1982) : M4-M5+.

Increasing U.S. circulation marks the success of British financial magazine, the ECONOMIST.

1785 Canape, Charlene. "Persistence Pays Dividends for MONEY." ADVERTISING AGE 55 (February 6, 1984) : M4-M5+.

Early problems for Time Inc.'s personal finance magazine, MONEY, seem to be overcome as ad pages rise and revenue grows. Comparison with its competitors, CHANGING TIMES and SYLVIA PORTER'S PERSONAL FINANCE.

1786 Crain, Rance. "Building the Crain Connection." ADVERTISING AGE 55 (July 26, 1984) : 12.

Cautious approach to fresh material will be key to Crain's NEW YORK BUSINESS, the newest business regional in Crain's stable.

1787 Elliott, Stuart J. "Happy With First Revamp, FORTUNE Sets Another." ADVERTISING AGE 53 (December 13, 1982) : 48.

Changes in FORTUNE as a result of its switch from monthly to fortnightly. Current redesign aimed at making FORTUNE more interesting and attractive.

1788 Elliott, Stuart J. "MANHATTAN, INC. Alters City-Business Skyline." ADVERTISING AGE 56 (October 14, 1985) : 46.

MANHATTAN, INC. executives expound on the success of their local business magazine.

1789 Elliott, Stuart J. "VENTURE Story One of Corporate Intrigue." ADVERTISING AGE 54 (April 11, 1983) : 3+.

Founder-investor conflicts at VENTURE magazine, fast-growing, four-year-old publication that offers advice to entrepreneurs.

1790 Emmrich, Stuart. "Giving Each Other the Business: Tough New Ads Hammer Away at the Competition." ADVERTISING AGE 53 (May 3, 1982) : M2-M3+.

Competition among business and financial magazines is highlighted by their tough new promotion and advertising campaigns.

1791 Emmrich, Stuart. "Ten-Year Payout for TIME's MONEY." ADVERTISING AGE 52 (November 30, 1981) : 32.

Synopsis of ten-year's steady growth for Time Inc.'s MONEY magazine.

1792 Fannin, Rebecca. "Business Paper Shoot-Out Headed for New York." MARKETING & MEDIA DECISIONS 19 (October 1984) : 62-63+.

Three business publications compete for the same audience in New York: MANHATTAN, INC., NEW YORK CITYBUSINESS, CRAIN'S NEW YORK BUSINESS.

1793 Flanigan, James. "Vision Goes Only So Far in Business." LOS ANGELES TIMES, 26 August 1984, sec. 5, p. 1.

Hodgepodge about magazine publishing--increase in new business and finance magazines, Time Inc.'s problems with HBO, and rumors about a new weekly stock market magazine from Time Inc.

1794 Francis, David R. "HARVARD BUSINESS REVIEW: A Giant Broadens its Appeal." CHRISTIAN SCIENCE MONITOR, 9 August 1983, p. 11.

To compete with other business magazines, HARVARD BUSINESS REVIEW has shortened article length, adopted a simpler, more direct style, and broadened its scope. Its objective is to be an educational arm of the school.

1795 Friedman, Barbara J. "Local Business Press." PRESSTIME 7 (February 1985) : 6-7.

More than thirty local business publications exist, but daily newspapers don't yet feel threatened.

1796 Geozi, Michael. "Magazines Battle for Readers, Ads." LOS ANGELES TIMES, 10 March 1983, sec. 4, p. 2.

FORBES and FORTUNE gain on BUSINESS WEEK. A heated battle for the top spot among the three largest business magazines.

1797 Hall, Peter. "Making Quirkiness Work: While Our Economy Flounders, the Offbeat British ECONOMIST is Thriving in the U.S." COLUMBIA JOURNALISM REVIEW 20 (March-April 1982) : 51-52+.

1798 Hanson, J. J. "Business Regionals: After the Heyday." 14 FOLIO (April 1985) : 15.

There's a lot of life in business regionals yet, and national ad accounts will multiply so long as editorial quality improves. Some competition in the catagory may be lethal to a few.

1799 Hogan, Bill. "The Big Business in Business Magazines." WASHINGTON JOURNALISM REVIEW 3 (July-August 1981) : 32-34.

Competition between the three leading business magazines (BUSINESS WEEK, FORTUNE, and FORBES) is spirited but gentlemanly, lately fueled by growing interest in business and economic news. Although aimed at the same general audiences, each magazine claims to reach a specific segment of the audience most efficiently. Other articles in this issue of WJR deal with business reporting in other media, with some comments on magazines.

1800 Hogan, Bill. "The Boom in Regional Business Journals." WASHINGTON JOURNALISM REVIEW 4 (July-August 1982) : 35+.

City, state, and regional business publications are growing fast. Two-page article describes major publishers and titles, competition between them, and initial editorial dependence on news and public relations press releases.

1801 "How MONEY Talks to Your Clients." MADISON AVENUE 25 (April 1983) : 116-120+.

Advertising sales presentation from MONEY magazine suggests the magazine's emphasis on major spending and investing decisions attracts a high level of readership.

1802 "Insane? Magazine Slashes Price." MONEYSWORTH 12 (June 1982) : 24.

AMERICAN BUSINESS, a monthly financial periodical, offers a one dollar introductory subscription price, gambling that new subscribers will renew.

1803 Jay, Margaret. "The ECONOMIST Formula: Elitism, Anonymity, 'Successful Coziness.'" WASHINGTON JOURNALISM REVIEW 7 (April 1985) : 52-54.

London news magazine, the ECONOMIST, has greater circulation outside of Britain. North America is its largest overseas market. Profile of the magazine and its editorial policy.

1804 Kanner, Bernice. "Trimmer FORTUNE Carries its Weight Well After 50 Years." ADVERTISING AGE 51 (February 4, 1980) : 32-33.

Brief profile of FORTUNE on its 50th anniversary with emphasis on changes over its history.

1805 Keller, Rip. "How the Regional Books Help Advertisers Fill in the Gaps." MAGAZINE AGE 4 (July 1983) : 30-32+.

Growing numbers of regional business magazines offer advertisers an opportunity to reach local markets. A consortium of CALIFORNIA BUSINESS, TEXAS BUSINESS, AND FLORIDA TREND was among the first to persuade national advertisers of their high demographics.

1806 Kelsey, Patricia A. "On Top of the Trends." ADVERTISING AGE 55 (January 9, 1984) : M25.

Brief profile of FLORIDA TREND, the state's twenty-five-year-old business magazine.

1807 Koten John, and Johnson, Robert. "Crain Brothers Take on Tough Turf with their NEW YORK BUSINESS Weekly." WALL STREET JOURNAL, 14 June 1985, p. 28.

Specialty-business magazine publisher launches a regional business magazine in a very tough market. Profile of Rance and Keith Crain and Crain Communications.

1808 Lazzareschi, Carla. "Magazine Targets the 'Working Affluent.'" LOS ANGELES TIMES, 2 December 1984, sec. 6, p. 1+.

PERSONAL INVESTOR, a new how-to magazine aimed at the working affluent, exemplifies the growing interest in financial news and the increasing number of financial journals.

1809 "Manhattan Ink." FORTUNE 110 (August 6, 1984) : 7-8.

Launch of MANHATTAN, INC., a new business magazine, is illustrative of the growing trend in business journalism--city business publications.

1810 Massing, Michael. "MANHATTAN, INC.--Yuppie Power Tool." COLUMBIA JOURNALISM REVIEW 23 (March-April 1985) : 54-55.

MANHATTAN, INC., newly published in September 1984, is well-suited to "the spirit of its times." It is a magazine for the upwardly mobile.

1811 "New Journals Tell the Local Business Story." BUSINESS WEEK (October 5, 1981) : 126+.

Rapid growth of local business publications exploits public interest in economics and finance. In response, some newspapers widen business coverage.

1812 "New York Rival Bought by Crain." ADVERTISING AGE 56 (August 19, 1985) : 3+.

Crain Communications has purchased NEW YORK CITYBUSINESS, local competition for Crain's NEW YORK BUSINESS.

1813 Peer, Elizabeth. "The High Life of Malcolm the Audacious." NEW YORK 17 (January 30, 1984) : 30-37.

Profile of Malcolm Forbes and FORBES magazine.

1814 Powell, Joanna. "INSTITUTIONAL INVESTOR: Journalism's Showcase for Stock Pickers Who Make the Team." WASHINGTON JOURNALISM REVIEW 7 (July 1985) : 44-46.

Stock analysts named to INSTITUTIONAL INVESTOR's yearly list of top analysts usually receive important career benefits. Though impact is strong, survey may be as unreliable as a voice vote.

1815 Salmans, Sandra. "A Magazine Numbers Game." NEW YORK TIMES, 20 April 1984, p. D1.

Competition between FORBES, FORTUNE, and BUSINESS WEEK.

1816 Thackray, John. "Business Press Boom." MANAGEMENT TODAY (May 1980) : 80-83.

Growing interest in business and finance and the trend toward magazine specialization are factors in the rising revenues of national and regional business magazines.

1817 Thompson, Sarah Anne. "A Profile of Regional Business Publications." M.A. thesis, University of Missouri, 1983.

The growth of local business publications that fill a void between national business magazines and daily newspaper business sections. Readership consists of affluent, influential executives who are a prime advertising target.

1818 VandenBergh, Bruce G; Fletcher, Alan D.; and Adrian, Mary A. "Local Business Press: New Phenomenon in the News Marketplace." JOURNALISM QUARTERLY 61 (Autumn 1984) : 645-649.

Local business publications that combine attributes of both newspapers and magazines are attracting affluent, influential readers.

1819 Wadyka, Steven. "Local Business Journals Target the Affluent and Influential." MADISON AVENUE 24 (September 1982) : 112+.

Combination of affluent audience, local business editorial, and lack of competition from national business magazines has brought recent success to new genre. Advantages for advertisers listed.

City & Regional Magazines

1820 Allen, Hamilton. "YANKEE'S Reach Exceeds its Deep Roots." LOS ANGELES TIMES, 17 November 1983, part I-B, p. 14.

New England-based YANKEE magazine circulates nationwide, and has revenues of $25 million annually. Offers a positive approach avoiding problems unless solutions may be offered. Refuses cigarette advertising.

1821 Alter, Stewart. "City Magazines Reach for the Sky." MAGAZINE AGE 1 (January 1980) : 22-24+.

The similarities and diversities of city magazines as a group. Advertiser benefits include reader loyalty, isolated markets, high reader demographics.

1822 "Arts Magazine in Ohio Shows Steady Growth." ADVERTISING AGE 52 (March 3, 1981) : M37.

NORTHERN OHIO LIVE successfully competes with CLEVELAND magazine.

1823 "The Battle of New York." TIME 109 (January 17, 1977) : 53-56+.

The unfriendly takeover of NEW YORK magazine by Rupert Murdoch from editor and part-owner Clay Felker. Includes profiles of each man.

1824 Berry, John D. "Regional Cultural Magazines." CO-EVOLUTION QUARTERLY (no. 38, Summer 1983) : 112-113.

Critical review of six regional cultural magazines that range from tabloid to elegant format.

1825 "California's Magazine War." TIME 110 (August 29, 1977) : 68.

Competition between LOS ANGELES and NEW WEST magazines.

1826 Carlson, Eugene. "Flashy Texas-Style Magazine Seeks a Niche in New England."

Brief item about the forthcoming NEW ENGLAND MONTHLY, founded by veterans from TEXAS MONTHLY. Typical New England folksy content will be avoided, publisher intends.

1827 Cekay, Thomas. "OREGON MAGAZINE: A Radical Publication Goes Straight." M.A. thesis, Northern Illinois University, 1981.

Role of advocacy journalism and reform magazines in periods of social unrest. As social climates cool, reform magazines may adopt less controversial editorial stance. The regional magazine OREGON (formerly OREGON TIMES) is profiled as an example.

1828 "City & Regional Magazines." ADVERTISING AGE 52 (March 30, 1981) : S1-S30.

Special report contains a variety of articles on city magazines, including an alphabetical, annotated listing of titles. Lead article covers development of the genre.

1829 "City and Regional Magazines." ADVERTISING AGE 53 (April 5, 1982) : M7-M27.

Articles in this special section deal with upscale readership, current success of the type, and numerous specific titles or regions (e.g., Texas, California, Chicago magazines). Also provides results of a poll of editors on the top ten city and regional magazines (p. M27).

1830 "City and Regional Magazines." ADVERTISING AGE 56 (January 17, 1985) : 11-27.

Emphasis on the growth of city and regional magazines since 1970. Most target affluent audiences seeking the "good life," and therefore attract advertisers. Articles in this special section deal with what makes a city or regional magazine successful, editorial content, research and marketing, networks for advertising sales, specific titles, and local business magazines.

1831 "City Magazines Are the Talk of the Town." BUSINESS WEEK (February 18, 1967) : 184+.

Expanding market for city magazines in 1967. Sophisticated and attractive periodicals, they aim for affluent audiences.

1832 Cook, Bruce. "LOS ANGELES: The Monthly that Wants Respect." WASHINGTON JOURNALISM REVIEW 6 (April 1984) : 31-34.

LOS ANGELES magazine, among the most financially successful city or regional magazines in the U.S., believes critics unfairly judge its editorial content.

1833 Cote, Kevin. "PHILADELPHIA Magazine Mixes Fun with Serious Journalism." ADVERTISING AGE 51 (January 28, 1980) : S20-S21.

Brief profile of award-winning PHILADELPHIA

magazine. Editorial blends witty gossip with serious investigative reporting.

1834 Curtis, Tom. "How the NEW WEST was Won." WASHINGTON JOURNALISM REVIEW 3 (April 1981) : 39-43.

Profile of the award-winning TEXAS MONTHLY. Founded in 1972 by Mike Levy and Bill Broyles, it began as a "city magazine for the whole state of Texas," and has since attracted national advertising. In 1980, it acquired NEW WEST. The strong contribution of editor Broyles is stressed--could either magazine succeed without him?

1835 Davis, Rod. "For Rich Texans Who Can Read." PROGRESSIVE 45 (December 1981) : 17.

As of September 1981, ULTRA circulates free to the estimated 70,000 Texans with incomes over $150,000. The magazine celebrates the lives and interests of the wealthy, and according to PROGRESSIVE does it badly.

1836 Duke, Paul, Jr. "WASHINGTONIAN'S Capital Readership Sets It Off from Big-City Magazines." WALL STREET JOURNAL, 23 September 1985, p. 20.

This profitable, award-winning city magazine has a reputation for excellent journalism and attentive, influential readership.

1837 Elliott, Stuart J. "NEW YORK Weathers 14 Years of

Storms." ADVERTISING AGE 54 (January 31, 1983) : 40+.

Editorial changes at NEW YORK lead to financial stability. Unlike most city magazines, 75 percent of NEW YORK'S advertising comes from national advrtisers.

1838 Emmrich, Stuart. "TEXAS MONTHLY No CALIFORNIA Road Map." ADVERTISING AGE 54 (May 2, 1983) : 4+.

Three years after purchasing NEW WEST (now CALIFORNIA), owner Michael Levy's successful techniques with TEXAS MONTHLY have failed to make CALIFORNIA profitable.

1839 Enterline, Joyce. "Ohio Magazines Growing Fat Fast." ADVERTISING AGE 51 (November 17, 1980) : S6+.

Comparison of four Ohio magazines: CLEVELAND, COLUMBUS MONTHLY, CINCINNATI, and OHIO. Each has distinct editorial emphasis and tone.

1840 Fannin, Rebecca. "Regional Magazines Gain National Impact." MARKETING & MEDIA DECISIONS 17 (August 1982) : 64-66+.

City and regional magazines attract national advertisers because of their editorial quality and highly interested readers. Discussion of specific regional magazines and the types of advertising they attract.

1841 Fletcher, Alan D. "City Magazines Find a Niche in the Media Marketplace." JOURNALISM QUARTERLY 54 (Winter 1977) : 740-743+.

City magazine editors relate the success of their publications to the excitement and local information they can offer a highly segmented audience.

1842 Fletcher, Alan D., and VandenBergh, Bruce G. "Numbers Grow, Problems Remain for City Magazines." JOURNALISM QUARTERLY 59 (Summer 1982) : 313-317.

Fast growth in city magazines is the result of selective advertising to specific markets. Biggest problems are rising production and postal costs.

1843 Goolrick, Chester. "One Way to Succeed in Sun Belt Is Simply to Sing Its Praises." WALL STREET JOURNAL, 25 November 1981, p. 1+.

Successful SOUTHERN LIVING magazine owes its success to a positive image of the South. Features are simply written, a mixture of recipes, travel, advice, and Southern city profiles.

1844 Gruen, Erica. "CRMs Deliver for National Advertisers." MADISON AVENUE 24 (September 1982) : 104+.

As city and regional magazines grow in content, circulation, revenue, prestige, they seek national advertisers. Lengthy discussion of the pros and cons aimed at advertising buyers.

1845 Hayes, John P. "City/Regional Magazines: A Survey/Census." JOURNALISM QUARTERLY 58 (Summer 1981) : 294-296.

Growth of city and regional magazines. Much magazine content is obtained from free-lancers.

1846 Hynds, Ernest C. "City Magazines, Newspapers Serve in Different Ways." JOURNALISM QUARTERLY 56 (Winter 1979) : 619-622.

The roles of city magazines and newspapers compared. Survey indicates some city magazine editors see their publications as possible alternative voices to newspapers in coverage of public issues.

1847 Jurgens, Frans. "Enter WASHINGTON WOMAN." WASHINGTON JOURNALISM REVIEW 6 (March 1984) : 13-14.

City magazine, WASHINGTON WOMAN, aims for more affluent audience with glossy paper and expensive format.

1848 Kanner, Bernice. "Murdoch Makes a Move on CUE." ADVERTISING AGE 51 (March 10, 1980) : 3+.

Merger of CUE and NEW YORK magazines--will Rupert Murdoch emerge the winner?

1849 Kanner, Bernice. "NEW YORK Rebounds from Hard Times." ADVERTISING AGE 50 (June 18, 1979) : 3+.

NEW YORK under owner Rupert Murdoch is again making a profit. A brief look at some of the magazine's problems.

1850 Kelly, Pat. "City and State Magazines." MARKETING & MEDIA DECISIONS 17 (March 1982) : 175-176+.

Growth of city and regional magazines from 1976-1980, including statistics on average audience demographics and reasons advertisers find them useful.

1851 Kurtz, Patricia. "A Study of the Relationship Between Metropolitan Magazines and Locally Edited Sunday Newspaper Supplements." M.A. thesis, California State University, Fullerton, 1982.

Comparison of eighty-five competing pairs. Most editors did not feel competitive for readers. Audiences were similar in age but differed in education and economic status.

1852 Lentini, Cecelia. "Magazines for Suburbia." ADVERTISING AGE 51 (July 28, 1980) : S10+.

Even with good, upscale demographics, some suburban regional magazines are having problems attracting advertisers. Deep penetration of narrow markets is unappreciated by local, unnoticed by national advertisers. Profiles of four magazines illustrate the problem.

1853 McClintick, David. "Murdoch Takes Over NEW YORK Magazine and Appoints James Brady as its Editor." WALL STREET JOURNAL, 10 January 1977, p. 10.

Unfriendly takeover of Clay Felker's NEW YORK by Rupert Murdoch. See WSJ January 7, 1977, p. 1 for more information.

1854 MacDonald, J. Fred. "Clinging to an Investigative Tradition." ADVERTISING AGE 56 (January 17, 1985) : 14.

While many city and regional magazines exude upscale commercialism, a few still publish in-depth investigative reports.

1855 MaGrath, Peter. "The Peters Principles." NEWSWEEK 103 (February 6, 1984) : 69.

Profile of the fifteen-year-old WASHINGTON MONTHLY under founder Charles Peters. The neoliberal regional magazine reaches an influential audience of politicians, government officials, and journalists.

1856 McGraw, Anita Grant. "The Role of City and Regional Magazines and Their Publishers in Society Today." M.A. thesis, University of Mississippi, 1982.

Overview of city and regional magazines. Emphasis on editorial content, readership, advertiser appeal, influence of publisher on the magazine. Publishers tended to reflect the demographic characteristics of their audiences.

1857 Mack, Toni. "Home, Sweet, Home?" FORBES 131 (April 25, 1983) : 80+.

Profile of Michael R. Levy, founder and publisher of the successful TEXAS MONTHLY. His new acquisition, CALIFORNIA, (formerly NEW WEST) is losing money.

1858 Maresca, Carmela C., and Wolff, Leslie R. "SOUTHERN LIVING Turns Regional Image to Gain." ADVERTISING AGE 52 (March 3, 1981) : M36.

How SOUTHERN LIVING successfully competes for advertising revenue. Promotional tools include publication of its own trade magazine, publicity-generating events, special sections.

1859 Marshall, Christy. "CALIFORNIA Still Seeking Gold." ADVERTISING AGE 52 (September 14, 1981) : 44+.

Formerly NEW WEST, CALIFORNIA has yet to make a profit under owners of one year.

1860 Marshall, Christy. "Texas Books in Numbers Game." ADVERTISING AGE 51 (October 13, 1980) : 56.

TEXAS MONTHLY and five other Texas magazines battle for circulation.

1861 Marshall, Christy, and Emmrich, Stuart. "Another Owner for CALIFORNIA." ADVERTISING AGE 54 (August 8, 1983) : 3+.

CALIFORNIA is sold to its fourth owner, Alan Bennett, publisher of SAVVY magazine. CALIFORNIA has been successful editorially but not financially.

1862 Merry, Howard. "City Magazines Grow More Numerous, Stir Sharp Controversies." WALL STREET JOURNAL, 16 June 1967, p.1+.

City magazines were a new and growing phenomenon in 1967. Many covered controversial issues. Others were promotional, covering mostly local economic issues.

1863 Moreland, Pamela. "CALIFORNIA Magazine in New York Hands Again." The LOS ANGELES TIMES, 15 August 1983, sec. 4, p. 1+.

SAVVY publisher and New Yorker Alan Bennett is

new owner of CALIFORNIA. Bennett bought the magazine from TEXAS MONTHLY's Michael Levy and is the fourth owner.

1864 "The Most Profitable Magazine in the U.S." FORBES 119 (June 15, 1977) : 30-31.

Financial comparisons of SOUTHERN LIVING magazine with the rest of the industry.

1865 Murphy, William S. "A New Slant on California History." LOS ANGELES TIMES, 18 November 1984, sec. 6, p. 18-19.

Two-year-old magazine, the CALIFORNIANS, deals with state history. It is as accurate as academic journals, but written in lively prose to appeal to non-academic readers.

1866 "NEW YORK Magazine to Absorb CUE/NEW YORK." FOLIO 9 (May 1980) : 12.

Rupert Murdoch purchases his biggest competitor, CUE.

1867 Oney, Steve. "The Silencing of a Southern Voice." COLUMBIA JOURNALISM REVIEW 24 (November-December 1985) : 50+.

How the ATLANTA WEEKLY, the second oldest Sunday newspaper magazine in the country, became one of the best of its type. Why it is ceasing publication even though it attracted both advertising and upscale readers in the early 1980s.

1868 Pool, Gail. "Magazines." WILSON LIBRARY BULLETIN 56 (March 1982) : 538-539+.

Comments on regional magazines as a type, evaluative reviews of major titles, and comments on excellent though relatively unknown publications.

1869 Rausch, Steven F. "The First Lustrum of TEXAS MONTHLY." M.S. thesis, University of Kansas, 1982.

History and description of TEXAS MONTHLY in its first five years. Emphasis on editorial content.

1870 Reddicliffe, Steven. "Print: Magazines Put Accent on Miami." ADVERTISING AGE 52 (April 6, 1981) : S16-S17.

Magazines for Hispanic Americans flourish in Miami.

1871 Reddicliffe, Steven. "ULTRA: The Ultimate Read." ADVERTISING AGE 53 (April 5, 1982) : M22-M23.

Comments on the content and circulation of Texas' ULTRA, the magazine for the very rich Texan.

1872 Riley, Sam G. "Specialized Magazines of the South." JOURNALISM QUARTERLY 59 (Autumn 1982) : 447-450+.

Editors of city, regional, and specialty magazines in the South surveyed about advertising, editorial content, article sources, forecast, audiences.

1873 Scarffe, John A. "The Rise and Fall of OKLAHOMA MONTHLY, Including Comparisons with TEXAS MONTHLY." M.S. thesis, University of Kansas, 1983.

History of OKLAHOMA MONTHLY, published 1975 to 1981. Comparisons to determine reasons one publication succeeded and the other did not.

1874 Seelig, Anita. "In Texas, Elite Publications Satisfy Big Appetite." ADVERTISING AGE 54 (April 4, 1983) : M30.

Between 1981 and 1983 at least eight magazines were developed for the growing numbers of affluent Texans.

1875 Smith, Lee. "The Payoff in City Magazines." DUN'S REVIEW 104 (November 1974) : 69-72.

Successful as a genre, many individual titles have failed. Suggestions for a successful formula and profiles of some particular titles.

1876 Sobczynski, Anna. "Magazines Project Community Identity." ADVERTISING AGE 50 (September 3, 1979) : S22.

Brief look at some glossy suburban magazines.

1877 Spadoni, Marie. "ACCENT Adds Spice to SIU Students' Lives." ADVERTISING AGE 54 (October 17, 1983) : M62-M63.

ACCENT ON SOUTHERN ILLINOIS, a regional magazine designed to create a positive image of the area, was founded by magazine journalism students at Southern Illinois University.

1878 Strazewski, Len. "Paging Through Texas Magazines." ADVERTISING AGE 56 (August 8, 1985) : 24.

Brief overview of the Texas magazine market.

1879 Stroud, Ruth. "CALIFORNIA Boasts its First Profit." ADVERTISING AGE 55 (March 5, 1984) : 53+.

How fourth owner Alan Bennett engineered a first-time profit for CALIFORNIA magazine (formerly NEW WEST).

1880 Truscott, Lucian K. IV. "Requiem for a Winner." NEW TIMES 8 (March 4, 1977) 21-24+.

Lengthy account of Rupert Murdoch's takeover

of Clay Felker's holdings--NEW YORK magazine, NEW WEST, and VILLAGE VOICE.

1881 Walker, Ruth. "City Magazines: Fat with Ads--and Serious Prose." CHRISTIAN SCIENCE MONITOR, 17 September 1984, pp. 23-24.

City magazines may be viewed as general interest magazines in one sense and specialty magazines in another. Marketed to an upscale local audience, emphasizing lifestyle stories, coverage is not necessarily parochial. Brief historical background of the type and comments on the seriousness of some city magazine journalism.

1882 Zuckerman, Laurence. "Charlie Peters and his Gospel Singers." COLUMBIA JOURNALISM REVIEW 22 (September-October 1983) : 40-44.

All about Charlie Peters, WASHINGTON MONTHLY, and its philosophy of neo-liberalism.

News Magazines

1883 Burriss, Larry L. "Accuracy of News Magazines as Perceived by News Sources." JOURNALISM QUARTERLY 62 (Winter 1985) : 824-827.

Survey of persons quoted in news magazine articles (TIME and NEWSWEEK) December 1983-March

1984. Respondents reported accuracy in most cases, except for quotes being taken out of context.

1884 Canape, Charlene. "The Race Among Newsweeklies: Can Bill Broyles Blast NEWSWEEK out of Second Place?" WASHINGTON JOURNALISM REVIEW 5 (January-February 1983) : 18-20+.

Speculation about NEWSWEEK's future under new editor Bill Broyles, formerly of TEXAS MONTHLY. Plans include improving the back-of-the-book, cleaner and bolder graphics, more investigative articles, more big-name writers. Editors of all three news magazines compared.

1885 Christ, William G., and Johnson, Sammye. "Images through TIME: Man of the Year Covers." JOURNALISM QUARTERLY 62 (Winter 1985) : 891-893.

Analysis of subjects of TIME magazine covers 1927-1984. Subjects represent individuals of great influence, and thus "provide benchmarks to history."

1886 Colford, Steven W. "Conservatives Try for New National Voice: WASHINGTON TIMES Developing New INSIGHT." ADVERTISING AGE 56 (September 2, 1985) : 47.

Conservative new magazine, linked to the WASHINGTON TIMES, debuts September 1985. INSIGHT will be ad-supported with controlled circulation. See also entry 1901.

1887 Culbertson, Hugh M. "Veiled Attribution--An Element of Style?" JOURNALISM QUARTERLY 55 (Autumn 1978) : 456-465.

The use of unnamed sources in news magazines. Comparison with data from earlier study on unnamed sources in newspapers.

1888 Diamond, Edwin. "The News About U.S. NEWS." NEW YORK 17 (August 27, 1984) : 48-49+.

Profile of U.S. NEWS & WORLD REPORT in relation to its competitors, TIME and NEWSWEEK. How will new owner Mortimer Zuckerman use and change the magazine?

1889 Diamond, Edwin. "NEWSWEEK's Testing Time." NEW REPUBLIC 188 (February 28, 1983) : 13-15.

A comparison of TIME and NEWSWEEK over the years. TIME is committed to its traditional formula, while NEWSWEEK is looking for change.

1890 Elliott, Stuart J. "Known Quantity Smith Over NEWSWEEK." ADVERTISING AGE 55 (January 9, 1984) : 62.

NEWSWEEK editor Broyles' resignation and replacement by staffer Richard Smith. Part of

Broyles' dissatisfaction may have resulted from lack of agreement by him and others regarding his role on the magazine.

1891 Elliott, Stuart J. "Mr. Broyles Charts a Prudent Course." ADVERTISING AGE 54 (July 4, 1983) : M4-M5+

Everyone seems satisfied with the changes made and proposed by NEWSWEEK's editor of one year, William Broyles.

1892 Elliott, Stuart J. "NEWSWEEK Tests Health-Market Strength." ADVERTISING AGE 56 (September 2, 1985) : 58.

NEWSWEEK plans test market of new NEWSWEEK ON HEALTH.

1893 Elliott, Stuart J. "U.S. NEWS, at 50, Works at Evolution." ADVERTISING AGE 54 (May 30, 1983) : 50.

U.S. NEWS executives comment on the differences between U.S. NEWS and other news magazines. While changes are necessary over time, U.S. NEWS aims for slow almost imperceptible change.

1894 Friendly, Jonathon. "NEWSWEEK's New Line-Up: Broyles Out; Smith In." WASHINGTON JOURNALISM REVIEW 6 (March 1984) : 50-51.

Richard M. Smith replaces William Broyles as editor of NEWSWEEK, the fifth change since 1972.

1895 Glynn, Lenny. "NEWSWEEK's New Editor." MACLEANS 97 (January 16, 1984) : 43.

William Broyles resigns editorship of NEWSWEEK. His preference for feature-oriented cover stories clashed with the hard-news preference of senior editors.

1896 Gupta, Udayan. "The Content is General, the Target is Female." ADVERTISING AGE 54 (October 3, 1983) : M36.

NEWSWEEK WOMAN, introduced in 1980, is a demographically segmented edition of NEWSWEEK, available to advertisers thirteen times per year.

1897 Henry, William A. III. "Change of Command at U.S. NEWS." TIME 123 (June 25, 1984) : 75.

With the usual background information, TIME reports Mortimer Zuckerman's purchase of U.S. NEWS & WORLD REPORT.

1898 Henry, William A. III. "NEWSWEEK's Outsider Bows Out. And an Insider Steps Up as its Sixth Top Editor Since 1972." TIME 123 (January 16, 1984) : 63.

Richard Smith succeeds William Broyles as editor of NEWSWEEK.

1899 Hirschfeld, Neal. "NEWSWEEK Tackles Serious Issues, Advertisers." ADVERTISING AGE 55 (July 19, 1984) : 38.

Special edition NEWSWEEK ON CAMPUS, distributed on four-year college and university campuses, seeks to reach the smartest and most affluent students.

1900 Hogan, Bill. "Behind the Grab for U.S. NEWS." WASHINGTON JOURNALISM REVIEW 6 (September 1984) : 20-26.

The sale of U.S. NEWS & WORLD REPORT to Mortimer Zuckerman was surrounded by secrecy and speculation among employees and shareholders.

1901 Hogan, Bill. "No Profit INSIGHT: The WASHINGTON TIMES' Conservative Newsweekly." WASHINGTON JOURNALISM REVIEW 8 (March 1986) : 34-36.

Owner of INSIGHT apparently traces to the Unification Church. Although graphic design is attractive, editorial features rely on shadowy attribution and unidentified sources. Distribution is by controlled circulation, and as yet, there is no paid advertising. WJR questions where the money comes from.

1902 Johnson, Hillary. "Deep in the Heart of NEWSWEEK." COLUMBIA JOURNALISM REVIEW 22 (January February 1984) : 37-41.

Problems at NEWSWEEK under new editor William Broyles.

1903 Jones, Alex S. "Libel Suits Show Differing Approaches of Papers, TV and Magazines." NEW YORK TIMES, 31 January 1985, p. B9.

Use of separate reporters and writers on news magazines differs from the newspaper approach of one person doing both jobs.

1904 Kaiser, Charles. "Too Good a Correspondent." NEWSWEEK 100 (August 16, 1982) : 60.

NEWSWEEK's Moscow bureau chief is expelled by the Soviets for "impermissable methods of journalistic activities."

1905 Lee, Richard. "The TIME-NEWSWEEK War." WASHINGTONIAN 20 (July 1985) : 124-130.

Personality-oriented article about the traditional rivalry between TIME and NEWSWEEK. Suggests "TIME is bigger and more establishment" while NEWSWEEK "is faster on its feet."

1906 MacDougall, A. Kent. "TIME, NEWSWEEK Vie with Polished Prose and Reams of Research." WALL STREET JOURNAL, 12 July 1967, p. 1+.

TIME and NEWSWEEK compared and contrasted. The competition between them is as relevant today as in 1967 when this article was written.

1907 Machalaba, Daniel. "New Editor Shifts NEWSWEEK's Emphasis and Stirs up Staff, Trying to Gain on TIME." WALL STREET JOURNAL, 17 February 1983, p. 33.

NEWSWEEK worries about competition from TIME and television in its number two spot. New editor, William Broyles, sparks controversy with editorial, design, and graphics changes.

1908 McNichol, Tom, and Carlson, Margaret. "A Developer Remodels U.S. NEWS, or, the High-Rise Ambitions of Mort Zuckerman." COLUMBIA JOURNALISM REVIEW 24 (July-August 1985) : 31-36.

Changes at U.S. NEWS since its purchase by Zuckerman include selection of Shelby Coffey as editor and some cosmetic changes.

1909 Mayer, Caroline E. "Judge Frees Proceeds from U.S. NEWS Sales; Says Employees can Get their Cut." WASHINGTON POST, 29 March 1985, p. B3.

Proceeds from U.S. NEWS sale to Mortimer Zuckerman may be freed for distribution to employees and retirees under profit sharing plans. Further litigation is suggested.

1910 "NEWSWEEK is Adding New College Edition." NEW YORK TIMES, 19 April 1982, p. 6.

NEWSWEEK ON CAMPUS, unlike a demographic edition, has content different from NEWSWEEK. It will be inserted into student publications on major campuses.

1911 "NEWSWEEK Measures the Gold." AMERICAN DEMOGRAPHICS 7 (August 1985) : 17.

NEWSWEEK produces six different U.S. editions targeted at demographically different audiences. Editorial content is identical, advertisements differ. Many subscribers are unaware they are targeted. Variety of editions established to meet advertisers' needs.

1912 "NEWSWEEK Tests Theme Magazine." FOLIO 9 (June 1980) : 46.

NEWSWEEK FOCUS is an extension of the news magazine, dealing with one issue in depth.

1913 "Position Filled: A New Editor at U.S. NEWS." TIME 125 (April 1, 1985) : 72.

New editor at U.S. NEWS, Shelby Coffey, pledges "evolutionary" not radical change.

1914 Romano, Lois. "Scrambling for Covers: The Newsmagazines' Debate Deadlines." WASHINGTON POST, 10 October 1984, p. D1+.

Difficulties and costs for news magazines when deadlines overlap presidential news conferences. Comparisons.

1915 Rosenstiel, Thomas B. "New Publisher Tries to Revive U.S. NEWS." LOS ANGELES TIMES, 7 April 1985, sec. 1, p. 4.

Can Mortimer Zuckerman transform U.S. NEWS from something more than the "poor cousin of the news weeklies"? His views and first steps.

1916 Shaw, David. "Fierce Rivals: NEWSWEEK Versus TIME." LOS ANGELES TIMES, 1 May 1980, p. 1+.

Review of a critical 1970 analysis of TIME. Lengthy comparison of TIME and NEWSWEEK, and the competition between the two. Excellent commentary on news magazines. See also part two of this feature which appeared May 3, 1980.

1917 Shaw, David. "Men at Top are Key to TIME, NEWSWEEK Battle." LOS ANGELES TIMES, 3 May 1980, sec. 1, p. 1+.

Second of two-part feature describes the TIME-NEWSWEEK competition through the 1960s and 1970s. Highlights the differences in style and approach between the two magazines, and the role of the news magazine in general.

1918 "There's a New Newsweekly Style." FOLIO 15 (April 1986) : 119-121.

A look at the graphic commonalities of the three U.S. news magazines. Extensive layout comparative illustration; limited text.

1919 "Time." ADVERTISING AGE 54 (March 21, 1983) : M17-M80.

Advertisement showing every TIME magazine cover from 1923-1982.

1920 "U.S. NEWS Gets 4th Editor in 52 Years." U.S. NEWS & WORLD REPORT 98 (April 1, 1985) : 11.

Brief announcement of Shelby Coffey's new role as editor of U.S. NEWS.

1921 "U.S. NEWS May not be Such a Catch After All." BUSINESS WEEK (May 7, 1984) : 32.

Weak profits of U.S. NEWS have discouraged buyers despite its prestige and growth potential.

Political & Serious Magazines

1922 Adler, Jerry. "Storms in the ATLANTIC." NEWSWEEK 98 (July 20, 1981) : 74.

Fiscal problems still trouble the ATLANTIC one year after Mortimer Zuckerman bought the magazine. His dollar input has upgraded editorial quality, but he claims deception by the previous owners in their sale of the magazine.

1923 Armstrong, David. "Remodeling MOTHER." COLUMBIA JOURNALISM REVIEW 24 (January-February 1986) : 12-13.

As MOTHER JONES turns ten years old, it suffers from a growing debt and steady circulation drop. Reasons suggested for the decline include a smug editorial tone and lack of conflicting viewpoints in editorial content. New management plans changes, from redesign to possible name change.

1924 Barrett, William. THE TRUANTS: ADVENTURES AMONG THE INTELLECTUALS. Garden City, N.Y.: Anchor Press/Doubleday, 1982.

The story of PARTISAN REVIEW and the intellec--tual elite who edited and wrote for it.

1925 Boylan, James. "Drifting Left: Four New Magazines." NATION 226 (April 22, 1978) : 454-456.

Descriptions of four political magazines new in the late 1970s: INQUIRY, MOTHER JONES, POLITICKS & OTHER HUMAN INTRESTS, SEVEN DAYS.

1926 Bogart, Beth. "SATURDAY REVIEW Adds Fun to New Formula." ADVERTISING AGE 56 (October 3, 1985) : 46-47.

The latest editorial concept for SATURDAY REVIEW.

1927 Bogart, Beth. "Signs of Growth in the NEW REPUBLIC." ADVERTISING AGE 54 (October 17, 1983) : M10-M11.

Profile of the NEW REPUBLIC, and its recent efforts to boost newsstand sales and advertising pages. According to publisher, its new independence was not bought at the price of editorial integrity.

1928 Bourne, Tom. "Whatever Happened to the RAMPARTS Gang?" QUILL 68 (March 1980) : 13-14+.

The radical RAMPARTS magazine, 1962-1976, and what happened to its writers and editors. Comparison of RAMPARTS with today's MOTHER JONES.

1929 Brown, Kevin. "MOTHER JONES Adds a Little Life to its Politics." ADVERTISING AGE 55 (October 18, 1984) : 28.

Although MOTHER JONES' readers have a high annual income, advertisers often avoid the left-wing editorial style of the magazine. MJ editor feels the magazine is more life-style oriented than other political magazines. Comments on advertising and editorial policies.

1930 Brown, Kevin. "Times are A-Changin' at MOTHER JONES." ADVERTISING AGE 57 (January 13, 1986) : 40.

MOTHER JONES has a new publisher, and hopes

to attract new readers and advertisers as changes in format are planned. Like other political magazines, MJ has trouble attracting enough advertising.

1931 Clutterbuck, David. "Martyrdom of MOTHER JONES." INTERNATIONAL MANAGEMENT 35 (February 1980) : 24A.

MOTHER JONES uses a democratic management system, in which editor and publisher are elected annually. Majority of the non-profit foundation's directors are elected from the magazine's staff.

1932 Cockburn, Alexander. "One-Way Street." NATION 240 (June 29, 1985) : 789.

Criticism of the NEW REPUBLIC for not allowing reply by author of negatively reviewed book.

1933 Colford, Steven W. "Movers and Shakers Buy NATIONAL JOURNAL." ADVERTISING AGE 57 (February 24, 1986) : 43.

Profile of the NATIONAL JOURNAL, a small circulation, middle-of-the-road, opinion magazine with a highly influential readership in the nation's capital.

1934 Cook, Bruce. "The Fight to Control HARPER'S." WASHINGTON JOURNALISM REVIEW 5 (December 1983) : 43-46+.

Power struggle between former editor, new editor, and foundation credited with rescuing a financially troubled magazine. With former editor reinstated, HARPER'S plans new format.

1935 Cousins, Norman. "Birth of SR/W." WORLD 2 (July 31, 1973) : 10-12+.

Continuation of the SATURDAY REVIEW saga. Norman Cousins, now editor of WORLD, merges WORLD with SATURDAY REVIEW when Charney and Veronis file for bankruptcy after one year of ownership.

1936 Cousins, Norman. "An Epitaph for the SATURDAY REVIEW--and Culture, Too." LOS ANGELES TIMES, 23 August 1982, sec. 2, p. 7.

Long-time SATURDAY REVIEW editor describes the magazine's goals and philosophy.

1937 Cousins, Norman. "A Postmortem on the SATURDAY REVIEW: The High Cost and Risk of Intellectual Journalism in Contemporary Society." CENTER 16 (May-June 1983) : 33-40.

A backward look at the problems of SATURDAY REVIEW in the early 1970s by its editor of four decades. A round table discussion follows, covering such topics as the revival of SATURDAY REVIEW, difficulties of general interest and intellectual magazines, role of the editor.

1938 DeVries, Hillary. "ATLANTIC Magazine Finding New Friends." CHRISTIAN SCIENCE MONITOR, 12 October 1983, p. 1+.

Strong financial backing and good editing have brought new success to the ATLANTIC.

1939 Diggins, John Patrick. "The NEW REPUBLIC and Its Times: Seventy Years of Enlightened Mistakes, Principled Compromises, and Unconventional Wisdom." NEW REPUBLIC 191 (December 10, 1984) : 23-34+.

Start of lengthy section devoted to thoughtful historical overview of NEW REPUBLIC.

1940 Dixler, Elsa. "Rich Eccentrics, Red-Baiting and Jameson's Dog." NATION 240 (June 8, 1985) : 702-704.

Highlights discussions which occurred during the NATION'S conference on critical journals of opinion. Considers their role, audience, ownership, distribution.

1941 Donath, Bob. "New Owner Takes SATURDAY REVIEW Reins." ADVERTISING AGE 48 (March 14, 1977) : 3+.

Norman Cousins sells SATURDAY REVIEW to Carll Tucker.

1942 Doudna, Martin K. CONCERNED ABOUT THE PLANET: "THE REPORTER" MAGAZINE AND AMERICAN LIBERALISM, 1949-1968. Westport, Conn.: Greenwood Press, 1977.

The birth, death, and staff of the REPORTER magazine. Reports extensive interviews with founder Max Ascoli. Though the magazine survived only nineteen years, its readership included very influential subscribers, including the U.S. president, vice-president, seven cabinet members, and one-third of the Senate.

1943 Dougherty, Philip. "The Latest SATURDAY REVIEW." NEW YORK TIMES, 2 November 1984, p. D17.

SATURDAY REVIEW's new publisher and editor are its tenth owners since its founding sixty years ago. Brief background of the magazine and future plans.

1944 English, Deirdre, and Hazen, Don. "Don't Let Our Voice be Silenced." MOTHER JONES 10 (October 1985) : 6+.

MOTHER JONES calls for financial support from readers, emphasizing the need for independent, diverse information sources in a period when media moguls are buying smaller publishers, multinational corporations are buying the media that report on them, and the influence of advertisers is increasing.

1945 Fenn, Donna. "HARPER'S New Foundation." ADVERTISING AGE 54 (October 17, 1983) : M11+.

HARPER'S editors since the MacArthur Foundation bought the bankrupt magazine in 1980.

1946 Gallanis, Bess. "ATLANTIC's Sea Changes." ADVERTISING AGE 54 (October 17, 1983) : M10+.

Although not yet out of financial difficulties, the ATLANTIC has returned to its role as a forum for discussion of serious issues.

1947 Gerry, Roberta. "Thoughtleaders: Why Advertisers Look Beyond the Numbers." MAGAZINE AGE 3 (August 1982) : 20-22+.

Readers of magazines like the ATLANTIC, HARPER'S, FOREIGN AFFAIRS, AMERICAN HERITAGE may be few in number but are long in power and influence. Thoughtleader genre defined, readership described, titles reviewed. The Leadership Network is a consortium of eight publications responsible for attracting national advertisers.

1948 Gordon, Richard L. "Reagan in REVIEW Role." ADVERTISING AGE 55 (January 16, 1984) : 1+.

Conservative political journal, NATIONAL REVIEW, uses news clip of the president's praise for the magazine as an advertising endorsement and attracts "tens of thousands" of new subscribers.

1949 Grover, Stephen. "The NATION Magazine Increases its Readership by Courting Controversy; but Deficits Continue." WALL STREET JOURNAL, 13 December 1979, p. 48.

Current status of the NATION. New emphasis on publicity features editor of this influential magazine praising TV GUIDE in advertisement. Comments on its financial worries, influential readership, and use of unpaid journalism students for reporting and research.

1950 Heckman, Lucy. "HARPER'S Magazine." SERIALS REVIEW 7 (January-March 1981) : 49-56.

History of HARPER'S from its founding in 1850 to its rescue by the MacArthur Foundation in 1980.

1951 Henry, William A. III. "Breaking the Liberal Pattern: Quirky and Provocative, the NEW REPUBLIC is Surging in Influence." TIME 124 (October 1, 1984) : 78.

Part of the NEW REPUBLIC's appeal derives from its openness to multiple points of view. Martin Peretz, owner since 1974, has increased the magazine's revenues and heightened its influence.

1952 Hentoff, Nat. "An Editor Who Stands Up to His Readers." WASHINGTON POST, 18 April 1985, p. A23.

Hentoff's opinion favors PROGRESSIVE's efforts

to publish "H Bomb Secret: How We Got It. Why We're Telling It."

1953 Herman, Tom. "NATION Magazine is Underdeveloped, Buying Group Says." WALL STREET JOURNAL, 27 December 1977, p. 13.

New owners have plans to turn a profit after 112 years of deficits.

1954 Hochschild, Adam. "RAMPARTS: The End of Muckraking Magazines." WASHINGTON MONTHLY 6 (June 1974) : 33-42.

A former RAMPARTS reporter writes about its muckraking stories in the 1960s and its internal problems during the 1970s.

1955 "In Praise of Smallness." NATION 240 (April 13, 1985) : 417.

The important role of small, independent magazines in American intellectual life. Should left, liberal magazines like the NATION join other small magazines (even if right-wing, religious, or value-free) in seeking solutions to current problems exacerbated by the trend towards conglomerates and the impact of rising costs?

1956 "Inside the ATLANTIC." BOSTON MAGAZINE 74 (September 1982) : 145.

1957 "Inside MOTHER's Pocketbook." MOTHER JONES 3 (January 1978) : 3.

Brief notes on the economies of publishing independent magazines.

1958 Jaroslovsky, Rich. "Racial Purist uses Reagan Plug." WALL STREET JOURNAL, 28 September 1984, p. 56.

Publisher of politically, conservative academic journals has received letter of praise from Mr. Reagan. The White House objects to its use in advertising for the MANKIND QUARTERLY and the JOURNAL OF SOCIAL, POLITICAL AND ECONOMIC STUDIES.

1959 Kesler, Lori. "SATURDAY REVIEW Revisited." ADVERTISING AGE 54 (June 27, 1983) : M59.

New owner Jeff Gluck's plans for SATURDAY REVIEW.

1960 Kinney, Jay. "Keeping Track of the Arguments: Religion and Politics in Print." CO-EVOLUTION QUARTERLY 39 (Fall 1983) : 46-49.

Survey of sixteen magazines and journals that combine religion and politics. Brief critical comments on each title, including individual slants and focus.

1961 Lapham, Lewis H. "In the American Grain." HARPER'S 288 (February 1984) : 6-8+.

A brief look at HARPER'S history and an introduction to HARPER'S new image.

1962 Lescaze, Lee. "In the Nick of Time. Three General Interest Magazines Rescued ... for Now." WASHINGTON JOURNALISM REVIEW 2 (September 1980) : 17-19.

Will rescues of HARPER'S, ATLANTIC MONTHLY, and SATURDAY REVIEW be long-lived? Their editorial product is less in demand as newspapers develop magazine format opinion pages and television offers magazine shows.

1963 Levey, Robert. "How Hot it is at the ATLANTIC Magazine." THE PRESS 10 (February 1982) : 9-10.

Circulation rises at the ATLANTIC in response to a feature on David Stockman. But one successful issue does not guarantee a turnaround in ATLANTIC's recent record as a financial loser.

1964 Little, Stuart. "What Happened at HARPER'S." SATURDAY REVIEW 54 (April 10, 1971) : 43-47+.

Account of dispute between HARPER'S publisher and editors. Interesting as background and history.

1965 McManus, Kevin. "Rick MacArthur: How a Romantic Journalist Stepped in to Give HARPER'S a New

Lease on Life." ADVERTISING AGE 56 (August 29, 1985) : 4-5.

Profile of Rick MacArthur, who engineered the MacArthur Foundation's rescue of HARPER'S and the rehiring of former editor Lewis Lapham.

1966 McWilliams, Carey. "Is Muckraking Coming Back?" COLUMBIA JOURNALISM REVIEW 9 (Fall 1970) : 8-15.

Brief history of muckraking and the social factors that spawned the movement. Commentary on contemporary muckraking magazines, and forecast for an upsurge in reform journalism.

1967 McWhorter, Diane. "The ATLANTIC: In Search of a Role." NEW YORK TIMES MAGAZINE, 14 February 1982, p. 20+.

Can quality, general-interest, issue-oriented magazines survive financially? The ATLANTIC is trying under its new ownership.

1968 Mayer, Milton. "Only Seventy-Five: Still Time enough to Change the World." PROGRESSIVE 48 (July 1984) : 82.

Editorial on the PROGRESSIVE magazine--still fighting to make a better world.

1969 Merry, Robert W. "The Ferment at the NEW

REPUBLIC." WASHINGTON JOURNALISM REVIEW 7 (July 1985) : 22-24+.

The NEW REPUBLIC "probes, tests, fights and debates ideas like no other magazine," leading to inconsistency and "ideological schizophrenia" in content. The magazine has grown more conservative, though it clings to a liberal label.

1970 Meyers, Janet. "NEW REPUBLIC Ad Pitch Leaning to Right." ADVERTISING AGE 57 (February 10, 1986) : 32.

The liberal opinion journal, NEW REPUBLIC, seeks advertising from conservative corporations for its financial improvements.

1971 Morgan, Frederick. "Setting it Straight." AMERICAN SCHOLAR 50 (Autumn 1981) : 567-570.

Recent exchange of correspondence between the editors of PARTISAN REVIEW and HUDSON REVIEW about content of those magazines.

1972 "Mortimer Zuckerman, Boston Businessman, Buys ATLANTIC MONTHLY." WALL STREET JOURNAL, 3 March 1980, p. 7.

Although currently losing money, ATLANTIC magazine hopes to become a successful business enterprise while remaining independent. New owner will bring substantial financial backing.

1973 "MOTHER'S Call: A Shout from the Left?" TIME 116 (July 21, 1980) : 62.

Brief description of MOTHER JONES and a few of its notable exposes.

1974 Navasky, Victor. "Role of the Critical Journal." NATION 240 (June 8, 1985) : 698-702.

Excellent consideration of the opinion journal's role in times of increasing concentration in media ownership. Multiple, critical, and new ideas find expression in these publications.

1975 "New Cash For an Old Bostonian." TIME 115 (March 17, 1980) : 97-98.

Musings on the 123-year history of the ATLANTIC, the reasons why "smooth, non-Yankee" real estate developer, Mortimer Zuckerman bought it, and its chief rival, HARPER'S.

1976 Peter, John. "The SATURDAY REVIEW: A Quicker Read." FOLIO 14 (October 1985) : 157-158.

The new SATURDAY REVIEW is an "elegant exploration" of a widely recognized approach in communications--brief, condensed information for readers who want to save time.

1977 Pool, Gail. "ATLANTIC MONTHLY." SERIALS REVIEW 8 (Spring 1982) : 29-32.

A profile of the ATLANTIC details its history, ups and downs, forecast for the future under new owner Mortimer Zuckerman.

1978 Richter, Paul. "HARPER'S Will Limit Format to Opinion." LOS ANGELES TIMES, 13 July 1983, sec. 4, p. 2.

Under rehired editor, Lewis Lapham, HARPER'S will carry primarily opinion articles, hoping to attract affluent, well-educated readers.

1979 Schardt, Arlie. "The Torch Passes at SR." NEWSWEEK 95 (June 2, 1980) : 55.

Crises for serious, general-interest magazines are reviewed. SATURDAY REVIEW sale to Robert Weingarten is compared to Mortimer Zuckerman's purchase of the ATLANTIC and the proposed sale of HARPER'S.

1980 Schram, Martin. "Osborne Remembered." NEW REPUBLIC 184 (May 16, 1981) : 9-11.

Detailed eulogy for John Osborne, senior editor and columnist for NEW REPUBLIC.

1981 Shah, Diane K. "Feisty MOTHER." NEWSWEEK 91 (April 24, 1978) : 111.

Brief look at MOTHER JONES, a radical journal fast gaining a reputation for "hell-raising." Its success is based on a compromise between investigative ideals and captalist business practices. For example, it is critical of harmful products but accepts cigarette advertising.

1982 Shaw, David. "Care and Feeding of a Magazine." LOS ANGELES TIMES, 6 February 1983, sec. 1, p. 1+.

Thought-leader magazines, liberal and conservative, regularly lose money. Among their problems are increased postal and paper costs, and high costs of obtaining new subscribers. The NATIONAL REVIEW frequently cited as an example.

1983 Shaw, David. "Elite Magazines Struggle to Leave Slough of Deficits." LOS ANGELES TIMES, 7 February 1983, sec. 1, p. 1+.

HARPER'S and the ATLANTIC face economic problems. HARPER'S is taking an austerity route to survival. The ATLANTIC is taking a luxury route, backed by money of its new owner.

1984 Shaw, David. "Frugality Helps One 'Thought-Leader' Journal Earn a Profit." LOS ANGELES TIMES, 6 February 1983, sec. 1, p. 25.

WASHINGTON MONTHLY is one political magazine that often turns a profit.

1985 Sherrill, Robert. "The New Regime at the NEW

REPUBLIC." COLUMBIA JOURNALISM REVIEW 14 (March-April 1976) : 23-28.

Mid-70s disputes between owner and editors of the NEW REPUBLIC. Recent historical background.

1986 Shribman, David. "Magazine's Grasp of Government." NEW YORK TIMES, 6 June 1982, sec. 3, pp. F5-F6.

After twelve years, the NATIONAL JOURNAL is making a profit. Its small circulation goes to very influential members of the government.

1987 Simonds, C. H. "A 25-Year Frolic." NATIONAL REVIEW 116 (December 31, 1980) : 1606-1634.

Twenty-fifth anniversary article gives overview of some personalities that helped shape the NATIONAL REVIEW. Other articles in the issue discuss the magazine over its life--its covers, cartoonists, the last five years, looking back and looking forward.

1988 Stein, M. L. "Opinion Journals Meet. Editors of these Small Magazines Ponder their Future: Should They Rake Muck or Leave it to the 'Big Media'?" EDITOR & PUBLISHER 118 (April 27, 1985) : 18+.

Editors of opinion journals met to discuss the functions of their magazines. Some felt big media should be the crusaders; others felt corporate advertising pressure was limiting such investigation. Meeting expenses also discussed. Suggestions for coping included non-profit status, low budgets, low salaries.

1989 Suplee, Curt. "Moving Magazine: SATURDAY REVIEW Sold, Coming to Washington." WASHINGTON POST, 22 June 1984, p. B1+.

News item on purchase of SATURDAY REVIEW by investment group. New owner Paul Dietrich anticipates increased profitability and influence.

1990 Thomas, Bill. "Two-Upmanship." WASHINGTON JOURNALISM REVIEW 6 (September 1984) : 15.

Increasing competition between two highly respected political journals--NATIONAL JOURNAL and CONGRESSIONAL QUARTERLY.

1991 "Trinity Day: A New Journal is Born." TIME 126 (October 21, 1985) : 72.

PUBLIC INTEREST, the neoconservative quarterly devoted to domestic issues, will have a sister publication, NATIONAL INTEREST, devoted to foreign policy.

1992 "A Very Good Magazine in Trouble." WASHINGTON POST, 6 August 1983, p. A17.

High circulation and high production costs

yield financial problems for the influential, liberal PROGRESSIVE.

Science & Computer Magazines

1993 "An Avalanche of Personal Computer Magazines." BUSINESS WEEK (August 22, 1983) : 90.

The rapid growth of computer magazine titles is leading to a shakeout. Many titles owned by small entrepreneurs are being bought by large publishers.

1994 Bennett, William. "Science Hits the Newsstand." COLUMBIA JOURNALISM REVIEW 19 (January-February 1981) : 53-57.

New general interest science magazines to compete with forty-year-old SCIENTIFIC AMERICAN. Most are long on advertising and short on editorial promises.

1995 Benoit, Ellen. "Our New Astrology." FORBES 131 (February 28, 1983) : 93.

Overview of computer magazines. Their popularity is compared with the popularity of movie magazines in the 1930s and 1940s. Discussion of content, advertising, specific titles, and the importance of finding a unique niche in the market.

1996 Berg, Eric. "The Computer Magazine Glut: Only a Few May Survive." NEW YORK TIMES, 8 September 1984, p. 31-32.

1997 "Boom in Computer Magazines." NEW YORK TIMES, 9 November 1983, p. D1+.

Computer magazines' growth and health is reflected in increased advertising and high page count.

1998 Camilleri, John. "Overview of the Science Magazine Category." MARKETING & MEDIA DECISIONS 20 (April 1985) : 124+.

Can the market support four new and one old science magazines? Brief profiles of the five titles.

1999 Chace, Susan. "Kids to Have Own Magazine on Computers." WALL STREET JOURNAL, 24 June 1983, p. 25.

Children's computer magazines offer advice to children, provide information on what computers can do, review computer systems. Several new titles mentioned. Some involve children in writing and editing.

2000 Chace, Susan. "An Old-Fashioned Spat Breaks Out in World of High-Tech Magazines." WALL STREET JOURNAL 13 December 1982, p. 13.

Ownership of PERSONAL COMPUTING magazine is contested by founder and financial backer, when financial backer sells magazine to Ziff-Davis.

2001 Collins, Glenn. "Children's Magazines for a Computer Age." NEW YORK TIMES, 10 September 1983, p. 48.

Computer magazines for children. Some involve children in writing and editing.

2002 "Computer Magazine Overbyte." FORTUNE 110 (November 26, 1984) : 9-10.

Computer magazine shakeout is beginning as many titles are failing to reach the circulations promised to advertisers.

2003 "Computer Magazines' Programs for Reader Friendliness." ECONOMIST 293 (November 10, 1984) : 84-85.

A major problem for computer magazines is reaching the reader advertisers want to reach. Advertising revenues decide which magazines will survive. One solution is to use controlled circulation.

2004 Diamond, Edwin. "That New Time Religion." NEW YORK 18 (July 22, 1985) : 17-19.

On relaunching of Time's DISCOVER magazine. Ads, criticism of "dull copy."

2005 Elliott, Stuart J. "It's a Man's World to SCIENCE DIGEST." ADVERTISING AGE 55 (September 24, 1984) : 14.

Having discovered a general science audience does not exist, Hearst's SCIENCE DIGEST is repositioning. Still a science magazine, its targeted audience will be "young men of the baby boom generation." Its role will be that of a service and lifestyle magazine for the "citizen of high technology."

2006 Endicott, Craig. "Machine Specific: Perilous Publishing at Best." ADVERTISING AGE 55 (March 5, 1984)) : M60.

Problems faced by machine-specific computer magazines, with reference to 99ER HOME COMPUTER.

2007 Endicott, Craig. "Machines Face Terminal Illness." ADVERTISING AGE 55 (March 5, 1984) : M60-M61.

A shakeout is expected in the market for machine-specific computer magazines.

2008 Engstrom, Theresa. "Personal Computers Inspire a Rash of Magazines, but Shakeout is Seen." WALL STREET JOURNAL, 9 April 1984, p. 37.

Computer magazines over 700 pages per issue find it difficult to avoid editorial redundancy while filling pages between ads.

2009 Fannin, Rebecca. "The Computer Magazine Maze." MARKETING & MEDIA DECISIONS 18 (October 1983) : 71-72+.

Hefty computer magazines are loaded with ads. Difficult for media buyers to select publications. Proliferation of titles is expected to lead to a shakeout.

2010 "55 Computer Books 'Byte' the Dust." MARKETING & MEDIA DECISIONS 20 (April 1985) : 8.

Brief article announcing the start of a shakeout in the computer magazine field. Graph illustrates start-ups and failures in the field.

2011 Francis, David R. "The Boom in Sci-Tech Magazines: Is It Going to Last?" CHRISTIAN SCIENCE MONITOR, 2 February 1984, pp. 21-23.

Problems at some newer science magazines which assume there is a mass market for science. The oldest, SCIENTIFIC AMERICAN, is one of the most profitable, but does not aim at a mass market.

2012 Friedman, Mel. "Cashing in on the Computer Explosion." MADISON AVENUE 25 (December 1983) : 58-59+.

Growing number of computer magazines range from "fan" magazines for specific computers to service manuals for eager learners.

2013 "The Hot New Competiton in Science Magazines." BUSINESS WEEK (July 14, 1980) : 58+.

Time Inc. will launch DISCOVER, a science magazine. Is public interest in science strong enough to support DISCOVER and its competition?

2014 Inger, Dina, and Alter, Stewart. "The Expanding Universe of Science Magazines." MAGAZINE AGE 1 (August 1980) : 22-26+.

How advertisers feel about the growing number of science magazines. Statements from five major corporate advertisers suggest positive response. Review of major science magazines and their targeted audiences.

2015 Kanner, Bernice. "'Parasite' Power: The Computer-Magazine Boom." NEW YORK 16 (July 25, 1983) : 18+.

Computer Magazines, the fastest growing segment of the magazine industry today, are popular with readers and advertisers.

2016 Kanner, Bernice. "Scientific Experiments." NEW YORK 17 (October 29, 1984) : 16+.

New science magazines lose advertisers and readers while SCIENTIFIC AMERICAN, established 1845, keeps on going. Problems among science magazines relate to targeting the wrong audience. Science magazines are repositioning to survive.

2017 Kaufman, Lionel M. "Scorecard Needed for Science Books." MARKETING & MEDIA DECISIONS 18 (June 1983) : 64-65+.

Advertising in the science magazines. Profiles of the five major publications.

2018 Klingel, John. "The Computer Market Shakeout." FOLIO 12 (November 1983) : 64+.

Computer magazine glut means some magazines will fail. Trends and problems in the computer magazine business.

2019 Kolgraf, Ron, and Loring, Lisa D. "What the Science/Technology Books Have to Offer." MAGAZINE AGE 3 (February 1982) : 46-50+.

Advertisers face problems in distinguishing various science magazines from each other. Comparison of seventeen titles, their readerships, and ad rates.

2020 Marbach, William D. "A Byte and a Bonanza." NEWSWEEK 100 (October 4, 1982) : 75.

PC: THE INDEPENDENT GUIDE TO THE IBM PERSONAL COMPUTER is one of dozens of new, specialized computer magazines. The magazines vary in editorial quality. Content ranges from hardware and software reviews to how to make a fortune with your personal computer. See also PUBLISH--with first of bi-monthly issues on desktop publishing.

2021 Marsh, Jeffrey. "Politicizing Science." COMMENTARY 77 (May 1984) : 51-53.

Profile of SCIENTIFIC AMERICAN with particular emphasis on its redesign and editorial changes in 1948. Examination of the magazine's stance on nuclear weapons. Implied criticism of SCIENTIFIC AMERICAN's opposition to strengthening U.S. military position. The magazine has not demonstrated how to apply scientific thought to an important political issue.

2022 Marshall, Christy. "Who Will Survive Science Book Shoot-Out?" ADVERTISING AGE 52 (February 23, 1981) : 30+.

Science magazines battle for affluent readers and advertisers.

2023 Maryles, Daisy. "A Title Wave of Computer Magazines." PUBLISHERS WEEKLY (December 2, 1983) : 58+.

Booksellers provide a major outlet for computer magazines. PW reports a telephone survey of booksellers on their handling of computer magazines and the special problems involved.

2024 "Media Growth Mirrors Science Interest." ADVERTISING AGE 52 (October 19, 1981) : 64.

Suggests recent increase in science magazines is a result of current popular interest in science.

2025 Meyers, Bill. "The Advance of Science." WASHINGTON JOURNALISM REVIEW 3 (November 1981) : 36-37.

A brief comparison of new magazines created in the late 1970s in response to growing public interest in science. Among the titles discussed are OMNI and DISCOVER.

2026 Moran, Brian. "Computer-Book Market Shakes Out." ADVERTISING AGE 55 (July 30, 1984) : 70.

Brief news item reports the beginning of computer magazine shakeout, as unsold magazines are returned in large numbers to publishers.

2027 Nash, Ed. "Computers Take a Big Byte of Magazine Field." ADVERTISING AGE 53 (October 25, 1982) : M10+.

As more people become interested in computers, the magazine market serving them expands rapidly.

2028 Pool, Gail, and Comendul, Michael. "The Computer Magazines' Puffery Problem." COLUMBIA JOURNALISM REVIEW 24 (September-October 1985) : 49-51.

Computer companies seek positive editorial coverage in computer magazines, and magazines appear to cooperate. Many are filled with favorable, upbeat product reviews.

2029 Pool, Gail. "Magazines." WILSON LIBRARY BULLETIN 56 (January 1982) : 376-377+.

Overview of the computer magazine field, and evaluative reviews of specific titles.

2030 Schardt, Arlie. "The Science Boom." NEWSWEEK 94 (September 17, 1979) : 104+.

Do new science magazines reflect growing public interest in science or publishers' search for a new market? An overview of new titles and the impact of science journalism.

2031 Tangorra, Joanne. "Technology: Computer Periodicals." WORKING WOMAN 9 (April 1984) : 62+.

Background on the genre, and reviews of six computer magazines. The reviewer considers audience, writing, and contents of the publications but does not address the ethical question: how much of the magazines' content is puffery?

2032 Tchong, Michael. "Computer Magazines: A Perspective." MARKETING & MEDIA DECISIONS 20 (June 1985) : 66+.

Drop in computer magazine advertising pages as advertisers turn to mass-circulation magazines. More machine-specific magazines failing. Stagnation in the computer industry may be a factor in the decline of computer magazines.

2033 Wylie, Kenneth. "Guides Through the Information Maze." ADVERTISING AGE 54 (November 14, 1983) : M34-M35.

Profiles of twelve computer magazine titles for perspective advertisers.

Scholarly Journals

2034 Ceci, Stephen J., and Peters, Douglas P. "Peer Review: A Study of Reliability." CHANGE 14 (September 1982) : 44-48.

Peer review process on top academic journals favors submissions from recognized scholars and institutions. An enlightening review of a process vitally important to most academics.

2035 Cross, Nigel. "The Economics of Learned Journals." TIMES LITERARY SUPPLEMENT, no. 4260 (November 23, 1984) : 1348.

British journalist comments on the big business in academic journal publishing. Factors contributing to profitability include pre-paid subscriptions, print-runs dictated by predetermined buyers, unpaid authors, expensive cover prices. Many journals exist to fill the needs of writers rather than readers.

2036 Delorme, Charles D., Jr., and Wood, Norman J. "Grant Support for Economics Journal Articles 1950-1977." REVIEW OF BUSINESS AND ECONOMIC RESEARCH 16 (Fall 1980) : 104-109.

The proportion of economic journal articles produced with research grants has increased from 13.8 percent to 35.9 percent, and is evidence of the importance of such grants to the university community.

2037 Dyson, Stephen L. "Two Paths to the Past: A Comparative Study of the Last Fifty Years of AMERICAN ANTIQUITY and the AMERICAN JOURNAL OF ARCHAEOLOGY." AMERICAN ANTIQUITY 50 (April 1985) : 452-463.

Ideas on the purpose of scholarly journals and a comparison of the approaches used by two archaeological journals.

2038 Ellsworth, S. George. "Ten Years: An Editor's Report." WESTERN HISTORICAL QUARTERLY 10 (October 1979) : 421-436.

The founding, editorial concept, and function of the WESTERN HISTORICAL QUARTERLY.

2039 "The Journals Division: ' ... Forums for Debate and Exchange.'" CHANGE 16 (October 1984) : 43-44.

The Journals' Division of the University of

Chicago Press produces forty-five titles and half the Press' annual income. How subjects for new journals are decided on. The role of the academic journal as a forum for debate.

2040 Kahn, Joseph P. "My Magazine, The Doctor." ESQUIRE 94 (November 1980) : 56.

Selection of articles for the NEW ENGLAND JOURNAL OF MEDICINE. How the JOURNAL attained its influential position in the world of medical journalism. Are the JOURNAL's experts the best arbiters of what the public should know?

2041 Koch, James V., and Cebula, Richard J. "The Curious Case of the Journal Manuscript Market: Ethics Versus Efficiency in Academe." AMERICAN ECONOMIST 26 (Spring 1982) : 30-34.

Discussion of manuscript submission to economic journals, with particular emphasis on the inefficiency of prohibiting simultaneous submission of manuscripts to multiple journals and payment of submission fees by authors.

2042 Lacy, William B., and Busch, Lawrence. "Guardians of Science: Journals and Journal Editors in the Agricultural Sciences." RURAL SOCIOLOGY 47 (Fall 1982) : 429-448.

Survey of journal editors and agricultural scientists on the value of journals and criteria for publication. As major outlets for scientific research results, journal editors are "guardians of science" in their gatekeeper roles.

2043 Lee, Hermione. "American Assembly-Line." TIMES LITERARY SUPPLEMENT, no. 4028 (June 6, 1980) : 649-650.

British journalist briefly surveys the vast field of scholarly and literary journal publishing in American academic institutions, labeling it a "hyperactive industry."

2044 Lerner, Rita G. "The Professional Society in a Changing World." LIBRARY QUARTERLY 54 (January 1984) : 36-47.

How the goals of the professional society publisher differ from those of the commercial publisher, with emphasis on boards of directors and prospects for capital growth. Publishing is a major part of professional society activities.

2045 Lowry, Dennis T. "Evaluation of Empirical Studies Reported in Seven Journals in the 70s." JOURNALISM QUARTERLY 56 (Summer 1979) : 262-268+.

Based on content analysis of seven journals, author concludes communication research has "a severe case of tunnel vision." It fails to study trends, focuses too much on individuals, relies too heavily on survey data and subjective response.

2046 Moore, Laurence L., and Taylor, Bernard W. "Study of Institutional Publications in Business-Related Academic Journals, 1972-78." QUARTERLY REVIEW OF ECONOMICS AND BUSINESS 20 (Spring 1980) : 87-97.

A count of scholarly research articles in fifteen business journals to determine which universities have been most productive. Comparison with data from an earlier study, 1961-1971.

2047 Morton, Herbert C., and Rutimann, Hans. "A Profile of Scholarly Journals: The MLA Findings." CHANGE 15 (May-June 1983) : 54-55.

Compilation of statistical findings on language and literature journals, derived from Modern Language Association's new database. Deals with numbers of journals, subscription rates, advertising, submission fees, elapsed time between manuscript submission, decision and publication.

2048 Over, Ray. "Representation of Women on the Editorial Boards of Psychological Journals." AMERICAN PSYCHOLOGIST 36 (August 1981) : 885-991.

Between 1972 and 1977, the number of women on the editorial boards of fourteen psychology journals increased from 6.8 percent to 17.8 percent, and approximated the sex ratio of published authors in the journals.

2049 Ricklets, Roger. "Publish or Perish? Professors Discover Perishing is Simpler." WALL STREET JOURNAL, 25 May 1979, p. 1+.

Publishing in scholarly journals is a delayed, non-financially compensated process. Academics depend on it for job tenure.

2050 Rogers, Pat. "Current and Unbound." TIMES LITERARY SUPPLEMENT, no. 4028 (June 6, 1980) : 648.

Examination of writing, publishing, and reading scholarly papers in academic journals and literary magazines.

2051 Soley, Lawrence C., and Reid, Leonard N. "Advertising Article Productivity in the U.S. Academic Community." JOURNALISM QUARTERLY 60 (Autumn 1983) : 464-469.

Both academics and professionals published. Among academics, 41 percent of the articles came from 13 percent of the schools.

Other Specialized Magazines

2052 "The Affluent Market." ADVERTISING AGE 55 (August 23, 1984) : 11-47.

Special section on reaching the affluent market. Includes several articles on magazines targeted to affluent audiences, such as TOWN & COUNTRY (p. 13), CONNECTICUT (p. 14), and SOUTHERN ACCENTS (p.18).

2053 Alter, Jennifer. "Able Publisher for the Disabled." ADVERTISING AGE 52 (June 8, 1981) : 66+.

Founded as POLIO LIVING, ACCENT ON LIVING celebrates twenty-five years of publication. Content covers disability assistance devices, architectural barriers, success stories, medical breakthroughs, adjustment.

2054 Alter, Stewart. "SELF & OMNI: Two New Viewpoints." MAGAZINE AGE 1 (May 1980) : 56-58.

Comparison of two special interest magazine successes illustrates how magazines work and how advertisers use them. Both draw readers involved in a variety of lifestyles. Neither is narrowly focused. Both have acceptable demographics and are in touch with societal trends.

2055 Alward, E. "Science Fiction: Magazine Growth Industry." SERIALS REVIEW 9 (Fall 1983) : 27-32.

2056 Anderson, Elliott, and Kinzie, Mary, eds. "The Little Magazine in America: A Modern Documentary History." TRIQUARTERLY, no. 43 (Fall 1978).

The entire 750-page volume is devoted to the little magazine. The aim is to present "a sense of the living reality of the publications," not a historical overview. Contributions include essay-memoirs from editors and contributors to many varied literary magazines.

2057 Anderson, Elliott, and Kinzie, Mary, eds. THE LITTLE MAGAZINE IN AMERICA: A MODERN DOCUMENTARY HISTORY. Yonkers, N.Y.: Pushcart Press, 1978.

This volume is the same as entry 2056, except that it has an index.

2058 Anson, Robert Sam. "Citizen Wenner." NEW TIMES 7 (November 26, 1976) : 16-18+.

Profiles Jann Wenner and his creation, ROLLING STONE. Article continues December 10, 1976, pp. 22-26+.

2059 Atwater, Tony. "Editorial Policy of EBONY Before and After the Civil Rights Act of 1964." JOURNALISM QUARTERLY 59 (Spring 1982): 87-91.

After 1964, EBONY increased civil rights coverage and served as an advocate for social change through the use of photo editorials.

2060 Barth, Jack. "Fanzines." FILM COMMENT 21 (March-April 1985) : 24-30.

Critical description of fanzines, "the alternate press of film criticism." Includes lengthy list of fanzines, ranging from homemade magazines to tabloids.

2061 Bass, Paul. "Lockout at Yale." COLUMBIA JOURNALISM REVIEW 21 (November-December 1982) : 15+.

Changes made by new owner of the YALE LITERARY MAGAZINE prompt Yale University to instigate a lawsuit.

2062 Beckman, Jody. "Four Year Effort is Making it--So Far: Focusing on the Nitty-Gritty for First-Time Job Seekers." ADVERTISING AGE 54 (January 3, 1983) : M18.

MAKING IT, a new magazine for recent graduates and job-jumpers looking for employment. This article is part of a twenty-four-page ADVERTISING AGE MAGAZINE special report on job hunting.

2063 Beitler, Stephen. "Sportsmen Go by the Books." ADVERTISING AGE 52 (March 23, 1981) : S6+.

Leisure-time sports magazines cover the field and offer much competition for each other. An overview of titles for prospective advertisers.

2064 Bell, Arthur. "Oh, Those Movie Magazines." COSMOPOLITAN 179 (February 1975) : 169-172+.

Non-academic overview of the business and functions of movie magazines.

2065 Benoit, Ellen. "No Lambs, Bears or Talking Down." FORBES 135 (June 17, 1985) : 162.

Telepictures Publications markets slick magazines to kids that are modeled on popular adult magazines. Examples are MUPPET MAGAZINE, BARBIE MAGAZINE. Briefly mentioned is competition from Scholastic Inc. and Children's Television Workshop.

2066 Berling-Manuel, Lynn. "Reaching the Gay Market." ADVERTISING AGE 55 (March 26,1984) : M4-M5+.

Includes profile of the ADVOCATE, an upscale gay news magazine with 83,000 circulation.

2067 " ... the Best Friend the Industry Ever Had." BROADCASTING 103 (August 23, 1982) : 27-34.

Biographical obituary on Sol Taishoff, founder and editor of BROADCASTING magazine. Includes history and objectives of the book.

2068 Bhatia, Gauri. "Jann Wenner: Publisher of ROLLING STONE." FOLIO 11 (November 1982) : 68-69.

Profile of ROLLING STONE's founder. How the book has "grown up."

2069 Birnbaum, Jeffrey H. "With 1,134 Editions, FARM JOURNAL Labors to Please all of its Readers." WALL STREET JOURNAL, 1 January 1983, p. 25.

Wide variety of readers has led to profitable approach of printing different versions to meet everyone's needs.

2070 Blakken, Renee. "SCHOLASTIC Offers a Lesson in Making the Grade." ADVERTISING AGE 54 (October 17, 1983) : M56.

New and old magazines at Scholastic Inc. Types of advertising successful in Scholastic publications.

2071 Block, Chip. "The Personalized Magazine." FOLIO 10 (May 1981) : 81-83+.

An editorial service which allows readers to select from a wide range of materials.

2072 Blount, Roy, Jr. "In-House Effect." COLUMBIA JOURNALISM REVIEW 19 (September-October 1980) : 42-43.

Humorous article on the increasing specialization of magazine titles.

2073 Brin, Geri. "How Special Interest Publications Capture Specialized Audiences." MAGAZINE AGE 1 (September 1980) : 64-69.

Special interest magazines are defined here as newsstand publications appearing infrequently, with limited circulation, specific subject matter, high cover price, and not audited. They offer advantages to advertisers but do not substitute for general interest magazine advertising.

2074 Broeske, Pat H., and Latuner, Cheryl A. "Teenzine: A Loss of Innocence." LOS ANGELES TIMES, 25 August 1985, sec. Cal., pp. 42-46.

First of a five-article series on fan magazines and the coming of age of American girls. Teenzines aimed at girls 11 to 13 years old are read by 8 to 15 year olds. They reflect popular culture, from celebrities to fashion, and combine attributes of fan and confession magazines. Includes guidelines for aspiring writers and editors.

2075 Broeske, Pat H., and Latuner, Cheryl A. "Teenzine: Heartthrob's Marriage Isn't the End of the Story Anymore." LOS ANGELES TIMES, 28 August 1985, sec. 6, p. 1+.

Teenzines exist to introduce young girls to male stars. Today's teenzines offer more reality with romantic fantasies than magazines of the 1970s.

2076 Broeske, Pat H., and Latuner, Cheryl A. "Teenzine: Paths to Pinup Popularity: How About that Tried-and-True Vulnerable Look--or the Pout?" LOS ANGELES TIMES, 26 August 1985, sec. 6, p. 1+.

What makes a good teenage idol or cover pinup for a teenzine.

2077 Broeske, Pat H., and Latuner, Cheryl A. "Teenzine: Readers Find Relevancy Among the Fab Fax on all Their Faves." LOS ANGELES TIMES, 27 August 1985, sec. 6, p. 1.

Birth of teen magazines in the 1940s. Editors seek balance between celebrity publicity and consideration of relevant issues.

2078 Broeske, Pat H., and Latuner, Cheryl A. "Teenzine: Who's Who and What's What with their Hottest 'Babes.'" LOS ANGELES TIMES, 29 August 1985, sec. 6, p. 1+.

Interviews with some teenage readers.

2079 Campbell, Colin. "Magazine Sold by Yale Fights to Retain Name." NEW YORK TIMES, 21 February 1985, p. B2.

Under new ownership, the YALE LITERARY MAGAZINE has become a conservative, slick national quarterly with increased advertising, no longer staffed by students. Yale University seeks to legally prevent the use of its name in the magazine's title.

2080 Canape, Charlene. "The Chase is On: Can TV-CABLE WEEK Catch TV GUIDE?" WASHINGTON JOURNALISM REVIEW 5 (June 1983) : 24-28.

Analysis of TV GUIDE and its new competitor suggests the market for tv magazines may be big enough for both publications and other guides as well.

2081 Canape, Charlene. "If You Love Fine Food, Read On: Five Upscale Magazines Battle for the Epicurean Market." ADVERTISING AGE 54 (September 12, 1983) : M4-M5+.

Editorial variations and ad rates in five food magazines for affluent readers.

2082 Christian, Elizabeth. "Retiree-Aimed Magazine has Come of Age." LOS ANGELES TIMES, 17 February 1984, sec. 5, p. 1.

MODERN MATURITY has the third largest domestic magazine circulation in the U.S.

2083 Christopher, Maurine. "TV WORLD New Challenge for TV GUIDE." ADVERTISING AGE 50 (September 3, 1979) : 52.

Will local cable-based guide expand to include network listings as TV GUIDE expands its New York City edition to include cable listings? Brief comparison of New York tv magazines and update on competition among titles.

2084 Clemons, Walter, and Lehman, David. "Sting of the Gadflies; Three 'Little Magazines' Stir

Up Big Cultural Waves." NEWSWEEK 106 (August 12, 1985) : 65-66.

Reviews of three little magazines: GRANTA: A PAPERBACK MAGAZINE OF NEW WRITING, THE NEW CRITERION, and GRAND STREET.

2085 Cohn, Howard. "Differences Narrow Between Consumer and Trade Magazines." ADVERTISING AGE 45 (November 18, 1974) : 99-100.

Suggests specialized magazines are the best job sources for college-trained newcomers. Business magazines are broadening their readership base by broadening editorial concerns. Meanwhile, consumer magazines cut circulations to reach more select audiences.

2086 Condon, Garret. "'Little' Magazines Growing: A New Appreciation for Serious Literature." HARTFORD COURANT, 27 December 1985, sec. C., p. 1+.

Little magazines, like PARIS REVIEW and PLOUGHSHARES, are enjoying new popularity. More than one thousand little magazines publish serious short fiction, poetry, essays, criticism.

2087 Cook, Michael L. MYSTERY, DETECTIVE, AND ESPIONAGE MAGAZINES. Westport, Conn.: Greenwood Press, 1983.

Alphabetical listing of three hundred mystery

magazines, with annotations, bibliographic information, history, reference sources. Introduction offers valuable insights into the genre, with references to pulps, digests, and fanzines. Some foreign titles. Bibliography covers pulps, mystery writing, and related popular culture sources.

2088 Cooper, Ann. "Jann Wenner Grows from Gonzo to Gotham." ADVERTISING AGE 56 (January 1, 1985) : 3+.

Profile of Wenner and his shaping and founding of ROLLING STONE.

2089 Cowan, Wayne H. "In 25 Years You Pick Up a Lot of Memories." CHRISTIANITY AND CRISIS 39 (September 17, 1979) : 210-211+.

An editor's personal remembrances through a period of change and uncertainty for CHRISTIANITY AND CRISIS, 1954-1979.

2090 Daniel, Walter C. BLACK JOURNALS OF THE UNITED STATES. Westport, Conn.: Greenwood Press, 1982.

A directory of black magazines and journals, including publications of the nineteenth century. Each entry provides title, descriptive notes, publication history, and bibliography of sources.

2091 Denniston, Lyle. "New Breed of News Hound: The

Legal Beagle." WASHINGTON JOURNALISM REVIEW 3 (March 1981) : 26-28.

Three tabloids (two weekly newspapers and one monthly magazine) scrutinize the legal profession and attract more readers outside the profession than within. Description and comparison of LEGAL TIMES OF WASHINGTON, AMERICAN LAWYER, and NATIONAL LAW JOURNAL.

2092 Dougherty, Philip H. "Magazines on Black Culture." NEW YORK TIMES, 24 October 1985, p. D29.

AMERICAN VISIONS, a magazine of Afro-American culture, will debut in January 1986 with a controlled circulation of 1.5 million upscale blacks.

2093 Drew, Bernard A. "From Pulp to Celluloid." FILM COMMENT 14 (July-August 1978) : 65-67.

Pulp magazine heroes of the 1930s and 1940s did not transfer successfully to the movies, probably because they were usually featured in low-budget films.

2094 Duke, Judith S. CHILDREN'S BOOKS AND MAGAZINES: A MARKET STUDY. White Plains, N.Y.: Knowledge Industry Publications, 1979.

Primarily about books, one chapter deals with children's magazines and comics. 1970s circulation and advertising statistics for some specific titles. Division of children's magazines into six categories--teenage service and fan, religious, educational, general, comics. Sections on various publishers and non-profit magazines.

2095 Ebisch, Robert. "New Magazines Get a Reading on the Industry." ADVERTISING AGE 53 (November 15, 1982) : M12.

Trade magazines and program guides that serve the cable tv industry.

2096 "EBONY Responds to a Changing Market." MADISON AVENUE 24 (May 1983) : 122-126+.

EBONY is influential in reaching black consumers. It highlights black achievement with success stories and how-to-do-it advice. Sales presentation gives advice to EBONY advertisers on the use of ethnic ads and ads using white models.

2097 Elliott, Stuart J. "Change Marks TV GUIDE 30th." ADVERTISING AGE 54 (April 4, 1983) : 74.

TV GUIDE experiments with changes in response to the forthcoming TV-CABLE WEEK.

2098 Elliott, Stuart J. "Health Kicks Into Magazines." ADVERTISING AGE 56 (September 9, 1985) : 120.

Some health magazines find profitability and

less risk in controlled circulation to medical care facilities (e.g. doctor's offices, hospitals).

2099 Elliott, Stuart J. "Magazines in Battle for Real Estate Turf." ADVERTISING AGE 57 (April 21, 1986) : 36+.

Market for real estate magazines is booming as publishers anticipate increased home sales. Time Inc. is distributing editions of REAL ESTATE to high demographic areas in N.Y., N.J., and Conn. New ground for Time Inc. in specialized subject, regional focus, and controlled circulation.

2100 Elliott, Stuart J. "The Muppets Make Good in Print." ADVERTISING AGE 54 (October 10, 1983) : M4-M5+.

The MUPPET magazine is a clone of the tv show. It differs in tone, objectives, and policy from SESAME STREET, which also features muppets. It carries advertising, and is a humor magazine for children.

2101 Elliott, Stuart J. "RUNNER'S WORLD Clears Hurdles." ADVERTISING AGE 56 (July 8, 1985) : 61.

Rodale Press' newly acquired RUNNER'S WORLD is running down.

2102 Elliott, Stuart J. "SEVENTEEN Hits 40: Numbers Tell the Story." ADVERTISING AGE 55 (August 30, 1984) : 24.

Profile of SEVENTEEN MAGAZINE over its forty-year lifetime.

2103 Emmrich, Stuart. "How TV GUIDE Opened Door for Time Inc." ADVERTISING AGE 54 (April 25, 1983) : 20.

TV-CABLE WEEK has filled a void created by TV GUIDE'S unwillingness to carry complete cable tv listings. Strong competition between the two magazines prompts the question: is there room in the market for both?

2104 Emmrich, Stuart. "TV GUIDE Attacks Flat Sales, Cable Books." ADVERTISING AGE 53 (March 29, 1982 : 92.

Challenge for TV GUIDE as it responds to competitors and tries to satisfy increasing reader and advertiser demands with regard to cable tv.

2105 Endicott, Craig. "Ag Books' Incomes Sapped; But Profiled Farm Publications Weather the Weather and Economy." ADVERTISING AGE 51 (November 24, 1980) : S2+.

Ad revenue of farm magazines hurt by the weather and economy. Profiles of four farm publication publishers.

2106 English, Mary McCabe. "Black Publishing: Words in the Future Tense." ADVERTISING AGE 53 (November 29, 1982) : 21.

Brief article forecasts a healthy future for black magazines because they fill an important reader need.

2107 "An Era that May Mean Red Ink for Newsletters." BUSINESS WEEK (January 25, 1982) : 109-110.

Problems for a newsletter designed to inform businessmen about government regulations as they adapt to Reagan's deregulatory climate.

2108 "FARM JOURNAL Now Up to 1,106 Versions--More to Come." FOLIO 12 (February 1983) : 19-20.

FARM JOURNAL has more demographic editions than any other magazine.

2109 "Farm Media." MARKETING & MEDIA DECISIONS 15 (January 1980) : 100+.

A brief overview of farm magazines and how advertisers use them. Includes a list of the top advertisers. Article is part of a special report on "America's Largest Business"--farming.

2110 "Farm Media: Planting Now for Bigger Harvests." SALES AND MARKETING MANAGEMENT 126 (April 6, 1981) : 34-35.

Brief overview of farm magazines. Trends in content and advertising.

2111 Feinberg, Andrew. "Magazine Madness." MARKETING & MEDIA DECISIONS 16 (February 1981) : 68-69.

Humorous look at the ultra-specialization of magazines. One-liners for professors and speech-makers on plausible to mostly ridiculous theoretical magazines. "Madness" gets A laugh but hardly more for its make-believe editorial concepts.

2112 Ferman, Edward L. THE MAGAZINE OF FANTASY AND SCIENCE FICTION: A 30-YEAR RETROSPECTIVE. New York: Doubleday, 1980.

Brief history and overview. Body of book consists of twenty-four articles published in the magazine 1946-1980.

2113 Fife, Sandy. "A Debate Over 'Free' Magazines." MACLEAN'S 98 (May 27, 1985) : 41+.

Canada's controlled circulation magazines, distributed free in affluent neighborhoods and competing with paid-circulation magazines for advertising, are under pressure from advertisers to prove the magazines are read.

2114 Fletcher, Marilyn P. "Science Fiction Magazines and Annual Anthologies: An Annotated Check-list." SERIALS LIBRARIAN 7 (Fall 1982) : 65-71.

Annotated list of science fiction magazines, annual anthologies, reviewing journals, and library selection tools.

2115 "Flying in Magazine Heaven." TIME 113 (March 26, 1979) : 87.

East/West Network publishes in-flight magazines for ten airlines. East/West pays five clients for the right to publish their magazines.

2116 Freeman, Laurie. "Many Children's Publishers Turn to Toys." ADVERTISING AGE 55 (October 18, 1984) : 51.

Some children's magazines follow tv trends and others center around toys like Barbie dolls.

2117 Freeman, Laurie. "New Magazines Deliver Professional Niche." ADVERTISING AGE 55 (November 19, 1984) : 45.

Targeted to upscale readers, new black magazines have editorial quality and slick appearance, but fail to attract advertisers.

2118 Fuller, Doris A. "Parent Magazines Ride Baby Boomlet." LOS ANGELES TIMES, 15 August 1985, sec. 4, p. 1+.

Current rise in birth rate is reflected in five new parenting magazines. American Baby Inc.

has grown from a single-magazine publisher to a baby-oriented conglomerate. Elaboration of social changes in family life as they affect magazines.

2119 Gage, Theodore J. "Consumer Books Carve Niche." ADVERTISING AGE 52 (March 9, 1981) : S4-S5.

Rising public interest in health and fitness has resulted in new special interest magazines and more health content in existing publications. Publishers argue among themselves about which magazines are truly health publications.

2120 George, Nelson. "Black Fanzines Growing in Importance and Impact." BILLBOARD 95 (January 29, 1983) : 6+.

Importance of fanzines in providing media exposure to entertainers. Black fanzines cited as examples. Several titles are improving editorial graphics to reach wider audiences.

2121 Gerbner, George. "The Social Role of the Confession Magazine." SOCIAL PROBLEMS 6 (Summer 1958) : 29-40.

Early confession magazines attracted non-magazine readers from the working classes. Notes on the editorial formula of the genre, its appeal and relation to problem-solving for its readers, and audience demographics.

2122 Giges, Nancy. "PENNY POWER Incites Child Ad Critics." ADVERTISING AGE 53 (February 22, 1982) : 52.

PENNY POWER, published by Consumers Union for children aged 8 to 12, criticizes commercials that don't provide useful facts.

2123 "'Grand Street': Belles Lettres With an Edge." NEW YORK 18 (January 21, 1985) : 23.

A look at literary magazines with some snippets of how-to and history.

2124 Greene, Bob. "Boy at his Best." ESQUIRE 95 (June 1981) : 17-18.

BOY'S LIFE, published by the Boy Scouts of America, relies on subscription revenue and continues to publish adventure, camping, sports stories that exude optimism. Is this magazine an anachronism?

2125 "Grove Press Relaunches EVERGREEN REVIEW." PUBLISHERS WEEKLY 225 (March 23, 1984) : 56.

EVERGREEN REVIEW is an avant-garde literary magazine previously published 1957-1973. It will now be published irregularly.

2126 Grover, Stephen. "Winds of Change Blow in Editorial Suites of Movie Magazines." WALL STREET JOURNAL, 6 March 1974, p. 1+.

Concern about decreasing sales in the movie magazine business 1974 may prompt content changes--less sensationalism and more factual reporting.

2127 Gupta, Udayan. "This BABY's Come a Long Way." ADVERTISING AGE 55 (March 26, 1984) : M42-M43.

Profile of AMERICAN BABY, and its successful ventures in reaching the new parent audience.

2128 Gurevitz, Susan. "PBS Viewers Use DIAL to Tune In." ADVERTISING AGE 53 (October 25, 1982) : M48.

PBS publishes DIAL, a program guide to PBS shows, to create revenue.

2129 Haas, Charlie. "Sons of Pulp." MOTHER JONES 3 (April 1978) : 56-58+.

Pulp fiction magazines of the 1920s and 1930s are reborn as paperback book series. Commentary on some of the modern heroes.

2130 Handler, David. "TV GUIDE's Doubtful Attempt to Include Editorial Matter." THE PRESS 9 (May 1981) : 4.

Brief report on TV GUIDE's attempts at investigative reporting.

2131 Hanson, J. J. "ON CABLE Publisher Undaunted by Time Inc. Entry into Market." FOLIO 12 (August 1983) : 93-95.

Circulation growing for ON CABLE despite competition of TV GUIDE and TV-CABLE WEEK.

2132 Hechinger, Fred M. "About Education." NEW YORK TIMES, 18 January 1983, p. C6.

HIGHWIRE--THE NATIONAL STUDENT MAGAZINE is aimed at upper level high school students with one-third paid circulation. Content deals with current issues and doesn't avoid controversial topics such as cheating, sex, and death.

2133 Hechinger, Fred M. "Magazines for Children Address Serious Topics." NEW YORK TIMES, 11 June 1985, p. C7.

COBBLESTONE: THE HISTORY MAGAZINE FOR YOUNG PEOPLE is one of several children's magazines combining fun and serious information. Useful as education tools.

2134 Henry, Charles P. "EBONY Elite: America's Most Influential Blacks." PHYLON 42 (June 1981) : 120-132.

Analysis of EBONY'S lists of the "most influential blacks" suggests black and white elite groups have similar education and professional levels. Few blacks actually wield national power.

2135 Henry, DeWitt. "Public Publishing in Boston." ANTIOCH REVIEW 38 (Spring 1980) : 218-226.

The story of PLOUGHSHARES, a little magazine published by a non-profit organization "dedicated to literary education," formed during the 1960s.

2136 Herman, Tom. "Some News Reporters Put Out Newsletters as a Lucrative Sideline." WALL STREET JOURNAL, 22 May 1985, p. 1+.

Some use their subject specialty expertise to publish newsletters. Is this a conflict of interest with their salaried positions?

2137 Hirschfeld, Neal. "GUIDE TO CAREERS Means Business." ADVERTISING AGE 55 (July 19, 1984) : 40.

Readership of BUSINESS WEEK's spin-off GUIDE TO CAREERS. Publisher McGraw Hill seeks bright, ambitious upscale students.

2138 Hogue, William P. "The INSIDE SPORTS Story." FOLIO 11 (May 1982) : 81-85+.

INSIDE SPORTS from its founding to its second owner. Lengthy play-by-play account of its near-successes and defeats.

2139 "How Time Inc. Might Elbow in on TV GUIDE." BUSINESS WEEK (April 19, 1982) : 35-36.

How the competition between TV GUIDE and the forthcoming TV-CABLE WEEK appeared.

2140 Hulin-Salkin, Belinda. "Media Cool--But Not to College Crowd." ADVERTISING AGE 53 (August 2, 1982) : M7+.

Advertisers trying to reach the college market are using magazines specially targeted at college student audiences.

2141 "Humor and the Single Girl." FORTUNE 110 (September 17, 1984) : 7.

Parody publications, a growing specialty business. Brief article describes the latest entrant, COSMOPARODY, a humorous takeoff on COSMOPOLITAN.

2142 Jacobs, Sanford L. "Specialty Magazine Publisher Succeeding with a Difference." WALL STREET JOURNAL, 14 September 1981, p. 33.

Business management techniques of John Tillotson, publisher of the WORKBASKET, FLOWER AND GARDEN, and WORKBENCH.

2143 James, Frank E. "Why a Magazine for Disabled Ignores Handicapped Heroes." WALL STREET JOURNAL, 11 January 1985, p. 1+.

DISABILITY RAG, a journal for the disabled, is on a shoestring budget, with small circulation and great influence in the disabled rights movement. Why the magazine has no medical stories, advertising, or disabled hero stories.

2144 Jaspersohn, William. MAGAZINE: BEHIND THE SCENES AT SPORTS ILLUSTRATED. Boston: Little, Brown, 1983.

Explanation in detail of how, by whom, and of what SPORTS ILLUSTRATED is made. Covers idea assignment through circulation simply but without talking down. Thorough and impressive. Written for youth, and suitable for elementary schoolers through college freshmen. Extensive photographs on most of its 127 pages.

2145 Johnson, Edna Ruth. "Humanism's Many Allies." HUMANIST 44 (September-October 1984) : 26-27+.

A few humanist newsletters and magazines described.

2146 Johnson, Mark. "In-Flight Magazines: They're Showing New Ability to Land Blue Chip Advertisers." MAGAZINE AGE 1 (February 1980) : 54+.

Growth of in-flight magazines over the past few years. Earlier identity crisis has yielded to better understanding of their purpose within the advertising world.

2147 Kaiser, Charles. "A Bouncing Year-Old Baby." NEWSWEEK 101 (February 21, 1983) : 76.

AMERICAN HEALTH is established as a most successful specialty magazine. A brief portrait of the magazine's content, staff, and audience.

2148 Kaiser, Charles. "The Clash of the Titans." NEWSWEEK 101 (April 18, 1983) : 53.

Time Inc. launches TV-CABLE WEEK, marketing exclusively through cable television systems. Fearful of competition, TV GUIDE is spending millions to improve its cable listings.

2149 Kanner, Bernice. "Fan, Romance Books Face Sagging Numbers." ADVERTISING AGE 50 (April 9, 1979) : 22+.

Romance and fan magazines directed at blue collar women experience declining circulation and advertising pages.

2150 Kastor, Elizabeth. "The Man Who Loves Being Bill Regardie: With His Magazine, Making a Business of Success." WASHINGTON POST, 12 April 1985, p. C1.

Snippets of profile on creator of REGARDIE'S. Casts him in eccentric light.

2151 Katz, Milton S. "COMMENTARY and the American

Jewish Intellectual Experience." JOURNAL OF AMERICAN CULTURE 3 (Spring 1980) : 155-166.

The role, influence, and content of COMMENTARY, founded 1945 by the American Jewish Committee. Regarded as representing the viewpoint of American Jews on politics and other controversial issues.

2152 Kelly, R. Gordon. CHILDREN'S PERIODICALS OF THE UNITED STATES. Westport, CONN.: Greenwood Press, 1984.

Extensive, annotated list of children's periodicals with bibliographic, historical, content descriptions. Surveys history of magazine publication for children.

2153 LeRoux, Margaret. "Reaping the Benefits of TV's Daytime Affairs." ADVERTISING AGE 53 (October 25, 1982) : M11+.

Fan magazines for daytime tv's soap operas.

2154 Levine, Art. "Reader's Guide to Video Magazines." AMERICAN FILM 7 (March 1982) : 30-32.

Textual descriptions and annotated list of magazines about cable and video.

2155 Liff, Mark. "Spanish Language Magazines Begin to Soar." ADVERTISING AGE 55 (March 19, 1984) : M32-M33.

The DeArmas Hispanic Magazine Network distributes fifteen Spanish-language magazines, including some with ties to American publications like COSMOPOLITAN, HARPER'S BAZAAR, and POPULAR MECHANICS.

2156 Logan, Frenise A. "Twenty Years of the JOURNAL OF NEGRO HISTORY, 1958-1978: An Appraisal." JOURNAL OF NEGRO HISTORY 65 (Winter 1980) : 1-5.

Description of the contributors to the journal.

2157 Love, Barbara. "Small Magazine Publishers Roundtable." FOLIO 15 (June 1986) : 102-105+.

Special needs, problems, opportunities for majority of all magazines--small ones. From computers to commissions, from associations to ancillary activities, the conference report covers much ground in eight pages.

2158 MacDougall, A. Kent. "Confession Magazine Revenue Keeps Rising Despite Same Tales, Misleading Headlines." WALL STREET JOURNAL, 2 August 1968, p. 28.

Brief history and commentary on the economically successful formula of confession magazines. Dated but author's excellence still relevant.

2159 McFadden, Maureen. "Growing Up with PARENTS."

MAGAZINE AGE 6 (November 1985) : 60.

One-page overview of PARENTS (1927-), old and new versions. How the magazine now reaches its audience.

2160 Machalaba, Daniel. "State Your Subject; Somebody Will Start a Newsletter on it." WALL STREET JOURNAL, 24 December 1979, p. 1+.

Concise format for quick reading and specialized content make newsletters a fast growing journalistic medium.

2161 Machalaba, Daniel. "TV GUIDE Struggles to Reverse Slide in Sales, Say Analysts." WALL STREET JOURNAL, 25 March 1982, p. 22.

Personnel changes are indicative of TV GUIDE'S problems. Recession and price increases are blamed for decreased sales. Plans to capitalize on growing cable tv market.

2162 "Magazines that Zero in on the Super-Rich." BUSINESS WEEK (May 23, 1983) : 47.

Growing business in controlled-circulation (free) magazines catering to the rich.

2163 "Magazines Your Kids Will Like." CHANGING TIMES 37 (August 1983) : 45-47+.

General comments on types of magazines enjoyed by specific age groups, followed by an annotated, illustrated list of children's magazines.

2164 "MODERN MATURITY." MADISON AVENUE 26 (October 1984) : 102-106.

Sales presentation from MODERN MATURITY emphasizes the large market and the advantages of controlled circulation (to AARP membership). Ads showing active people are preferred.

2165 Moore, Thomas. "Why Cable TV is Unraveling TV GUIDE." PHILADELPHIA MAGAZINE 72 (July 1981) : 108-111.

Problems at Triangle Publications include the increasing complexity of tv with the advent of cable, its geographic distance from New York City, its lack of imagination, its unsuccessful launch of PANORAMA in 1980. Article includes comments on Triangle's competition.

2166 Morehead, Joe. "The Pentagon's Magazine Publishing Empire." SERIALS LIBRARIAN 5 (Fall 1980) : 7-12.

Review of a few of the Pentagon's more than one thousand periodical titles.

2167 Morehead, Joe. "Tattered Coat Upon a Stick: Aging, the Process and the Periodical." SERIALS LIBRARIAN 4 (Spring 1980) : 269-274.

History and content of AGING, published by the government as the official publication of the National Clearinghouse on Aging.

2168 Morse, Susan. "In the Write Frame of Mind." WASHINGTON POST, 24 September 1985, p. B5.

A local magazine for children's writing debuts in the District of Columbia.

2169 "The Moving Target." MARKETING & MEDIA DECISIONS 14 (November 1979) : 64-65+.

Public interest in physical fitness is a trend not a fad, and magazines serving sports activists are attracting advertisers. Discussion of the more successful magazines in this category.

2170 Mulcahy, Jerry. "Other People Magazines: A Somewhat Irreverent Look at Single Author Journals." CHANGE 14 (April 1982) : 48-51.

A review of the more interesting and least known journals and newsletters that deal only with the life and works of a single author.

2171 Neher, Jacques. "Personalized Magazines Near?" ADVERTISING AGE 50 (November 12, 1979) : 47.

Brief description of plans for page-by-page personalized magazine.

2172 Neher, Jacques. "Video Boom Spawns Magazines." ADVERTISING AGE 52 (January 12, 1981) : S10-S11.

Boom in video electronics has resulted in a boom in video magazines. Several titles including PANORAMA.

2173 "New Voice for Latinos." TIME 109 (April 18, 1977) : 52.

Ethnic pride is becoming a new area of specialization for magazines. Includes descriptions of several new publications addressed to English-speaking Americans with foreign backgrounds.

2174 "Opinions Differ on Why Personalized Magazines Have Not Taken Off." FOLIO 13 (February 1984) : 12.

Technology exists to produce personalized magazines, but publishers seem reluctant to use it.

2175 Patner, Myra Mensh. "Kids: Magazines with a Special Interest." WASHINGTON POST, 24 January 1983, p. B5.

Review essay on a wide variety of children's magazines. Reference to the effects of television on the genre.

2176 Perry, Susan. "Kids Put their Creativity in

Print." LOS ANGELES TIMES, 26 December 1983, sec. 4, p. 35.

YOUNG PEOPLE TODAY, a magazine for youth, is written, edited, and illustrated by young people.

2177 Pool, Gail. "Magazines." WILSON LIBRARY BULLETIN 56 (February 1982) : 457-458+.

Development, editorial formula, and critical review of TV GUIDE. While the magazine includes network criticism, it is conservative. See also entry 53.

2178 Pool, Gail. "Magazines." WILSON LIBRARY BULLETIN 58 (November 1983) : 220-221.

Review of MODERN MATURITY and 50 PLUS, two publications for senior citizens.

2179 "PREVENTION Enjoys Good Health." MADISON AVENUE 25 (December 1983) : 84-85+.

Sales presentation by PREVENTION executives emphasizes the magazine's strengths and guidelines for prospective advertisers. Since advertising acceptance denotes editorial endorsement of products, PREVENTION refuses advertising for certain unhealthful products.

2180 Quimby, Harriet B. "Periodicals for Children: A Selection." SERIALS LIBRARIAN 5 (Spring 1981) : 73-79.

Thoughts on what makes a magazine appropriate for children. Review essay on numerous children's magazine titles, written as a guide for library selection.

2181 Randall, Michael. "Confession Magazines." SERIALS REVIEW 7 (January-March 1981) : 43-47.

Overview of the genre and reviews of seven high circulation titles from a variety of publishers. Includes BRONZE THRILLS, aimed at a black audience, TRUE STORY, MODERN ROMANCES, TRUE CONFESSIONS.

2182 Randall, Michael H. "Teen Fan Magazines." SERIALS REVIEW 8 (Winter 1982) : 47-49.

Brief overview of genre and its audience is followed by reviews of five representative titles. Attractive reading materials for teens who have difficulty reading.

2183 Reed, Robert. "Flying Those Not-Always-So-Friendly Skies." ADVERTISING AGE 53 (July 5, 1982) : M2-M3.

Four publishers compete for reader attention and ad dollars in in-flight magazines. Chart compares largest circulation magazines of this genre.

2184 Richardson, Selma K. MAGAZINES FOR CHILDREN: A GUIDE FOR PARENTS, TEACHERS, AND LIBRARIANS. Chicago: American Library Association, 1983.

Annotated list of children's magazines for readers aged 2 to 14. Lengthy annotations describe targeted audience, physical appearance, content, purpose.

2185 Richter, Paul. "Telling How to Succeed is Big Business." LOS ANGELES TIMES, 10 January 1985, p. 1.

Success of SUCCESS magazine.

2186 Rom, Christine. "Little Magazines: Do We Really Need Them?" WILSON LIBRARY BULLETIN 56 (March 1982) : 516-519.

A good overview of the field written for acquisition librarians. Brief historical background of the genre, its importance, economics, and reasons libraries frequently fail to subscribe.

2187 Rout, Lawrence. "The Special Business of 'Elite' Magazines is to Flatter the Rich." WALL STREET JOURNAL, 22 July 1980, p.1.

Magazines, often with controlled circulation, sent to the very rich. An example is LEADERS, for leaders of nations, world religions, international businesses and educational institutions.

2188 Sage, Lorna. "Academic Growth Industry." TIMES LITERARY SUPPLEMENT, no. 4028 (June 6, 1980) : 649.

Critical review of literary journals that focus on criticism of the novel.

2189 Salmans, Sandra. "Health Magazine is in Fine Shape." NEW YORK TIMES, 14 December 1983, p. D1+.

AMERICAN HEALTH is a sturdy newcomer to the magazine industry when more lavish and heavily-financed magazines are failing. The magazine's demographics, circulation, content, financing.

2190 Schardt, Arlie. "Magazines to Turn the Viewer On." NEWSWEEK 96 (October 27, 1980) : 101-102.

Brief overview of several new television guides, including PANORAMA and DIAL. The fate of this genre is unpredictable.

2191 Schinto, Jeanne. "Facts of Fiction." WASHINGTON POST, 21 February 1984, p. D7.

Lament of a fiction writer striving to publish in little magazines.

2192 Sesser, Stanford. "Critics Hit Magazines Published by Airlines, but Admen Like Them." WALL STREET JOURNAL, 31 October 1969, p. 1+.

The first airline magazines were dull "publicity puffery." Although airlines viewed magazines as revenue-losers, increase in advertising rose rapidly enough to break even.

2193 Shiver, Jube, Jr. "Big Business From Small Ads." LOS ANGELES TIMES, 21 February 1985, sec. 4, p.1.

TV Fanfare Publications distributes program guides free at supermarkets.

2194 Sitomer, Curtis J. "An Outspoken Journal Enters its Second Century." CHRISTIAN SCIENCE MONITOR, 24 September 1984, p.21.

Comments on the CHRISTIAN CENTURY on its one hundredth birthday.

2195 "Smart Sell for Hard Times." NATION'S BUSINESS 71 (April 1983) : 62-63.

Published by a small marketing firm, STREET-FIGHTER is a successful newsletter aimed at helping small merchants promote their stores cheaply.

2196 Sonenschein, David. "Process in the Production of Popular Culture: The Romance Magazine." JOURNAL OF POPULAR CULTURE 6 (Fall 1972) : 399-406.

How romance magazines for black and white readers obtain and edit their fiction. Most is free-lanced by white middle-class housewives.

2197 Sorenson, Laurel. "In FARM WIFE NEWS, Rural Readers Write of Mice and Women." WALL STREET JOURNAL, 15 June 1982, p.1+.

Profile of FARM WIFE NEWS, "chummy," slick magazine for rural women, largely written by readers.

2198 Springer, P. Gregory. "U.of I.'s TUMOR Still an Annual Happening." QUILL 70 (April 1982): 32.

Brief description of University of Illinois underground publication, TUMOR, 1927 to present.

2199 Stepp, Carl Sessions. "Looking Out for #1: Magazines that Celebrate Success." WASHINGTON JOURNALISM REVIEW 7 (November 1985) : 41-44.

Magazines, aiming for upscale and successful readers, focus on trendy topics--fine living, fashion and style particularly for men, fitness and health, career development, celebrities.

2200 Stevenson, Richard W. "Fitness Magazine Explosion." NEW YORK TIMES, 15 June 1985, p. 35+.

Popular interest in physical fitness has led to numerous start-ups from health and nutrition to exercise magazines, from well-financed to one-shot publications. Problems include finding the right advertisers and credibility of editorial copy.

2201 "Supplement for Blacks Makes Headway." EDITOR & PUBLISHER 112 (July 21, 1979) : 36.

NATIONAL SCENE circulates monthly in fifty-four black weekly newspapers with over a million circulation.

2202 Svilpis, J. E. "Science-Fiction Magazine Illustration: A Semiotic Analysis." SCIENCE FICTION STUDIES 10 (November 1983) : 278-291.

Academic analysis of the functions and meanings of illustrations in science fiction magazines, particularly covers.

2203 Sweet, Neesa. "Can INSIDE SPORTS Make it this Time Around?" ADVERTISING AGE 54 (November 7, 1983) : M40-M41.

INSIDE SPORTS has third new publisher.

2204 Thomas, William V. "MAD Magazine: Past and Future." THE PRESS 10 (August 1982) : 36-37.

Profile of publisher William Gaines and his creation, MAD. Like PLAYBOY, MAD is a product of the "repressed 50s." Gaines believes MAD is a teenage publication, but has never undertaken reader surveys. Audiences are harder to please today and circulation has dropped.

2205 Tobias, Andrew. "Jeff Butler's Pie in the Sky Mag Money Machine." MORE 7 (March 1977) : 22-24.

East/West Network's in-flight magazines reach

large numbers of businessmen. Business is good as advertising sales increase.

2206 Trager, Cara S. "Monitoring the Pulse of America." ADVERTISING AGE 55 (March 26, 1984) : M48.

Profile of AMERICAN HEALTH magazine.

2207 Tsianter, Dody. "Taste of Success." WASHINGTON POST, 26 December 1984, p. B2.

Both "yuppies" and the industry apparently gobble up Joan Steuer's CHOCOLATIER magazine. Fluffy look at editor's delightful fringe benefits without predictions about what will happen to her waistline as her market of 425,000 grows.

2208 Tuthill, Mary. "Let a Newsletter do the Walking." NATION'S BUSINESS 70 (July 1982) : 74-75.

Two-year-old travel newsletter is a one-man profit-making operation that reviews unusual vacation resorts.

2209 Ubinas, Luis. "Publishers Hope Video-Game Fans Have Time--and Ability--to Read." WALL STREET JOURNAL, 11 August 1982, p. 25.

At least six magazines are aimed at video-game players.

2210 Walling, Donovan R. "It's Time to Consider a School Magazine." CLEARING HOUSE 58 (November 1984) : 116-117.

A variety of alternatives to consider when planning a school magazine.

2211 "WASH. JOURNALISM REVIEW, Crain Link." ADVERTISING AGE 55 (July 9, 1984) : 3+.

WJR and Crain Communications form partnership.

2212 Waters, Harry F. "The PEOPLE Perplex." NEWSWEEK 89 (June 6, 1977) : 89-90.

A superficial glance at celebrity magazines that mimic PEOPLE WEEKLY, and a critical look at the "personality journalism" they depend on.

2213 Watkins, Linda M. "Big Growth in Health Publications Might be Bad for Readers' Health." WALL STREET JOURNAL, 24 April 1985, p. 33.

Increasing social interest in health and the corresponding rise in health magazines is prompting publication of misleading and inaccurate information.

2214 Wertham, Fredric. THE WORLD OF FANZINES: A SPECIAL FORM OF COMMUNICATION. Carbondale, Ill.: Southern Illinois University Press, 1973.

A fanzine is an uncommercial, nonprofessional, small-circulation magazine, dealing with fantasy literature and art and privately distributed. Types and characteristics of fanzines, lists of titles, content, style, jargon, production, significance. Not part of the established communication networks, fanzines represent a "paraculture" and are personal publications that successfully speak to small groups, not the masses.

2215 "What's New? Old People." SALES AND MARKETING MANAGEMENT 123 (October 15, 1979) : 14+.

The rising percentage of elderly people in the population is "suddenly energizing the communications world, especially magazines." Short listing of several new magazines for older persons.

2216 Wolseley, Roland E. "How Good are J-Magazines?" ASNE Bulletin, no. 644 (September 1981) : 33-37.

List of journalism publications with evaluative annotations by nationally-known magazine scholar and educator.

2217 Woods, Richard D., and Graham, Ann Hartness. "Hispanic American Periodicals for Libraries." SERIALS LIBRARIAN 4 (Fall 1979) : 85-98.

An annotated list of magazines for Hispanic Americans.

2218 "Youth Media Market Diverse." ADVERTISING AGE 51 (April 28, 1980) : S2+.

An annotated listing of youth-oriented publications compiled by AA through questionnaire survey. Publications from ethnic to religious, for elementary school to college students.

2219 Yovovich, B. G. "Leisure Reading for Sports." ADVERTISING AGE 51 (December 1, 1980) : S2+.

Trends in leisure sports magazines since the fitness craze began in the 1970s.

2220 Zonana, Vince. "Publishers, Lured by 'Great Demographics,' Rush to Put Out Magazines for Joggers and Runners." WALL STREET JOURNAL, 28 April 1978, p. 42.

Fast-growing RUNNER'S WORLD is facing competition from other new magazines for joggers.

==

Index

==

NUMBERS REFER TO ENTRIES, NOT PAGES.

FIRST SEE TABLE OF CONTENTS.

Items are NOT indexed by chapter subject heading. For example, all history entries appearing in the chapter on history are not also indexed under "history." Entries appearing elsewhere in the book, and dealing with history, will be indexed under "history." For greater explanation, see p. 7 in the preface.

With few exceptions, magazine titles are indexed only when three or fewer titles are mentioned in an article. The index refers only to the bibliograpic entries in Part II.